The Communist League of America 1932–34

James P. Cannon
Writings and Speeches, 1932–34

THE COMMUNIST LEAGUE OF AMERICA 1932–34

PATHFINDER

New York   London   Montreal   Sydney

Edited by Fred Stanton and Michael Taber

Copyright © 1985 Pathfinder Press
All rights reserved

ISBN 978-0-87348-950-8
Library of Congress Catalog Card Number 85-72188
Manufactured in the United States of America

First edition, 1985
Fifth printing, 2022

PATHFINDER
www.pathfinderpress.com
E-mail: pathfinder@pathfinderpress.com

Contents

About the author	11
Introduction	13
Foreign-language work of the CLA *(Published January 2, 1932)*	43
Proletarian Party split *(Published January 9, 1932)*	47
Clarence Darrow and the Scottsboro case *(Published January 16, 1932)*	51
A sorry adventure *(Published January 23, 1932)*	53
Public apology for article on Lassalle *(Published February 13, 1932)*	57
NC statement on the situation in the International Left Opposition *(March 1932)*	59
The threat of illegality and the mood of the workers *(Published March 19, 1932)*	63
A false antiwar slogan *(Published March 19, 1932)*	69
Internal problems of the CLA *(March 22, 1932)*	73
Fifty years of Israel Amter *(Published April 2, 1932)*	123
Mobilize white workers for Scottsboro prisoners *(Published April 9, 1932)*	127
Lay the whole matter before the membership *(April 10, 1932)*	131
The 'degeneration of the old guard' *(April 21, 1932)*	137
Trade union unity and the ILGWU *(Published April 23, 1932)*	151
'Under rank-and-file leadership' *(Published April 30, 1932)*	159
The anti-Cannon bloc *(April 30, 1932)*	165

Centrist–right wing unity? *(Published May 7, 1932)*	177
Weisbord blows the whistle *(Published May 7, 1932)*	181
The fight is here *(May 7, 1932)*	185
For genuine reunification of communist forces *(Published May 14, 1932)*	193
A debate with the IWW *(May 14, 1932)*	199
More on slogan of 'rank-and-file leadership' *(Published June 11, 1932)*	207
Results of the June plenum *(July 1932)*	217
Draft on the internal struggle *(July 1932)*	225
Stalinist-pacifist collaboration *(August 9, 1932)*	255
Organizing in the Illinois mine fields *(September 23, 1932)*	259
On relations with B.J. Field *(October 6, 1932)*	265
Minority maneuvers and problems with Trotsky *(October 1932)*	269
For more field organizing *(November 5, 1932)*	277
The international delegate question *(December 20, 1932)*	281
Financing the international delegate *(December 20, 1932)*	287
Results of discussion and voting on the plenum resolutions *(Published December 29, 1932)*	289
Our delegate will be on the boat *(January 1, 1933)*	297
On the 'money' question *(January 10, 1933)*	307
The new party turn *(Published January 21, 1933)*	309
The New York unemployed conference *(January 22, 1933)*	313
Breaking out of the narrow groove *(January 24, 1933)*	319
The Left Opposition at Gillespie *(Published February 11, 1933)*	323

Show by concrete example what we can do *(February 11, 1933)*	333
External advances, internal turmoil *(February 11, 1933)*	337
Resolution on the Red Army and the German revolution *(March 1, 1933)*	343
The conflict sharpens *(March 2, 1933)*	355
Speech at Albany unemployed conference *(March 6, 1933)*	357
The Left Opposition in Springfield *(March 15, 1933)*	363
Albany: three years of party policy *(Published March 18, 1933)*	365
Open letter to the Central Committee of the Communist Party *(Published March 18, 1933)*	373
Errors of the majority *(March 27, 1933)*	377
NC motions on Gillespie conference *(March 29, 1933)*	379
For a realistic policy at Gillespie *(March 30, 1933)*	385
Deadlock in the National Committee *(April 7, 1933)*	391
Concessions to the minority *(April 1933)*	395
Our work in the PMA *(April 10, 1933)*	399
On collaboration with Allard *(April 10, 1933)*	405
Allard at the turning point *(April 20, 1933)*	409
Red-baiting in the Illinois mine fields *(Published April 29, 1933)*	411
For a united front to defend Mooney *(May 2, 1933)*	417
Financial factionalism *(May 29, 1933)*	419
Support for a Fourth International *(September 11, 1933)*	421
Membership discussion of the new turn *(September 16, 1933)*	423

The left wing needs a new policy and a new leadership *(Published September 16, 1933)*	425
Initial discussions on forming the new party *(September 25, 1933)*	433
The British section and the ILP *(September 27, 1933)*	437
For a new party and a new international *(September 30, 1933)*	441
Negotiations with the Gitlow group *(October 11, 1933)*	449
The AFL, the strike wave, and trade union perspectives *(Published October 14, 1933)*	453
CLA activity among Jewish workers *(October 17, 1933)*	461
Relations with the United Workers Party *(December 6, 1933)*	465
The lynching wave and American fascism *(Published December 9, 1933)*	469
Striking out on an independent path *(Published December 23, 1933)*	475
Strike the hotels! *(Published December 30, 1933)*	481
Field's policy in the hotel strike *(February 15, 1934)*	487
Steps toward fusion with the American Workers Party *(February 26, 1934)*	489
Internationalism and the new party *(Published March 10, 1934)*	491
The furriers and the needle-trade unions *(Published March 24, 1934)*	499
Reaction hounds Trotsky! *(Published April 21, 1934)*	505
All out to Madison Square on May Day *(Published April 28, 1934)*	513
New defense organization needed *(Published May 19, 1934)*	525

Learn from Minneapolis! *(Published May 26, 1934)*	529
Victory in Minneapolis *(May 29, 1934)*	535
Minneapolis and its meaning *(June 1934)*	537
The Socialist Party convention *(June 1934)*	547
Report and motions on SP developments *(June 25, 1934)*	561
The strike wave and the left wing *(September 1934)*	565
For fusion with the AWP! *(Published September 15, 1934)*	573
Textile strike debacle *(Published September 29, 1934)*	579
Report on situation in the French section *(October 31, 1934)*	583
For a new revolutionary party *(Published November 17, 1934)*	589
Record of the CLA leadership *(November 30, 1934)*	601
The *New Militant* *(Published December 15, 1934)*	611
Non-Partisan Defense *(Published December 15, 1934)*	615
The real issues in the Soviet Union *(Published December 29, 1934)*	619
Appendix: Four letters by Trotsky on CLA crisis	623
Glossary	637
Notes	659
Index	701

About the author

James Patrick Cannon was born in Rosedale, Kansas, on February 11, 1890, into a working-class, Irish family. Won to socialist ideas by his father, he joined the Socialist Party in 1908 and the Industrial Workers of the World in 1911. In the IWW Cannon worked with Vincent St. John, "Big Bill" Haywood, and Frank Little as a strike organizer and journalist. As a leader of the Socialist Party left wing after the Russian revolution, he became a founder of the communist movement in September 1919 and was elected to the Central Committee of the United Communist Party in 1920. When the Workers Party was founded in 1921 as the legal arm of the communist movement Cannon was elected its national chairman. One of the key leaders of the CP during its first decade, he served on the Presidium of the Communist International in Moscow (1922–23) and headed the International Labor Defense (1925–28). Won over to Trotsky's Bolshevik-Leninist opposition while attending the Sixth World Congress of the Comintern in Moscow in 1928, he was expelled from the CP later that year for Trotskyism. With Max Shachtman and Martin Abern he was a founding leader of the Communist League of America and served as editor of its newspaper, the *Militant*.

Cannon was a founder of the Socialist Workers Party in January 1938 and a participant in the founding conference of the Fourth International held in France later that year, where he was elected to its International Executive Committee. Convicted with seventeen other leaders of the SWP and of the Minneapolis Teamsters union in 1941 for opposing the imperialist war policy of the U.S. government,

Cannon served thirteen months at Sandstone penitentiary in 1944–45. Cannon was the national secretary of the SWP until 1953. Thereafter he was the party's national chairman, and later national chairman emeritus until his death on August 21, 1974.

James P. Cannon's more than sixty years of active struggle in the cause of socialism are recorded in his many books. Published in his lifetime were *Socialism on Trial* (1942), *The Struggle for a Proletarian Party* (1943), *The History of American Trotskyism* (1944), *America's Road to Socialism* (1953), *Notebook of an Agitator* (1958), *The First Ten Years of American Communism* (1962), *Letters from Prison* (1968), *Speeches for Socialism* (1971), and *Speeches to the Party* (1973). This volume is one of a posthumous series of his writings and speeches, which includes *The Socialist Workers Party in World War II*, *The Struggle for Socialism in the "American Century,"* and *The Left Opposition in the U.S., 1928–31*.

Introduction

As this volume opens in January 1932, the U.S. labor movement had reached the low ebb of its devastation by the Great Depression, which had begun more than two years earlier. By December 1934, when the book closes, labor had begun to score some initial victories against the employers—victories that were to lead to the explosive rise of the Congress of Industrial Organizations (CIO) in the latter half of the decade.

This shift in the U.S. class struggle was reflected in the changing political fortunes of the Communist League of America (CLA)—precursor of today's Socialist Workers Party. The CLA had been formed in 1929 by revolutionists expelled by the Stalinist leadership of the Communist Party (CP). The year 1933 marked the beginning of the end of what CLA leader James P. Cannon called the "dog days" of the young organization. During the final year and a half covered by this volume, the CLA made a turn toward centering its activity in the mass working-class organizations—the trade unions, union organizing committees, and organizations of the unemployed. It threw its energies into building a new communist party and a new revolutionary International.

Cannon's writings and speeches during these years show how the revolutionary workers' movement grappled with the problems and responded to the challenges and opportunities of this period. This collection helps complete the story of the CLA begun in *The Left Opposition in the U.S., 1928–31*, which recounted the Communist League's formation and first three years. The present book ends with the CLA's fusion with another organization to found the new Workers Party of the United States.

Together, these two volumes are useful source material for and companions to Cannon's *The History of American Trotskyism,* which was originally given as a series of talks in 1942. These books record an important chapter in the struggle in the United States to maintain the revolutionary course charted by the Communist International in its first five years (1919–23), led by the Bolshevik team around Lenin.

Following Lenin's death at the beginning of 1924 the Comintern, under the growing influence of a privileged bureaucratic caste in the Soviet Union headed by Joseph Stalin, was abandoning its revolutionary orientation, carrying the majority leadership of the U.S. Communist Party in its wake. These policies were being fought by Soviet Communist leader Leon Trotsky and the political current led by him within the Soviet CP and the Comintern. The Bolshevik-Leninists sought to defend the Leninist program and strategy that had been the Comintern's guide through 1923.

They attacked the Stalin leadership's flight from revolutionary internationalism. This regression to "national communism" was symbolized by Stalin's attempt to foist on the Comintern the subordination of the world revolutionary movement to the task of "building socialism in one country"—a term Stalin coined in 1924 to claim that socialism could be achieved within the borders of the Soviet Union alone.

Stalin caricatured the views of those who opposed this anti-Marxist innovation. He charged that they advocated simultaneous revolutionary uprisings in all countries, and that they doubted the Soviet Union's capacity to develop its economy and raise the living standards of the workers and peasants. These charges were false. What Trotsky and other Communist leaders opposed was Stalin's policy of shaping Comintern policy to serve the shifting diplomatic needs of the Soviet government bureaucracy, rather than the interests of the world revolution.

Within the Soviet Union, Trotsky and other Communist leaders sought to preserve the worker-peasant alliance that was the social bedrock of the revolutionary regime against the policies of Stalin and Nikolai Bukharin—policies that benefited a relatively small layer of state and party functionaries, exploiting peasants, and speculating traders at the expense of the urban working class, rural wage earners, and the vast peasant majority.

Within the Comintern the Bolshevik-Leninists warned against the dangers of a "second wave of Menshevism," best exemplified by the class-collaborationist line imposed by Stalin and Bukharin on the Chinese CP during the 1925–27 revolution in that country. That policy, which contributed decisively to the revolution's defeat, sacrificed the interests of workers and peasants to the objective of maintaining a bloc with bourgeois-nationalist leader Chiang Kai-shek. The disastrous result of this course was the massacre of thousands of Chinese workers and peasants by Chiang's armies in Shanghai, Wuhan, and outlying rural districts in mid-1927.

Finally, Trotsky and other Soviet CP leaders attacked the Stalinists' bureaucratic suppression of alternative points of view. They demanded a return to the democratic internal functioning and revolutionary centralism that characterized the party and Comintern under Lenin's leadership.

Adherents to the Bolshevik-Leninist opposition inside Russia were met by slander, abuse, expulsion from the party, and exile to Siberia. In 1929 Trotsky was banished from the Soviet Union and deported to Turkey. From there he helped organize the International Left Opposition (ILO) as an international movement fighting for the regeneration of the Comintern with a Marxist program and leadership.

The Great Depression in the United States bottomed out in 1932–33, with 16 million people—one-third of the work force—unemployed. The Gross National Product had plummeted to 54 percent of its 1929 level. The employers were driving workers who still had jobs to produce more for less. Real wages had fallen by 20 percent since 1929.

The American Federation of Labor (AFL) lost almost half a million members between 1929 and 1933, continuing the decline it had suffered throughout the 1920s. In the needle trades, the Amalgamated Clothing Workers collected dues from only 7,000 members in 1932. With coal production at its lowest point since 1904, few members of the United Mine Workers were working sufficient hours to earn a living. Construction, transportation, and communications workers' unions were hard hit.

In the unorganized production industries, conditions were even worse. In auto, 207,000 production workers lost their jobs from 1929 to 1932—almost half of the total work force.

The U.S. working class needed strong organizations and united action to fight for emergency relief, public works programs, and a shorter workweek with no cut in pay to spread around the available jobs. The need to organize the unorganized, who comprised the vast majority of the working class, was more acute than ever before.

Yet during the first few years of the depression there was no organized resistance on a mass scale to the employers' attacks. Instead of fighting and organizing, the unions that did exist were in retreat. There were few strikes, and most of those that did occur were defeated.

The perspective of the officialdom of the AFL had reached a dead end. Based on the relatively better-off workers in the skilled crafts, the union bureaucrats in their big majority opposed the organization of production workers in steel, auto, rubber, and other industries. They were dead set against the industrial form of organization, whereby all production workers in the same factory and industry—whether on the assembly line or in the tool room—belong to the same union. Industrial unionism threatened the lucrative positions of the officialdom of the AFL's craft unions.

Identifying labor's interests with those of preserving capitalism and boosting the bosses' profits, the AFL bureaucracy could present no way for either organized or unorganized workers to resist the mounting attacks on their rights and living standards. While some labor misleaders talked about cutting the workweek, they looked to Democratic and Republican party "friends of labor" to accomplish this. Meanwhile, the best they could do was to make agreements for so-called work sharing—workers would work fewer hours, so a few more people had jobs, but the weekly pay check went down proportionately, or even more.

The AFL bureaucracy's passivity toward the bosses contrasted sharply with its steadfastness in policing the union ranks. In this, its overriding goal was to keep a grip on its dues base—the trough from which the officials fed to maintain their own privileged lifestyles. They were determined to beat back any attempt by the workers to utilize the unions as an instrument of militant struggle to defend their interests and organize the unorganized majority of their class. That would require a massive social movement going beyond the narrow framework of the trade unions as they existed; such a struggle would rock the boat, and the bureaucrats feared that they would be among those swept overboard.

Many AFL craft unions refused to admit Blacks as members. In addition to helping preserve the Jim Crow system of segregation, this racist policy of the bureaucracy was another factor weakening the unions themselves. It was a blow to the solidarity among the ranks that is the touchstone of unionism. Moreover, since the vast majority of Black workers were concentrated in the mass-production industries, the officialdom's refusal to organize the unorganized reinforced the oppression and superexploitation of these workers by the ruling class.

Lacking effective unions to fight for their interests, workers did what they could as individuals or in small groups to weather the crisis. Since many workers were from farm families, some tried going back to the land to raise a little food. Some workers organized small cooperatives and other self-help schemes. Others organized demonstrations to demand relief. Many were forced into destitution, begging, and onto food lines.

Various organizations of the unemployed began to be set up, largely at the initiative of left-wing organizations. The CP-led National Council of Unemployed organized squads of workers to fight evictions; in 1931 and 1932 it sponsored hunger marches that were often attacked by the cops. The Socialist Party and the Conference for Progressive Labor Action (CPLA) also built organizations to fight for the rights of the jobless. But the unemployed workers, dispersed in their homes and often demoralized, were not easy to organize on a large scale. The organized social power of the unions was needed to bring the unemployed together as a fighting force, and this did not begin to happen until prospects for some victories became a little brighter toward the mid-1930s.

The procapitalist policies of the AFL bureaucracy received enthusiastic support from the class-collaborationist "Old Guard" leadership of the American Socialist Party, which at the time had a membership of about 10,000. While not a major force in the top AFL officialdom, SP members were prominent in the leadership of the needle-trades unions, especially in New York City.

There was also a small left wing within the union movement. A layer of militant workers looked for leadership to the Communist Party, which had a slightly larger membership than the SP. These workers, however, were increasingly handicapped by the disorienting effects of the CP's political degeneration.

In 1929, the Stalinist leadership of the Comintern proclaimed that post-World War I capitalism had entered its "third period," the period of its final crisis and collapse. This cataclysmic prognosis was designed as a justification for an ultraleft turn initiated by Stalin in the wake of domestic and international reverses at the end of the 1920s, resulting from the Soviet Communist Party leadership's course since the middle of that decade. Accompanying this sharp turn to the left was the ouster from the leadership in 1929 of the right wing of the Soviet Communist Party led by Bukharin, who since 1926 had been the most prominent leader of the Comintern. The purge of the right-wing opposition was carried out in Communist parties throughout the world. In the U.S. CP the current associated with Jay Lovestone, a supporter of Bukharin who had been the party's general secretary, was expelled.

As part of the ultraleft "third period" schema, the

social-democratic parties of the Second International were termed "social fascist" and presented as the workers' chief enemy. The Stalinists no longer called on the leaders of social-democratic parties or the unions to enter into alliances for joint action to advance the interests of exploited working people. The perspective of the working-class united front, formulated by the Comintern under Lenin's leadership, was abandoned. Only a "united front from below" was permissible—that is, a call on the ranks of social democratic organizations to break with their leaders and join in united actions with the Communists. This sectarian approach could influence only the tiny handful of workers already convinced politically of the need to break with the leadership of their organizations.

In pursuing this line, the Comintern advanced a new "dual union" policy of splitting militant workers away from the established unions to form their own, "red" unions. The CP applied this policy in the United States by pulling its members and others influenced by them out of the AFL to establish new organizations. Through this action, the CP isolated many vanguard workers from the rest of the organized working class, thereby leaving the AFL officialdom a freer hand in its class-collaborationist practices.

The CP's ultraleft course was also reflected in the farmers' protest movement when the party refused to support the Farm Holiday Association founded in 1932. Characterizing this group as "social fascist," the CP set up its own separate farm organization.

The pressures from the political situation during the early 1930s bore down heavily on the 150–200 members of the Communist League of America. The CLA was largely isolated from active participation in working-class struggles, and it was plagued by a severe lack of funds.

During these years the CLA's weekly newspaper, the *Militant*, and its public activities were oriented primarily to the working-class vanguard that continued to belong to and look toward the Communist Party. Cannon explained this orientation in *The History of American Trotskyism*.

The CLA directed its "main efforts, appeals and activities, not to the mass of 40 million American workers, but to the vanguard of the class organized in and around the Communist Party," Cannon said. Its approach was that, "We must first get what is obtainable from this vanguard group, consisting of some tens of thousands of Communist Party members and sympathizers, and crystallize out of them a sufficient cadre either to reform the party, or, if after a serious effort that fails in the end—and only when the failure is conclusively demonstrated—to build a new one with the forces recruited in the endeavor. Only in this way is it possible for us to reconstitute the party in the real sense of the word."

"By remaining partisans of the Communist Party and the Communist International," Cannon said, "by opposing the bureaucratic leaders at the top, but appraising correctly the rank and file as they were at that time, and seeking contact with them, we continued to gain new recruits from the ranks of the Communist workers. The overwhelming majority of our members in the first five years of our existence came from the CP. Thus we built the foundations of a regenerated Communist movement."

The Communist Opposition, however, did not have an easy time getting the ear of the thousands of revolutionary-minded workers in the CP. It faced the obstacle of the CP bureaucrats' physical attacks and verbal slanders. Moreover, some CP members who were initially influenced by the CLA misinterpreted the Stalinists' ultraleft "third period" policies as embodying the essence of the program of the Bolshevik-Leninist opposition.

"The Stalinist 'left turn' piled up new difficulties for us," Cannon recounted in *The History of American Trotskyism*. "This turn was in part designed by Stalin to cut the ground from under the feet of the Left Opposition. . . . They used to say to us: 'You see, you were wrong. Stalin is correcting everything. He is taking a radical position all along the line in Russia, America and everywhere else.' . . .

"There were, I would say, perhaps hundreds of Communist Party members, who had been leaning towards us, who gained the same impression and returned to Stalinism in the period of the ultra-left swing."

"Those were the real dog days of the Left Opposition," Cannon said.

Despite all these obstacles, the CLA did not succumb. Although perpetually scrambling for funds, the CLA continued the regular publication of the *Militant,* never missing an issue of it. The CLA was able to publish and distribute the most important political and programmatic articles by Trotsky and the International Left Opposition. It educated and trained a disciplined and self-sacrificing cadre that would be capable of responding to political opportunities when they arose.

Nonetheless, the combination of the pressures bearing down on the working class as a whole at the beginning of the 1930s and the particular obstacles confronting the CLA inevitably took their toll on the organization. In his *History* Cannon paints a vivid picture of this period:

"We had no friends, no sympathizers, no periphery around our movement. We had no chance whatever to participate in the mass movement. Whenever we tried to get into a workers organization we would be expelled as counter-revolutionary Trotskyists. We tried to send delegations to the unemployed meetings. Our credentials would be rejected on the ground that we were enemies of the working class. We were utterly isolated, forced in upon ourselves. Our recruitment dropped to almost nothing. The Communist Party and its vast periphery seemed to be hermetically sealed against us.

"Then, as is always the case with new political movements, we began to recruit from sources none too healthy.... Many people came to us who had revolted against the Communist Party not for its bad sides but for its good sides; that is, the discipline of the party, the subordination of the individual to the decisions of the party in current work. A lot of dilettantish petty-bourgeois-minded people who couldn't stand any kind of discipline, who had either left the CP or been expelled from it, wanted, or rather thought they wanted to become Trotskyists. Some of them joined the New York branch and brought with them that same prejudice against discipline in our organization....

"All the people of this type have one common characteristic: they like to discuss things without limit or end. The New York branch of the Trotskyist movement in those days was just one continuous stew of discussion.... Walled off from the vanguard represented by the Communist movement and without contact with the living mass movement of the workers, we were thrown in upon ourselves and subjected to this invasion. There was no way out of it. We had to go through the long drawn-out period of stewing and discussing."

The predominantly petty-bourgeois composition of the league's New York City organization formed a breeding ground for cliques that spent their considerable energy complaining, factionalizing, and sniping at the leadership. "The greatest movement, with its magnificent program of the liberation of all humanity, with the most grandiose historic perspectives," Cannon recalled, "was inundated in those days by a sea of petty troubles, jealousies, clique formations and internal fights. Worst of all, these faction fights weren't fully comprehensible to the membership because the great political issues which were implicit in them had not yet broken through."

One factor exacerbating these conflicts was the CLA leaders' training in the CP during the middle and late 1920s. The Comintern leadership, rapidly fleeing from Leninist policies during that period, could no longer serve as an example and source of assistance to its still young national sections in the hard task of forging a mature, objective, and politically homogeneous leadership. Lacking such counterbalancing influences, the U.S. CP had become a jungle of permanent factions. Cannon described this situation in *The First Ten Years of American Communism:*

"The factional struggle became bankrupt for lack of real political justification for the existence of the factions. For that reason nothing could be solved by the victory of one faction, giving it the opportunity to execute its policy, since the policies of the others were basically the same. There were differences of implicit tendency, to be sure, but further experience was required to show where they might lead. The factions lived on exaggerations and distortions of each others' positions and the anticipation of future differences."

Pressures similar to those confronting the CLA at the outset of the 1930s, and their organizational and political effects, also took a toll on the International Left Opposition as a whole. The ILO's European sections, too, had difficulty in forging leaderships that worked collectively to build their organizations around a revolutionary Marxist program. They went through numerous faction fights and splits, sloughing off politically disloyal groupings and individuals, cliques, traffickers in "inside dope" and personal intrigue.

Many leaders of the International Left Opposition who were miseducated in the factional jungles of the degenerating Comintern were now challenged to develop the political skills to deal with these problems. The best help in this regard was to be found in the political experience and capacity that Trotsky had learned as part of the leadership team of the Soviet republic and Comintern forged by Lenin.

The CLA had some advantages over the majority of European organizations in dealing with these problems. In general, it was a more politically homogeneous leadership, and more working-class in composition. Many, including Cannon—a veteran of the Industrial Workers of the World and a leader of the CP-led International Labor Defense founded in 1925—had backgrounds as leaders in working-class struggles going back a decade or more. In addition, most had previously been leading members in the Communist Party, where they had been won to a revolutionary working-class perspective. Of special note was the CLA's Minneapolis branch, which included virtually the entire former leadership of the CP in that city, leaders with considerable experience inside the labor movement.

Under the impact of the formidable pressures the CLA confronted, however, this collaboration began to fracture. In particular, frictions that had developed in 1929 between Cannon and Max Shachtman—the CLA's two most prominent founding leaders—broke out into a bitter faction fight in early 1932.

The factional struggle divided the nine-person National Committee elected in 1931 as follows:

The Cannon group included Vincent R. Dunne and Carl Skoglund, formerly central leaders of the Minnesota

CP, who were seasoned revolutionists with long experience in the trade unions; Hugo Oehler, an organizer with experience in miners' struggles in the West and in the CP's textile-organizing drive in the South; and Arne Swabeck (referred to as Ben Webster in *The History of American Trotskyism*), a founding central leader of the CP with many years' experience in trade union work in Chicago.

The Shachtman group included Shachtman himself, who had spent most of his time in the CP as an editor for the youth paper or for the International Labor Defense's monthly journal; Martin Abern, a founding leader of the CP youth with experience as a district organizer and an assistant to Cannon in the ILD; Maurice Spector, a founding leader and former national chairman of the Canadian CP, who had edited its paper and was working as a college professor after his expulsion; and Albert Glotzer, who had been a leader of the CP youth.

By early 1933 the faction fight had reached such a degree of intensity that the CLA faced the danger of a split lacking a sufficient political basis. Such an outcome would have dealt a body blow to revolutionary Marxism in the United States for many years to come.

There were some differences between Cannon and Shachtman, especially over Shachtman's work as international representative of the league in Europe. Shachtman had intervened on the side of various cliques and groupings in several European sections, giving the misimpression that his views on these internal disputes reflected those of the CLA leadership. This had led to political conflicts between Shachtman, on the one hand, and Trotsky and other European ILO leaders, on the other.

Cannon and Shachtman also had a different approach on how to go about building a professional staff and effective leadership committees.

None of these differences, however, were either deep enough or sufficiently clear at this point to explain the factional heat generated around them in the National Committee.

Although the National Committee was unanimous on every big political question, it was nonetheless often paralyzed. The committee of the NC members resident in New York—the day-to-day leading body—often found itself deadlocked, unable to act on practical matters. In addition, the league's finances, on shaky ground to begin with because of high unemployment and inexperience in organizing financial matters, were further disrupted by factionalism, as Shachtman's followers expressed their disagreement with some projects by withholding contributions to the national office.

The Cannon group, which had a slim majority on the National Committee as a whole, grew increasingly impatient with this situation. Following a unanimous vote on the international resolution at the June 1932 NC plenum, which appeared to signal a resolution of the conflict, the Cannon group moved to coopt two more of its supporters onto the NC to assure a working majority on the resident NC in New York. This proposal was then submitted to the membership for approval in a referendum, since the CLA constitution provided that NC members could be elected only by a convention. Heated discussions erupted in the branches. Not only Shachtman's supporters but other CLA members asked: Why do we need cooptations when the National Committee is unanimous on all questions? The majority of the membership voted against the cooptations.

In early 1933 Swabeck was scheduled to go to Europe as the CLA representative for discussions with Trotsky and the European sections. Prior to Swabeck's departure, he and Cannon proposed a new reorganization of the resident NC. They formed a Political Committee composed of Cannon, Oehler, and Shachtman. As a result, Abern was now the only NC member resident in New York not on the new body, which had a two-to-one majority for Cannon's faction.

The Shachtman faction protested these moves by the NC majority. Shachtman demanded a quick national conference, where—on the basis of the referendum vote—he expected to gain a majority.

This was the situation when Swabeck and Trotsky began to discuss the fight in the CLA during their meetings in Turkey in February 1933. Trotsky was soon able to convince Swabeck, and through him Cannon, that organizational concessions by the majority were necessary to deescalate the internal tensions, avoid a split, and enable the CLA to advance. Trotsky also convinced Shachtman, who had been sent by the CLA to Europe around this same time, of the need for steps to lessen organizational frictions, including an end to his supporters' financial and leadership boycott. (The transcripts of some of Trotsky's discussions with Swabeck on this and other subjects have been published in *Writings of Leon Trotsky (1932–33)*, *Writings of Leon Trotsky Supplement (1929–33)*, and *Malcolm X, Black Liberation, and the Road to Workers Power*, all published by Pathfinder Press.)

It was through Trotsky's assistance that the CLA leaders were able to extricate themselves from the factional war. Four of Trotsky's letters are included as appendices to this book, containing his views of the CLA's crisis and his suggestions for overcoming it. In one of these letters, "The Situation in the American League," Trotsky analyzed the causes of the conflict:

"The lack of progress in the movement which has been the case aroused all sorts of personal antagonisms, group antagonisms, or local antagonisms. The same lack of progress in the movement does not permit these antagonisms to take on a political character. This has given and still gives the struggle an exceedingly poisoned character in the absence of a principled content clear to everybody. Members of the organization do not learn anything from such a struggle. They are forced to group themselves according to personal attachments, sympathies and antipathies. The struggle of the groups becomes in its turn an obstacle to the further progress of the movement."

"It is quite possible," he went on, "that in this struggle there are contained valid principled differences in embryonic form. Nevertheless it is unfortunate that the two groups anticipate too much and sharpen the organizational struggle between the groups and the members altogether out of proportion with the development of political work and of the questions raised by the latter."

Trotsky added that "it is impossible not to see the harmful influence of the methods and the procedure of the epigone Comintern, which has accustomed an entire generation to seek a way out of all sorts of difficulties through apparatus combinations at the expense of the whole organization."

It was these factors that were leading the CLA to a split. "A split under these conditions," Trotsky wrote, "would have a purely a priori character, a preventive one, so to speak, one that is incomprehensible to all except those who initiate the split. If it is difficult for us, the leading members of the International Left Opposition, to grasp the motives of the ferocious struggle, the American workers, including the members of the League itself, would be all the less capable of understanding the causes of a split. This kind of split at the top would infinitely shatter the authority of both groups and compromise the cause of the

Left Opposition in America for a long time."

Trotsky was confident that an expansion of the CLA's work within the organizations of the working class and the recruitment of workers would facilitate the league to find a solution to the crisis. For this to occur, however, it was necessary to buy some time for a change in the political situation. Trotsky suggested a series of proposals designed to restore normal leadership functioning within the organization and prevent a split.

The result of Trotsky's political guidance was an agreement in May 1933 by the leadership of both factions to end the fight. This achievement made possible the CLA's further political advance and organizational strengthening over the next period.

As Trotsky predicted, the next round of differences that emerged in the CLA leadership did not reproduce those from the past, but revealed new alignments on the basis of new tasks and challenges facing the movement. One of the documents toward the end of this book, "The Record of the CLA Leadership," notes how the differing political perspectives that emerged in the National Committee in late 1934 cut across the previous factional divisions. In particular, the collaboration of Cannon and Shachtman was restored, lasting until 1939.

"To be sure," Cannon later acknowledged, "the definitive split did eventually take place—in 1940. But that was seven years later, over principled differences and political disputes of such depth and scope as to be clear to everybody. Meantime the party did some good work despite internal friction. Following the truce and the developments of mass work new alignments took place and the eventual split, which came in 1940, after the political differences were fully matured and explainable to all, had a salutary effect on the further development of the party, as we all know." The record of the 1939–40 political struggle against Shachtman's anti-Marxist opposition can be found in Cannon's *The Struggle for a Proletarian Party* and Trotsky's *In Defense of Marxism*.

The resolution of the factional struggle in the CLA took place against the background of big changes in the political situation both in the United States and internationally. These developments posed a series of major new tasks and challenges.

On January 30, 1933, Adolf Hitler was appointed chancellor of Germany, and in March he seized dictatorial power. The victory of German fascism and the crushing defeat of capitalist Europe's largest and most powerfully organized working-class movement was a historic blow to the proletariat internationally. It set the stage for the onset of the second interimperialist world war.

The Nazi victory in Germany had not been inevitable. It was hastened by a betrayal by the two mass German workers' parties: the Communist Party and the Social Democratic Party. Together these two parties had the support of the overwhelming majority of the German working class.

For several years prior to 1933, the Nazis had been rapidly expanding their mass base among small business people and professionals, as millions became desperate at the prospects of being ruined by the capitalist crisis. It also attracted certain layers of declassed and permanently jobless youth. Moreover, dominant sections of the German bourgeoisie had become convinced that a Nazi accession to power was now the only way to destroy the organized working-class movement and prevent a challenge to capitalist rule.

Escalating attacks by armed Nazi gangs on the unions,

CP, and Social Democrats posed the need for a united front of the two main workers' parties to defend the interests and organizations of the working class through militant action. Such a united front had the potential power to defeat the fascist forces. Through decisive action and by presenting a program to offer a way out of the capitalist crisis, the working-class forces could have rallied large sections of the disoriented middle classes to the side of the proletariat. It could have forged a fighting alliance with the exploited farmers, a substantial proportion of Germany's population at the time.

The International Left Opposition urgently campaigned for a CP-Social Democratic united front against the Nazis and in defense of the interests of working people. The ILO pointed out that if the CP launched such a campaign, pressure from the workers who still looked to the reformist Social Democratic Party could force it to participate. The Stalinists, however, adopted the opposite course. Under the influence of the ultraleft "third period" line, the CP centered its fire not on the Nazis but on the Social Democrats, terming them "social fascists." Until a few months prior to Hitler's victory, the CP was still spurning all calls for joint action with the Social Democrats to fight Nazism. The CP's sectarian policy suited the Social Democratic officials. These misleaders put their faith in liberal, "democratic," capitalist forces, and were not eager for a working-class united front against Hitler.

This default by the CP and the Social Democrats opened the door to a Nazi victory that encountered virtually no opposition, stunning class-struggle-minded workers around the world—including many who had previously looked to the Stalinists and Social Democrats. A certain number began to listen for the first time to Trotsky and the International Left Opposition, who had been sounding the alarm and presenting a Marxist perspective for the fight against fascism in Germany since the outset of the 1930s.

In the wake of this historic defeat, the leadership of the German CP and the Comintern refused to assess the errors of its disastrous policy and return to a revolutionary course. The ranks of the Stalinist-led organization had been so whipped into line by the preceding purges and slander campaigns that this betrayal by their leaders did not result in any significant shake-up or reassessment of views regarding the policies of the bureaucratic caste in Moscow.

This default convinced the International Left Opposition that the Comintern could no longer be looked to as the force from which a new revolutionary Marxist leadership would emerge. Those seeking to restore a consistent internationalist course of advancing the fight against world imperialism could no longer focus their energies on winning a majority committed to reforming these organizations. New parties and a new International would have to be built. Consequently, in August 1933 the International Left Opposition issued a call for the construction of a Fourth International.

The CLA leaders enthusiastically endorsed this shift in strategic orientation. No longer would their axis in building the CLA be that of convincing CP militants to wage a battle to return the party to revolutionary Marxism. The task of building a revolutionary party in the United States now necessitated looking in other directions—toward increasing the CLA's participation in the organized working-class movement, which in the fifth year of the depression was finally starting to organize and fight back on a significant level. The CLA now set out to win workers from the CP, SP, and other forces to this party-building orientation in the midst of the labor upsurge that was beginning.

In 1933 workers in the United States were beginning to recover from the initial shock of the Great Depression. This coincided with a partial economic upturn. As many workers returned to the job and the unions began to reverse their decline in size, a feeling of rising confidence and willingness to struggle emerged in the ranks of labor.

Democrat Franklin D. Roosevelt had been inaugurated as president in March 1933 and went on to proclaim a "New Deal," raising the expectations of many workers. The aim of Roosevelt and the Democratic Party, however, was to make the workers and exploited farmers pay for the measures that could help stimulate an upturn in the capitalist economy. Spending from government New Deal programs flowed overwhelmingly to the big industrialists, bankers, and landlords.

Roosevelt had no intention of "giving" the workers and working farm families anything. They had to fight for each and every improvement in their conditions. Gains won by the working class over the next half decade such as industrial unions, social security, unemployment insurance, and cash relief were conquered through hard-fought and often bloody struggles involving millions of workers. These gigantic battles reinforced the fight of working farmers, who also won important gains, including government-funded credit programs and rural electrification. These fresh winds also gave an impetus to the struggle by Blacks against Jim Crow segregation and lynchings in the South, as well as miserable slum conditions and racist discrimination in the North.

The first strike wave of the decade began in early 1933.

As a result of this upsurge, the Roosevelt administration and Congress were pressured to include provisions expanding workers' rights to organize as part of the first major New Deal reform bill—the National Industrial Recovery Act (NRA). The NRA was by no means a prolabor policy, however. It set up production codes that exempted industries from antitrust laws, established low minimum wages, and upheld the employers' "right" to victimize union militants on the basis of "merit." Nonetheless, unions made use of the NRA to sign up new members. The United Mine Workers grew by 300,000 in two months; the International Ladies' Garment Workers' Union by 150,000; and the Amalgamated Clothing Workers by 50,000.

Washington quickly showed where it stood when workers fought for union rights. The government used injunctions, troops, police, special deputies, labor spies, and criminal syndicalism laws against the workers. In the second half of 1933, fifteen strikers were killed, two hundred injured, and hundreds arrested. The 1933 strike wave ended in a series of defeats, although it signaled a new wave of militancy and willingness to struggle.

Despite the gains registered by some unions, the AFL leaders as a whole did little to organize the unorganized under the NRA. But the workers had shown in 1933 that they were ready to move. And it was the cadre of socialist and communist organizations who provided leadership for the first successful organizing strikes of that period in 1934, working through AFL unions.

Through militant and nationally publicized strikes in February, May, and July–August 1934, Teamsters General Drivers Local 574 in Minneapolis won union recognition and forced significant concessions from the employers. Among the central leaders of these strikes were members and sympathizers of the CLA, including National

Committee members V.R. Dunne and Carl Skoglund, and Farrell Dobbs, who was won to the CLA during these struggles. Organized democratically to mobilize the power of the ranks, Local 574 built alliances with unemployed workers and with farmers, organized a women's auxiliary, published a daily strike newspaper, held daily mass strike meetings, fielded flying picket squads, and effectively defended itself against armed attacks by cops and special deputies. The victories scored by Local 574 opened the way to organizing truck drivers, including over-the-road drivers, and warehouse workers on an industrial basis throughout the Midwest.

At the Toledo Electric Auto-Lite plant, members of an AFL federal local (chartered by the national federation, not by one of its craft-based affiliates) went on strike in mid-April and were hit with an antipicketing injunction. They looked for help to the local unemployed league, which was led by the American Workers Party, and more than 10,000 people were mobilized to defy the injunction. The strikers and their supporters held their ground in a six-day battle with police and the National Guard that nearly led to a general strike. The union won a contract, which helped open the way for the organization of the auto industry.

A third battle came in July 1934 in San Francisco. There a strike by longshore and maritime workers was being led by radicals, some in or around the CP, others influenced by syndicalist notions. The chief leader, Harry Bridges, was close to the CP but did not follow its policy of sectarian abstention from the AFL unions. After police killed two workers, the union movement shut down the city with a general strike lasting four days and involving 125,000 workers. After the city's AFL leaders called off the general strike, vigilante gangs and cops smashed the headquarters of the left-wing groups and jailed more than 300 people.

The eleven-week longshore strike finally ended with an agreement to arbitrate. Through continuing job actions over the next year the workers won the union hiring hall, thereby reducing the bosses' ability to discriminate against union militants in hiring and increasing the workers' power on the job. This struggle opened the way for the organization of industrial labor on the West Coast.

These three class battles in 1934 set the stage for the massive organizing drives in steel, rubber, auto, and other mass-production industries that were the key element in the rise of the CIO, which was founded the following year.

These changes in the objective situation enabled the CLA to begin breaking out of its isolation. As Cannon described it, the CLA now had the opportunity to make a "turn to mass work" in the trade unions and other organizations of the working class. Opportunities began to open up for work within unemployed organizations, including those led by the CP that had previously excluded CLA members.

In early 1933 the CLA faced its first significant opening for trade union work, among Illinois coal miners who had recently formed the Progressive Miners of America. Many of Cannon's articles and letters in this volume were written to help guide CLA members involved in this work. They contain useful lessons about the CLA's efforts to work out and apply a communist approach to strategy and tactics in the trade unions.

This collection also includes writings by Cannon on the CLA's participation in the leadership of two 1934 trade union battles: the New York hotel workers' strike, and the Minneapolis Teamsters strikes, the latter of which brought the CLA to national attention. Through its leadership of the Minneapolis Teamsters movement, the CLA was also gaining rich experience in relating to the reformist-led Minnesota Farmer-Labor Party. During this period the CLA was not calling for the creation of a labor party based on the trade unions, but its experiences in Minnesota were useful to the league when it changed its policy in 1938, placing the labor party demand in a central place in its program.

As a result of taking advantage of the new political openings in 1933–34, recruitment began to pick up, and by the end of this period the CLA had grown to 400 members. The circulation of the *Militant* was climbing.

In *The History of American Trotskyism* Cannon describes why the CLA was able to respond effectively to the new openings: "After five years of struggle our ranks had become consolidated on a firm programmatic foundation. They had been educated in the great principled questions, had acquired facility in explaining them, and in applying them to the events of the day.... It was precisely that period of isolation, hardship, discussion, study and assimilation of theoretical ideas that prepared our young movement for this new time of bloom when the movement was opening up in all directions."

The CLA also began to look more closely at other left-wing organizations that were being affected by these political developments and that seemed to contain currents moving in a class-struggle direction. "In all workers organizations there was ferment and change," Cannon pointed out. "One who had a political eye could see that things were really happening now, and that this was not the time to be sitting in the library mulling over principles. This was the time for action on these principles; this was the time to be right on top of things, to take advantage of every opportunity presented by the new developments in the other organizations and movements. . . . We invited all groupings, whoever they might be, who were interested in forming a new revolutionary party and a new International, to discuss with us the basis of the program."

Most important of these forces was the American Workers Party, led by A.J. Muste. The AWP had developed from the Conference for Progressive Labor Action, founded in 1929. Its politics had become more radical through participation in struggles of miners, textile workers, and the unemployed; and it was attracting revolutionary workers.

In January 1934 the CLA took the initiative and proposed discussions with the AWP. These discussions began soon after, and in December led to the fusion of the two groups. This marked the first significant fusion on the U.S. left since 1921.

The new party was named the Workers Party of the United States. It continued to pay particular attention to the development of new revolutionary currents, especially to the militants who were joining the Socialist Party. The SP had been in decline throughout the 1920s, but the radicalizing conditions of the early 1930s were attracting militant workers and students to it. This helped lead to the development of a significant left wing that clashed with the policies of the right-wing leadership. The WP sought to influence this current, at first from outside, and later by entering the SP in 1936. That will be the subject of a future volume in this series.

James P. Cannon did all he could to further the CLA's turn to mass work. Even during the "dog days," Cannon had always sought to respond to any openings in the trade unions and other mass organizations. He recognized that the best conditions for overcoming the league's problems would be created when it began to recruit workers and transform its internal political life. He spoke to conferences of miners and the unemployed, wrote about them in the *Militant,* and collaborated with CLA trade unionists in strike battles they were involved in. He argued within the National Committee for more leadership attention to and involvement in this work.

Cannon eagerly embraced the new opportunities in 1933–34 to turn the league outward toward the broader labor movement. As he remarked in an unpublished interview before his death in 1974, "My aspiration was always outward. I started in the Wobblies as a soapboxer, an agitator."

The CLA's turn to mass work affected him personally to a degree that was noticeable even to his factional opponents. Albert Glotzer remarked in a letter to Shachtman in February 1933 that Cannon appeared warm and happy for the first time in four years after his trip to the Illinois coal fields.

None of the material by Cannon included in this collection is currently in print. In addition to previously published articles from the *Militant* and elsewhere, this volume contains a number of unpublished items from Cannon's private papers. Among these are many of Cannon's letters and circulars, as well as reports and motions contained in the CLA National Committee minutes.

This volume does not contain all of Cannon's writings and speeches that are available from this period. Left out are articles and letters of a routine character, or those of less general interest, as well as those which are repetitive of other items that are included. Since almost all of Cannon's speeches from this period have been preserved in the form of outline notes rather than transcripts, only three speeches are included.

In addition, Cannon's articles from the *Organizer,* the daily strike newspaper of Minneapolis Teamsters Local 574 in 1934 are contained in *Notebook of an Agitator* (New York: Pathfinder Press, 1973), and are therefore not included here.

Since many of the events and individuals mentioned in this volume will be obscure to present-day readers, extensive editorial notes have been provided, along with a glossary of names and organizations at the end of the book.

Fred Stanton
Michael Taber
JULY 1985

Foreign-language work of the CLA

Published January 2, 1932

The following is excerpted from a column in the *Militant*.

The appearance of a Greek organ of the Left Opposition in America, and the projected early publication of a Jewish paper, will no doubt extend the propaganda effectiveness of our movement to a considerable extent.[1] At the same time, these developments pose before the Communist League, for the first time in its experience as a distinct organization, one of the most difficult and complicated problems—the problem of coordinating and centralizing a movement which is compelled, by the force of circumstances in the country, to speak in many tongues.

Foreign-language-speaking workers constitute an important—even if not the most decisive—section of the American proletariat. To carry the message of communism to them and to unite them with the native workers in a single movement is a task that American communism has stumbled over more than once in the past. We ought to learn from the costly mistakes of the past party experience in order to avoid them in our own work as a faction.

The problem is political, first of all. Organizational difficulties, which have in the past assumed tremendous importance, flow from the political essence of the question. As Marxists we can do no other than aim at a centralized movement which carries an identical message in every language, and always acts as an organizational unit. Special language organizations cannot have an independent existence under our banner. The Left Opposition has no use for autonomous language groups.

The strength of the Left Opposition, in all of its manifestations, is the strength of its ideas, its granite foundation of principle. Every special language grouping or propaganda expression must be built from the very start on this conception. It follows from this that all of our language papers, as well as all other propaganda mediums, are organs of a single National Committee. The references all our language organs make to specific problems of the immigrant workers have to be subordinated entirely and directly related to our fundamental principled line.

The right wing of American communism is also having an experience in this field.[2] In the contrast between that experience and ours can be seen the contrast between a movement that lives from day to day, as best it can, and a movement that goes by principle. *Revolutionary Age* complains about its Lithuanian twin *Naujoji Gadyne,* which has recently made its first appearance.

"There is a distinct tendency to treat the struggle of the Lithuanian Opposition as if it were an isolated 'Lithuanian' fight. The fundamental political struggle . . . is almost completely neglected. . . . It does not as much as mention the Communist Party (Majority Group)."

Well, what do you expect? Of course they leave aside

the big questions and devote themselves to the comparatively petty "national" issues, to catch the support of people with transitory grievances. The opportunists always do that. *Naujoji Gadyne* is only repeating the method it learned from *Revolutionary Age.*

Such exhibitions cannot happen in the Left Opposition. *Revolutionary Age* also criticized the manifesto of the Communist League in the Greek language—but from an opposite standpoint. The manifesto, it said, talked too much about the Anglo-Russian Committee and the Chinese revolution, and not enough about the so-called Greek questions. We need not worry about such criticism. Let us go to the workers in all languages with a uniform propaganda on the fundamental questions of world import. In that way we will build a movement among the foreign-language-speaking workers that is ideologically united with the Communist League and an integral part of its organization. If we go ahead with this aim we will be armed in advance against most of the difficulties and contradictions which hampered the party in the past in the foreign-language field.

Proletarian Party split[3]

Published January 9, 1932

The following article was published in the *Militant*.

Engels once wrote that every workers' party must necessarily develop in a process of internal struggle, according to the dialectical laws of development in general. This observation is again called to mind by the factional struggle now taking place in the ranks of the Proletarian Party. It is a sign of vitality that is well worth watching.

For over a decade this sectarian offshoot of American communism devoted itself to a tranquil observation and "explanation" of social phenomena. The depression in the American labor movement during the period of prosperity, and the indifference of the workers to revolutionary propaganda which ensued from it, created special conditions for the existence of such a group. And this was further facilitated by the errors and exaggerations of the official Communist Party. The pseudo-Marxist policy of Keracher and Company was a complement to Pepperistic adventurism. Thus a number of revolutionary workers were maneuvered onto a sidetrack. Everything was quiet in the Proletarian Party. The leadership walled it off from the class struggle and from the fierce disputes which raged within the general communist movement.

But that state of affairs could only be temporary. The accentuation of the class struggle in the country and the great conflicts over principle which have brought the world movement of communism to a crisis, have posed questions which can no longer be evaded. Controversy is sweeping through the Keracher party like a tornado, making up in fury for its long postponement. Almost overnight the Keracher group of leaders, who ask only for peace and quiet, has been confronted with a stormy internal struggle.

Following the national convention of the organization, where criticism was smothered and all the burning questions of the moment were met with evasive opportunism, an opposition has come to life and is waging a militant struggle on a national scale. The opposition is publishing its own bulletin and has even gone so far as to project a national conference. A split appears to be the inevitable outcome of the conflict.

In fact, the split has already begun. The leaders of the Proletarian Party, who borrow so much in principle from Stalinist revisionism, have revealed themselves also as apt pupils of the administrative methods. The criticisms of the opposition everywhere are being answered not with arguments but with expulsion. According to the *Proletarian Opposition Bulletin,* six of the leading oppositionists in Chicago have been expelled and twenty-five members have resigned from the party. Members of the NEC are being sent out on a witch-smelling and heresy-hunting campaign, with power to expel, suspend, or otherwise punish members, without the formality of a "trial." Three members have been suspended and one expelled in Elkhart, Indiana. The entire branch of forty in Buffalo has been expelled. In New York and other places secessions have taken place.

The course of the opposition movement within the Proletarian Party remains unclear. It is quite obvious, from a reading of its campaign material, that the opposition has not yet undertaken to answer the main question which arises inevitably from its struggle against the leadership and policy of the party. That question is: Where are we going, and why? *Proletarian Opposition Bulletin* no. 2, which we have at hand, directs a sharp criticism against the bureaucratic regime within the party; it condemns the opportunistic election campaign in Detroit, and insists on a struggle for immediate demands on the question of unemployment.

On all these points the opposition is undoubtedly in the right as against the leadership. But when all is said and done these questions have a secondary importance. They are by no means an adequate armament for a real political struggle. The opposition must equip itself with an all-around platform. It must take a position on the basic questions of principle, and make its tactical deductions accordingly. Otherwise it will not be able to avoid a rapid disintegration. Such a fate will threaten it immediately.

One thing at least may be said with certainty: the opposition cannot stand alone as an independent movement. Having made a decisive break with the sterile circle of Keracherism—and this is a sign of its vital proletarian impulse—the opposition confronts the necessity of attaching itself to the living movement of communism. This is the first and most pressing implication of the revolt.

With which faction will the new grouping affiliate? That is the question. Those who seek to evade that question, who hold up the prospect of a "fourth" faction, can only deceive and mislead the movement. That is only the Keracher policy on a small scale; and the present upheaval is, in the first place, a sign of the utter bankruptcy of this policy. The fact that a part of the insurgent elements in New York and other places have already gone over to the Stalin faction without waiting for the movement as a whole to clarify its policy, is a warning against temporizing and delay with this fundamental problem.

To save the new movement, or at least a substantial part of it, from this fate is the task of the serious communist elements within it. Keracherism is only a weak sprout of Stalinism; the ideology at bottom is fundamentally the same. A transfer of affiliation from the Proletarian Party to the Stalin faction signifies nothing more than an organizational secession and a capitulation in principle. Every tendency to limit the opposition to the secondary tactical points is a preparation for such a debacle. A serious study and consideration of the great principled questions, and the adoption of a precise attitude toward them, are now indispensable for a fruitful outcome of the revolt in the Proletarian Party.

Clarence Darrow and the Scottsboro case[4]

Published January 16, 1932

The following article was published in the *Militant*.

The withdrawal of Clarence Darrow and Arthur Garfield Hays from all participation in the legal side of the Scottsboro case has called forth a chorus of praise from the bourgeois press. Darrow didn't like the agitational methods of the International Labor Defense. "You can't mix politics with a law case," he said. He would take part in the legal defense only on the condition that the ILD keep out. The withdrawal of the famous lawyer on these grounds affords the brass-check newspapers—whose attention was drawn to the Scottsboro case by the stormy agitation of the ILD—another occasion to point a moral about the harmful effects of "Communist interference" on behalf of any victim of bourgeois justice. Liberal snivellers and muddleheaded workers, whose thinking is done for them by the ruling class, are echoing this judgment.

Such arguments are not worthy of a moment's consideration. The ILD was absolutely right in rejecting the presumptuous demands of Darrow and Hays, and the Scottsboro prisoners showed wisdom in supporting the stand of their defense organization. Any other course would have signified an end to the fight to organize the protest of the masses against the legal lynching; and with that would have ended any real hope to save the boys and restore their freedom.

There are people, of course—and too many of them—who hold a contrary view. But they are the credulous ones, who have faith in the justice and fairness of the class courts. We rejoice at the blow that has been dealt to this servile and treacherous philosophy. It is true that the lawyers in question are celebrated in their trade. But from our point of view, that fact only invests the calling of their bluff with a greater significance and merits for it a warm approval.

"You can't mix politics with a law case"—that is a reactionary lie. It is father to the poisonous doctrine that a labor case is a purely legal relation between the lawyer and client and the court. It was under that sign—with the same Darrow in the leading role—that the McNamaras and Schmidt and Kaplan were sacrificed, and the labor movement was dealt a blow from which it has not yet recovered. It was the influence of this idea over the Sacco-Vanzetti Defense Committee which paralyzed the protest mass movement at every step and thereby contributed to the final tragic outcome. Not to the courts alone, and not primarily there, but to the masses must the appeal of the persecuted of class and race be taken. There is the power and there is the justice. The affair of Darrow, the Scottsboro prisoners, and the ILD will help to inculcate this lesson.

A sorry adventure

Published January 23, 1932

The following article was published in the *Militant*.

It is just about a year since Weisbord, having failed to convince us by argument, set out to prove by example that he alone possessed the secret of organizing a mass movement and steering it on the straight revolutionary path.[5] If we still remain skeptical it is not because his adventure has been devoid of interest or because he failed to make contributions of a certain kind to the movement in general. You have to give him credit for trying.

He didn't prove his own case, it is true, but he proved something else. What his exploits lacked in heroic quality they made up in a unique humor that was all the more infectious because of its apparent unconsciousness, like the comic act of a sad-faced clown. Therefore we maintain, against those who want to cross him off as a total loss, that the man has his uses. Revolutionists remain human, all too human; we need diversion and amusement. We live parlous lives, beset with griefs and difficulties, and one who can make us laugh is not to be utterly scorned. A brief account of the life and deeds of Albert Weisbord during the past year is justified by this consideration.

As the world knows, or ought to know, the Herculean endeavors of Weisbord have recently culminated in a split of his organization. From this we learn that the total membership of the mass movement—at the time of the split—was thirteen people. Out of these thirteen, six seceded or were expelled, leaving a net membership of seven in the parent organization, including Weisbord himself and his immediate family.

Thereupon—it is alleged—some members of the split-off faction, who had never belonged to any other organization and whose sole instruction in revolutionary ethics had been imparted by him, made an uninvited visit to the headquarters and carried off some books. Weisbord announced this depredation in a characteristic manifesto and submitted it to the whole revolutionary movement as the question of the day.

We are not in favor of burglary and larceny, and it is easy to incite us against practitioners of these arts—principle in this matter being reinforced by personal grievances. We were just on the point of passing judgment on the alleged culprits when Weisbord forestalled us by an appeal to other authorities. The incomparable revolutionist took his whilom comrades and pupils to court and there prayed for the justice that had been denied him.

And then, to make sure that this lesson in Marxism would not be restricted to the defendants, he published a letter in the *New York Forward* explaining his action. He went to court, he said, on the advice of Roger Baldwin. That ought to satisfy anybody who is satisfied with Roger Baldwin as a moral, legal, and political authority.

Moreover, he protested, it was a civil suit and not a criminal case, which—as they say in Missouri—is a distinction if not a difference.

So what can we do now? We have never yet testified against anybody in court and cannot go as witness. We are also barred by ethical scruples from expressing any opinion which might prejudice the case of the defendants. And besides, if it is a matter of law, cannot the seceding faction claim minority rights in the property? We have heard of cases where minority groups of stockholders sued for an accounting and division and were granted it. We raise here also a hypothetical legal question: suppose the defendants plead insanity and cite as proof that they were still suffering from the influence of Weisbord at the time of the alleged offense? It would be a cruel judge indeed who would turn a deaf ear to such a plea.

One may think that these performances would be enough for one man for one year—or for a lifetime. But no, the comic resources of our hero are inexhaustible. On top of all this—to round out the year, so to speak—Weisbord addressed a letter to the Communist League proposing that we get together and talk things over with a view of unity. This proposal, he blandly informed us, is designed to be a "bridge" to the Communist League. But he is separated from us in such a way that a bridge can hardly be the medium of connection. What this fellow needs is a ladder or, better yet, a rope.

New York CLA branch picnic, 1930. Seated on ground: unidentified, Jane Rose, Max Shachtman, Joseph Carter, Rose Karsner. Middle row: Mac Rose (seated), James P. Cannon (seated), Billie Shachtman (in bathing suit), Edith Harvey (kneeling), unidentified, Morris Lewit, unidentified, George Ray (far right). Standing at rear: unidentified, Von Borstel, Morris Kent, unidentified, Cornelia Hansen, Peter Hansen, Ruth Cannon (obstructed), unidentified.

Public apology for article on Lassalle

Published February 13, 1932

The following article was published in the *Militant*.

The editorial board of the *Militant* owes an apology to its readers for the publication, in the issue of January 30, of the book review dealing with a recent biography of Lassalle.[6] The superficial quality of this article, as well as its flippant and presumptuous tone, have been remarked as more appropriate for the *New Masses* than for our paper. The entire article contradicts our attitude toward the great historic figures of the proletariat, among whom we count Lassalle. Its appearance in these columns was entirely accidental. We are decidedly against the attitude expressed in the article, and we are still more against the spirit of it.

The founder of the German labor movement was not without shortcomings in the field of theory and tactics. Marx, who was his contemporary, explained them sufficiently, and they are known to the students of socialist history. But, for every serious revolutionist, Lassalle remains

Lassalle, the sword and the flame of the proletariat. We do not grant to anyone the right to disparage and belittle him—and thereby to distort him altogether and to obscure his grandiose historic import.

Lenin, who was not so presumptuous, spoke of Lassalle many times, and always with respect. He began his famous brochure *What Is to Be Done?* by quoting, in thesis form, from a letter of Lassalle to Marx. In another place he speaks of "the historical service Lassalle rendered to the German labor movement." Trotsky has referred to him in the same manner in *Our Revolution* and in other works. Such examples were lost on the reviewer who appraised Lassalle in the *Militant*.

It is necessary to protest against the utterly false evaluation of Lassalle in the review under consideration. But it is no less important to react against the spirit it manifests. We have to be careful that such a movement as ours, which is obliged, especially under present conditions, to emphasize the critical side of its work, does not become a playground for smart-aleckism and parvenu self-assurance. Tendencies of this kind are to be seen now and then, especially among the youth. The parvenu spirit is the petty-bourgeois spirit. It is alien to an organization of proletarian revolutionaries and has no legitimate rights within it.

NC statement on the situation in the International Left Opposition[7]

March 1932

The following article, signed by the National Committee of the CLA, was first published in the April 23, 1932, *Militant*.

The National Committee, having considered and discussed the most important parts of the material bearing on the present situation in the International Left Opposition, and the French section in particular, has come to the following conclusions:

1. The most important feature in the internal life of the International Opposition in the past two years has been the struggle to free the movement from the influence of alien elements who paralyzed its activities by sterile intrigues, distorted its principles in practical application, and hampered its development as the guiding force of the proletarian vanguard. We are and have been fully convinced of the progressive and revolutionary quality of the struggle for these ends which has been led by Comrade Trotsky. It has been an unavoidable and necessary stage

in the preparation of the International Left Opposition to fulfill its great historic tasks. The National Committee is in full solidarity with the estimate of this struggle and the perspectives of the International Left Opposition outlined in the circular letter of Comrade Trotsky under date of December 22, 1931.[8]

2. The correctness and necessity of this struggle to purge the movement of alien elements is demonstrated, among other things, by the positive results in the German section after the liquidation of the worthless intrigues of Landau and the freeing of the section for its actual revolutionary tasks. The leadership of the German section, which has taken shape in the struggle against Landau and his sterile factional regime, must be given all possible international assistance and support in its tremendous responsibilities and opportunities.

The necessity of the struggle for internal renovation is shown with no less force—although in a negative manner—by the present state of affairs in France. The demoralization there ensues directly from the fact that the two-year struggle has not been brought to a conclusion.

3. In our opinion the present situation in the French [Communist] League—which ought to be a matter of grave concern to the entire International Opposition—is not a new one. We regard it rather as the rear end of the struggle to clear the section of the influence of unassimilable and careerist elements, which has been unduly prolonged. The task there, as we see it, is not to seek a solution of the crisis from the standpoint of the episodic questions and differences. This only blurs the real issue. What is necessary is a decisive course toward the liquidation of the crisis by a firm stand against the representatives of the disintegrating tendencies.

Among these we count the leaders of the Jewish group,

and we particularly condemn their attempt to set up a *nationality group* as a faction within the league and their resignation from the National Committee in the name of such a group. Such methods and practices are incompatible with communist organization. No less harmful, in the drawn-out internal crisis of the league, have been the ambiguous and diplomatic maneuvers of Naville, against which we have recorded ourselves in our previous resolution.[9] In our opinion it is most necessary for the French league to bring the internal controversy to a conclusion, to draw clear and precise lines and make a selection on that basis.

4. The proposal of Comrade Trotsky for the reorganization of the International Secretariat, by constituting it out of representatives of the most important sections who will be responsible to their sections, is the most feasible plan under the circumstances. As the experience of the past few years has shown, the International Opposition has not yet developed to the point where a secretariat based on the selection of persons—free from accountability to the respective sections—could fulfill the office. The secretariat must become a responsible body standing above the intrigues and helping to liquidate them.

We are of the opinion that Comrade Mill misused the office of international secretary and erred fatally by identifying himself with the factional struggle in the French league against the leadership. Thereby he helped to negate the whole progressive struggle against Landau-Naville-Rosmer and, at the same time, undermined the authority and discredited the International Secretariat. The reorganization of the secretariat as a responsible body will help to shield it against such a fate by rendering it less susceptible to personal moods and vacillations.

5. The difficulties of distance, etc., make a timely and

effective participation of the American league in the internal questions of the European sections extremely difficult, and preclude altogether any pretensions on our part to play a leading role in their solution. We must not undertake that. Nevertheless, we consider it desirable to participate more directly in the work of the International Secretariat through an elected representative, and the National Committee will propose to select such a representative of the American league as soon as possible.

It is necessary to acknowledge a slackness in our international activities and duties, the nature of which and its basic causes have been accurately described in Comrade Trotsky's circular letter. In order for our league to be useful in the solution of the internal problems of the European sections, and to educate itself in internationalism in the process, it must firmly organize a *collective* participation. The National Committee as a whole must familiarize itself with the international questions and bring a collective judgment to bear upon them. The most important material must be translated and supplied to the league membership for information and discussion. The progressive elements in all sections, which are struggling for the liquidation of circle psychology, sterile intellectualism and worthless intrigues, and for the consolidation of genuinely revolutionary cadres, must be assured at every step that they have a conscious and resolute ally in the American league.

The threat of illegality and the mood of the workers

Published March 19, 1932

The following article was published in the *Militant*.

American capitalism is already giving advance notice of the bloody answer it is preparing to the slaves whom it denies a living within their slavery. In the roar of gunfire at Detroit it said to the workers whom it has thrown onto the streets: "We cannot employ you and we will not provide you, and if you protest we will shoot you." The massacre at Detroit was followed a few days later by the murderous attack on the Chicago demonstration of the Communists before the Japanese Consulate.[10] Here, as in Detroit, the police were clearly the aggressors. The demonstration was designed as a peaceful one; with Communist direction it could not be otherwise under the given conditions, for it is no part of Communist policy to substitute the futile violence of an individual or of a small group for the intervention of the masses, who are not yet active.

We do not credit the story by means of which the police

murderers are attempting to cover themselves—that the first shots were fired from the crowd, and by a "Communist agitator" at that. Such individual reactions to the regime of brutal repression are of course possible; one may say inevitable. Even if that had been the case in Chicago, the police who forcibly deprived the manifestants of their rights would bear the whole responsibility. But their attempt to pin the accusation on a "known" Communist discredits their story from the start. It is a transparent subterfuge to justify themselves and to frame up the party.

They are proceeding in the same way in Detroit. The four victims of their gunmen had not been laid away before they began a wild manhunt for Communist leaders and set the legal machinery in motion to grind out wholesale indictments. They are drawing the noose tighter around the workers' vanguard. They are starting to isolate it from the great mass of discontented workers and to outlaw its activities. The labor passivity that has attended the Kentucky prosecutions and convictions only encourages a similar procedure after every skirmish in other places.[11] The ruling capitalists and their government hirelings, shivering in fear at the coming storm of labor rebellion, would like to cut off and proscribe the conscious and articulate section of the class and deprive the germinating mass movement of legal spokesmen and organizers.

The menace of illegality for the communist movement is undoubtedly growing, and it calls for the most serious and all-sided consideration. There is no prescription by the aid of which the party can be guaranteed a legal existence. With the present weakness and isolation of the party, with the intensification of war danger increasing, and with a powerful ruling class panic-stricken at the prospect of a workers' mass movement to come, but not yet matured and merged with the vanguard, the revolutionary wing may be driven underground in spite of anything it can do.

There is no prescription that will guarantee legality. But within certain limits it can be safeguarded and strengthened by a correct policy. The experience of 1919–21 must be recalled and its lessons assimilated by those militants who have been drawn into the movement, under legal conditions, since that time.[12] The first of these lessons is to value legality; and, without surrendering a single point of revolutionary doctrine or evading a single duty, to fight for it to the end. A retreat into illegality under the present conditions, or even under much more aggravated ones, would signify a retreat from the coming class battles.

One of the most important problems of American Communist tactics is to maintain an open legal, or at least semilegal, position until a significant workers' mass movement has caught up with the conscious vanguard and joined with it in a common struggle on the concrete questions of the day. Then the suppression of the party will be a thousand times more difficult. The numerically weak party, isolated and fighting virtually alone, is only a threat. The party supported by a workers' mass movement is a power.

If we are going to find our way in the charged social atmosphere of these days, the first obligation laid upon us is to see things as they are. History assigns an enormous role to the conscious revolutionaries, who foresee the line of march theoretically; but it does not allow us to force events by our own wishes. Marxism is no doctrine of social miracles wrought by small minorities. It has nothing in common with putschism. Even if one is convinced—as we are convinced—that we are near the threshold of great events and great changes in the life of the American working class, it is not permissible to forget for a moment that we alone will not and cannot be the authors of these changes and these events. The future of American communism is bright with promise, but we will move toward that great future only insofar as the working masses move with us at every step.

The material conditions are long ripe for a tremendous upsurge of militant labor. This we know and this is the foundation of our perspectives. But the workers do not react automatically to the material pressure upon them, and there is no rule by which to foretell the extent and tempo of their movement in advance. That must be judged and estimated as it actually unfolds or, at least, as it is clearly intimated. A clear-sighted study of the mood and temper of the workers must precede and regulate the daily tactics and working methods of the revolutionary party if it really aims to accelerate and influence the collisions of class forces.

Unemployment on the one side and wage reductions on the other are weighing down upon virtually the whole working class of America and ruthlessly changing all the accustomed conditions and standards of life. But in spite of that—and this is the most singular and inescapable fact in the situation—the workers have not yet begun the inevitable movement of revolt. Under pressure of conditions that become more and more intolerable, the workers are undergoing a profound mental change. But the outward signs of this change are not yet manifest to any appreciable extent. It is like the slow accumulation of steam in a sealed boiler that has not yet reached the explosive point. The explosion will come, and it may come unannounced; but it is not the storm—it is but rather the dead calm before the storm—that characterizes the present situation.

The sporadic movements which flare up here and there are organized by the small communist vanguard and, for the most part, carried through by them in almost every case.

In these actions the communist workers are distinguishing themselves by their courage and resolution. Thereby they are storing up capital and prestige for the future. But the masses are not moving with the communists. In this disparity there is a great danger that the vanguard will become exhausted and demoralized and unable to handle the real movement when it breaks.

The communist workers are not the working class. They are only its conscious section, and at present in America they are a small and numerically insignificant section. The communist workers alone cannot fight real class battles. Their function is to fight with the workers, and in their front ranks. The task of the communists at the moment is to prepare the workers for the coming struggles. The center of this task is the "patient work of explanation"; of agitation and propaganda to win the workers over to a course of struggle. There is no substitute for this prosaic task and there is no way to leap over it. A renovation of the party's tactics in this sense is an absolute necessity. Only in this way can it prepare the coming workers' movement and entrench itself within it.

A false antiwar slogan

Published March 19, 1932

The following article was published in the *Militant*.

The revolutionary fighting spirit of the Communist workers who demonstrated before the Japanese consulates last Saturday is not to be questioned.[13] The firm will to fight against the imperialist warmongers was their animating impulse. And that is all the greater reason for protest against the manner in which the energies of the militants are being misdirected by the false tactics of the party leaders. It is a cruel irony that the brave demonstration of the Chicago revolutionists, inspired by a hatred of "their own" imperialists, could give the outward appearance of an "anti-Japanese demonstration," and be so described by the capitalist press. Such a direction of the struggle does not in the least hamper the war plans of American imperialism. On the contrary it gives them unwitting support.

Of course we support the Chinese people; we ought to expose and denounce the Japanese militarists in our general campaign in America against the government of Japan. And this is precisely the impression that, in the present situation, the demonstrations before the Japanese consulates are bound to create in the minds of the masses. In actions of this kind only the salient facts stand out. The subsidiary slogans, the other issues which are "linked up" with the main event, are lost in the shuffle. How quickly wrongly formulated slogans exact their penalty! The popular impression of the Saturday demonstrations as an "anti-Japanese" affair is the price already paid for the asinine slogan of the party leadership: "Drive the Japanese diplomats from the country!"

In this slogan there is the basis for a complete disorientation of the proletarian struggle around the question of the coming war. It fits in with the pseudopacifist policy of American imperialism in the East and facilitates its work of delusion at home. "The Japanese are mad with militarism; they are provoking a world war; but our own government strives for peace, and if it is finally forced into war it will be the fault of Japan"—this is the imperialist propaganda for the coming year which is seeping into the minds of the American people day by day. Does the "anti-Japanese" agitation of the party counteract this poisonous delusion or does it contribute to it? In the event of war with Japan the Communists will be disarmed if the American imperialists can say: "You were more eager than we were; you demanded the expulsion of the Japanese diplomats while we were still striving for peace."

"The enemy is in our own country!"—this is the revolutionary slogan of Liebknecht and Lenin, the guiding line of the proletarian struggle against imperialist war. Those who forget this for one moment are already on the toboggan to social patriotism. The proletariat in every country has to wage its own specific fight against its own imperialists and work for their defeat. The central task of the American communists in the question of war is the systematic exposure of the policy of America which masks the most monstrous imperialist designs with the phrases of pacifism. The fire of the communists must be concentrated mainly on this Hoover policy if it is to serve the interests of the proletariat. The anti-Japanese slogan contradicts this task, confuses and disorganizes the struggle, and even contains the germ of chauvinist deviations. The slogan should be withdrawn before it does further harm.

Internal problems of the CLA

March 22, 1932

The following article by Cannon and Arne Swabeck was printed in the CLA's Internal Bulletin no. 3.[14]

Comrade Trotsky's remarks, in his circular letter of December 22, 1931, about the general perspectives of the league[15]—which coincide with what has been said on this subject in our second conference thesis and in other articles and documents—ought to be supplemented at the present time by a consideration of the prospects of the more immediate future, as well as by an estimation of the specific part which our league as an organization may play in the further development of the American communist movement.

The objective conditions of the moment, within which the great future possibilities of American communism are slowly ripening, press very heavily upon the Opposition. The ideas are at work, thanks to our fairly good propagandistic activities, and there is no doubt that our cause is making silent gains in the ranks of the Communist workers. But it appears to us most probable that the real chances for rapid organizational growth will come only later, after the impact of great events has shaken the party more profoundly. That such opportunities for the Opposition to advance in great leaps will present themselves, we can have no doubt. And in this connection a most important question presents itself: Will the nucleus which we have previously organized be prepared to meet the situation and take command of the party, or a substantial section of it? Or will it turn out that the ideas of the Opposition have to find their eventual organizational medium only after longer delays, by a more roundabout way and through some other door than ours?

The vindication and the victory of our ideas in time is assured. But this may take place in a drawn-out fashion and after much waste of time if our league falls short of its tasks. If it transpires that the present nucleus shall have exhausted itself in the preliminary propaganda tasks—the popularization of the fundamental ideas of the International Opposition—and shall have failed to raise the necessary cadres to carry them through, this will undoubtedly be the case. On the other hand, if we succeed in the time that is allotted to us in assembling and training a politically "hard" and genuinely revolutionary group, the rapid reconstruction of the party—with our nucleus as its core—may be accomplished in a few decisive steps after the inevitable smash-up of centrism.

This latter, in our opinion, ought to be our deliberate aim. From this point of view it is essential now to submit the present situation in the league to a thoroughgoing consideration and to examine the trend of development. The strength of the American section of the Opposition, and its advantages over a number of the European sections—as we have maintained against many critics (Weisbord, Carter, and others) who saw the thing upside down—consisted in the homogeneous group, trained and prepared by years of struggle, as a single faction, in the party. The leading group, which had been assembled over a period of years in the party in the party struggles, was united by a community of opinions on the concrete questions of domestic policy as well as by an accord with the fundamental principled line of the International Left Opposition. It was this experience and this general homogeneity which gave the leadership an exceptional authority and enabled it to guide the organization firmly; to reduce capitulationism to insignificance and to liquidate oppositional attempts without crises and without even serious internal disturbances (Fox, Weisbord, Malkin).[16]

But during this whole period, in which a general external unanimity was displayed, the organization became aware, from time to time, of alarming frictions within the National Committee which gave the impression of personal quarrels. This state of affairs was signalized by the disruption of the work of the committee for several months after the first conference in 1929, by protracted abstentions on the part of individual members, and especially by an open conflict at the second conference over the selection of the new NC.

The facts which were known gave rise to uneasiness and dissatisfaction among the members, and to demands for an explanation of the political reasons for the friction. To all such demands the members of the committee answered that there were no serious differences on questions of the league policy. And this answer was not a deception of the organization, as some comrades charged. Episodic disputes, of course, occurred quite frequently, and at times there were heated discussions, but when it came to the actual formulation of the committee's position on the important questions, we found a common language. This was the case at the First National Conference in 1929; at the plenum in the spring of 1930; and in the resolutions presented to the Second National Conference in August 1931.

In spite of that, the delegates to the second conference witnessed a struggle over the new NC, initiated by Comrade Shachtman's attempt to change its composition, which they were obliged to decide.[17] From the acrimony of this dispute it became obvious there to the conference delegates, and especially to us, that the unity of the committee was by no means as firm as the unanimous political resolutions seemed to indicate. Nevertheless we assured the delegates of our confidence that the conflicts would be overcome in the course of common work and comradely discussion without plunging into a crisis.

These hopes were not realized. We have not been able to construe the conduct of Comrade Shachtman since the conference otherwise than as a series of blows to the organization. And finally, at the meeting of the NC held on March 15, 1932, Comrade Shachtman presented a document couched in such terms and filled with such accusations against us as to preclude the possibility of harmonious collaboration. Rejecting our proposals for a prior discussion of the questions within the committee, Comrade Shachtman had already gone outside the committee with this attack. It has become the material for a factional campaign in the New York branch on the part of comrades who have been at odds with the NC right along. Comrades Abern and Glotzer have associated themselves with this document of Comrade Shachtman. As a result of all this it is obvious that the organization is placed before a situation which cannot be solved by the committee itself. Nothing remains but to submit the disputes to the organization as a whole, and, simultaneously, to transmit the material to the other sections.

The ostensible basis for this attack, and the factional agitation in the New York branch inspired by it, is the publication in the *Militant* of March 5 of an article by Comrade Swabeck which sharply condemns the interpretations of Engels's "Introduction to *The Class Struggles in France*" made by Comrade Carter in *Young Spartacus* no. 2. It is claimed that Comrade Swabeck's contentions are incorrect, and strong objections are also made to the harsh tone of his article. But even if these allegations were well-founded—which we dispute—it is quite obvious that such an incident, by itself, is not and cannot be the real cause of the tumult. No grown-up communist will believe for a moment that a National Committee of more or less experienced people can be disrupted overnight for the sake of a remote historical dispute or an insult to a comrade. The situation can become comprehensible only if the real causes are laid bare. The muffled differences and half-differences of the past, which have matured to the point where they upset the unity of the committee, must be brought to light before the organization.

To place the discussion on this, its real, political basis, is the aim of the present statement. On this background the specific dispute in question, which has been seized upon as the pretext for the attack, can be assigned its proper proportional place and discussed with the necessary objectivity. The dispute over Comrade Swabeck's article, which, while it has a certain importance in itself, and will be discussed here at full length, will then be revealed in its real significance as an incident in a larger conflict—one that can no longer be confined to the National Committee.

In order to bring the necessary clarity into the discussion, the first requirement is to put the disputed questions as they really are. For the past year or so, within the resident

National Committee, and particularly between Comrade Shachtman on the one side and the present writers on the other—upon whose collaboration the practical work and direction of the league rested—there has been a slowly but steadily developing divergence over questions which we consider decisive for the future of our movement. These questions are the following:

1. The position of our league on the struggle within the International Left Opposition for the consolidation of revolutionary cadres and the break with alien elements and tendencies which stood in the way of this consolidation.

2. The conclusions and lessons to be drawn from this international struggle of the past three years. And, organically connected with the first two—

3. The attitude of the leadership of the league toward various nonrevolutionary and intellectualistic tendencies in the New York branch.

The international questions

In his document, referred to above, Comrade Shachtman refers to the disagreements on the international questions in a most peculiar way. On the one hand, he accuses us of "tacking on the international questions" to other disputes arbitrarily. On the other hand, he charges us with disloyalty in mentioning the international differences. He writes: "Cannon has disloyally taken advantage of views I have expressed in letters to Comrade Trotsky, etc." These arguments contain their refutation, both in fact and in principle. Moreover, they betray their irreconcilable difference between his *approach* to these questions and ours.

In the first place, our disputes with him *began* with the international questions, especially on the way of approaching and dealing with them, and could not be "tacked on" to other disputes that did not exist in any clearly defined form. And, in the second place, we know of no obligation whatever to keep silent about the international questions, or to put them on one side as something abstract and entirely disconnected from the life of our league. If we have so far confined our discussions of them to the close circle of the leadership, and even more than that to personal conversations with Comrade Shachtman, it was not because we considered them "cabinet" secrets, but only for the purpose of helping him to alter his course while there was yet time. If Cannon, with the full agreement of Swabeck, spoke at the [1931] national conference on the *concrete lessons* of the fight against Landau-Naville—after Comrade Shachtman had overlooked this side of the question in his report—and did not mention Comrade Shachtman's name, nor his half support of these elements, it was not because we lack any right to speak openly, or because we wish to fight him with "insinuations" and "hints." It was only to warn him that we cannot agree that our league should skip over these international experiences without discussing what they really signified.

These efforts to influence Comrade Shachtman without appealing to the organization yielded absolutely no results. The breach, which we did not yet consider unbridgeable at the conference, became wider and *our league became further compromised in the International Opposition as a result of Comrade Shachtman's conduct.* That is why we have come more sharply into conflict with him. It is necessary to speak out loud about it now. Comrade Shachtman will have no reason to complain of "insinuations," nor of any indirectness whatever.

The evolution of our differences with Comrade Shachtman on the international questions into the open conflict of the present moment has been recorded all along the line by a chain of facts which speak for themselves and leave no possibility of doubt as to their meaning. The mere recital of those facts—which are clearly established—will show how futile are the assertions of Comrade Shachtman that the present differences have been invented and "tacked on" in some kind of a "frame up" against him.

We consider Comrade Shachtman's approach to the functions of international representative of the league and his method of conducting them just as false as the position he took on the struggles in the other sections. And we made our objections known to him not once or twice, but many times, and not since yesterday, but for more than a year past.

On the side of *methods:* Comrade Shachtman conducted himself as the international representative and correspondent of the league in an irresponsible and purely personal way. In these affairs, which have the deepest interest for the committee as a whole, he acted as an individual, not as the representative of the committee and responsible to it. He did not even find it necessary to make the information about the development of struggles in the European sections, which came to him by virtue of his office, available to the committee.

Incredible as it may seem to one who thinks in terms of organization and collective work, *especially in a committee that is presumably united in its policy,* Comrade Shachtman regarded the correspondence of Comrade Trotsky, on matters relating to the most acute crises in the European sections, as a purely personal correspondence. He would convey the contents of these letters to the committee in snatches and brief extracts, or not at all, as he saw fit.

It was impossible for us to agree to such a procedure. We could not think of Comrade Trotsky as an individual, passing his time in a purely individual political correspondence to America, when there is an organization here in harmony with his views that attaches the greatest importance to every word he writes about the International Opposition. We tried to explain this point of view to Comrade Shachtman, both in committee meetings and in personal conversations, beginning more than a year ago, *but without the slightest success.*

We could understand Comrade Trotsky writing especially to a minority of a national section, or even to a single individual, in cases where he found the committee against him—as in Germany in Landau's time—or in cases where the committee itself was divided into factions and he found it necessary to intervene. But here was the committee of our league, united in its own policy, which had not taken issue with Comrade Trotsky on any question and had not been criticized by him. Why then should his letters dealing with political questions such as the affairs in the French and German sections be withheld from the committee? This is the point of view we tried to explain to Comrade Shachtman—in the most patient and friendly tone but nonetheless in an insistent way—*but without the slightest success.* Comrade Shachtman only became insulted, only considered our position an invasion of his "personal rights."

Comrade Shachtman's attitude, especially at the time when the struggle against Landau-Naville, etc., was becoming most acute and we were most eager to know more about it, forced us to consider the advisability of asking Comrade Trotsky to address his political letters directly to the committee. We held back from this step, not because we were thinking of a "campaign" against Shachtman, but for precisely opposite reasons. We hoped that a solution would be found. We did not want to sharpen relations with him, and we did not wish to injure his standing with Comrade Trotsky by the implication of a lack of confidence in him. This action was taken eventually by the committee on the motion of Comrade Abern.

At the committee meeting of June 12, 1931, in connection with a discussion of the crisis in the German and French sections, the following motion was carried:

"That the secretary [Swabeck] inform Comrade Trotsky that he acts officially for the NEC and ask him to address official communications to the league in care of the secretary."

Even then Comrade Swabeck could not bring himself to carry out the instruction. The letter was never sent, because he felt it would be a blow to Comrade Shachtman and he hoped for a milder way out of the difficulty. These incidents speak very eloquently about the origin of the disputes.

On the *position* of Comrade Shachtman on the international questions: It became gradually impressed upon us that our quarrel with Comrade Shachtman over this method and procedure in the international questions was merging into a difference of position in regard to them. While we still had apparently "general" agreement, there was to be noted a decided difference in emphasis and definiteness. From the limited material at our disposal (Comrade Shachtman was much better supplied) the general character of the Landau-Naville elements was clear enough to us and we favored a resolute struggle against them. Even without Comrade Trotsky's illuminating open letters it was sufficient for us to read a couple of the translated polemics of Landau, and to take note of the ambiguous and shifty tactics of Naville in his struggle against the leadership of the French league, to get a definite impression of these people. After all that we learned in the party struggle with elements of this type it was impossible for us to be in doubt as to our position. Comrade Shachtman—upon whom the experiences of the past left fewer traces—was less definite, less concrete, and, as we later learned, much less convinced.

We got a sharp reminder of the way things were drifting and of the way they were being taken abroad, by the arrival of a letter from Comrade Trotsky [dated May 23, 1931] in which he criticized our National Committee for its delay in acting against Landau, and held us partly responsible for Landau's actions. If Landau had known that he could not count on the support of our section among others, said Comrade Trotsky, he might not have gone so far in his criminal course as to bring the German section to the split. We did not feel that this criticism properly belonged to the committee, for we had not been put on guard. We made no protest against the criticism—perfectly correct in itself but sent to the wrong address by mistake—but we began to look into things more closely.

We saw that the resolution on the situation in the International Opposition, which Comrade Shachtman had been assigned to write at the meeting of June 12, with definite instructions as to its contents, was delayed from week to week. It was not ready until more than two months later, on the eve of the conference, and it was lacking in that quality of definiteness which we began to insist on more and more. It condemned Landau—who had already split from the International Opposition—but it avoided mention of Naville, who was remaining inside the French league for reasons of factional strategy. The specific condemnation of Naville which appeared in the resolution when it was published in the *Militant* was written into the document on the linotype box by Comrade Cannon.[18]

The common resolution on the situation in the International Opposition began to seem like another of those worthless agreements "in general" which concealed real differences. Comrade Shachtman's international report at the conference was simply a factual chronicle of what had happened. The lessons of the struggle as they applied particularly to that part of the process which remained unfinished, were left out of account altogether. It was this circumstance—coming after all that had gone before—that called forth Comrade Cannon's speech at the conference. Comrade Shachtman has referred to that speech as "insinuation filled," and as marking the height of a "campaign" against him. He is quite mistaken. It was a warning to quit trifling with the problems of the European sections and join us in a common fight on the side of the revolutionary elements.

We didn't know then as clearly as we know now how much actual support he had given to the elements of disintegration in the International Opposition. We only began to realize that the differences were deeper than we had thought, and to fear that the actions of Comrade Shachtman were not entirely accidental.

The attitude toward the problems of the New York branch

Comrade Shachtman's rather ambiguous role on the international questions had its counterpart in his attitude toward the New York branch. Here also the differences with him grew slowly and gradually, and appeared to consist of differences in shading and emphasis. For a long time they were not clearly defined, and, in such circumstances, it would have been futile to think of an open conflict around them. We had a more or less "general agreement" on these problems and, as in the case of the international disputes, were in no hurry to expand the differences into open conflict.

We had fought together against Weisbord and other

oppositional movements, and these struggles exerted a certain unifying influence. But in the conflicts with the Carter grouping we had less agreement. As subsequent events, and the present disruption of the committee in particular, have shown, our apprehensions as to the significance of the first—apparently slight—disagreements were not unfounded.

The characteristic of this grouping—as we estimate it—is pedantic sterility and scholasticism combined with incapacity to judge the actual questions politically. Comrade Shachtman speaks of Carter's criticisms as "frequently exaggerated and petty." And in addition to that it is politically false. This grouping acts as a medium through which the propaganda of our political enemies, including their slander, filters into the Opposition in a moderate form. Carter gave partial support to Weisbord, and as a rule he has selected the acutest moments of our fight with pronouncedly false tendencies to sharpen his attacks on the National Committee. This grouping lacks many things. But its chief shortcoming is the lack of communist proletarian spirit.

We have conceived it as a duty to liberate the branch from this influence by a straight-out, systematic, and unyielding political struggle. Comrade Shachtman went with us part of the way. "In general" we were agreed. But when it came time to clinch the point in a given dispute with this grouping, and to extract a lesson from it, so that the same thing would not have to be gone over again, Comrade Shachtman would draw back. This, as always, only muddled things. The real values of the discussion were lost, and they had to be repeated continually.

What these unformulated differences between us and Comrade Shachtman really signified was intimated rather sharply at the branch meeting prior to the [1931] national conference. After weeks of discussion by the branch, marked by false political criticisms and attacks on the National Committee, the local executive committee brought in a "unanimous" resolution, agreeable both to the Carter group and the alleged supporters of the NC. We rose in opposition to such an unprincipled conclusion of the discussion, which left everything just where it was before, and demanded a clear resolution one way or the other. With this design Comrade Cannon introduced a resolution specifically supporting the NC and rejecting the criticism of Carter. This reopened a discussion which showed conclusively that *there was not real agreement.*

Comrade Shachtman sat silent during this discussion and did not vote on either of the resolutions. Other "supporters" of the NC closest to Comrade Shachtman concentrated their attacks on our resolution.

These were disturbing signs. And though they did not seem to us of enough importance to break up our general solidarity, they contained a warning of future conflicts. This warning sounded louder on the last day of the conference, when Comrade Shachtman insisted on adding to the NC one of those comrades who had not been able to distinguish between the tendency of the NC and the tendency of Carter, and who, at the critical moment, concentrated his attacks on us.

The overwhelming defeat of this proposal by the conference did not in any way serve to convince Comrade Shachtman that he had misjudged the attitude of the organization. And least of all did it suggest to him the idea of respecting that attitude. He appeared to take the matter as a personal affront, from which he has not yet recovered.

This affair threw a spirit of gloom over the closing hours of the conference. The irresponsible and politically incorrect action of Comrade Shachtman—from which all the committee members had tried to dissuade him—gave new encouragement to the Carter group. They began to speculate more actively on divisions in the National Committee—which Carter had repeatedly hinted at in the branch discussion without any rebuke from Comrade Shachtman—which would facilitate oppositional movement. The members began to be apprehensive of coming conflicts, the reason for which was not entirely clear to them.

This unsettled feeling in the organization has been directly fostered by the whole course of Comrade Shachtman since the conference. The mere listing of his irresponsible acts since the conference gives convincing proof of this. These actions have led him straight, step by step, to his present position.

1. Immediately after the conference he demanded a two months' vacation. Assenting to his proposal, we tried to prevail on him to delay it for a short time so that it would not appear to the membership as a reaction to the conference disputes and cause further uneasiness among them. All these arguments were wasted. Comrade Shachtman would not listen, and insisted on his point.

2. He elected to go to Europe on his vacation. Much as we opposed the idea of international relations being caricatured by individuals touring from one country to another on personal responsibility, we did not raise objections to this kind of a vacation.

3. While on his European tour, Comrade Shachtman interested himself in the acutest conflicts in the European sections, passed judgments and took sides in them, without so much as sending the National Committee a single word of information. We had to hear from Comrade Trotsky himself, in an indignant letter of protest against the conduct of Comrade Shachtman in Europe and the false appraisal he had made of the disputes.

4. Following the return of Comrade Shachtman, and the receipt of Comrade Trotsky's letter [of December 25, 1931], the National Committee held a meeting to act on the proposal of Comrade Trotsky. He had asked the committee to say whether the views and acts of Comrade Shachtman in international affairs were his own personal views and acts, or were representative of the committee's opinion. To that the committee could only reply that it had not even known of the views formulated by Comrade Shachtman in Europe and that it could not take any responsibility for them. This statement was formulated in a very moderate resolution, which did not condemn Comrade Shachtman but only deferred its final judgment on the questions pending the receipt of more detailed material. The discussion was conducted in a moderate and friendly tone, and Comrade Shachtman was elected by unanimous vote to resume his work as editor of the *Militant*. This Comrade Shachtman refused to do.

5. On top of all this we now find Comrade Shachtman coming out against us, in alliance with an oppositional grouping which obstructs the political education and development of the New York branch, and hurling at us a document which proclaims the end of collaboration with us.

In the light of the foregoing, Comrade Shachtman's document, which would be otherwise absolutely inexplicable, can be analyzed and its real meaning demonstrated. From the foregoing it will be quite clear that Comrade Shachtman has not composed such a document merely for the purpose of "correcting" a misunderstanding of Engels's introduction on the part of Comrade Swabeck, nor for the purpose of protecting a member of the organization from injustice and insult. No, Comrade Shachtman has drawn up his document as a protest against our insistence on a firm and unambiguous position on the international questions, and as a demonstration of solidarity with an oppositional faction in the New York branch which is false in its political criticisms and permeated with a spirit that is out of place in a really serious proletarian organization.

And to do this he has been obliged to resort to a polemical method which is foreign to the Bolshevik method of putting questions squarely and discussing them honestly. He had to spin a web of specious argumentations in which he himself got hopelessly entangled. This document, designed to discredit us, gives in fact the appearance of a terrific self-revelation. It can only bring us nearer to the conclusion which flows from what went before it: his half support of Landau-Naville, his present support of the Mill-Felix group in France against the leadership of the French league, his growing antagonisms to us and his corresponding solidarity with the Carter group and others whose political orientation consists primarily of opposition to us—all these events have a certain connection and have not happened by chance.

The dispute over Engels's introduction

Comrade Swabeck's article was written in reply to statements in the article of Comrade Carter regarding the position taken by Engels in his introduction to Marx's *Class Struggles in France*. Were these statements true or false? Did they serve a revolutionary or a reactionary cause? These are the real questions at issue as we see it. But Comrade Shachtman, in his defense of Comrade Carter and his attack on Comrade Swabeck, twists away from this issue at the beginning of his polemic and does not return to it in any direct way. He has space for pages of quotations, but he does not once quote the statement of Carter which Comrade Swabeck answered. To restore the discussion on this question to its real basis we must begin with this quotation.

Comrade Carter wrote: "Rosa [Luxemburg], in her inaugural address, again investigated the new problems brought forth by the conditions of the war and post-war period. She re-examined the teaching of Marx and Engels on the questions of *armed insurrection, guerilla warfare, force and violence* and concluded that history had once again placed on the agenda the tactic advocated by Marx and Engels in the Communist Manifesto in 1847–48, *but later proclaimed by Engels as outlived.* (Introduction to *The Class Struggles in France*—Marx.)" (Our emphasis.)

This statement is not true. Thrown into an agitational article to be read by unschooled young workers, it could only mislead them in regard to Engels's teachings. As it stands it is a slander against Engels which serves the reformists, and in this country particularly the Socialist Labor Party, which preaches legalism on the "authority" of Engels. "The tactic advocated by Marx and Engels in the Communist Manifesto" is the tactic of "the forcible overthrow of all existing social conditions." Engels never proclaimed this tactic "outlived," he never said that "the teachings of Marx and Engels on the questions of armed insurrection, guerilla warfare, force and violence" were "outlived." It was the revisionists who perfidiously ascribed this renunciation to him, utilizing the published version of his introduction to Marx's *Class Struggles in France,* out of which they had blue-penciled the most direct and striking revolutionary passages, as their authority. In this country the SLP printed this mutilated work of Engels under a misleading title, with a preface which falsely claims the authority of Engels for their program of legalism.[19]

It is this principled issue between reformists and revolutionists that Comrade Swabeck had in mind when he attacked and refuted the statement in Carter's article which misrepresents Engels and helps the reformists. We cannot allow such a statement to stand unchallenged in our press, and the proper place to refute it was in the official organ of the league.

Here is what the Socialist Labor Party says in the preface to the paper edition of the introduction: "But here comes Engels—Marx's life-long co-worker—and who is more fit to interpret Marxism than he—showing by facts and figures that the day of the barricade, of street-corner revolution, of military action against the capitalist military forces, was a thing of the past already in the last half of the nineteenth century."

Comrade Carter's assertion only paraphrases the words of the SLP. True enough, he does not draw their conclusions, and Comrade Swabeck never accused him of that. But he concedes their premise, repeats in almost the same words what they say about the position of Engels, and thereby grants them the right to refer to Engels as their authority. Comrade Swabeck's article disputed this concession to the treacherous legalists of the SLP. And that was right and necessary, for the heritage of Engels belongs exclusively to us. The revisionists have no claim on his authority.

As is known, the revolutionary Marxists always maintained this in the prewar period, even before the original manuscript of the introduction was discovered in the archives of the German Social Democracy and brought to light by Riazanov. But in this struggle against the revisionists who claim the authority of Engels they were handicapped by the one-sided emphasis on legal methods in the published version of the introduction and by certain statements in it which, without the qualifying and complementary clauses in the original, gave ground for confusion and misunderstanding. They had to rely on a Marxist *interpretation* of the document, on the scattered references to the state as a "covenant" which was not binding on the people if the rulers break it, on the remark that "the right of revolution is, in the last analysis, the only real 'historic right,'" and on the Engels letters of protest against the attempt to paint him as a "pacifist worshipper of legality at all costs."

The revisionists of the time—as now the SLP—took full advantage of the one-sided emphasis on legal methods in the edited introduction, and Bernstein, as Riazanov points out, attempted to pass it off, after Engels's death, which occurred a few months later, as a political testament repudiating the revolutionary past of himself and Marx. With what success this treacherous game was played with Engels's introduction is revealed most pointedly by Rosa Luxemburg in her speech at the founding congress of the German Communist Party. She said: "Two important conclusions were drawn from this reasoning. In the first place the parliamentary struggle was counterposed to direct revolutionary action by the proletariat, and the former was indicated as the only practical way of carrying on the class struggle. Parliamentarism, and nothing but parliamentarism, was the logical sequel of this criticism." And further: "Thenceforward the tactics expounded by Engels in 1895 guided the German social democrats in everything they did and in everything they left undone, down to the appropriate finish of August 4, 1914."[20]

The deletion of some of the most vital sections of the original document, so far from having no significance—as the SLP and after it Comrades Shachtman and Carter maintain—greatly facilitates the colossal deception of the masses undertaken by the revisionists. Kautsky, according to Riazanov, knew that the published version differed significantly from the original, and he wrote, "If the revolutionary viewpoint *(Weltanschauung)* of Engels does not manifest itself with *the necessary clarity and decisiveness,* then it is not he who bears the guilt, but his German friends, who forced him to dispense with the conclusion, *because it was too revolutionary.* They believed that the introduction spoke clearly enough without that. However, as Figura [?—JPC and AS] has shown, this is not the case."[21]

In their pamphlet *Who Are the Falsifiers?* the SLP-ites say: "The alleged omissions," (which they carefully refrain from quoting), "do not serve the Comesoonist [Communist] purpose at all . . . but that is neither here nor there and has nothing to do with the case." Comrade Carter in his statement to the National Youth Committee on March 5 argues: "The Socialist Labor Party replied to Trachtenberg [who quoted the deleted sections from Riazanov—JPC and AS]. I have not been able to find a comeback in any of the Communist publications." And Comrade Shachtman, pressing harder along the same line, adds: "The whole introduction, ungarbled, uncut, undistorted, was printed by Kautsky."

But Kautsky himself had a different opinion. He thought then, as we think now, that the claims of the revisionists could be fought more effectively if the original document were published. Whereupon, says Riazanov, Kautsky made the following proposal to Bernstein:

"Bernstein is in possession of the manuscripts left by our master. If the manuscript of the introduction should be among them, together with the omitted conclusion, then I demand that he publish this conclusion, which Engels omitted for external considerations and not because of inner reflections. That will prove distinctly what little cause Bernstein had to take recourse to Engels."

But, says Riazanov, Bernstein did not react to this challenge. And that did not stop him from stubbornly repeating in all the later editions of his book the contention that the renunciation of revolutionary action was the last testament of Engels.

In the light of these facts appears the enormous value to the revolutionists of Riazanov's discovery of the original manuscript. It does away with the confusion as to Engels's active position at the time and makes his meaning crystal clear, *not only to educated Marxists,* but to anyone who wants to know the truth. From the original manuscript one can prove, not by interpretation only, but *by Engels's own direct words,* that he never renounced an iota of his revolutionary views, to say nothing of proclaiming them "outlived." If he said—in the published version—that "the fighting methods of 1848 are today obsolete in every respect," he outlines—in the suppressed sections—other fighting methods no less forceful and no less revolutionary. If he remarks—in the published introduction—that "the rebellion of the old style, the street fighting behind barricades, which, up to 1848, gave the final decision, has become antiquated," he leaves no room for doubt in the original manuscript that he means only "the old style" and the old form and not rebellions and street fights as such. No wonder the revisionists concealed the original document! It was necessary for their purpose. A few quotations will suffice to show what the deletions signified.

The published version said: "Therefore, even during the classic period of street battles, the barricade had a moral rather than a material effect. It was a means to shake the solidity of the military. If it held until that had been accomplished, the victory was won; if not, it meant defeat." There they stop. The following is left out: *"This is the point of view to be borne in mind even . . . in an investigation of the prospects of the future street battles."*

We have here in Engels's own words, as Riazanov comments, "not a renunciation of street battles nor even of barricades, but ultimately a more diligent evaluation of the chances for them."

Another quotation, with the deleted sections underscored: "And finally, the newly built quarters of the large cities, erected since 1848, have been made out in long, straight and wide streets as though made to order for the effective use of the new cannon and rifles. The revolutionary, who would himself select the new working class districts in the north and east of Berlin for a barricade battle, would have to be a lunatic. *Does this mean that the street battles will play no part in the future? Not at all. It simply means that conditions have become far more unfavorable for the civilian fighters since 1848, and far more favorable for the military forces. Street battles in the future may be successful only if this unfavorable situation can be neutralized by other factors. Such fights will therefore be far less usual in the earlier stages of a great revolution than in its later course, and will have to be fought with greater resources of strength. Such battles will rather resort—as in the great French revolution, and as on September 4 and October 31, 1870, in Paris— to open attack than to the defensive tactics of the barricades.*"

What basis is there whatever, in the face of these words of Engels, for the SLP to represent him as showing that "military action against the capitalist forces was *a thing of the past* already in the last half of the nineteenth century" or for Comrade Carter to limp after them and, without weighing his words or thinking what he was doing, to corroborate their false contention with the no less false assertion that Engels *proclaimed the tactic which he and Marx had advocated in the Communist Manifesto "outlived"*? How much truer, more to the point, and more worthy of a place in our press is the observation of the Marxist scholar Riazanov: "These words of Engels appear to one like a prophecy of the October [1917] revolution!"

Did the revisionists blue-pencil the original document, striking out these and other vital, direct statements, or did

Engels strike them out himself? Shachtman makes a great point of this, and so does Carter. The SLP "proves" that Engels made the excisions: "from which," says the SLP, "it is evident that if anything appears in a discovered manuscript that did not appear in the *Neue Zeit*, it was at one time or another expunged by Engels himself." Comrades Shachtman and Carter press this deduction very insistently, as though they are scoring a point thereby against Comrade Swabeck, and without stopping for a moment to consider who has an interest in this contention.

We do not have sufficient facts at hand to give a positive answer, and we do not consider it decisive for a revolutionist. The SLP's "proof" is full of loopholes and is convincing only to those who want to be convinced. In either case the original manuscript gives the same indisputable proof of Engels's real thought and intent, and confounds the legalists who misused his authority. If Engels agreed to the deletions under the pressure of the exceptional conditions of the moment—the situation created by the drafting of the new Anti-Socialist Law—and the insistence of the party leaders—it only means to a revolutionist that Engels was betrayed and that his death soon after prevented his punishment of the betrayers.

One can understand why the SLP is so anxious to prove that Engels made the deletions of his own accord. But why should Comrades Shachtman and Carter be so positive and insistent? They don't know any more about it than we do. Riazanov is a man of great prestige among revolutionists. Comrade Trotsky in a recent article spoke of his "incomparable Marxist erudition" and also emphasized his exceptional conscientiousness, particularly in matters of historical facts concerning our heritage. In his article in *Unter dem Banner des Marxismus* no. 1 he gives the definite impression that the changes were made in Berlin. In one place he even makes a distinction between the parts struck out of the manuscript by the "editorial blue-pencil" and a "correction made by Engels himself in the proof-sheets." One may take his choice between this representation of Riazanov and the dubious "circumstantial evidence" of the SLP according to his fancy.

But Shachtman has got himself into such a position, he is so concentrated on the design of "making a case" against Comrade Swabeck that he passes over the principled issues of the dispute, and its aims on each side. And, without realizing what he was doing, or the spirit he reveals in doing it, he undertakes the same task, if not for the same ends, as that undertaken in the SLP pamphlet *Who Are the Falsifiers?*: to *discredit Riazanov's* discovery of the original manuscript.

He hammers on all keys: "The whole introduction, ungarbled, uncut, undistorted, was printed by Kautsky." ". . . The whole which Kautsky printed with Engels's authorization and proof corrections." "The deleted sections are obviously those which Engels himself had blue-penciled." And then, having completely convinced himself, he declares, "Neither Riazanov nor Trachtenberg dare to say the contrary openly." What do you mean "Riazanov does not *dare*"? Against whom is he fighting? Who should he be afraid of? Why do you challenge him in such a tone? Comrade Shachtman does himself no credit by this belligerent challenge to Riazanov. And Comrade Carter, who is in pursuit of "historical truth" for its own sake, follows in the path of Comrade Shachtman with some observations that are no less remarkable. Comrade Shachtman has explained that Carter expressed himself "awkwardly." And for that his actual trend of thought sticks out all the more crassly.

Comrade Carter is offended because Comrade Swabeck

brushed aside the quibblings of the SLP and paid no attention to them. He also is quite sure that Engels changed the introduction himself. And he actually complains—in his statement to the National Youth Committee—that Comrade Swabeck "does not so much as mention the SLP pamphlet *Who are the Falsifiers?*" This negligence convinces him "that Comrade Swabeck's interest was not in correcting a misinterpretation of facts and historical documents." Comrade Carter is undoubtedly against the conclusions of the legalists, but he gives their "historical impartiality" a trusting confidence in his dispute with Swabeck.

The refutation of the revisionist and SLP claims to base themselves on the authority of Engels, and the purging of our press of any remarks that could in any way help these claims—this is the question which interested us as revolutionists. This was the obvious aim of Comrade Swabeck's article in the *Militant*.

The criticism of Luxemburg and Trotsky

Comrade Shachtman overlooked this side of the question—or at any rate referred to it only in passing—and released instead a flood of quotations from the discussion over the introduction which took place in the revolutionary camp before the World War. This discussion, of course, had its own value, but it has very little to do with the real question in dispute: the misrepresentation of Engels's position in *Young Spartacus*. But even on this side of the question we cannot find a common standpoint with him.

Comrade Shachtman assures us that the paragraph in Carter's article, to which Swabeck replies, is merely a paraphrase in a very condensed form of what "Rosa (he means Luxemburg) herself said" in her speech at the first congress of the German CP. We didn't know that, and no one could know it from a reading of the paragraph, and we don't know it yet, after all the explanations, including that of Shachtman. Such may have been Carter's intention. We shall not dispute that—but his statements are in no sense a "condensed form" of Luxemburg's remarks, not even an "awkward" one. Luxemburg did discuss and *criticize* Engels's introduction in her speech, but an examination of its text will show very conclusively that her position is in no way related to the one defended by Shachtman and Carter.

In the first place, Luxemburg did not have the opinion which Shachtman and Carter advance—in dubious solidarity with the SLP—that the introduction in the published version represented the "undistorted" views of Engels on the question. And every line of her speech shows that she could not have agreed with their idea that the deleted sections—discovered after her death—have no significance. To say that Engels's introduction is fully correct and that Luxemburg's speech is also correct—as they do—is to play with words as well as with ideas. She *criticized* the position of Engels, as it is presented one-sidedly in the published version of the introduction, and not from the standpoint that *it was right at the time it was written* and later became "outlived," precisely because it appeared to leave out of consideration *those phases of the question directly handled in the deleted sections,* which were just as valid in 1895 as today.

How far removed from the casuistical argument that the published version of the introduction is a whole and fair presentation of Engels's actual revolutionary position is Luxemburg's comment on the document. In an earlier polemic, which Shachtman quotes, she interpreted and defended the introduction in general. But in her speech at the party congress she submitted it to a closer examination and found grave faults in it. But for those faults *she did not hold Engels personally responsible,* as Shachtman and Carter do when they deprecate the importance of the deleted sections and ascribe their deletion to Engels himself. She blamed the party leaders for the shortcomings of the published version. This is what she said: "I must remind you of the well-known fact that the introduction in question was written by Engels under strong pressure on the part of the parliamentary group. . . . They assured Engels, who lived abroad and naturally accepted the assurance at its face-value, that it was absolutely essential to safeguard the German labor movement from a lapse into anarchism, and in this way they constrained him to write in the tone they wished."

Here was a straight-out condemnation of the party leaders for their imposition on Engels—for their abuse of his good faith, for the game they played, as Riazanov says, "with marked cards." And she never accused Engels of a principled deviation. She said in that same speech: "We take our stand upon the ground occupied by Marx and Engels in 1848, we adopt a position from which in principle they never moved." If Comrades Shachtman and Carter were really to stand on the position of Luxemburg it would signify a big step forward. But even then they would not be entirely right, for in the light of the original manuscript, Luxemburg was not entirely right in her speech.

Luxemburg stated plainly—in contradistinction to Comrades Shachtman and Carter, who agree with the introduction and also agree with her speech—that "the introduction was the formal proclamation of the nothing-but-parliamentarian tactics." And further: "When Engels's preface declares that, owing to the modern development of gigantic armies, it is positively insane to suppose that proletarians can ever stand up against soldiers armed with machine guns and equipped with all the latest technical devices, the assertion is obviously based upon the assumption that anyone who becomes a soldier becomes thereby once and for all one of the props of the ruling class. It would be absolutely incomprehensible in the light of contemporary experience, that so noted a leader as Engels *could have committed such a blunder,* did we not know the circumstances in which the historical document was composed."

Could Rosa Luxemburg have said these words and in this way if she had known what Engels actually wrote in the original manuscript, *directly after the passage to which she refers?* Instead of speaking of this "blunder" would she not rather have said as Riazanov said: "These words appear to one like a prophecy of the experiences of the October revolution"?

The same applies to the quotation from Trotsky which Shachtman has thrown in as some kind of a proof against Swabeck, although it serves an opposite end.

Continuing his scholarly exposition of "dialectics" to prove that everybody was right—Engels's introduction and those revolutionists who criticized it in the form in which it was published—Shachtman has recourse to Trotsky. The bringing in of this quotation reveals even more clearly the empty verbalism with which he is playing around the whole question. Here is the full quotation as Shachtman gives it:

"In his well-known introduction to Marx's *The Class Struggles in France* Engels created room for great misunderstandings, by counterposing the military-technical difficulties of the uprising (speedy shifting of troops with the aid of railroads, destructive effect of modern arms and ammunition, wide, long and straight streets in the modern cities) to the new chances of victory resulting from the evolution of the class composition of the army. On the one side, Engels showed himself to be pretty one-sided in the appraisal of the role which is due to modern techniques in revolutionary uprisings; on the other side, he did not consider it necessary to present the fact that the evolution in the class composition of the army can be brought out only when people and army are 'confronted.' . . . The Russian revolution has once more brought proof of the fact that it is not arms, cannon and armored ships which prevail over people, but, in the final analysis, people who prevail over arms, cannon and armored ships." (Trotsky, "The Balance of the Revolution," from *1905*, pages 202–4.) [22]

This, says Shachtman, who claims the published introduction said all that needed to be said for the Marxists to understand and that the deletions add nothing essential, "showed how Engels's standpoint *was no longer applicable.*" One must have very little regard for the meaning of words or the intelligence of his readers to ask them to put such a construction on the quoted remarks of Trotsky.

Trotsky didn't criticize Engels for what the introduction said, but for what it left unsaid. He found that the introduction, as it was printed, "created room for great misunderstandings," that Engels was pretty "one-sided," that he did not consider that the evolution of the army can be brought out by "confronting" it.

But it was just this "one-sidedness" that is balanced by the inclusion in the introduction of these deleted sections which have been quoted above—and which Riazanov appraises as "a prophecy of the October revolution." We do not believe that Trotsky, any more than Rosa Luxemburg, would have made these criticisms of Engels if the whole introduction, as Engels wrote it, had been before him at the time.

Revisionist premises

Comrade Shachtman has undertaken a factional defense of Comrade Carter's indefensible statement. To accomplish this, in an indirect way, he had to discredit Comrade Swabeck's reply to Carter. Every step on this path led him so much deeper into the morass of sophistry, passed off as "dialectics." To judge by his exposition, dialectics is some kind of legerdemain in which things never stand as they appear to stand, a mystery in which plain statement and definite, easily verified facts have no place.

The fact, for example, that Comrade Swabeck, in refuting Comrade Carter's misrepresentation of Engels, quoted the plain, simple, direct words of the original text is only a proof of his ignorance of the Marxist method. It reveals to Comrade Shachtman that Swabeck "has not understood the first thing about the historical dispute" and, in his bungling ignorance, "actually approaches the question from opportunist premises." Let us see.

Even before the war, says Shachtman, the leading Marxists in the Second International *interpreted* the introduction *in a revolutionary sense.* That is true, and they had the right on their side; they represented the true, revolutionary thought of Engels. But Shachtman leaves out of account—or, rather, mentions only in passing, the fact that the revisionists, among whom there were not a few "dialectical" jugglers, also *interpreted* the introduction in a *revisionist sense.* And he passes over altogether the success of the revisionists in deceiving the socialist workers. The one-sided statements in the introduction, unqualified by the sections which they had deleted, were weapons in their hands, and gave them an advantage before the socialist masses, who respected the authority of Engels. That is why Kautsky, according to Riazanov, blamed the party leaders because Engels's "blue-penciled" introduction did not manifest his views with the *necessary clarity and decisiveness.* That is why he demanded that *Bernstein publish the original manuscript.*

One would think, from Comrade Shachtman's presentation of the question, that real Marxists are distinguished by indirection of speech, that they never use plain words to explain things. If Engels appears to speak one-sidedly, or to leave something unsaid for the moment, in consideration of the pending Anti-Socialist Law, and "the timidity of our Berlin friends," or because these same "friends" themselves mutilated his manuscript—then that, according to Shachtman's twaddle about "revisionist premises," is the correct way to speak under all conditions. And if Swabeck now does not rest upon the prewar interpretation of the Marxists and refers to the new facts and cites the plain words, he "doesn't understand the first thing about the historical dispute."

The conduct of the present "historical dispute" about socialism in one country shows how much this conception of "dialectics" has to do with the fighting methods of the Russian Marxists. They can demonstrate, and they have demonstrated, the falsity of this theory on political and theoretical grounds without resorting to a single direct quotation from any Marxist authority. But when the epigones advance this theory *on the authority of Lenin,* as the revisionists claimed the authority of Engels, the Russian Oppositionists did not rest with a purely theoretical explanation of the question. They knew what Shachtman leaves out of account—that the masses are not educated Marxists. They understood what Shachtman has not thought of—that the masses have a great regard for the authority of the classic teacher and can be deceived by treacherous references to them.

Therefore, when Stalin began to quote Lenin for "socialism in one country," Russian Opposition brought the *direct words of Lenin* himself to refute them, just as Swabeck brought the direct words of Engels. In one section of Trotsky's "Criticism of the Draft Program" alone—although quotation is not his customary polemical method—he makes *twenty-two quotations from Lenin to show that the advocates of socialism in one country had no right to his authority.*[23]

Carter's article was a newspaper article to be read by unschooled young workers. He made a statement that misrepresented Engels. Swabeck cited the words of Engels himself to refute it. Under the circumstances, that was the simplest, most effective, and therefore the most correct way to dispose of the misrepresentation.

False issues and strange methods

A large part of Comrade Shachtman's document is devoted to a very learned elucidation of the idea that legal and illegal methods of struggle are not mutually exclusive, that the emphasis shifts from one to the other and back again according to conditions of the time, without necessarily affecting principle. This instruction was necessary for us because we didn't know it before. To be sure, it was precisely we who initiated the struggle in the party more than ten years ago now against the "armed insurrection" propaganda of that time; we were likewise in the front of the fight to bring the party out of its underground sectarianism and establish a legal existence; it is true that we are even now pressing the party to emphasize the fight for democratic rights and to guard its legality—and in all that time we remained communists. But Comrade Shachtman found it necessary to explain to us—at length, in detail, and with patient reiteration, so that even a very dull person could understand the instructions—that Engels did preach "peacefulness and antiviolence" for the time in Germany in 1895, that we should not be afraid to admit it, and that Engels did not, because of that, "cease to be a revolutionist."

When Swabeck denied the statement of Comrade Carter that Engels had "proclaimed the tactic of the Communist Manifesto outlived," Comrade Shachtman asks: "Is it possible that Comrade Swabeck has not even read the foreword, where the change is advocated in just so many words?" And then he goes on to accuse Swabeck of fearing to quote Engels's letter to Lafargue to the effect that "I preach this tactic (peacefulness and antiviolence) only for the Germany of today and even then with substantial reservation," because "it would upset all his contentions."

But Comrade Shachtman has practiced just a little sleight-of-hand here and put the object in a different box. Comrade Swabeck refuted the claim that Engels had declared revolutionary tactics—"armed insurrection, guerrilla warfare, force and violence"—"outlived." Comrade Shachtman makes him deny that Engels preached "peacefulness and antiviolence" *for the moment* in 1895 and makes him imply that such a position would have meant "that Engels became a revisionist, à la Bernstein"—"That is what I mean," he says, "by saying that Swabeck approaches the question with revisionist premises!"

And then, having put Comrade Swabeck, without his knowledge or consent, in a position which neither Swabeck nor anybody else we know of in the American party has defended since the fight with the "leftists" ten years ago, Comrade Shachtman proceeds at full swing to demolish Swabeck. With erudite historical references, quotations, sneers, quips, and rhetorical flights—to say nothing of the inevitable appeal to "dialectics," which has served so often as a cover for mere verbalistic tricks—Comrade Shachtman demonstrates the absurdity of Comrade Swabeck's "position."

To all this it is only necessary to reply: Comrade Swabeck's article never maintained the position which Comrade

Shachtman attributes to him, and nobody could honestly read such an implication into it. When he said in the article: "Engels in his introduction draws a sharp distinction between the conditions of 1848 and those of 1895. This is as it should be," he said all that needed to be said on this side of the question. The inference from that regarding the party method of the moment is perfectly clear, and especially so to Comrade Shachtman, who knows the part we played in the fight with the "leftists" on just such points. There is no possibility whatever for him to have been deceived as to Swabeck's meaning. His gymnastics around this point have no bearing at all on the question in dispute. The polemical method he has introduced represents a sharp departure from our practice in discussing things. We have known this method only from our struggle against it. In our ranks we encounter it now for the first time.

Concerning 'tone' and 'procedure'

The agitation around Comrade Swabeck's article began, as has so often been the case with factional movements which do not want to proclaim their political aims, with protests against the "tone" of the article and the "procedure" of its publication. The attempt to work out a political defense of Carter's statement about Engels began only later and has already gone through a curious evolution. At first it never occurred to anybody, except Carter himself—and least of all perhaps to Shachtman, who made no comment at all when he first saw the article—to offer a justification for this scandalous document. That came only after the atmosphere had been sufficiently heated about the "tone" and "procedure" to prevent a really objective discussion of the principled issue at stake. This lack of objectivity undoubtedly played a part in pushing

Comrade Shachtman from one false position to another since the publication of the article in question.

If there were nothing involved but a mistake in procedure, and a wrong tone in the article, the matter could easily have been rectified. Comrade Shachtman could have appealed to the resident National Committee of five. Failing there, he could have submitted his protest to the nonresident members, whose impartiality and fairness in matters of relations between comrades is well known.

But Shachtman did neither. He insisted on making his attack on the article known to the New York branch members before the National Committee had an opportunity to hear his criticism.

At the meeting of the National Committee on March 7 he insisted on discussing the whole question—and making the most violent accusations in the presence of Comrades Carter, Ray, and Basky—and twice rejected our proposals to consider the matter first in the committee.[24] Thus the disruption of the committee and its inability to act as a body was deliberately advertised to the members of the branch, for Comrade Shachtman knew as well as we that Comrades Carter and Ray were there as representatives of an oppositional grouping that would learn of the situation and take courage from it. This, of course, is what happened.

It is argued that Comrade Carter's meaning was misrepresented. In reply to that we can only say that we understood his statement to mean what it said. We were not under the impression that Comrade Carter—who will admit on any occasion that his education, in a formal and literary as well as in a political sense, is superior to ours—is so "awkward" a journalist as to say "armed insurrection" and "force and violence" when he means only certain forms of such action, and "outlived" when he means inapplicable at the moment. However, if we really misjudged his meaning, he had and still has an easy means of redress. He had only to reformulate his statement in a correct way that would do justice both to himself and to Engels and the matter could have been disposed of by a correction of everything, including the tone of the criticism, in the *Militant*. We have no wish to misrepresent the position of a comrade. Our political method does not misrepresent the position of anybody, not even the Stalinists or the right wing. We always aim to state their position fairly in every polemic we conduct against them. We challenge anybody to show the contrary.

But Comrade Carter had no thought of reformulating and correcting his statement. He was not interested in justice but in factional capital. Before coming to the National Committee he first went to the National Youth Committee and induced it to pass a resolution against the "tone" and the "procedure" of Comrade Swabeck's article. And at the meeting of the National Committee on March 7 he was directly asked by Comrade Swabeck if he wished to reformulate his statement and he declined to do so. And he hasn't reformulated it yet. On the contrary, he has written an article defending it as it stands.

There is a certain comic interest in the fact that the meeting of the National Youth Committee—a subordinate, appointed subcommittee—which adopted Comrade Carter's protest against the "procedure," was held without the participation of a representative of the National Committee. Comrade Swabeck, who was sitting at his desk in the next room, was not even informed that the meeting was passing judgment on his article and was not invited to come in and explain his point of view before the motion was passed to condemn him. Formal procedure, which is raised into a principle on one side, is completely forgotten on the other—as is usually the case when deeper issues are really involved.

And matters stand exactly the same way about the "tone" of the dispute. At the same meeting of the National Youth Committee where he demanded the protest against Swabeck's tone, in Swabeck's absence, Comrade Carter submitted a statement which refers to Comrade Swabeck in such terms as "noncommunist action"; "breaks with that essential Bolshevik loyalty and honesty"; "illogical, stupid, puerile, and dishonest piece of writing," and similar comradely salutations which belong to the language of one who is interested above all in lubricating personal relations by polite speech. This document of Comrade Carter's, says Comrade Shachtman, is "inside the organization" and therefore doesn't count. We do not care a fig for this distinction, and we care even less for the hypocritical pretense that condemns the "tone" on one side and condones it—and employs it—on the other.

But Comrade Shachtman advises us with patriarchal wisdom: Swabeck "should be a teacher of the young comrades, ought to have made him 'aware' before cracking open his skull in public." This advice about the way to deal with the mistakes of Comrade Carter would have more weight if there were no previous experience to judge by.

Haven't efforts been made, not once or twice, but scores of times, to explain things to Comrade Carter in the branch meetings, and in friendly, more or less private conversations? And can Comrade Shachtman tell us of a single occasion when Carter ever learned anything, acknowledged anything, or corrected anything as a result of such efforts? Comrade Shachtman ought to know better than anyone the futility of such a method with wiseacres and know-it-alls. He has set up and employed this method in contrast to our inclination for a political struggle against the upstart spirit they represent. By this shoddy "cleverness," this wise method of handling an abominable parvenu tendency by personal diplomacy, Comrade Shachtman only muddles things, flatters and encourages the tendency, and hampers the revolutionary education and development of the New York branch.

Comrade Shachtman's complaints about procedure on his own account could easily be adjusted with our full agreement in the National Committee, even if we are not very fond of the psychology which puts such stress on personal rights and personal grievances. Insofar as it is a question of a really collective control by the committee over the contents of the *Militant,* of the right of every member to bring his protest against a given article to the body before its publication, or of establishing safeguards against arbitrary acts of an individual or a minority—he will not have to quarrel with us. We stand firmly by this principle and have explained it to him on more than one occasion. On this point it was only necessary for him to make the necessary motions regulating future procedure and we would have voted for them, or to point out a transgression on our part—if it was really a transgression and not a misunderstanding—and we would acknowledge it.

Our understanding of the circumstances under which Comrade Swabeck's article was published is not exactly the same as that presented by Shachtman. He admits that the question of Carter's reference to Engels was raised at a meeting of the National Committee by Swabeck and that he then announced his intention to reply to it, and that nobody spoke against Swabeck's intention. This is exactly what happened in regard to the Lassalle article. At the same meeting Cannon said he would answer it in an editorial note. No formal motion was made in either case. The reply to the Lassalle review appeared without any further consultation and evoked no protest. The assignment for the writing of scores of articles in the past has been indicated in this semiformal way without mention in the minutes. There is nothing wrong with this method—in practical work all editorial boards function this way to a certain extent, when there is general agreement.

It is a different matter, of course, when differences of opinion are expressed as to the contents of an article or the advisability of printing it at all. Then a formal vote is necessary. But Shachtman's remarks show that no differences were expressed on the article in question. When he says "nobody spoke on it," he admits that nobody protested against it. According to our usual procedure that was an assignment to write the article—at least we so understood it. Therefore when Comrade Shachtman says: "In no sense was Swabeck 'commissioned' to reply to Carter, nor was there any understanding or decision that a reply was required," he is squeezing the procedure of the committee on editorial matters into a strict formality that it has never observed, and that in the past concerned him least of all.

In many instances articles have been written on such informal assignments and printed without showing them to the other members of the committee for criticism or corrections. The fact that Comrade Swabeck didn't find the time for several weeks to write the reply to Carter, and that after writing it he took the trouble to show it to the various members of the committee, is sufficient to show that Comrade Swabeck was in no hurry to circumvent the committee. Even then the article was published without its formal consideration by the committee only because of the postponement of the meeting.

It is quite true that the article might have waited another week. But Shachtman had seen the article and made no criticism of it. How was anyone to know that he was "reserving his opinion" for the meeting and that this opinion would flower into a principled objection? We have always been in the habit of exchanging opinions frankly in looking over each other's articles, and that is the communist way to work together. Comrade Abern made no principled objections to the article, but expressed doubts as to the advisability of public criticism.

The objections of Comrade Abern might be considered reason enough to postpone the publication of the article till the committee meeting. We should have done that under the circumstances, and if the matter had been fully considered, would have done so. We can acknowledge the justice of criticism on this score all the more readily because we stand for the principle of collective responsibility for the paper in the real, and not merely in the formal, sense.

This was precisely one of the subjects of discussion at the plenum in the spring of 1930. It arose in connection with the publication of an article by Shachtman on the needle trades.[25] In that article Comrade Shachtman certified to the correctness of the charge that the left wing had bribed the police. Against this shameful article, giving aid to the *Forward* and the whole Black Hundred gang against the left wing, which is a blot on the record of the *Militant,* Comrade Cannon had raised a violent objection, and had insisted that the paragraph in question be stricken out. This Comrade Shachtman refused to do, and likewise found it unnecessary to delay the matter for a committee meeting on it. At that plenum we advanced the idea of a really collective control of the paper and of the right of any member of the committee to delay an article until his objections shall have been duly considered. Comrade Shachtman could not see the justice of this criticism at the plenum, and could not acknowledge any fault in his action. That is why his clamor at the present moment about strictly formal procedures has such a hollow sound, and argues so convincingly that the real source of his indignation lies elsewhere.

About 'Stalinism'

From what has been said above it is quite clear that Comrade Shachtman had no ground to attack the article of Comrade Swabeck on principle and that in attempting to do so he only succeeded in confusing the real question at issue and filling the air with extraneous arguments based on a flagrant misrepresentation of Comrade Swabeck's position and his purpose. If one can find a certain merit—even if there is no consistency—in his objection to the procedure and the tone of the article, the way to redress these offenses was open to him, as has been indicated, by normal methods within the National Committee or at least within the full committee by referendum or by a plenum.

He chose another way. By his action, and by his document, he has elected to hurl the dispute into the membership in an atmosphere of crisis. And by the presentation of this document—which only formulates and systematizes the agitation carried on by his friends in an even cruder and more outspoken form—he is asking that we be adjudged as Stalinist bureaucrats and as people who approach theoretical questions "from opportunist premises." On the latter accusation we have already spoken. It is now time to speak of the alleged identity of our methods with the methods of Stalin; about our "fundamentally bureaucratic procedure," which, it appears, is not an incidental digression but a "characteristic" one, "characteristic of bureaucratism."

If Comrade Shachtman really means these accusations seriously, if they are not merely journalistic flourishes, then they can only be a summons to the organization to draw the necessary conclusions in regard to its leading staff.

The members of the Left Opposition cannot and will not allow accusations of this character to be bandied about loosely. Some of them, at least, learned about Stalinist bureaucratism through blows over the head in reply to their criticisms, and in the course of the struggle they assimilated the idea that "characteristic bureaucratism" is not an independent phenomenon, but rather represents and is necessitated by a systematic political course that violates the interests and the Marxist traditions of the movement and has to be imposed on it by violence and deception. No, the Left Oppositionists will not reconcile themselves with "characteristic bureaucratism" and will not tolerate those who represent it.

Neither can they let the question, once projected, remain undecided. If the accusation is really true; if a section of the leadership which helped to educate the members to understand and to hate Stalinist bureaucratism has been playing a double game; if they are in reality Stalinists in disguise, and not very well disguised at that—then the organization will settle accounts with them in short order. On the other hand, if the accusation is a light-minded slander, and can be shown to be such, then the slanderers must be called to order. One way or the other—*but no middle way!*

If the actions of Comrades Swabeck and Cannon in the incident under discussion were Stalinist actions, if our treatment of Carter was "as comradely as our expulsion from the party was comradely," as Comrade Abern stated at the committee meeting of March 7, in the presence of several branch members, and if it was "characteristic" of us, then it follows that we have left a fairly clear bureaucratic trail in our conduct over a period of time. And right here we ask for an examination of this record, and a proof of this characteristic and systematic line, not with loose generalities but with concrete facts. Our part in the leadership of the league has been conducted before the eyes of the membership. Show us how and wherein the "characteristic" bureaucratic quality has been manifested.

In order to assist those who wish to examine the record over a period of three and one-half years since our expulsion from the party, and to judge us by our part in the making of that record, we cite here a number of facts and events in the life of the organization which we consider most significant and most revealing as to the "method" of the leadership, and of ourselves in particular.

1. *Disputes with the branches.* We had differences, more or less serious, with various branches of the league, including Minneapolis, Boston, Toronto, and Philadelphia. Has any one of these branches at any time ever protested against our method of conducting the disputes? Not one.

2. *The First National Conference.* After six months of preparation following our expulsion from the party, we consolidated the organization at our First National Conference. The conference was arranged and conducted in a fair, democratic way, full rights of discussion were enjoyed, and the leadership was selected by general and unanimous agreement. What was bureaucratic about this conference?

3. *The Second National Conference.* This conference summed up the experience of three years of the Opposition struggle as an expelled faction. It was preceded by more than two months of free discussion after the publication of the National Committee thesis. More space was accorded in the discussion pages of the *Militant* to criticism than to defense of the thesis. The delegates from the branches were freely elected without pressure from above and they recorded their agreement with us on every important question—almost unanimously where the committee stood united, and by an overwhelming majority

when Comrade Shachtman made different proposals (the selection of the new NEC). What did the management of this conference have in common with the methods of Stalinism?

4. *The Fox incident.* Shortly after the First National Conference an oppositional movement was started by Fox in the New York branch on a manifestly false political basis and with a highly disruptive form of activity. We continued the discussion on those questions for meeting after meeting until the issues were fully clarified and a number of conscientious comrades who had at first given Fox a certain sympathy, got a clearer view of things and broke away from him. Expulsion eventually took place, only after the branch had convinced itself of the necessity for this action and began to protest against our prolongation of the discussion. The branch itself, by unanimous vote, expelled two members, and two others withdrew. Following the liquidation of this affair the activity of the branch took a forward jump. The further evolution of the expelled members testifies to the correctness and the necessity of the organizational measures. Where was the "characteristic bureaucratism" manifested in this conflict?

5. *The Weisbord affair.* It will be recalled that Weisbord at one time had a factional grouping in the New York branch and had some sympathy from other members. His factional method was personal slander against the leadership with his political platform smuggled in under the cover—after the usual manner of opportunists. We put the *real questions of policy* on the agenda and discussed them fully with the branch, giving Weisbord, who was not even a member of the organization, an opportunity to present his views at the same time. The result, which is well known, was a complete defeat for Weisbord in a political sense and at the same time a demonstration of the futility of slander

in disputes within our league (a warning to others). One expulsion and one resignation were the total of the organizational measures which the branch found necessary to wind up the conflict. Did we defeat Weisbord, and have we since that time demolished his attempts to split the league or set up a rival against it, by Stalinist bureaucratic methods, or by a genuine political struggle?

6. *The Toronto branch.* A grouping in the Toronto branch quite similar in composition to the Carter grouping in the New York branch, developed a line of policy which we had to characterize as semicapitulationist. For example, rejecting the proposals of Comrade Spector, they declined to send official delegates of the league to the United Front Conference Against the Sedition Law in order to avoid a conflict with the party. They had no more respect for the opinions of the NC on these questions than for the personal advice of Comrade Spector, and rejected our directions. After some more experience by the branch, which gave sharper proof of the original error, the policy was corrected. What disciplinary steps, to say nothing of bureaucratic actions, were taken, except to explain our views in correspondence and in a few remarks in the *Militant*?

Yes, there were a few organizational measures taken by the New York branch at our suggestion, and the NC itself threw out two or three people from the national organization—in a political movement, that cannot be entirely avoided. But in every case these measures only disposed of personal obstructions *after* the political issues had been firmly decided, and the necessity of the steps was understood and agreed to by the membership. Over a period of three-and-one-half years, the league maintained a firm unity. It got rid of a few miserable capitulators who tried to sow demoralization, beginning with slander against us. Without any serious convulsions we isolated and sloughed off a few disrupters who also, before their departure, pelted us with filth they had gathered from the garbage pails of the political enemies of the Left Opposition. But was anybody expelled unnecessarily or unjustly? Did a single one of those whom we threw out show by his subsequent conduct that we had misjudged him, or did not their further evolution confirm our judgment in every case? Has anyone been denied the right to criticize or been expelled for criticizing?

In this series of incidents and events in the internal life of the league, the method of the leadership has been clearly recorded. Where in this record, from start to finish, has the Stalinist abuse of authority been seen? And—more important—where has been the false policy imposed upon the organization by such an abuse? Comrade Shachtman, of course, cannot show that because it did not exist and no one can discover it. If he answers that the leadership as a whole conducted these struggles and unfolded this method—which is quite true—it does not change matters with regard to his accusations. For he cannot show in any case where he demanded a different line, and our part in the execution of the committee's policy is known.

There are indeed remnants of Stalinism and other political maladies in the New York branch. And it could not be otherwise, for it contains comrades who have not fully overcome the effects of their miseducation in the party, who are impressed by the propaganda of the Stalinists, especially by their slander, and repeat it in slightly moderated forms. And along with them there are others who never had any party or other experience in the class struggle, and show it sadly. These are the comrades who concern themselves unduly over personal matters; who have time and inclination for gossip and go around with their ears cocked for scandal, and who arrive at their "position" in disputes on the basis of these trivial considerations. Along with them the New York branch has besides some earnest young workers, a grouping of youth elements of the scholastic student type, who have not yet assimilated the communist proletarian spirit, who combine a sterility of ideas and criticism with a detestable parvenu self-assurance. And there are others who are excited about nothing in the world so much as the fact that somebody stepped on their toes. At the present moment, under the stimulus of Comrade Shachtman's attack, we see these elements converging into a sort of faction, insofar as such a heterogeneous combination, which has nothing in common except paltry grievances, can be so designated. *But it is not our faction!*

Our aims run along different lines, and we will not conceal them. We conceive of the league as the potential nucleus of the future party, and we want a deliberate course to bring the organization, and especially the New York branch, more into harmony with this conception. That means, first of all, to translate the lessons of the internal struggle in the International Opposition into the American language, and assist the entire organization to assimilate them. This will not be accomplished in a day and without struggle. But we are late. We must begin.

The key to the present problem is the New York branch. The present composition of the branch is, in general, unfavorable for its development as a proletarian-revolutionary organization. The elements of superficial intellectualism and scholastic sterility, of preoccupation with mere quibbling, and indifference to real questions and practical tasks of the day—these elements, leaning on Comrade Shachtman, exert a disproportionate influence. They represent in reality an unwholesome tendency which, on the one hand, hampers the activity of the branch and obstructs the political education of its members, and, on the other hand, renders it inaccessible to serious workers.

The improvement of the situation requires, as the first step, a frank statement of the problem and then the beginning of a genuine political selection of forces by the method of political education. The selection must take place no less among the "young" than among the old, separating the revolutionary elements from the mere triflers, the proletarian militants from the scholastic quibblers. The serious elements amongst the youth will find their place beside us, and they will be most resolute fighters against the attempt to ignore political tendencies in favor of a division according to age. And to the extent that they grasp the real questions at issue, they will reject flattery and the demagogic suggestion that their function is to lead. Before the youth can lead they must learn, and not from books only but from life; they must go through some tests and give some proofs of their revolutionary qualities—of their courage, stability, endurance, and capacity to sacrifice for the cause.

The ability to find one's way in the present discussion is one of those tests, of which there will be many, by means of which the selection of forces for the future will gradually take place. To the degree that the comrades, and especially the young comrades, resolutely put aside superficial, incidental, and personal factors, occupy themselves with serious and decisive questions, and judge them by political criteria, the discussion will bring fruitful results. On that basis the unity of the league will be more firmly established, and we can undertake the next steps toward the fulfillment of our historic tasks with a surer confidence.

Fifty years of Israel Amter

Published April 2, 1932

The following article was published in the *Militant*.

The hard life of the revolutionist is not without its compensations. The fret and travail of the struggle and the gray details of daily work are relieved from time to time by ceremonial affairs and jubilees at which, in contemplation of great men and great events of the past, the militant may refresh his soul and renew his inspiration. The anniversaries of the illustrious dead have been such occasions.

But nowadays, with so many heroes still among us in the flesh, the birthdays of our living chiefs become occasions for official celebration. Not long ago the masses were invited to felicitate Stalin on his fiftieth birthday. And now, according to reports in the *Daily Worker,* Israel Amter is about to reach the half-century mark, and a great outpouring of spontaneous enthusiasm is to be given outlet at an official "mass celebration" of his birthday.

It is needless to say that we welcome this event, for we

were converted long ago to the doctrine of "flowers for the living"—that is, if one feels flowery about them. And who could feel otherwise about Amter, who has done so much and isn't finished yet? It is probable that we will not get to the celebration. But anyway we will weave a garland of encomiums in the hope that it will not be entirely buried under the floral offerings.

The ceremonial articles and official greetings which have been printed so far review his life and deeds. We will follow the same pattern. And if we fill in some neglected details, it can be attributed to the fact that we write under less constraint than the others and therefore can speak more freely and sincerely.

Our hero began his career as a piano player, and they say he was a good one. But the tunes he extracted from that classic instrument were nothing to the rhythms he produced when he began to play didoes with the communist movement. Like the jazz composers in the musical field, he specialized in the bizarre and the unique. His self-expression, through the medium of the revolutionary movement, took a distinctly individualistic form. In all that he said and did he was strictly Amter, and nobody else.

Amter made his debut on the national stage of the party at the first underground convention of the party, where he attracted attention by his fearless and uncompromising demands for the propaganda of "armed insurrection," to be promoted by leaflets hurled into the midst of the masses from ambush. Soon after, he appears, or rather one of his leaflets appears, in the strike of the Brooklyn transit workers for a wage increase of five cents an hour. With that mastery of the dialectic which already distinguished him, he "linked up" this "everyday demand" of the unsuspecting streetcar men with the final goal of their struggle, and called on them to rise, arms in hand, and capture the powerhouse.

Failing in this maneuver, because of the unreadiness of the workers and the fact that the "third period" had not yet arrived, Amter made a slight strategical retreat; but only for the purpose of gathering strength for another leap. Keeping his plans to himself, he took the capitalist forces by surprise with a sudden leaflet in the spring of 1921 entitled "May Day of Revolution." Due to a hitch somewhere, this leaflet didn't overthrow the class regime, but it did overthrow the Central Committee of the party at a convention a few weeks later. All the members of the CEC swore they had had nothing to do with the leaflet and knew nothing about it, but this did not save them. Amter's propaganda had set a movement in motion that could not be appeased without some sacrifices, and the heads even of the innocent had to fall.

Amter next appeared as one of the co-authors of the famous "Ford-Dubner" thesis, and leader of the "Goose Caucus." In this thesis our hero, disguised from his enemies by the pseudonym of Ford, advanced the idea that the illegal existence of the party was a matter of principle, and that the advocacy of a legal organization was in itself a sign of counterrevolution—a subject in which he later specialized and took several degrees. In this affair, Amter suffered a temporary setback due to the Trotskyist influence then prevailing in the Comintern.[26] His thesis was rejected, the movement was legalized, and Amter, defeated but not terrified, went into a temporary eclipse.

It was at this stage in his career that he began to display that remarkable adaptability that enabled him to keep alive politically in any weather. Unlike the illegal leftists who kept muttering about armed insurrection after the season had passed, Amter got in step with the times. The Farmer-Labor period had arrived, the Pepper-Lovestone group of leaders came to the front and took the place of the wild men of the "Goose Caucus." Amter was one of those who saw the light. He not only joined the Lovestone faction but became vociferous about it. For several years, right up to the day that the Comintern telegram against Lovestone arrived, Amter was a Lovestoneite in all things great and small.

But even after these years of habituation to the Lovestone formulae and the Lovestone politics he did not become rigid and doctrinaire about it. He retained his flexibility, and finally gave an exhibition of it that will always stand in the history of the party as an example for people who want to know how to change their opinions and change them quick. This was on the day the CI cablegram against Lovestone came. He awoke on that fateful morning as loyal and as red-hot a Lovestoneite as you could find with a search warrant, and went through a few morning chores of cursing Fosterites in a routine fashion. At twelve o'clock he received a copy of the telegram to the effect that Lovestone was no longer kosher. One hour later he was hunting for Lovestoneites to expel from the party, and was as thick with Foster as one liberty bond with another.[27]

A man with such a political biography could not be denied recognition. He has a fitting place in the top circle of the hierarchy. His fiftieth birthday is a public event and deserves a public demonstration of some kind. We disagree with the official plans only on one point. Why should it be a "mass celebration"? Why not a mass trial?

Mobilize white workers for Scottsboro prisoners

Published April 9, 1932

The following article was published in the *Militant*.

The Scottsboro case reveals American capitalism in one of its most hideous aspects, and offers to the Communists an exceptional opportunity to deal the whole system a mighty, world-resounding blow. The deliberately planned assassination of the unfortunate Negro children is notice to the entire world that imperialist America, this pretended pacifist and friend of justice, is in fact a monster. The endeavor to thwart its bloody designs in the present case calls out the deepest and best human instincts.

The words *solidarity* and *justice* acquire fresh values, they become new again in the struggle for the liberation of the helpless young Negro boys who await their fate in the Alabama jail. It is hard to think of a cause that could appeal more strongly to the hearts of the workers and all the oppressed than that of these obscure and friendless symbols of a doubly persecuted race and class.

From the revolutionary standpoint, the struggle, of course, goes far beyond the immediate objectives of the court appeals. To save the lives of the intended victims and restore their liberty is indeed our aim; but the only hope of accomplishing this is to set a really immense movement into motion. And such an achievement could have great implications for the strengthening of the Communist influence over the workers and the Negro masses. All of this is bound up together with the concrete fight for the freedom of the prisoners. To separate the one from the other, as the liberal and Socialist snivelers try to do, would only make the sacrifice of the prisoners doubly certain.

The problem consists primarily in the mobilization of the white workers for the fight. In our opinion it is incorrect to view the Scottsboro case as a "Negro issue"; it is wrong to direct the main agitation toward the Negro people and concrete organizational work around them, including their churches and lodges. Such a tactic will not be able to arouse a movement of the necessary breadth and power. And, moreover, it will fail even to make the desired impression on the Negro people.

There is no doubt that the Negro masses burn with indignation at the Scottsboro outrage and suffer their own thousandfold wrongs again in sympathy with the prisoners. But along with that, they cannot help being conscious of their position as a hopeless racial minority. What they need to inspire them for struggle is the prospect, or at least the hope, of victory. Direct agitation alone will never suffice for this. The sight of a significant movement of white workers fighting on their side is the agitator that will really move the Negroes and make them accessible to the Communist organizers of that movement.

The central problem of the Scottsboro defense movement is the organization of the white workers for the fight.

New York City demonstration in support of Scottsboro prisoners, December 9, 1933.

Once a good start is made along this line, the enlistment of huge Negro contingents in the common struggle will be a comparatively simple matter. In this question, as in every important undertaking in the class struggle, the trade union movement exhibits its decisive importance. The trade unions ought to be alive at this moment with Communist agitation on the Scottsboro case. Here is an unexampled opportunity to explain to the organized workers the necessity of solidarity with their Black brothers, and to dramatize the argument with the monstrous story of Scottsboro.

Assuming a Communist Party that knows how to work in the trade unions, a big response can be expected from this agitation. The sympathies of the organized workers can be quickly crystallized into a network of conferences. The movement of the unions in this direction will give a tremendous impetus to the propaganda among the Negroes; they will join in the movement with enthusiasm and hope. The concrete demonstrations of white and Negro solidarity, ominously foreshadowing their coming union in the revolution, will impress the judicial hirelings more than a thousand lawyer's briefs; will make them pause and weigh the possible consequences of their murders. The Communists, as the organizers and leaders of the unprecedented demonstration, as the loyal and capable champions of the most oppressed and persecuted, will gain an enormous prestige.

In such a perspective there is nothing fantastic. It assumes merely an active Communist Party which understands the essence of the Negro question, which applies the tactic of the united front, and which has not isolated itself from the trade union movement. Even in the present situation the deficiencies can be made up by a timely correction of policy. The best way to serve the Scottsboro case is to press for this.

Lay the whole matter before the membership

April 10, 1932

The following letter was written to Vincent R. Dunne in Minneapolis.

Dear Vincent:

By this time you will have digested the material on the disputes in the resident [National] Committee and will no doubt have come to the conclusion that the present exhibition of the old New York pastime requires a little looking into by the boys from the provinces. You will note from the minutes of the last meeting that Arne and I are disposed to lay the whole matter before the organization and let the members decide the disputes at a conference. It will come to this, and in my judgment it should not be delayed too long. We cannot play around with a chronic internal crisis in the French style.

However, since the committee meeting we have talked with a few of the most responsible members of the branch here and they seem to favor the idea of a plenum before the conference on the ground that it may give the others a final opportunity to retreat a bit before it is too late. We have no reason to be opposed to this, as long as it does not convey the idea of leaving things where they are now. The comrades around the country generally will probably expect us to show that we left nothing undone to keep the conflict within certain bounds. The best comrades here, who haven't a particle of sympathy with the course of Shachtman, have nevertheless cautioned us not to force him to go farther than he wants to go himself. This has also been our idea right along, but it would perhaps be advisable to make special concessions to the comrades who stress this point. When it comes to the final showdown, the unity of the league will be all the more secured if the members feel at every step that what was done had to be done that way and couldn't be done otherwise.

From this point of view we have come to the conclusion that you comrades should decide for the holding of a plenum in the very near future. I know very well that you will not relish such a trip, with the personal sacrifices and economic difficulties it entails, with the prospect of another journey to the conference. But in the long run it will probably be better for the organization. Shachtman's motion in this respect is simply a dodge to gain time—at the previous meeting of the committee they wanted to begin the discussion right away in the New York branch—but that does not need to affect our attitude toward the question. There is just a bare chance, although I think it is a very slight one, that the plenum may succeed in restraining these people a little. In any event, a resolution by the plenum to open the discussion will serve to convince the organization of its necessity and will exert a certain stabilizing effect. You must come to the plenum if it is at all possible, together with Comrades Coover and

Skoglund. Every possible weight must be put into the scale at the moment when the stability of the organization is being tested.

There seems to be no way to avoid the fight. And we should not deceive ourselves in regard to the difficulties it will present. Right now we are face to face with a financial crisis which threatens the whole structure of our enterprises—as you know, everything is tied up together and geared so high that a financial depression is more apt to mean a smash-up than a mere letdown here or there. Swabeck drew twenty-five dollars in wages for the month of March and has now gone off the payroll altogether. Take this situation together with the prospect of an internal factional struggle—and sabotage of the work, which is already to be noticed to a pronounced degree—and anyone can see that we are in for a siege. They have left the whole burden—of the work and the worries—to us.

You have probably noticed that Shachtman and Abern have quit writing for the *Militant*. This sort of thing goes hand in hand with a campaign to the effect that the *Militant* is deteriorating, etc. When it came time to decide finally whether we should go through with the project of the theoretical magazine or not, we had a very revealing situation, as you will see from the minutes. Swabeck and I took the position that the prospect of a faction fight, which had already begun in the New York branch and in the committee, together with the increasing financial difficulties of the national office, dictated a temporary retreat on this project. The other three *refrained from voting*, and the decision was made by a *minority*, Swabeck and Cannon. How is that for a picture of responsibility and "leadership"? Well, we will take the responsibility and we don't give a damn who abstains.

I only mention these perspectives from the standpoint

of realism, not of pessimism. We may as well know what we have to face. The leading group of the league on a national scale will have an opportunity to show how tough it is, and in my opinion it will show it in the most convincing way for the benefit of all who are in doubt about the matter. There is a lot of speculation about the leading group going to pieces, and similar twaddle. Just the opposite will be demonstrated, in my opinion. Those who are losing their sense of humor and their sense of proportion, and try to monkey with the unity of the basic cadre, will only give the league an opportunity to see the real strength of the group and their own futility. The unity of the organization, and the authority of the leading group on a national scale—and the strength of our group, as was revealed so distinctly at the 1930 plenum and on other occasions, consisted precisely in the fact that it had a national scope and was rooted in the districts, and was not confined to the functionaries in New York—will be firmer after the discussion than before. Neither Arne nor I have doubted this for a moment.

What do these people really want, and what is behind their virulent campaigns around such superficial and obvious pretexts as the Carter-Swabeck-Engels controversy? I will not try to answer that question, which everybody will ask, more than we answered it in our joint statement. Further than that we have not been enlightened yet. Shachtman's last statement intimates a new revelation on this point. Let us hope it will be forthcoming. I venture the prediction, however, that when all is said and done, it will be shown that we sized up the real motivation in our statement already sent out. Further discussion will only fill in and confirm that estimate.

We are inclined to take the controversy very seriously and to demand that all the experienced and serious comrades in the organization make it their first concern to probe the matter to the bottom and come to some absolutely firm and definite conclusions. If we have to go through such a fight it is best to take a little time out now, while we have the time, and do a thorough job of it. That is much better than to postpone it until we have a real chance to leap forward as an organization and then find ourselves paralyzed with an internal contradiction. There is a lot of loose talk about a "split." Shachtman seems to specialize in this chatter and, by accusing us of such intentions, thinks he will make us "responsible" for such an eventuality. That reminds me of a kid putting his fingers before his eyes and thinking others cannot see him. It will not be such a simple matter to split this group—that is, in a serious organizational sense. We expect the serious revolutionary men in the organization, who have been more than sufficiently modest in the daily work and struggles of the league, to come forward now and show who and what they are. The "split" talk, and all the rest of the empty verbalism, will soon be dissipated by such a demonstration.

You ought to begin to prepare the leading workers of the branch for the inevitable struggle. Also let us hear from you. This letter, of course, is for Comrades Skoglund and Coover also.

Jim

The 'degeneration of the old guard'

April 21, 1932

The following letter was written to Vincent R. Dunne in Minneapolis.

Dear Vincent:

One part of your letter in particular made an impression on us here—the matter-of-fact approach to the difficult and complicated problem of getting to a plenum and then facing the prospect of another journey to the conference. We have a general impression of the adverse economic circumstances of yourself and other nonresident members at present. That is why we thought it best to refer the question to you for final decision, rather than making the decision here out of hand and then notifying you all about it. We know, although you do not emphasize it in your letter, that the trip necessitates a hard squeeze and a real sacrifice for those who make it, especially for those whose personal responsibilities are not suspended by their absence.

In a recent letter to the Spanish comrades, the Old Man

said that in politics one must learn to look at small things, and even to form a judgment on them, when the larger things are not clear, when they are muffled up or concealed in some way. He cited as an example that the new centrist socialist party in Germany (the Socialist Labor Party [SAP]) declares in its program for the dictatorship of the proletariat and the soviet system. On the other hand, it speaks in its press of such black agents of imperialism as Otto Bauer and Leon Blum as "comrades." This little fact, says Trotsky, is a truer index of the character of the leaders than their program.[28] Well, without waiting for this wise suggestion of the old man, Arne and I have also been looking at the "little things" for quite a while now, all the more so since the main questions and the real intentions have been obscured and still remain so.

The point is this: For quite a while now we have heard mutterings and vague hints about the "degeneration of the old guard" and the necessity of a new, young leadership which presumably retains all of its capacity for activity and sacrifice. That is the idea hidden under Glotzer's "report" about the Minneapolis branch.[29] Now, I am no advocate of the idea of an old-timers' clique which hangs together for the sake of past memories and deprives younger people of the right to sweat and sacrifice for the cause, even in leading positions. But I have noticed that, in the main, it is just those who are allegedly "degenerated" who step forward, without any fuss or grumbling, when real sacrifices are called for, and that many of those who make the accusations display the greatest agility in dodging these responsibilities and sacrifices. The little fact that you comrades, who have not been backward in this respect in the past, calmly set about to discuss and arrange the practical sides of another burdensome undertaking in the interests of the organization deserves notice on this point. The other little fact that Swabeck, a man with family responsibilities, finds it possible to give up his job in Chicago, come to New York at his own expense, work full time for three months without pay while his savings are being consumed, then continue another full year at a weekly wage amounting to very little more than he is accustomed to getting for a day's work in his trade—and do this without whimpering—also deserves notice under the heading of "the degeneration of the old guard." I set against these two incidents, which very probably will not occur to the authors as anything to shout about but something to be taken for granted, a couple of characteristic incidents on the other side of the dispute. I could cite a score, but I will mention here two very little ones. A couple of recently graduated high school students, who are in the front ranks of the group that Shachtman appeals to and relies on against us—"the most valuable forces for the future"—are stenographers. They live at home, have no responsibilities, and can impose on their families, as revolutionists should, in a pinch. Each of them in turn was taken into the national office to do the necessary stenographic work. And each of them walked out as soon as they got two weeks back in their wages. I put these little symbolic facts side by side and conclude that the "young and old" argument in our league is a fake.

I learn from your letter, and recently heard vague mutterings in a roundabout fashion from other sources, that we are to be recognized henceforth as the "right wing"; and, since a right wing must have its corrective in a left wing, that honor is to go by default to Shachtman and his unterrified students, including the stenographers who don't believe in work without wages. We have seen a lot in our time, and our experience has taught us, or should have taught us, to be surprised at nothing. Therefore instead of flying into a fit about this "right wing" accusation, whispered out of the side of the mouth, suppose we ask for specifications. We had a conference six or seven months ago. The only people who opposed the resolutions of the National Committee were those who are now in the bloc against us. We have had a number of meetings of the National Committee since then. There have only been two differences of any importance that I know of. One related to the international questions and was raised by Trotsky's protest against the right wing in the European sections claiming the support of the American league. On that point the records show that Shachtman tried to sabotage any decisive action which would hurt his European friends. Abern and Glotzer tried to smother the whole thing with ambiguities and delays, while we, *after a three-month struggle,* pushed through a resolution that speaks clearly and out loud against this whole worthless clique of intriguants who are blocking the revolutionary development of the French league and of the International Opposition as a whole.

If they are going to fight on this ground they cannot do it very conveniently on the basis of the record as it now exists. The issues will have to be cooked up between now and the plenum. I should not wonder if we may be confronted with some fancy theses on that occasion, the basis for which is not yet revealed to us. We can face even this prospect without the least alarm, for we learned long ago to watch not only the theses, but, as the Old Man once remarked in the dispute with Landau, "to watch the fingers also." We remember that the Lovestone-Pepper faction passed itself off for a long time as the left wing, and that our expulsion from the party was advertised as a part of the campaign against the "right danger."

This "right wing" issue is just as fraudulent as the issue

of the "degeneration of the old guard." I haven't the slightest doubt that the plenum will fully reveal the complete falsity of their position on every point, and far more clearly and unmistakably than was the case at the plenum two years ago. We have had two years of experience since then. The organization has had a full opportunity to test out the disputants, to see what they stood for and what they are worth. I got the impression that you comrades, and Swabeck also, held your judgment in abeyance on that occasion. You had every right to do that, because the merits of the dispute seemed to hang on the say-so of the disputants—there was not much tangible material to go by. That is not the case now.

Swabeck, for example, has been here for sixteen months. He has had the opportunity of judging the question and the people involved day by day over that entire period. Others have had the opportunity, even if at a distance, to watch the developments in the National Committee, in the records, in the paper, at the conference, and in the activities of the individual members of the resident committee. At the plenum we can sum the whole thing up on the basis of tangible facts and records. No one can have the slightest grounds for remaining in doubt—the proof will be laid down before his eyes. You will not find it possible to support Shachtman-Abern-Glotzer on a single point.

This statement raises, of course, a very important question. It implies that we will demand of the plenum not a conciliation, such as was feasible at the first plenum, but a *decision*. We want the plenum to express itself definitely and firmly on every question that has been raised in the documents already presented, and others which will no doubt supplement them. We cannot promise that the plenum will solve the crisis, but it will take the first and most necessary step toward that solution by letting the organization know who's who and what's what. It is not a question of personal concessions here and there; we have always been ready for that and have given proof of it ten times over in the past two years. We do not fight over trifles, and have never involved others in fights over trifles. As long as the issues remain obscure, indefinite, or at least so indefinite that the organization as a whole would not be able to comprehend them, it was best to seek the path of conciliation in the committee and not stir up the members. You will recall that I never even wrote a line to you comrades before the plenum two years ago, although I had a hundred personal provocations under conditions of extraordinary personal troubles and complications. Even at the conference, with the record of a solid year of inactivity on the part of Abern, Glotzer, and Spector—three out of the four who had cried so much against me at the plenum on the same grounds—we never said a word to discredit them or to sharpen personal relations. Even a blind man could see that our aim was to leave every door open for future collaboration.

Matters stand differently now. That method is completely exhausted. It will be a waste of time, and stupid besides, to think that personal diplomacy can get us out of this impasse. Definite questions are posed, which in their totality come to this: who is to lead the league and along what lines? Only after that question is firmly decided can there be any value in attempts at conciliation, and then *only on the basis of the decision.* My views on this question have never been a secret. I think the basic group that was assembled in the party struggles and which founded the Left Opposition on a national scale is the legitimate and genuine representative of the International Left Opposition. It must form at the present time the basic core of the leadership. There is no other, and nearly four years of struggle and experience has not brought another forward. On the contrary the experience has only served to expand the capacities of this group and to strengthen its responsibility. By that I do not by any means present claims for the founding group as "natural rights" which it cannot forfeit. The basic group is also an organism, and like all organisms it goes through a process of change and differentiation. Some elements prove inadequate to the increasing demands and responsibilities and have to be sloughed off. That is what happened just prior to our expulsion when a whole section of the party faction proved unable to advance and was cast aside. The significance of that event—that ruthless split—was not so much the fact that nearly a half of the leading functionaries blew up, as that we broke with them and left them behind, in spite of all past traditions, personal ties, etc. The same applies to those whom we parted from since the Left Opposition was formally organized as an expelled faction. What does the expulsion of Carlson and the dropping of O'Flaherty signify from a political standpoint? That we are no clique of "old soldiers" imposing a mere tradition on the league and indifferent to the demands of life. That we do not hold on to anybody and compel the league to tolerate anybody in the leadership, or even in the league, for the sake of old friendship.

Contrariwise, I do not regard the leading cadre as a closed corporation. It has to draw in new blood, it must make room for new people who grow up and prove themselves in the struggle. But there again we have to set a hard face against any tinkering and irresponsible experiments. The new candidates for incorporation into the leading cadre must show that they are really growing up in a political sense; they must really give some proofs of their merits, not by their personal claims, and not by the ballyhoo of promoters, but by their own actions over a period of time. Oehler *graduated naturally* to the National Committee. I can think of several others who deserve to be considered and who should be watched carefully and given every possible assistance and encouragement from this standpoint.

Special attention should be given to the prospect of serious candidates for leadership from the youth that are being attracted to our banner. But I for one am going to fight to the last ditch against the idea of mere students graduating from the classroom to the leadership of the movement. They must show what they are made of first. They must prove that communism is in their blood as well as in their heads. We have every reason to believe that such bona fide candidates will show themselves in good time. And I have no doubt that the leading group, as it is now constituted, will do everything to help them find their rightful place.

Now, behind all the mumbling and muttering of Shachtman and the others there is some kind of a vague idea of getting rid of the "Cannon group." At bottom this is a capitulation to the propaganda of the party and Lovestone fakers, who, for some reason or other, direct a great deal of their slander to "Cannon." This was the first plank in Weisbord's platform. Malkin, as soon as he began to slide down to treachery, took up the campaign against "Cannon" and the "Cannon group," and has continued it ever since. Everybody that we had to throw out of the organization, especially here in New York, signalized the beginning of his break with our movement by this kind of agitation. If you would make a collection of the arguments to be heard right now on this point—and when all is said and done, this is the real point of the attack—and lay them beside the stereotyped slanders of the party and right-wing fakers, they would be shown to resemble the latter in the same way that commercially bottled milk resembles the stuff that comes from the cow on the farm—the same stuff, only a bit diluted.

Shachtman has gone through a number of vacillations and zigzags on this question. You will recall at the plenum two years ago that we had a slight exchange around it; this was the "hidden platform" which they finally decided to keep under the table. And it was this last-minute retreat that left them in such a helpless political position, as you remarked in your letter.[30] They evidently decided to wait until the further "degeneration of the old guard" would give more point and more plausibility to the campaign. Then things began to go awry for the theory. Out of the group of four that was to supplant the outlived leadership, three went to sleep, and not like the bear, for the winter months only, but for the whole year round. The necessity of establishing some kind of working relations with what was left of "Cannon" then suggested itself to Shachtman, since there were no others. I met him more than halfway, and together we soon began to pull the league out of the hole. When the Weisbord fight came along and really began to threaten the existence of the New York branch—and such things can be expected at any time in a dynamic political movement—the importance of this collaboration manifested itself very sharply.

The absolute identity of the anti-"Cannon" agitation with an attempt to disrupt the league was as clear as was the necessity for me to lead and organize the fight against Weisbord. I did not concede an inch to Weisbord's campaign against our "tradition"; on the contrary, I took that as the starting point and proceeded from it, as my speech, which was sent to you, will show. Shachtman, in a serious contest with a political enemy of the league, found it necessary to fight along the same lines. Then Swabeck came to

New York, and the three of us pulling together steered the league through the most gratifying and substantial progress it has yet recorded. There wasn't much room in that situation—the absence of the others did not seem to materially affect the progress—for the kind of agitation that preceded the first plenum and took place in a muffled form there.

The only ones to keep this talk alive were such people as Friedman (Carter) and others who are new in the movement, who have learned about the history of the party from the undercover gossip of the fakers, who hold our tradition against us and would like to supplant the present leadership with a leadership that has no tradition at all. Shachtman tried to smuggle a formulation into the conference thesis which would justify this point of view. Arne and I, who were on the committee with him, fished out these sentences—he was willing to pass them over without any discussion, probably thinking we would not notice them—and asked what he meant. It transpired, from his explanations, that we wanted "to take away the arguments" of Weisbord, Carter, and such critics by adopting their position. We couldn't agree to this clever maneuver because we see no need to falsify the history of the party and of the formation of the Left Opposition in order to avoid disputes. Shachtman retreated, but now he is back again with the same old stuff. We may as well have a showdown now on this point as well as on the others.

You ask, as have others here who cannot see any political basis for the venomous attitude toward us, where Shachtman is heading for. I will not undertake to answer that question with any positive assurance, except to say that if he keeps on the way he is going he will come to a bad end, and that, perhaps, sooner than anyone realizes. But I must say candidly that I am far less concerned with the destiny of Shachtman than with the problem of reducing the harm he can do to the organization to the minimum. I cannot regard this present sally as anything short of a criminal attack against the movement, and as a warning of what might be expected from him in a really critical situation. It is a piece of good fortune that we have the opportunity to face this problem now and to put the organization on guard for the future. We will have to pay for the experience; make no mistake about that. But we can afford it better now than later. There are certain positive sides of the fight that relieve the pessimistic perspective, even for the immediate future.

The New York branch, the largest and under the circumstances the most important, will have an entirely different aspect when this scuffle is finished. It has been a rather formless organization, reflecting the muffled conflicts in the National Committee and lacking a firm political core. The parvenu-student elements, relying on the backing and encouragement of Shachtman, have exerted far too much influence and, in reality, have dominated the executive committee. It was impossible to organize a genuine concentration of the proletarian-revolutionary elements as long as the National Committee could not take the lead in it. Now the situation is changing, and the worker elements are beginning to assert themselves. There need be no fears of the outcome here. Numerically the first test will probably show about an even division, but the *quality* will be all in our favor. While Shachtman's support will be made up of a heterogeneous collection which does not agree on any common program, our group will be a solid political unit which understands and agrees on all the main issues and is ready to fight for their ideas to the end. If we get the support which we have a right to expect from the experienced comrades in the other districts, the reshaping of the New York branch will not be a very difficult matter. That will be one of the strongest guarantees for the future stability of the league.

Another favorable aspect of bringing the conflict to a head now, without allowing it to smolder any longer, is the opportunity it will give us to elucidate a whole series of questions in open discussion. In the long document which Arne and I drew up in reply to Shachtman (which I assume you have received) we touched on some of the concrete questions raised in Shachtman's document. In addition to that we are preparing several other documents in which we will try to illuminate a number of fundamental questions connected with the problem of building a cadre that really aims at victory in the party struggle. Besides some new questions which have never yet been answered in the American movement, we will find it necessary to restate some fundamental conceptions which we assimilated in the experience of the old party fights, but which are unknown to many of our members.

I doubt very much whether the others will contribute anything of value to this educational work in the discussion. All that they have brought forward so far is directed not to the education of the new members but to an exploitation of their ignorance. That is why, as a rule, we find that the more experienced comrades reject the contentions of Shachtman, and see through their falsity and contradictions, without waiting to read our answers. Shachtman's "Statement on the Motion for a Plenum" is a sample of his self-refuting polemics. Pick that up and read it over again if you have the time and patience.

He begins with a hysterical accusation that "the aim of the Swabeck-Cannon statement is to split the league." And not only that, we want to do it "as rapidly as physically possible." One can imagine a greenhorn being taken in by such a presentation of the question. But this statement is sent out to members of the National Committee, which consists of people who have had a little experience and who have never failed to see splitters raise a hue and cry about the evil intentions of others and their own devotion to unity. We were called the "Trotskyite splitters" at the moment we were being pitched headlong out of the party for the mere demand for the right to speak. It was only natural for Oehler to write in and ask that if a split is unavoidable the issues that necessitate it should be explained. Those who talk about a split at the very beginning of the discussion, and before any principled lines have been contrasted, will bear watching—that is the most obvious deduction to make from this kind of talk.

If a split is to come, he says, "that remains for others besides Cannon and Swabeck to decide." Naturally. And why should Swabeck and Cannon object to others having something to say about it? They would be a couple of sorry blockheads to undertake a split all by themselves. How could anybody but a schoolboy, or one who thinks he is dealing with schoolboys, pose the question in this way?

In the statement of Shachtman we read about "three years of deliberate concealment of the disputes in the National Committee, and even the persistent denial of their existence." As to the meaning of this, if it has any meaning, we are just as much in the dark as you are. To such a statement one can only reply with a request for enlightenment. First, who concealed the differences and how could we conceal them if he wanted to make them known? Second, what are the differences that were concealed? We do not know of any differences that would justify a split, and none at all that are not also known to the other members of the National Committee.

It is true that we proposed a conference to pass judgment on the disputes—that is, we proposed the opening of a general discussion in the branches, on the basis of documents, with the objective of a conference. And that readiness to let the membership decide is construed as a proof of our determination to split the organization behind the backs of the membership. The statement says: "Cannon and Swabeck construe this conference as the consecration of the split, as the place where the organization will be confronted with a fait accompli." But even if one grants the bad will on our part, how could we do that? Landau was accused, and justly, of splitting the German league because he refused to call a conference and insisted on expelling his opponents first. But we are accused of intentions to make a split because we propose, on our own initiative, to follow the course which the International Opposition demanded of Landau. As a matter of fact we are a *minority* in the resident committee and have no power to expel anyone or to gerrymander the elections even if we wanted to. How can grownup people take such accusations seriously?

We are glad that the plenum will be possible and hope you will be able to remain here long enough to discuss everything thoroughly. We are by no means in a mood of panic and see no need to rush things unduly. We do insist on all the cards being put on the table before the whole organization. The more thorough the preparation, and the more adequate the discussion, the better securities will be established for the binding character of the decisions. But we must not tolerate a state of permanent crisis. We must not allow the league to be "Frenchified." For that reason, taking all the necessary time, and making all the required preparations, we must move deliberately for a solution of the crisis.

As ever,

Jim

Trade union unity and the ILGWU

Published April 23, 1932

The following article was published in the *Militant*.

The convention of the International Ladies' Garment Workers' Union stands in the center of a series of developments and events which signalize a new stage in the needle trades struggle. This occasion can be the starting point for the revival of a genuine labor struggle against the bosses and a new advance of the militant section of the movement. The conditions now are present for the transformation of the existing state of affairs in favor of the workers and their revolutionary vanguard.

In order to make this possible the left wing is obliged to make an objective examination of the whole situation as it exists in reality, and to elaborate a new line of tactics which proceed from it. The leading idea in this departure is a new and correct formulation of the slogan of unity. Bound up with it, and indispensable to its effective application, is a reconsideration of the present attitude with regard to the problem of work within the reactionary union.

The appearance at the ILGWU convention of seven delegates—five from Local 9, one from Local 1, and one from Local 38—even though their election was accomplished under shady circumstances[31]—denotes a recognition in fact of the necessity for a systematic struggle within the right-wing union. It is also a proof of the fruitful possibilities of this struggle. This was clearly indicated long ago, from a practical as well as from a theoretical standpoint, despite all the fulminating agitation to the contrary by the people who deduce tactics out of their own heads and not from the facts of life.

The election of the left-wing delegates is an expression of the fact that workers who are sympathetic to the aims of the left wing are compelled by the force of circumstances to belong to the right-wing union. The organized left wing, under the direct influence of the Communist Party, had to seek an approach to these workers and provide a focal point for their protest. This is the meaning of the left-wing campaign for the election of delegates to the convention. The party was dragged at the tail of a movement which came into existence in spite of the asinine "theories" which prohibited it. The problem now is to recognize the vital progressive character of the unauthorized movement and provide it with a bold and realistic leadership.

The program on which the left-wing delegates campaigned for election ("for a program of class struggle," "against clique control in the International," etc.) refutes in life the worthless contention, imposed upon the left wing by the Stalinist muddlers, about the International being a "company union" and therefore not a proper field for systematic work and not subject to reformation in its practices by an organized struggle of the militants within it. The circumstances which compelled the workers to reenter the right-wing union imperiously command the revolutionary militants to adjust themselves to the situation and organize a struggle there, in coordination with that of the [left-wing] industrial union. The old policy which has artificially divided and thereby demoralized this struggle must be replaced by a policy which unites and revitalizes it.

These developments, among others, are signs of a relationship of forces between the right and left unions in the field which cannot be ignored in the elaboration of the left-wing tactics of the day. On the contrary, they must be taken as the basis from which the tactics ensue. Aided by the bosses and the police on the one side, and the consistently false policies of the party leadership on the other, the Schlesinger union, which was badly shattered in the split, has been able to reconstitute itself to a very large extent.[32] At the same time, and by dint of the same factors, the organization of the industrial union has been reduced and relegated to a small sector of the trade, and has been unable to lead the struggles of the needle trades workers on a sufficiently broad scale to beat back the encroachment of the bosses.

The justified aspiration and the heroic struggle of the workers to replace the reactionary unions with a militant industrial union did not meet with success. The best militants were isolated into a small organization which, lacking a mass membership, lacked the power to enforce its demands. On the other hand, the masses of workers, driven by the pressure of circumstance into the faker-controlled union, and lacking the directing nucleus of conscious militants, could not organize an effective struggle within the union.

As a result of all this the fighting capacities of the

workers in the trade have been weakened and they have had to suffer a steady deterioration of their conditions. The strikes of the industrial union yielded no concrete results, and each failure had the effect of still further undermining the confidence of the workers in the prospect of any progress along that line. The traitors at the head of the International, freed from the pressure of a genuine fighting opposition, were able to transform the official strikes into decorative affairs which left the conditions of the workers no better than before, and in some cases worse. The morale of the masses in the needle trades has suffered heavily under these repeated blows. Pessimistic moods, induced by the apparent hopelessness of victory while the union organizations are split apart, spread a paralyzing influence over the "market" and undermined the struggles in advance.

The slogan necessary to revive the fighting spirit and fighting capacities of the needle trades workers, and to restore the decisive influence of the left wing, which is a condition for victorious advances, is the slogan of trade union unity.

This slogan can move the workers more than any other, precisely because it corresponds to their most burning needs and expresses their deepest impulses. But in spite of that, or rather just because of that, there can be no trifling, no phrase mongering bluster, no demagogic pretense with this great slogan. Whoever really wants to get the attention of the needle trades masses and to influence them seriously must remember one thing: they have been fooled enough; they are on guard for tricks in the name of unity; they have to be convinced that the slogan is both sincere and realistic.

The party bureaucrats overlooked this point, and this is one of the main reasons that their bombastic agitation around the question of unity and their gross perversions of the Lenin teaching on the subject yielded such miserable results and gave the game to the bosses and their labor agents every time. The demand for unity under the leadership of the Communists predetermined in advance—as the demoralized functionaries of Stalinism have been presenting the question—cannot unite anybody except those who are already convinced of the necessity of this leadership. The "unity from below" ballyhoo is part of the same futility.

But the problem of the day is to unite the great masses of the needle trades workers, including those who are indifferent and even hostile to communism, for a common trade union struggle for concrete demands. This is what the workers want, and this is what they need. The slogan of unity must be formulated in such a way that it conforms to this situation and appears to the workers as both realistic and realizable.

At the time when the industrial union still contested the field seriously with the International—when the struggle for supremacy remained undecided—the slogan of unity formulated by the Left Opposition was applicable to the situation: "The amalgamation of the unions into a single organization by means of a joint convention." The present conditions and relationship of forces between the unions dictate a reformulation of the slogan of unity which, without yielding anything in principle, will correspond more closely to the realities of the situation.

From this standpoint the latest meeting of the National Committee of the Communist League, in agreement with the needle trades group, decided to recommend to the party and the left wing that the slogan of unity with respect to the International be formulated as follows: "Readmission of the left wing into the International as a body, without discrimination and with full membership rights." Together with this, a general campaign should be carried on for the amalgamation of all the unions in the various trades into a single organization embracing the entire industry.

This slogan, which flows out of the actual state of affairs, will also impress the workers as both reasonable and realizable; it will reawaken their confidence and their aspiration for an effective union. At the same time it will open the way for the left wing to the masses of workers now separated from it in the Schlesinger union.

The industrial union, which holds its plenum on May 1, the day before the opening of the convention of the International, should put forward the slogan in this way and elect a delegation to present the question before the International convention. Simultaneously, the left-wing delegates to the International convention, acting in concert with the industrial union at every step, should begin a fight in the convention in favor of the slogan. Such an action on their part, following the action of the industrial union's plenum, will immediately change the character of the convention, and change it most radically.

The more-or-less sham battle between the Schlesinger machine and the "Progressive Bloc," with the left wing gesticulating on the sidelines—for which the stage is now set—will give place to a realignment of forces and a real fight. Let the "Progressive Bloc" dare to oppose this slogan! Their rank-and-file supporters, who want unity and a militant policy and mean it earnestly, will at once begin to shift over to the left wing. If the "Progressives" accept the slogan it will be the means of developing a struggle on a broad front that will soon go beyond the bounds of the pseudoprogressive program. In a few decisive steps the left wing can regain its position as the dynamic force in the whole needle trades situation, beginning with the International.

It goes without saying that this formulation of the slogan of unity has nothing in common with the liquidationist program of the Lovestoneites. The left wing suffered a defeat in its major undertaking to replace the reactionary union with another one. That must be frankly acknowledged. But it still retains its basic nucleus of the most reliable and tested militants. It still remains an organized force.

This force must be kept intact and demand reincorporation into the International as a fighting unit. This should be the line of its fight, not a capitulation and the individual reentry of its members into the International on the terms of Schlesinger. The masses will support this proposition, including those inside the International at present and thousands who are standing aside from both unions, discouraged and waiting for some new turn in the situation.

But, Foster and Browder will answer, Schlesinger and his black-and-yellow gang will not agree to this proposal. The slogan of unity, as the communists present it, is not designed to meet the approval of the labor fakers but to facilitate the struggle of the workers against them. The new campaign for unity, along the lines we have suggested, will start the reorganization of the workers around the banner of the left wing. The left wing will rise again as the authentic spokesman of the masses. On this basis the genuine unification of the needle trades workers' struggle will take place, with or without the wishes of the Socialist betrayers.

'Under rank-and-file leadership'

Published April 30, 1932

The following article was published in the *Militant*.

One of the demands in the program of the lefts who were elected to the convention of the International Ladies' Garment Workers' Union was for "a real strike under rank-and-file leadership." This slogan does not appear here for the first time. It did not originate with the workers who stood as the candidates of the left in the International elections, and they should not be blamed for it. There is no doubt that this antileadership slogan was imposed upon them by their own leaders, the Stalinists, whose "rank and file" ballyhoo is intended for the deception of others and by no means for their own guidance in relation to their own rank and file.

In their steadily losing battle of recent times with the traitorous leaders of the right-wing unions, the demoralized officials of Stalinism have been trying to outwit their opponents and to sneak into the leadership of the workers without their knowledge. This is the grand "strategy" which motivates the demagogic appeal for the leadership of the rank and file. The sad results which these unworthy maneuvers have brought, not the least of which has been the disorientation of the communist workers in the simplest and most elementary questions, justify a discussion of this ridiculous slogan from the standpoint of the ABC of Marxism.

The first thing which must strike the observant workers, and which in part accounts for the miserable failure of the slogan about rank-and-file leadership, is the howling inconsistency of its authors. On the one side they stand at the head of the party by virtue of appointment, and rule it with the most bureaucratic arbitrariness. If one is looking for an example of the leadership of the rank and file he will never find the merest trace of it in the Stalinized party.

The rank-and-file Communist who would venture to assert the modest right to say what he thinks in criticism of the leadership, to say nothing of the advocacy of the slogan which he propagates in the unions under party instructions, would soon be handed his passport. This is what has happened to many, and the workers in the unions know it. Integrity, common sense, and a decent respect for ordinary human intelligence all argue against this sordid attempt to fool the workers with an idea that is flatly contradicted in the practices of the Amters and all the other Fosters.

But hypocrisy and dishonesty are prime ingredients of Stalinism; and, in addition, contempt for the workers. Abusing the faith of the conscious proletariat in the Russian revolution and the Comintern, they imagine they can sanctify anything by mere command. This is what misleads them into such self-contradictory policies in relation to the general labor movement.

Ruling within the limited sphere of the party by decree, they forget that in order to influence the noncommunist masses it is necessary to convince them. And since the masses take nothing on faith, but test everything out in life and learn from their experience, the slogans of the party which do not correspond to reality are unavailing. Thus it happens that such manifest absurdities as the "leadership of the rank and file" leave the masses untouched, and succeed only in deceiving and disorienting the Communist workers.

Twelve years ago Lenin wrote a pamphlet for the purpose of clearing up some misconceptions in the newly formed Communist parties. One of these misconceptions was the prejudice, derived from syndicalism, regarding leaders and masses. Replying to the arguments of those "leftists" in the German party who contrasted the one to the other, he remarked: "What old and well-known rubbish! What 'left' childishness!" The simple explanations and ironical comments of the great teacher, regarding the masses and the leaders and the interrelations between them, apply so pertinently to the present aberration of the American Stalinists on the subject of "rank-and-file leadership" that a few quotations will be in order.

"One notices the superficial and incoherent use of the now 'fashionable' terms, 'masses' and 'leaders.' People have heard much and have conned by rote all the frivolous attacks on 'leaders'—contrasting them with the 'masses'—but failed to grasp the application and the inner meaning of these words."

"To a Russian Bolshevik . . . all talk of 'from above' or 'from below,' the 'dictatorship of leaders' or 'the dictatorship of the masses' cannot but appear as childish nonsense. It is something like discussing whether the left leg or the right arm is more useful to a man."

"People bend every effort to elaborate something extraordinary, and in their zeal to be intellectual they become ridiculous. It is common knowledge . . . that the classes are usually and in most cases led by political parties, at least in modern civilized countries; that political parties, as a general rule, are led by more or less stable groups of the more influential, authoritative, experienced members, elected to the most responsible positions, and called leaders. All this is elementary. It is simple and plain. Why then all this rigamarole, this new Volapük."[33]

These citations are taken from *The Infantile Sickness of "Left" Communism.* Have the new members of the party ever seen this pamphlet, and have the old members forgotten it? These teachings, like all the fundamental doctrines elaborated by the Comintern under Lenin, have been declared out of date; they are buried under the filth and confusion of the Stalin regime. The Communist worker who wants to find his way back to the Lenin path might well begin with a study, or a reexamination of the *Infantile Sickness.*

After that he would never be able to go around shouting such absurdities as "the leadership of the rank and file." He would not be able even to listen to such an instruction from his own "leaders" without laughing under the table.

The chatter about "rank-and-file leadership" is a disgrace for communists. Such horseplay can very well be left to the confusionists of syndicalism who object to the idea of a workers' political party on the ground that the masses need no leaders. This demoralizing nonsense only hampers the organization of the working class and thus serves the bourgeoisie. The mission of the communists is to educate the workers, not to muddle and confuse them; to aspire, frankly, to lead them in their struggle, not to trail behind them and cater to ignorance and prejudice with demagogic slogans.

The working class under capitalism is not and cannot be a homogeneous body. The enormous pressure of the ruling-class ideology presses heavily upon it. Bourgeois ideas, disseminated through the press, the schools, the movies, the political parties, and in other ways, demoralize and corrupt the thoughts of the workers. Besides that, the working class under capitalism is divided into various economic categories, with different standards of living and, to a certain extent, different immediate interests. The upper stratum, the aristocracy of labor, which is the most conservative and at the same time the best organized, becomes a means of strengthening bourgeois influences over the class. The labor bureaucrats, with their high salaries and petty-bourgeois standards of life, act as the agents of capital in the labor movement.

As a result of all this, it is possible under capitalism for only a minority of the working class to free itself from bourgeois influences and ideas and to understand the historical class position of the proletariat. These are the conscious workers, the vanguard of the class. In order to influence the class it is necessary for these conscious workers to organize themselves and to fight unitedly against the domination of the capitalists and their agents in the labor movement. From this arises the Marxist idea of the centralized workers' party. It is the first letter of the Marxist alphabet on the question of working-class organization.

This principle of leadership by the most conscious and resolute elements applies to strikes and other daily struggles as well as to the class struggle as a whole. The agitation for "the leadership of the rank and file" negates this principle and sows confusion. By this it only makes the leadership of the reactionary agents of the capitalists more secure. This harmful and anti-Marxist slogan should be cast aside. Instead of it, the Communist workers in the unions, as in every other field of the class struggle, should frankly contrast their policy and their leadership to the policy and the leadership of the labor lieutenants of capital. This is the only way to teach the workers and help them in their struggle. There is no roundabout way.

The anti-Cannon bloc

April 30, 1932

The following letter was written to Hugo Oehler in Chicago.

Dear Comrade Oehler:

I received your letter of April 27 and note what you said about the attitude of the Chicago comrades toward the conflict in the resident National Committee. I can very well understand why they shrink from the idea of a "fight" in the league over such a question as the Swabeck-Carter-Engels matter; and their hesitancy in committing themselves on one side or the other until they have a chance to see what issues are behind the furor is likewise comprehensible. The habit of judging disputes politically, on the basis of adequate information from all sides, is one of the marks which distinguishes a political grouping, such as we have aimed to build up over a period of years, from the factional gangs and cliques inflicted on the movement by such demagogues and careerists as Foster, Pepper, Lovestone, and similars. I wouldn't give a cent for the support of people who determine their position on this or that question of policy in advance, or who "line up" on one side or the other before they know what is really involved in the conflict. Such people are as useful to the Left Opposition as a wart on a man's nose.

But in the complexities of politics it often happens that people, in striving to avoid one mistake, fall into another, and sometimes a worse one. This can easily be the case at the present time with comrades who stand aside and wait for the presentation of "principled issues" of policy which may or may not be presented, and may not even be involved. In the meantime one must not close his eyes to the fact that the "fight" has already disrupted the resident National Committee and that the New York branch is being divided into factions. When this can happen without the presentation of principled political differences, this fact in itself becomes a decisive question and one cannot simply stand aside and ignore it. It is necessary to ask: How did this happen and who is responsible for it?

A year or so ago, the German league went through a period of factional paralysis which culminated in a split. But what are the "political issues" which rendered this result unavoidable? Nobody knows to this day. Comrade Trotsky said, "The differences between the groups in the German section were not principled differences, and still less irreconcilable ones." And yet the internal fight and finally the split occurred just the same, and we could not remain neutral. This example is sufficient to warn us against an oversimplification of the question and a too formal standard of judging "issues."

The Chicago comrades, yourself included, have read all the official material. And yet you say that they feel that "they know very little about the issues" and that "they are waiting for more material to judge." As I said before, this waiting attitude can be understood on broad political grounds. They see no reason for a fight on the basis of the material so far disclosed to them. We know as much about the serious political differences as they do, and no more. And for that reason we think, as they do, that a factional struggle in the league has no political justification and we tried to avoid it. But in spite of all that, the fight has been started. This "little fact" is the key to the whole puzzle. Shachtman has already convicted himself of plunging the league into a factional struggle on a false basis, without real political issues which would justify and necessitate the fight or, at any rate, without informing anybody as to what these basic issues are.

That is not to say that no "political issues" will be presented to the plenum. They have been asked so many times to say what they are really driving at that they may, and probably will, find it necessary to bring forward something "new." But such new issues are discredited in advance, and with them those who sponsor them. Really serious issues do not fall out of the air and cannot be invented overnight. It is only seven months since we had a conference. There the resident committee defended a common platform on all the important questions of external policy. Since the conference we have held meetings every week, or nearly every week. You have the minutes of these meetings. Look them over again. Can you find there in the record any trace, any hint, of real differences on important questions of external policy? No, it cannot be found there. The records show a difference on the internal questions of the International Opposition, on the Carter-Swabeck-Engels question, and a few episodic, incidental questions which were never raised the second time and on which the votes did not fall according to the present line of division in the resident committee. This is all the *material* that existed when Shachtman began the fight on the Carter-Engels question. If the Chicago comrades are eventually presented with some "new" material and some "issues," will they not be justified in looking them over with a slight skepticism? Will they not be obliged to ask: "Why didn't you think of that before? Why did you start the fight about something else if this is what you really had in mind?"

For our part, the comrades need expect no surprises. We have said our say in the document by Cannon and Swabeck in reply to the statement of Shachtman. We intend to write a great deal more, but it will be in elaboration and supplement to the points touched on in the first document, and in reply to anything brought forward by the other comrades. When all is said and done, the decision of the organization will be founded on the material *and the facts* already known.

One of these facts, which will aid the membership in judging the two groups, is the contrast between them with regard to their internal unity and homogeneity. We, and those comrades who support us, are a unit on all the important questions, both with regard to internal and external policy. The others are united completely on only one point, and that has nothing to do with communist politics: a common antagonism to us. We are accustomed to think of a bloc as a combination of two or more groups which are united on some main political objective, with some differences of a secondary character. But just take a look at this bloc and ask yourself what policy will guide the league if they prevail in the struggle and secure the leadership. They cannot win over the radical workers to the Opposition merely by cursing Cannon. The workers are not sufficiently interested in such a platform; and besides, others have preempted it.

Glotzer agrees with us, or says he does, on the internal questions of the International Opposition, which we consider the first and most important question. Abern takes the same position, with "reservations" and ambiguities. Shachtman, on the other hand, flatly opposes this view, and gives more or less support, directly or indirectly, to the careerists, triflers, and disintegrating elements in the European sections. But this little contradiction does not prevent them from presenting a "united front" against us in the committee.

When they extend outside of the committee, encounters new complications. In the New York branch the committee bloc is part of another bloc with Carter and his friends, who constitute a distinct grouping which also has internal contradictions and differences, and which disagrees with Shachtman-Abern-Glotzer on a number of important questions. For example, some of the Carterites agree with us on the international questions, and others will probably take a directly opposite position. Most of the Carter grouping fought the National Committee on the important question of the character of the youth clubs. They stubbornly defended an opportunist position on this question, maintaining that the clubs should be "broad" organizations in the political sense, admitting Lovestoneites, Stalinites, and others—and they still maintain this position. For months the main struggle in the New York branch occurred over this question, with the National Committee as a whole leading the fight on one side and Carter on the other. These are some of the many differences between them, but it does not in the least prevent them from making a bloc against us.

In addition to all these contradictions, there is still another. The New York branch contains a number of nondescript apolitical elements whose heads are not shaped in such a way as to make it possible for them to assimilate communist ideas, especially in the sphere of organization. They are oppositionists "in principle" and have drifted into the league by some accident or other. For a long time the leadership as a whole has had to combat them at meeting after meeting on the simplest and most obvious questions. They are always "against the leadership" and their main thesis is that all politicians are fakers. The bloc makes a place for these elements and caters to their ignorance and prejudice in the fight against us.

Even that is not all. When we discuss the question at the plenum, we will present a more thorough analysis of the bloc and ask them to say definitely which lines it stands on: Shachtman's, or Glotzer's, or Abern's, or Carter's, or all of them together, or none of them except the common platform of personal antagonism to Swabeck and Cannon? The bloc will hardly be able to survive the first serious test. In any case it will be clear that it can give no assurance of a responsible and consistent leadership for the league.

We have never asked anybody to "line up" with us on personal grounds or take a position on any question in advance on our say-so. There was a great deal of that sort of thing in the old party fights and we always regarded it as one of the most pronounced features of factional degeneration and corruption which hampered the revolutionary education and development of the membership. Foster and Lovestone sowed this demoralization consistently and it contributed heavily to the degeneration of both these factions. There are people who would like to picture the whole history of the party as a series of these senseless scuffles between the various leaders with all the factions on the same level. We cannot agree to that interpretation because it is not a true one. The rivalries among the leaders played a certain part, and always a harmful one, which should warn us to guard against these evil factors in our disputes. But we fought on a different basis in the party. That is one of the main reasons why we were able to find our way to the platform of the Left Opposition.

If we judge the course and the methods of the other comrades correctly, it represents an attempt—very likely not a conscious one—to drag us backward in this respect. As far back as 1925 we began to realize that the faction struggle between the Ruthenberg-Pepper-Lovestone group on the one side and the Foster-Cannon group on the other was degenerating more and more into a vulgar gang fight in which "political issues" were being conceived as pretexts for the struggle for power rather than motivating causes for it. Our break with the Foster group and our forming a separate one was inspired, among other causes, by the determination to liberate ourselves from these unprincipled feuds and to approach questions from a political standpoint. That split was accompanied by a bitter fight which will not be forgotten, and should not be forgotten by those who bore the brunt of it. The contrast in methods of the two groups at the time of the split—political arguments on the one side and personal attacks and slander on the other—symbolized and foreshadowed the whole future development of the two groups. The political method brought us eventually to the eminence of the Left Opposition; the personal method, the slander, the emphasis on incidentals, gossip, and similar trivialities, brought the Foster group eventually to the foul swamp of Stalinism. Let us not forget the road we traveled by.

The fate of the Foster group after the split with us is a terrific warning as to the significance of *method*. This group, as you know, was in the main a sound one in its composition. Under proper guidance it could have developed on the revolutionary path, for it was made up of proletarian militants, for the most part, who wanted to be communists. But Foster's method was not calculated to help them in this aspiration. His method was personal slander, personal incitement, appeals to prejudice and gang spirit and clique interests. Thus their political development was arrested; after their break with us, the group steadily deteriorated, and this political deterioration was in no way compensated for by numbers. The factional struggle is not only the factional struggle; it is one of the most important means whereby the party, and in our case the league, is either politically educated or politically demoralized.

Let us not forget the lessons of the past, and particularly the lessons which have been hammered into us by our experiences and the experiences of the party. In that light let us assume—if we can indulge ourselves in a pessimistic speculation—that the bloc succeeds in its fight and secures the leadership of the league along with our elimination. (This must be the aim if the attack means anything at all.) In that case there would not be a triumph of one line of principle and policy over another. It would rather be a victory based on personal antagonisms and attacks and the utilization of personal grievances and prejudices in general. Would the matter rest there? Would peace and harmonious collaboration be ensured for the future? No, one can say with certainty that the contrary would be the perspective. Anyone who wanted to push himself forward—and in such an atmosphere careerist elements of all kinds would raise their heads and grow bolder—would see that the way to accomplish his ends would be to tear down the others who stand in his way. Those who are animated primarily by ignorance, prejudice, and personal grievances—who support the present campaign against us—would soon transfer their support to the new opponent to the new leadership. Demagogy feeds on the triumph of demagogy. The downfall of the league as it exists today would inevitably follow. It would become necessary for the smaller group, which has been drowned out in the clamor of demagogy, to begin all over again.

I do not say this has to happen, because I do not think the bloc will triumph in the struggle. Comrade Swabeck and myself try to see things as they really stand and to picture them that way to others. You must have been impressed by the extensive material that we have already sent you, that we take the conflict very seriously. It is not a mere misunderstanding which can be straightened out by personal diplomacy and the intervention of some objective comrades from other districts. We regard this situation as a danger and as a test for the league. That is why we are concentrating our attention on it. We wish to remind all the comrades again: we do not fight over trifles. We regard the conduct of Comrade Shachtman since the conference, which is climaxed in his statement on Comrade Swabeck's article as an attack on the organization, on its national conference, on the internal policy of the revolutionary elements on an international scale, on the Bolshevik principled method of controversy. This attack must be repulsed in the most decisive fashion. The future of the league depends upon this.

The responsible comrades in the districts will not find it possible to stand aside in this conflict. If they think, "it is a personal squabble—tell them to make peace and get to work," they are due for some rude shocks. If they could attend one meeting of the New York branch they would quickly realize that sermonizing was out of place. Those who come to the plenum from the districts will have the situation presented to them squarely, and they will understand that the disputes must be decided firmly. That is the only possible foundation for future adjustment. After that we will see. You will not find us unwilling to consider a conciliation among comrades, or the reestablishment of personal relations which permit collaboration, once the basis for it has been firmly established by the political decision of the organization. We are not anxious to dispense with any of the forces of the league; we do not disparage the abilities of the comrades, or deny the value of the contributions they have made up till now; the personal aspect of the struggle comes entirely from the other side. Once this has been disposed of, that is to say, once the organization has decisively rejected it, we can consider the future organization of the work and the division of duties in a calm and deliberate manner. Before we reach that point in the conflict personal diplomacy is a waste of time.

You mention the reference in my letter to those who opposed the resolutions of the National Committee at the conference. By that I didn't mean those who offered amendments while accepting the main line of the documents. My reference specifically was to the Toronto branch which rejected the convention theses as a whole after the conference. And to that explanation I should add another qualification. The statement that "they are in a bloc against us" was an assumption—however, I think, a correct one. I know that this group established relations with the Carter grouping at the conference and that they have many points in common. The complete lack of discrimination Shachtman has shown in the acceptance of allies so far leads us to conclude that he will not reject these. We shall see. If my assumption is wrong, I will correct the statement, but I will not be wrong. It should be understood that Comrade Spector is not included in the Toronto group referred to. On the one hand, he, as you know, had a common political stand with the National Committee at the conference, and has not shared the views of the group in Toronto which rejected the thesis. On the present disputes he has not expressed himself officially and I do not know his position.

One more point about the conference thesis. The assumption that it is a specifically "Shachtman document" is completely erroneous. It is true that he wrote the draft, but by no means in the sense of a presentation of his personal views. The writing was preceded by a number of exhaustive discussions in which all the main points were considered. After that, the draft was gone over twice by a subcommittee, line by line, and still other additions and amendments were made as a result of discussion in the full committee. S., of course, contributed a full share of the thoughts and ideas. But the thesis was in every sense a collective document.

Fraternally,

[James P. Cannon]

Centrist–right wing unity?

Published May 7, 1932

The following article was published in the *Militant*.

The party members who have taken the official fulminations against the Lovestoneite "renegades" in good faith may be somewhat surprised to learn about the secret unity negotiations between the party CEC and these same "renegades," which have been going on now for some time. The letters printed on another page of this issue of the *Militant* from two sources give the essential facts about these negotiations.[34]

Behind a barrage of official denunciation of the Lovestoneites on the one side, and accentuated protests against the "ultraleft course" on the other, the chiefs of the centrist and right-wing factions are calmly talking business together. This much is clearly established. Of course the party members, who—so to speak—have an interest in the matter, were neither consulted nor informed about the negotiations. It has been a long time since the bureaucrats of Stalinism found it necessary to take the Communist workers into their confidence or to seek their approval before an action.

There is nothing really surprising, from a political standpoint, in the fraternal conferences of the right-wing and centrist factions. Neither is there any principled barrier to an actual consummation of the unity between them, although this does not appear the most probable outcome at the moment. The theoretical premise of each of the opportunist factions is the same—the reactionary theory of socialism in one country.

Lovestone's "exceptionalism" for the United States is only an American translation of Stalin's exceptionalism for Russia.[35] Revolutionary internationalism is a dead letter for both. Stalin doesn't care a fig for the policy of the American party as long as its support for his regime in the Russian party is assured. Lovestone will vote for anything in Russia, China, Germany, and all the rest of the world as long as he can have the American party to play with. In this mutual accommodation of special interests there is the basis for a bargain. It happened before. Why can't it happen again? Such are the real thoughts in the minds of the horse traders as they sit down quietly together to talk over terms.

Lovestone would prefer to wait for further developments in the American movement before taking any decisive steps one way or another. But he is not allowed to forget for a moment the fearful insecurity of his group's position. He is shaking under the pressure of the discontent in his own ranks like the lid on a steaming kettle. The debacle of the right wing on an international scale could not fail to have powerful repercussions within the Lovestone group, which includes not a few workers devoted to communism. The reaction of these workers against the orientation toward

Muste and the SP "Militants" convinced Lovestone that a decisive step in that direction could not be made without great internal difficulties. The shuttling back and forth between the left-reformist groups and the party—which characterizes the Lovestone politics—reflects the contradictions within the membership which have already resulted in numerous defections and small splits.

The Stalinists are not restrained from another deal with Lovestone and Company by scruples over principle, since they have no principles—or, to put it more precisely and correctly, no principles of their own. Their entire equipment in this respect consists of ideas furnished to them by the right wing and those borrowed in snatches from the Left Opposition by the method of routine denunciation. In the trade union field, and especially in the strategically important sector of the needle trades, the Lovestoneites, feeding on the crude errors of the party and adapting themselves to the pseudoprogressive wing of the bureaucracy, have strengthened their position. The Stalinists, confronted with a collapse of their policy in the trade unions, are seeking a way out by means of maneuvers and deals. Why not a bargain with Lovestone, which includes, it must be remembered, Zimmerman?

Who is there to object to such a proposition in the leading circles of the party, and for what reason? Certainly not those who shared the responsibility for the whole perfidious course of Lovestone over a period of years and left him only at the last moment, under command of Stalin. A serious objection on principled grounds can hardly come from Foster, who, we are informed in a recent article by Minor, is now "the foremost leader of the party." Foster believes in the "third period" trade union policy as much as we believe in reincarnation after death. Foster once proposed a bloc with Sigman. Why should he gulp over a bargain with Lovestone and Zimmerman?

The whole affair is a shocking revelation of the hollowness and futility of the official party campaign against the right wing. Those who were deceived by this "left turn"—which was calculated to disorient the proletarian elements in the party and arrest their development in the direction of the Left Opposition—may begin to come to life again and reexamine all that has transpired. There are signs of this.

A unity with the right wing—even though it takes the form of an organizational capitulation, as in Russia—will not be without a serious political effect. It is the method of Stalinism, which has no independent line and is incapable of formulating one, to appropriate, in whole or in part, the platform of opponents after their organizational defeat. The "defeat" of Bukharin and his retention in the party was followed by a swing to the right.[36] Let the revolutionary workers in the party look out for such a "defeat" and "capitulation" of Lovestone and his group.

Weisbord blows the whistle

Published May 7, 1932

The following article was published in the *Militant*.

There are more ways of judging leaders and would-be leaders of the revolutionary labor movement than to read their programs and theses, just as there are more ways of judging Texas steers than to measure the length of their horns. Sometimes a little act is more revealing as to the real character of a politician than a dozen statements and a hundred promises.

A few weeks ago we mentioned Weisbord's action in taking his erstwhile comrades to court in connection with the reams of advice he has offered to us on the art of "leadership," and concluded that advice from such a source would bear a close inspection. Now the same Weisbord, in order perhaps to throw a clearer light on the merits of his messianic claims, has demonstrated, by another action, his conception of how to wage the revolutionary struggle against the class enemy. For one who has read his theses, this performance will help to explain them; for those who haven't read the theses, it will make a study of them superfluous.

In the April 20 issue of *Class Struggle* we read the following remarkable summary of the marine workers' trial,[37] in which Weisbord, starting in where the state's attorney left off, invokes the testimony of the police stool pigeon Hoyle against the Lovestone group. He writes:

> It was stated *by the witness for the state,* Hoyle, and reported widely by the press, that when he went for the dynamite with Soderberg he went from "A Communist hall on East 27th Street" (which could be none other than Lovestone's headquarters) with several girls and in a car driven by a certain doctor. When the dynamite had been procured and they had returned, according to Hoyle, they stored the dynamite for the night and part of the next day at the same headquarters.
>
> *If this evidence is correct*, then we see why Lovestone, who expelled Soderberg after he had been arrested, never published his expulsion and why Lovestone . . . later entered the defense himself. *Did he feel they were all in the same boat?* [Our emphasis]

Let us rub our eyes and read this over again. Hoyle, whom Weisbord gives the euphemistic title of "witness for the state," is the stool pigeon and provocateur whose "evidence" sent the three marine workers to prison for long terms. Everything he said on the witness stand was denied by the three workers in the dock, and by that fact the testimony of Hoyle is completely discredited in the court of working-class opinion. It has no more standing there than the hounding demagogy of the district attorney, the biased rulings of the judge, or the class verdict of the jury.

But Weisbord is not satisfied merely to put Hoyle on the witness stand again in the columns of his filthy sheet, and to dress up the stool pigeon as a dignified "witness for the state." He has to bring out some of his testimony more clearly and to give it new implications against others in addition to those already sent to prison. To Hoyle's reference to "A Communist hall on East 27th Street," he finds it necessary to add in parentheses: "which could be none other than Lovestone's headquarters." And then he sharpens up the police tip with the observation that "if this evidence is correct" (when was the evidence of a stool pigeon ever "correct"?) it shows that "they were all in the same boat."

There is very little need for a revolutionist, or for an ordinary militant worker for that matter, to comment on this attempt to "put the finger" on the Lovestone group. The thing, like a policeman's badge, speaks for itself. But Weisbord, who published this rotten provocation, advertises himself as a communist; more than that, as a leader of communism; and still more, as an "adherent of the International Left Opposition." It is just the possibility that some unsuspecting worker might take these pretensions at face value that impels us to offer two words of comment.

The Left Opposition is opposed to the right-wing group of Lovestone; and Weisbord, as the above-quoted testimony would indicate, is not at present friendly to it. But there the similarity of positions comes to an end. We fight the right wing on principled grounds with the method of political argument addressed to the workers; Weisbord blows the whistle for the cops. Between these two methods there is a chasm that no bridge can span.

The fight is here

May 7, 1932

The following is an incomplete draft of a letter to Bernard Morgenstern in Moyamensing Prison.[38]

Dear Comrade Morgenstern:

Your release in the middle of this month will come before the plenum, which is scheduled for May 27, and this will give you the opportunity of participating in the discussion of the disputes before the resolution of the National Committee is adopted. The material that has already been sent to you, taken together with your previous knowledge of the difficulties that led up to the present rupture, will enable you to get a rough idea of how things stand now. Here I want to touch a few points concerning which I would like to have an exchange of opinions with you, if possible before the plenum. I cannot forget that your judgment proved better than mine, in one respect at least: after the discussion at the plenum two years ago, and the happenings at the Second National Conference, you had less confidence than I that matters could eventually be straightened out without an open fight. I am anxious to know what you think about things now.

The first essential fact to recognize is that the fight is here, whether we like it or not. And if I erred in thinking it might be avoided, I have no intention to repeat the error by minimizing the seriousness of the problem it presents or by relying on half measures to deal with it. No, the conflict and its causes must be probed to the bottom. We must go deep and find out what it really means. We must insist that the *causes* be laid bare and the necessary correctives firmly determined. The comparatively slow pace at which the movement is now developing is not without a compensating side. It gives us the time and provides us with the opportunity to examine some fearful internal weaknesses which would surely paralyze the league in the face of a real test of struggle.

As we see the situation, the American league is now beginning to manifest some of those internal contradictions which have disrupted the internal life of the European sections for the past few years. You know it has become a legend with us that the issues and struggles of the European communist movement have always repeated themselves on American soil—two or three years later. This, in a way, is the measure of our backwardness. I once wrote on this theme in the *Militant* and expressed the idea that, profiting by the experience of the European sections of the Opposition, we would skip over the crises that beset them. This expectation also proved too optimistic. At bottom the present conflict in our league signifies the American reproduction—it is to be hoped in a moderated form—of the internal crisis of the International Left.

By that I do not mean to say, of course, that we have an exact reproduction of the crisis of the European sections, nor that the specific disputes and errors and corrective measures are, or can be, mechanically transplanted here. My reference is to the essence of the problem, its foundation causes. Even in our faults and weaknesses we will remain Americans, but Americans bound up with the international communist movement no less inextricably than American capitalism is bound up with the world system of which it is a part. Our task consists in discovering wherein the peculiar, and apparently isolated, "American" issues are related to the international crisis, and in bringing to bear upon them the international experience. But a schematic application of this experience to America would be self-defeating. The Opposition did not originate and develop here along the same lines as in Europe; and in many respects the external characteristics of our league, its origin and progress, represent an opposite appearance. But the external differences, in spite of that, conceal a hidden fundamental similarity. To sweep away the fog of argument over pretexts and superficial matters and disclose the fundamental basis of the conflict is the first prerequisite for a real understanding of our disputes.

On the surface everything is different between the American league and, for example, the French and German and other European sections. The Opposition there was expelled from the party in 1923–24; here it did not take shape until 1928.

There the "original" Opposition—Urbahns, Van Overstraaten, Paz, Rosmer, etc.—had to be broken up and discarded before a real struggle on the lines of the Russian Bolsheviks could begin; here the fraudulent representatives of the Opposition (Lore) exhausted and discredited their claims without making the slightest impression on the party. The group which raised the banner of the Opposition in 1928 proved, over a period of four years already—and from the first—that it was the legitimate bearer of this banner.

In Germany, Belgium, and France the trade union question and the question of faction or party necessitated splits in 1928; in America the basic cadre remained untouched by these issues.

In the European sections the consolidation of a stable, more or less experienced and influential, leadership remains an acute problem; in our league the National Committee as a whole has had no serious opposition.

In Europe, notably Germany, the Opposition was expelled in the course of a struggle for control of the party, on a platform at variance with that of the Russian Opposition and, in many respects, contradictory to it. The adjustment of this contradiction had to take place later, at the cost of splits, in the expelled faction calling itself the Left Opposition. Here the faction that was destined to mature into the American section of the Left Opposition went through these contradictions, vacillations, and splits *within the party* before the final expulsion of its fundamental nucleus. This is what accounts for the fact that it could *begin* its existence as an expelled faction under the banner of the Russian Opposition.

If one looks closely into the matter, in the light of the preceding paragraph, it can be seen that the differences in the lines of development between our league and its European counterparts are more apparent than real. In any case they are not fundamental. The unavoidable crises and splits of the European sections stand out more clearly because they took place within the formal framework of the International Opposition as an expelled faction. Our evolution along substantially the same path was somewhat obscured, and the implications of our long and stubborn faction struggle preceding expulsion were muffled and distorted by the bureaucratic force of the International regime. It should not be forgotten that our eventual liberation from this regime, and our deliberate union with the Russian Opposition, had to be purchased at the cost of a deep split in the faction at the time of our expulsion.

Thus, if we look at the developments as they actually occurred—casting aside, of course, as unworthy of a moment's notice the theory of Weisbord, Carter, and other blockheads that the formal organization of the American section of the Opposition occurred in October 1928 by "accident" or as a result of a maneuver or trick by "Cannon"—that a considerable part of the dialectical process of development so clearly revealed in the European sections since the deportation of Comrade Trotsky, had its expression also here. The methods and the forms were different, but in our blundering way we traveled the same path. If we maintained a relative calm during the convulsions of the European sections in the Urbahns–Paz–Van Overstraaten affairs it was primarily due to the fact that this experience, *mutatis mutandis*, was behind us.

And by the same token, if we are now confronted with the symptoms of a crisis in the league which bears a certain resemblance to the crises which marked the course of the French and German leagues in the latter period, it is because we have not yet experienced these crises in our own ranks and have not assimilated the experiences of the other sections in them. We are obliged to search out and examine the root causes of our present difficulties in this light. We have to pay for our progress one way or another, either by a crisis of our own, by learning the lessons of the convulsions of the other sections, or by a combination of both. The latter alternative is the best we can hope for now. We waited too long in drawing the lessons of the internal struggle of the past two years in the

International Opposition to escape some kind of a disturbance in our league. The aim now must be to reduce this disturbance to the minimum. And for that we must look squarely into the sources of the international crisis, see what it means for us and what we can learn from it.

In the endeavor to get to the bottom of the present conflict in the league we encounter two arguments:

1. That we are artificially transplanting the French and German internal disputes to American soil, exaggerating and misrepresenting the differences, "framing up" Comrade Shachtman, automatically supporting Trotsky for reasons of factional strategy within the league, etc., etc. You see, there is no lack of accusations. But we learned long ago that a multitude of accusations does not necessarily signify a strong position, and quite often serves to cover up a weak one. However, I will take the time to answer these points.

2. On the other hand, and from the same comrades, either directly or by implication, we hear that these "international differences" are secondary and in reality have nothing to do with the actual causes of the controversy. Moreover, it is contended that we do not really know what the disputes in Europe are about, do not have sufficient information, etc. This idea seems to have a certain popularity with the young scholastics, who here, as always, occupy themselves endlessly with the study of texts, weighing and measuring, something on this side, something on that side, without in the least considering that a struggle is taking place which concerns the whole future of the movement.

I propose to deal with both of these arguments here in some detail. And if necessary I will return to the subject again. Before one can get down to the meat of the question it is best to clear away extraneous objections, answer accusations as to "motives" and other inconsequential contentions. It is regrettable that this is necessary, but we can take the time to do it if we have to. But only in order to clear the way for the discussion of the real issues. We learned how to do this, of necessity, in years of struggle, beginning particularly with the break with the Foster group. Thus we welded together a genuine political grouping that would not allow itself to be sidetracked from the essence of a question and would not determine its position on any other basis.

We will stop to explain and dispose of side issues if it is demanded. But on one condition: that we do not remain there! After the small and secondary matters are disposed of, we will return to the main question and form our judgments accordingly!

In our long statement, which Comrade Swabeck and I presented to the National Committee in reply to Shachtman's attack, we explained our point of view on the "international questions" and recounted the evolution of the differences which have culminated in the present conflict. The facts cited there—which are matters of record and cannot be disputed—speak more convincingly than mere argument.

For genuine reunification of communist forces

Published May 14, 1932

The following article was published in the *Militant*.

The revelations in last week's *Militant* about the secret negotiations between the [Communist] Party leaders and the expelled right wing have awakened a new interest among the Communist workers in the question of unity. And the informal discussion arising from it, according to the reports we have received, is not confined to the horse trade behind the scenes between the centrist bureaucrats and the Lovestone group. The revival of sentiment for unity with the left, that is, with the bona fide revolutionary faction, is noticeable.

There is a logic in this development that was never thought of by the machinators. In part, it is an expression of the fundamental solidarity which the proletarian militants in the party feel toward the Left Opposition. It is also a sign of resentment against the undercover maneuvers to readmit the right opportunist leaders; the proletarian elements want a revolutionary counterweight in the party. Therefore, our choice will be heard in the backroom conferences, even though we are not there as invited guests. The time is opportune for a restatement of the attitude of the Left Opposition on unity.

For communists, the unity of the revolutionary vanguard is not and cannot be the basis for any kind of maneuvers. It is no object of private understandings and agreements. Unity concerns the class whose interests are bound up with the organization of its political vanguard. Only people who are in reality separated from the party and the class and freed from their control can think of discussing unity, its terms and conditions, its possibility or impossibility at the moment, in secret.

What the Left Opposition has to say on the subject needs no concealment. Unity or division, like all other vital questions of the movement, must be understood by the party and decided by the party before the eyes of the proletariat. Only so can the decisions be firmly grounded. Therefore, our first demand is a discontinuance of the whispered negotiations behind the back of the party; for the elevation of the question from the level of a deal between businessmen into a discussion of principled considerations by the entire revolutionary vanguard. Bring the unity negotiations into the open!

Since the position of the Left Opposition on the subject of party unity, as on all other important issues, is founded on principle, a consistency in its expressions on the matter from time to time can be noted. From our first statement in regard to unity at the plenum which confirmed our expulsion three and one-half years ago, through the various occasions in which we again raised the question in timely communications to the party, until the present day, we have been guided by the example and teaching of our incomparable leaders, the Russian Bolshevik-Leninists. Just as they, in their platform and in all subsequent declarations, affirmed their desire to remain in the party, and their willingness to defend their views by the normal processes of party democracy and party discipline, so we have always protested against our enforced separation from the party. We never made any special demands that were not taken for granted and enjoyed by every party member in Lenin's time, and we do not make them now.

Our chief concern, which transcends all other considerations, is the return of the party and the Comintern to the foundation principles of Marxism. Since 1928, first within the party and afterward as an expelled group, we have advocated, on all the important questions of the day, the Marxist line of the International Left Opposition against the opportunist and adventurist zig-zags of official centrism. These views, the correctness of which has been confirmed in every case by the events of the class struggle, we still maintain. We have nothing to repent and nothing to retract.

Unity for us cannot be the formula for a reconciliation with the treacherous policy of the Stalinist bureaucracy, but a condition for the more advantageous struggle against it. The rectification of the truly enormous errors and crimes, not the least of which are the ruinous splits that have been imposed upon the workers' vanguard, will take place only in the course of the most relentless Bolshevik fight against the bureaucrats of Stalinism, and will be finally assured only with their downfall. In order that the workers who sincerely desire the unification of the party may have no illusions as to its actual meaning, this must be said directly, openly, and plainly.

They are deceivers of the communist workers who, abusing their good will, preach "unity" and capitulate to the general sentiment for it without speaking of the principal causes of the demoralization and splits. No better are those worthless *intriguants* who dicker over "unity" in a dark corner without even informing the workers what is going on, like commission merchants with so many head of livestock at their disposal. No, the first step toward a genuine unification of the communist forces must be a frank statement on the different positions and the present attitude toward them. All the wishes in the world will not bring unity for struggle in any other way.

This is not to say, of course, that the differences must be settled beforehand, or that the platform of the Left Opposition must be accepted as a condition for unity. We have never demanded that. The demand of the Left Opposition is for party democracy, as Lenin's party defined and practiced it. A free and open discussion of the disputes within the framework of the party. A convention whose delegates are fairly and honestly selected on the basis of the discussion. A leadership freely elected by the membership and subject to its control. The right of the minority to work in the party and to advance its viewpoint a second, a third, or a tenth time on proper occasion, within the limits of the party constitution. This is the way Lenin's party clarified its policies, corrected its errors, chose its leaders, and safeguarded its unity.

Nobody has invented any other method, and nobody can. The Stalinist substitute only succeeded in derailing the party from the Marxist track, crushing the initiative of the membership, and celebrating its "monolithic unity" with split after split. It is the horrible bankruptcy of this Stalinist substitute that compels the party membership to think of unity again in terms of Leninism, and to seek a way for the inclusion of the Left Opposition.

There is no doubt that the present objective circumstances

accentuate the harmful results of splits and the consequent weakening of the party before its class enemies. The sharpening of the class struggle at home, the increasingly heavy blows dealt to the militant workers by the entrenched reaction, the rumbling of impending revolutionary struggles abroad—all this gives a powerful impulse to the sentiments for unity within the party ranks. The Left Opposition, which has no special interests separate from those of the class and the vanguard, will do all in its power to strengthen this current and help it to realize its aims. From this point of view the last meeting of the National Committee of the Communist League decided to approach the party once again with an appeal for unity and a series of practical proposals for its realization.

The first of these proposals, which will be transmitted to the party within the week, will ask the reinstatement of the Left Opposition without any conditions except the rights of party democracy, and with an undertaking to assume any duties or responsibilities whatever which are assigned to us by the party.

The second proposal, to be applied immediately while the matter of formal reinstatement remains pending, is that the party accept the cooperation of the Left Opposition in class-struggle actions, in the trade unions and other organizations, and on every front where the pressure of the class enemy is heaviest. The Left Opposition will take its place in the front ranks of every struggle without exception and will demonstrate its revolutionary qualities there, now as it has in the past. The Oppositionists are ready to prove by deeds their right to work with the party militants. They will prove by deeds their right to be in the party.

In the party, or temporarily outside of it, cooperating with the party in united front struggles or denied the right to participate in them—whatever the circumstances of the moment, the Left Opposition will retain its principled positions, and above all its internationalism. We are united for life and death with the true inheritors of the October revolution, the Bolshevik-Leninists of Soviet Russia and the international organization of Bolshevik-Leninists which now embraces the world. We do not seek a solution of the problem of unity on a national basis; we do not separate our cause from theirs. If we are readmitted to the American party our first demand in free discussion will be:

Reinstate the expelled oppositionists in Russia and all other sections of the Comintern! Recall Trotsky from Constantinople and Rakovsky from Siberia! Release the thousands and tens of thousands of Bolshevik-Leninists from the Stalinist prisons and exile camps and restore them to their rightful place in the party. That and only that will give a revolutionary, international substance to the slogan of communist unity.

A debate with the IWW

May 14, 1932

The following are Cannon's handwritten notes from his presentation to a debate with Industrial Workers of the World leader Clifford B. Ellis.

1. The question we are debating is an old one. It has been the subject of heated controversy in the ranks of the international labor movement in various forms for the past eighty years.

2. That statement may appear to be a historical error. The IWW is not yet eighty years old; although, to judge by its vitality in the class struggle, it appears to be. My reference is to the ideas under discussion. Neither mine nor Ellis's are new. The modern communist position is the old, orthodox position of *Marxism*. The IWW represents at bottom a combination of the various schools of thought which fought Marxism and have been refuted time and time again, both in theory and practice.

3. The problem of how to emancipate the workers is

the problem of the revolutionary transformation of society—the problem of revolution.

4. This question transcends all others in importance.

5. It is not merely an abstract problem of the remote future, as it may appear to some people, but an actual question of our time.

6. We live in the epoch of wars and revolutions which are destined to change the face of the entire world.

7. Within the past eighteen years—that is, within our own lifetimes—we have seen:

a) The most devastating war in all history.

b) A proletarian revolution encompassing one-sixth of the surface of the earth.

c) Revolutions and attempts at revolutions in China, Germany, Bulgaria, Hungary, and Italy.

d) We see now what may be the beginning of a new world war in the Orient.

e) We have seen the first general strike of the British working class.

f) Italy has been under the iron heel of fascism for eleven years. Every trace of labor organization has been crushed out.

g) In Germany we see the issue hanging in the balance. The revolutionary proletariat and the fascist hordes stand face to face. The decisive struggle may be only a question of months or weeks.

h) And finally—to get back home—we see the boasted prosperity of the greatest capitalist power on earth, celebrated by 12 million unemployed, reduced living standards, and insecurity for the other workers.

8. Deep within the masses of the American workers—as a result of the happenings of recent years—a profound change is taking place.

9. This process is a slow one. It took time to implant

the illusions of permanent prosperity. It takes time to dissipate them.

10. But this process is going on with inevitably increasing momentum.

11. The workers are caught in the contradiction of capitalism. There is only one way for them to turn.

12. Slowly, but with inevitable certitude, the conviction will take shape in their minds that there is only one way to turn—toward the proletarian revolution.

13. These facts describe the general background of our discussion. They give it actuality, seriousness, timeliness. They give us—both those who speak and those who have come to listen—a conviction that it is no mere discussion that occupies us. In discussing the problems of the revolution we are discussing the central question of our lives.

14. I have enough respect for the audience to assume that you want to hear a discussion of principle and not an exchange of personal insults.

15. If we do nothing else in this debate except to raise the dispute from the gutter of personal slander to the level of an ideological dispute, it will be a victory for the movement as a whole.

16. We are both "social fascists." In view of that some present might wonder what we are debating about!

17. We have one thing in common—we both believe in free speech—even for people who call us funny names.

18. Free speech includes the freedom to talk like a fool. Because when you get right down to it a fool can't talk any other way.

19. The question we are debating assumes an anticapitalist attitude on both sides. The audience, I take it, needs no argument against capitalism, but a program for its overthrow.

20. Marxism teaches that human society is a process of evolution.

21. In the study of this historical process, on the basis of the materialist conception of history, one can understand the present and see also the line of future development.

22. We know that human society existed for tens of thousands of years in primitive communism, without classes or class struggles, without private property, and without a state.

23. The future society, toward which we strive, will be a return to that condition on a higher basis.

24. The institution of private property divided the people into classes, brought class struggles and the state.

25. The material conditions for the capitalist method of production matured within the framework of feudal society.

26. The capitalist method of production liberated itself from the fetters of the feudal order by means of revolution. No ruling class ever gave up without a fight.

27. Of what did that revolution consist?

a) The conquest of state power.

b) The use of the state power to (1) crush the remnants of the old order; and (2) keep the new wage class down.

28. I know that I am committing a sacrilege in mentioning the word "state."

29. The "state," we are told, is only a reflex—only a shadow. But it has not played a shadowy role in history.

30. When Robespierre and his Jacobins set up the guillotine in the public square [during the French revolution] the new state was not a shadow; it was a terrible reality for the aristocrats.

31. The state is the concentrated power of the ruling class in a class society.

32. Under capitalism it is: (a) the executive to regulate the common affairs of the bourgeoisie; and (b) an instrument to keep the exploited classes down by force.

33. Marx correctly defined the class struggle as a political

struggle, that is, a struggle for power.

34. This is the aim of every revolution. The proletariat cannot even make a good start toward its revolution until this is understood.

Ellis's arguments: "Revolutions come—they are not made." "The industrial revolution has already taken place." "The state is not the source of power."

Then: "They shoot us dead in the streets if we protest against their rule." "The world can't be run by preachers, lawyers, doctors, and politicians." (Who ran the World War? Politicians representing a class.)

"Give an instance in history where a group ever surrendered power—without more power being organized in industry?" "There can be no liberty until there is industrial liberty."

The material conditions for socialism have already matured within the framework of capitalism. The *economic* foundation of the new society is here. The problem is to make the social transformation. The question stands *politically*.

35. The revolutionary proletariat must aim: (a) to overthrow the state power of the capitalists; (b) to set up its own state power: the dictatorship of the proletariat.

36. The dictatorship of the proletariat is necessary: (a) to crush the resistance of the bourgeoisie and organize social production; (b) to defend the country against invasion and aid revolution in other countries; (c) to abolish all classes and class exploitation. Then it will wither away.

37. For the organization of the revolutionary struggle and victory the proletariat must form its own party.

38. All classes—exploiters and exploited—are led by parties. (Cite Germany and America)

39. A party is the conscious vanguard of the class.

40. We must take the working class as we find it.

a) Only a minority can become educated and conscious. [Reasons for this:]

b) Bourgeois influence, thanks to its control of the state, church, press, movies, literature and art, and political parties.

41. Besides this the class has various economic strata, with conflicting immediate interests: unskilled, half-skilled, aristocracy, slum proletariat, bureaucracy.

42. The organization of the whole class into the IWW will not take away these contradictions. ("No party" means backroom rule.)

43. A differentiation, a selection of the conscious elements and their organization into a party would be just as necessary.

44. If the revolutionary party does not lead the class—including the unions—some other party will.

45. "No party" means—no competition to the bourgeois and reformist parties. ("Form no party"—a favor to the capitalists since they have theirs.)

46. There are no "independent" unions anywhere: (a) England; (b) Germany; (c) Russia; (d) France (split); (e) America (New York City).

47. The general strike—its uses and limitations (Kapp putsch and Britain).[39]

48. Positive sides: (a) can play a great role (Russia); (b) a prelude to revolution.

49. Negative sides:

a) Strike alone cannot succeed in overthrow.

b) Unless it goes over to the armed insurrection it cannot succeed: (1) workers starve first; (2) violence of the state (Kentucky; what would happen in a general strike?); (3) fascist provocation (Butte; Italy); (4) "folded arms" targets.[40]

50. Failure of the British strike:

a) Political aims denied.

b) Weakness of the revolutionary party.

c) Betrayal of leaders.

d) What would the IWW leadership do with such a general strike?

e) To this we can answer: those who do not believe in an insurrection will never make one.

51. The Italian seizure of power (prelude to fascism).

a) Here is shown the real bankruptcy of syndicalism.

b) To organize production requires a proletarian state.

52. If one is really thinking of revolution—of expropriating the capitalists and destroying their institutions and their rule, then it is clear that the program of the IWW is by no means sufficient.

53. At best it is only a program for union organization within the framework of capitalism.

54. Insofar as it sets its program up as a complete program—denies the necessity for a proletarian party, for the forceful overthrow of the state and for the dictatorship of the proletariat—it becomes an obstacle to the revolution.

55. This is its great error and contradiction.

56. But in our day the problems of revolution are so closely bound up with the daily fight—which is a preparation for it—that those who have a false program regarding the goal have false tactics from day to day. This has been the fate of the IWW in recent years.

57. In revolutionary times, the revolutionary groups and parties thrive.

58. But in the case of the IWW—since the beginning of the great world advances of the revolution beginning in 1917—the IWW has been going down.

59. Let fellow-worker Ellis explain the phenomenon.

60. In order to bring out the position of the IWW more fully on the most decisive issues, I put the following

questions to him: How will the IWW proceed to "take possession of the industries"? How will they reply to armed attacks of the police and the army? What will the IWW do with the capitalist army and navy? [How will the IWW handle] foreign intervention?

More on slogan of 'rank-and-file leadership'

Published June 11, 1932

The following article was published in the *Militant*.

Some questions have arisen about the remarks in a recent issue of the *Militant* on the slogan of "rank-and-file leadership," which deserve a somewhat extended answer. The idea has been expressed that this slogan of the Stalinists really has some merits, that in reality it is only a restatement of the old demand of the left wing for trade union democracy, and that in any case the slogan is not wrong in principle.

In our opinion, such views are entirely erroneous in all respects, and only add to the confusion. And since the matter has a considerable importance—nothing will bring quicker disaster than a false direction in the trade union struggle—another attempt to clarify the issue will be worthwhile. The negative manner in which the slogan was discussed in the previous treatment, without reference to an alternative formulation, also came in for criticism and perhaps gave ground for misunderstanding. The present article, therefore, will undertake to deal with the latest trade union slogan of the Stalinists in a more rounded fashion and suggest a positive alternative.

Is "rank-and-file leadership" a new demand of the left wing, or is it simply the restatement of an old one? There are two answers to this question. It is an old idea that permeated the needle trades left wing more or less before the emergence of the Communist leadership. But its advocacy by Communists is something new—one of the many Stalinist "innovations" which are in reality borrowed from anti-Marxist schools. Before the rise of the Communist influence in the needle trades, the left wing was heavily tainted with the prejudices of anarchism and syndicalism in their various forms. The IWW, defeated organizationally in the needle trades, succeeded nevertheless in grafting a part of its ideology onto the militant section of the rank and file. The brilliant idea of "no leaders," of the rank and file leading the rank and file—which is just another way of saying "rank-and-file leadership"—gained a certain sympathy from the workers who were in revolt against the bureaucracy.

The leaders of the "company union" did not begin their treacherous work yesterday. The workers had good reason to learn about it before 1919. The old movement against the bureaucrats, which had not yet thought out its problems and formulated a clear program, had a tendency to identify the idea of leadership with the ruling clique and had to a certain extent fallen victim to nihilistic conceptions on the question of leadership, as preached by the anarchists and the IWW. In this respect, but in no other, it can be said that "rank-and-file leadership" is an old slogan of the needle trades left wing.

But ten years or more ago the Communists came to the

front and soon gained the decisive leadership of the left-wing movement by virtue of their superior policy. One of the first positive steps of the Communist left wing was to clear up the muddled ideology of the movement and sweep out the anarchistic rubbish which had paralyzed the struggles and strengthened the position of the reactionary bureaucrats. "Rank and file" demagogy and formlessness in the domain of organization gave place to the conception of democratic centralism.

The old and outworn reformist method of workers' organization makes an artificial division between the masses of the membership on the one side and the ruling bureaucrats on the other. This state of affairs created the conditions for the antileadership prejudices to gain a foothold. The Leninist idea of democratic centralism fuses the leaders with the masses and removes any ground for contrasting the one to the other. This idea gained hegemony in the left wing and was one of the most important reasons why its fighting capacities grew by leaps and bounds. From a chaos revolving around one spot, the left wing became a real contender for power in the unions, and in some cases achieved it.

In its struggle to break the backbone of the bureaucracy which was throttling the unions, the Communist left wing advanced along the line of principle in all questions, including the organization question. This was its strength. The Communists formulated their fighting slogans precisely and accurately, and in consonance with a general theory of organization. Confronted then as now with the sabotaging role of the bureaucrats in strikes, they did not attempt to leap over the difficulty by denying the necessity of an official leadership. On the contrary, they formulated a general demand applicable to the union as a whole, and a subordinate one, consistent with it, applicable to the management of strikes.

On the one hand, the Communist left wing raised the demand for honest, militant leaders in the union in place of the corrupt, reactionary fakers. In harmony with that, and consistent with the organization program which the left wing would apply when it gained control of the union, it demanded the democratization of the union, and particularly of the strike machinery. (At that time, you see, the left wing was not conducting a temporary excursion into the reactionary unions; it was aiming to conquer them, step by step, and it formulated its slogans accordingly.) The left wing did not bluster about rank-and-file "leadership," it demanded rank-and-file *control*. Moreover, it formulated this demand precisely, so that everyone could understand just what was meant.

In the program adopted at the Third Conference of the Needle Trades Left Wing, September 12–14, 1925, the idea is expressed as follows:

> It is only through a strike machinery thoroughly representative of the workers in the shops that the membership can effectively be mobilized for strike activity.... Therefore, foremost of our immediate aims during strikes is the democratization of the whole union machinery as provided in this program: (1) that the general strike committees and heads of the strike be elected by the delegates and chairmen from the shops and responsible to them; (2) that all strike assessments be collected as legally due to this strike committee, to be expended only for strike purposes; (3) that secret diplomacy be done away with and negotiations with the employers be conducted on an open basis.

Have these demands—so clear, so precise, and so consistent with the whole general program of the left wing for the renovation of the union on the basis of democratic centralism—anything in common with the latter-day mumbling about "rank-and-file leadership" of strikes? Are the Stalinists perhaps now saying, or trying to say, the same thing in a different way?

In reply to this question it is only necessary to ask: if they mean the same thing that the left wing meant in 1925, then why did they change the precise and correct formulation of that time for the present self-contradictory mishmash? The reason for the change is clear enough: the aims are different now and the slogan has a different meaning. In 1925 the left wing was fighting inside the union with the aim of wresting it out of the strangling grasp of the reactionaries. In 1932 the left wing, under the influence of the proconsuls of Stalin, are still monkeying around with the theory of "company unionism" and are searching for some kind of strike organization outside the existing union.

The fact that they hit upon a slogan that has no real sense or meaning, and that flatly contradicts Marxist conceptions of organization in favor of Wobblyism, is nothing to be surprised at. They always do something like this when they experiment with "theory." A short while ago it was "independent leadership of strike struggles." After they had cracked their heads on the rocks with this formula, they quietly dropped it. Now, with a "new" slogan, which is quite different in appearance, they are attempting to accomplish the same design that failed before, namely, to find a substitute for the existing union in the midst of a strike regardless of the attitude of the majority of workers.

Under pressure of the criticism we have brought against the slogan of "rank-and-file leadership," and no doubt also stimulated by the poor reception it has received from the rank and file, attempts are being made to interpret the slogan in a different way than was originally intended. Rose Wortis, for example, who strives to avoid obvious absurdities when the party bosses are not watching, speaks in the *Daily Worker* of May 31 about "a real strike for union conditions under rank-and-file *control*" (our emphasis).

Thus it would appear, according to the Wortis version, that rank-and-file leadership and rank-and-file control are synonymous expressions. But this is by no means the case, either in the field of organization or in the dictionary. In every democratic organization the ultimate control of the rank and file is presupposed; but the selection of the leadership and its functions remain a separate question. Only those who deny the role of leadership can solve the problem for themselves by a reference to "control." Wortis, for example, was a leader, but three-fourths of her leadership consisted in maneuvers to escape this "rank-and-file control" she talks about.

"Leadership is a necessary condition for any common action," says the resolution of the Third World Congress of the Comintern.[41] This principle, which does not at all exclude rank-and-file control of the leadership, implies however a selection of persons for leading functions. And it has the same force whether the persons selected are professional leaders or rank-and-file workers elevated to leading positions or committees. In every organization and in every action the question arises at once, and inescapably: Who is going to lead? You can answer: this group or that group; this committee or another. But if you wish to be taken seriously, do not say the rank and file is going to lead the rank and file. And do not try to pass the problem off with a statement that the rank and file will control. That is not the same thing.

In every organization certain persons are selected for leading functions or committees. By that fact they become "leaders," regardless of whether they have had previous experience or not. Such leaders, under the principle of democratic centralism, are inseparably fused with the rank and file, they are accountable to and controlled by the rank and file. This is understandable to anyone. But to confuse the leadership with the mass, or to contrast one to the other, as the slogan of rank-and-file leadership does, presents a muddle which no one can understand and for which everyone can have his own interpretation.

Leadership is one thing, control of the leadership is another. Democratic organization means, in the last analysis, rank-and-file control. But the communists who think things out and formulate their ideas clearly do not speak merely of democracy. The organizational form they advocate is *democratic centralism.* And what does that mean? On the one hand it means democracy in the organization. On the other hand—as against the anarchistic and IWW idea of "no leaders"—it means a recognition of the function of leadership. This leadership in the communist conception is not some kind of a clerical staff or informal bureau. It is invested with real functions and powers, that is, it is given the possibility to *lead.*

But—and herein lies the distinction from bureaucratism—the leadership is *selected* by the rank and file, is responsible to and, in the final analysis, is *controlled* by the rank and file. Democratic centralism, the communist organizational principle, therefore presupposes rank-and-file *control*, but excludes confusionist and demagogic demands for rank-and-file *leadership.* The 1925 program of the needle trades left wing was permeated through and through with this rounded conception. The slogan of today contradicts it in principle. The Wortis improvisation tries to smooth over the fundamental contradiction. She has had a lot of practice at that sort of business.

It has been said that our previous article on this question confused matters by contrasting the "rank and file" agitation of the Stalinists in the trade unions to their bureaucratic regime in the party. The party, it is urged, is not the same as the trade union, and therefore the comparison is inappropriate. True enough, a distinction must be made between the political organization of the vanguard and the economic organization of the broad mass. They differ fundamentally in many ways, including organizational *forms*, but according to the Lenin doctrine the *organizational principle* of each is the same. Rank-and-file leadership is an absurdity in either case; rank-and-file *control* is ultimately necessary in both.

Note the remarks of Comrade Trotsky on this point in the June 4 issue of the *Militant*: "As the first condition of the party control over the government Lenin put the control of party mass over the apparatus."[42] These will bear a careful reading several times. To shout for rank-and-file leadership in the union and soft-pedal about rank-and-file control in the party is a double mistake, a howling inconsistency all the way around. Some of the right-wing union fakers, it seems, snatched up our criticism of the inconsistency of the party bureaucrats and made use of it for their own purposes. But this by no means invalidates the criticism. The corrective for such parasitic exploitation of our exposure of party errors by the right wing is not to keep silent about the errors, but to compel the party to correct them. Let the party members exert some rank-and-file control in this respect in their own party. The same task in the trade unions will then be greatly simplified and facilitated.

In order to wage an effective fight in the trade unions today, and to fortify the victory of tomorrow, the left wing must have consistent slogans all along the line. As a minority it must defend those principles of organization which will govern the union when it comes under the control of the left wing. It must practice in the left-wing unions under its leadership that same method which it demands in the reactionary unions where it constitutes an opposition. If the left wing fails to do this, if it shuttles back and forth with a policy of expediency on every occasion, it will lose its principal guiding line, and with it the power to shape and lead a victorious movement of the masses.

This is what has been happening in recent years under the direction of full-blown Stalinism. The results speak for themselves; and in the catastrophic situation of the left wing in the needle trades they speak with an exceptional force and clarity. The most pressing task of the party and the left wing is to throw off this incubus that weights it down and halts its progress at every step. The general fight to liberate the movement from this paralyzing influence has to be supported by a concrete struggle on every point, against every error which contributes to the defeat of the left-wing workers. The slogan of rank-and-file leadership is one of these errors, the harmfulness of which is clearly demonstrable.

There can be no ground for compromise with such a policy. The Left Opposition, by its criticism, has driven the Stalinists from more than one false position. It must not halt for a moment the effort to do the same in this case. A correction of this error requires no new wisdom. With the aid of the Lenin teaching the left wing solved the problem in question in its program of 1925. What is needed now is a return to the 1925 formulation.

Results of the June plenum

July 1932

The following statement by the National Committee was sent to the branches in early July 1932. It was based on a report by Cannon to the resident NC on July 7 and a resolution approved by the NC on June 25.

Dear comrades:

In a previous circular the branches were informed that disputes had arisen in the resident National Committee which would be considered at a plenary meeting of the full committee. The plenum was held June 10–13, and we are transmitting herewith the minutes of the sessions and the resolutions adopted.

It was clearly established at the plenum that there were no serious differences regarding the general policy of the league as laid down by the national conference.

The two main questions of dispute, upon which the plenum adopted resolutions, were:

1. International questions

2. The situation in the New York branch.

In addition, the plenum considered the disputes and the disruption of the Toronto branch and heard representatives of the two conflicting viewpoints: Comrade Spector and Comrade Krehm. A self-explanatory resolution on this subject was also adopted by the plenum and is attached hereto.[43]

On both of the important questions in dispute, the plenum took a firm stand in support of the position which had been defended in the resident committee by Comrades Swabeck and Cannon against the opposition and obstruction of Comrades Shachtman, Abern, and Glotzer. The resolution on the situation in the International Left Opposition, which had been previously adopted by a referendum of the National Committee and sent to the branches, was ratified unanimously by the plenum. Comrade Shachtman, who up till then had opposed the resolution—which was aimed directly against the false position he had taken on the disputes in the European sections—withdrew his opposition and voted for the resolution. Likewise Comrades Abern and Glotzer, who had presented separate resolutions to the branches, withdrew their resolutions and voted for the official resolution. Comrade Spector, who had withheld his vote before, also voted for the official resolution and submitted a draft of his own which was accepted as a supplement to the original resolution.

The resolution on the situation in the New York branch also corresponds fully to the demands which had been made in the resident committee by Comrades Swabeck and Cannon in respect to the Carter group, with which, prior to the plenum, Comrades Shachtman, Abern, and Glotzer had acted in solidarity in their faction struggle. Under the pressure and insistence of the majority at the plenum Comrade Shachtman submitted a political characterization of the Carter group which is incorporated in the official resolution on the question, and on the basis of which a political struggle for the isolation of this group is to proceed.

At this point, having attained the major premises for the reestablishment of the unity of the National Committee and a renewal of the collaboration which had been disrupted in the conflict, the plenum took up for consideration the long document which had been submitted on the eve of the gathering by Comrades Abern, Glotzer, and Shachtman.[44] This document filled with personal accusations and slanders, with elaborate discussions of outlived and secondary questions and extraneous matters—by means of which it was sought to muddle up and divert attention from the real and actual concrete questions of the dispute—stood as a barrier to unity in the committee. The question was then squarely put to the three comrades mentioned: Do you wish the plenum to reply to your document in the form of a resolution, and take it to the membership for decision, or do you wish to withdraw it from the records?

Thereupon the three comrades, after taking a recess to give the matter due consideration, announced their decision to withdraw the document. On this basis, and on the basis of the further declarations of Comrades Abern, Shachtman, and Glotzer that they wished to restore the unity and collaboration of the committee on the foundation of the plenum decisions, the meeting, which up to then had been the scene of the sharpest struggle, was oriented toward a reestablishment of unity in the committee. The plenum refrained from passing resolutions of direct condemnation of Comrade Shachtman and the others for their previous false position and their indefensible methods of faction struggle. The plenum decided to accept as sufficient their political retreat on the really important questions of the moment and to give them another opportunity to correct their course without a direct appeal to the organization against them.

In this spirit Comrade Shachtman was again appointed to his post as editor of the *Militant,* which he had deserted five months before as a demonstrative protest against our intervention on the international questions. It was agreed to reconsider the original determination to call a national conference and, instead of that, to submit the results of the plenum to the membership for an objective discussion, free from faction spirit or faction struggle. In order to broaden the National Committee's composition and, at the same time, to bring the majority of the resident committee into consonance with the majority of the full committee, and thus guarantee the execution of its policy in the daily work, it was decided to coopt two new members with voting rights—Comrades Basky and Gordon—and one candidate, without voting rights—Comrade Clarke. This necessary action—which is submitted to the entire membership for approval by referendum—was taken only after the alternatives of a conference or of the reorganization of the resident committee as a political bureau reflecting the plenum majority, had been openly considered, and after Comrade Shachtman had stated that, while disagreeing with the cooption of the new members, he would accept the decision of the plenum and would not oppose it before the membership.

Thus the plenum adjourned on a note of unity, with a deep feeling of satisfaction on the part of the committee members, as well as on the part of the other comrades who had attended the sessions by invitation, that the league had safely overcome the threatened crisis on a principled basis and that the fundamental political solidarity of the leadership and its capacity to solve its difficulties without a convulsion in the organization had once again been demonstrated. The nonresident members returned home in an optimistic spirit, confident that the great danger of an unfounded faction struggle had been averted and that the league's forces could all be mobilized now for a new and broader program of constructive activity, including a more effective intervention in the class struggle of the workers, than before.

These hopes, which were grounded on the unanimous adoption of the important resolutions, and the declarations made at the plenum by Comrades Shachtman, Abern, and Glotzer, soon proved to be illusory. No sooner had the resident committee come together to put the plenum material in shape for the membership discussion, than the three comrades resumed their factional position and attempted to ignore the proceedings of the plenum as though nothing had happened and nothing was changed. The document which they had withdrawn from the records of the plenum "in the interest of unity and collaboration" was again introduced in the resident committee on June 30 in a different form, with the demand that it be sent out to the membership in the discussion. In this document the plenum, which called them to order and compelled them to retreat from their previous positions, is represented as a vindication of themselves on every point.[45]

The resident committee, at the meeting of June 30, reacted to the new statement of the three comrades with the following motions:

> 1. The document of Comrades Abern, Glotzer, and Shachtman, which they demand to be sent to the membership and which they refuse to withdraw, is a factional document that falsifies the decisions of the plenum, attempts to incite the membership to overturn

them, directly contradicts the action of the said comrades in withdrawing their document from the records of the plenum, and attempts to smuggle it back in a politer form, and by this means aims to give the signal for the maintenance of a faction in the organization against the line of the plenum of the NC.

2. The document, moreover, represents an unprincipled and uncommunist attempt to cover up and justify the really serious mistakes, particularly by Comrade Shachtman, on the international questions, which brought great harm to the European sections and compromised the league by the erroneous impression that he acted in the name of the National Committee, which had nothing to do with his position and did not approve of it.

3. The action of the three comrades, in violation of the obligations they assumed at the plenum, makes it now imperatively necessary to inform the entire membership of the complete facts and to call upon them to condemn and repudiate these unprincipled methods and this irresponsible trifling with the responsibilities of leadership.

4. We demand of Comrade Glotzer, who wrote into the minutes of the NC of January 13 on his return from Europe that he disagreed with Comrade Shachtman's position on the international questions, to discontinue his unprincipled attempts to promote factional struggle out of personal considerations for Comrade Shachtman, to shield him at the expense of truth and the interests of the organization, and join the NC in its efforts to correct the abominable methods of Comrade Shachtman—his attempts to pass off the disputes created by his own fully established errors as a "frame-up" against him by other members of the NC who insisted on a

firm position in support of the revolutionary elements in the European sections.

5. Comrades Cannon and Swabeck are commissioned to draw up a comprehensive statement on the whole matter.[46] The secretary is instructed to inform the nonresident members of the NC of the actions of Comrades Abern, Glotzer, and Shachtman in violation of the plenum decisions and propose to them the immediate decision to call a conference of the league to pass the judgment of the organization on the whole matter.

In compliance with the foregoing motions the NC is now preparing all the documentary material bearing on the disputes and will transmit it to the membership for information and discussion. The statement of the three comrades of the minority will be included in the forthcoming internal bulletin, together with the reply of the NC. In addition to this we deem it now necessary to hand over to the membership all the essential documents which have accumulated in the records of the committee in the course of the conflict. With this material before them the members of the league will be able to gain a clear understanding of the disputes which disrupted the resident committee and to form a decisive judgment.

This is the only course open now. The National Committee has endeavored up to the last moment of the plenum to maintain peace in the organization as long as it could be done without compromising any essential policy. It held the door open to the minority, passed no resolutions against them, and approached them in good faith on the basis of unity and collaboration the moment they complied with the minimum political demands. The minority members are trying to frustrate these designs with a double-dealing maneuver. They retreated from their positions and spoke for peace at the plenum, and a week later they wrote a factional appeal against the plenum. They are trying to play hide-and-seek with the National Committee. They are trifling with the unity and stability of the National Committee, which is especially necessary now and which they have no principled ground to attack. The membership of the league must call a halt to this unprincipled faction game.

We are confident that the league members, with all the information before them, will firmly support the political standpoint of the plenum and the organizational measures taken to guarantee its execution, and give a stern warning to those who are trying to sabotage and overthrow them. It is up to the league members now to demonstrate that four years of struggle under the banner of the International Left Opposition have not been in vain, that the profound internal conflicts in the European sections have not passed by without leaving deep traces in the consciousness of the American Oppositionists. Not to fly into a panic, not to be led astray by secondary and personal issues, but to examine calmly the whole matter, to search out the important questions and decide them firmly—this is now the task of the membership of the league. We can have no doubt that such an approach to the problem will result in the categoric rejection of the irresponsible maneuver of Shachtman, Abern, and Glotzer. The safeguarding of the league against similar undertakings in the future depends on this.

Draft on the internal struggle

July 1932

The following unedited and unpublished draft was found in the Cannon archives.

The conflict within the NC, which is now before the membership in the discussion, has revealed from the beginning two different methods of approach, as can be seen by a study of the documentary material in the internal bulletins. On our side one can trace the insistent effort to put in the foreground the most important and actual questions which require definite decisions at the moment, namely the international question and the question of the New York branch, which is organically connected with it. On the side of the Shachtman group there has been, as their controversial documents show, a constant attempt to *shift* the discussion away from these actual disputes to secondary, incidental, outlived, and personal questions which do not require a decision at the moment, and concerning which they do not even demand a decision.

Shachtman replied to our intervention against his "false and damaging" position on the international questions with a venomous polemic in defense of Carter's semi-Menshevik interpretation of Engels's introduction to *The Class Struggles in France*, and in this attack he blandly added the accusation that Swabeck and Cannon were "characteristic" bureaucrats of the type of Stalin, no less (see Bulletin no. 3). Thus he began the open factional struggle. I leave aside for the present the intrinsic merits of this polemic. It is dealt with elsewhere (Bulletin no. 3).[47] Here I wish merely to point out that the document primarily represented an attempt, so to speak, to "change the subject."

In the new and somewhat lengthy document "The Situation in the American Opposition: Prospect and Retrospect," we are presented with another illustration of the same technique. This document, from first to last, is a personal attack against Cannon. Even those sections of the document which purport to deal with "political" issues and differences pursue one and the same aim throughout: to discredit Cannon as a person, as a revolutionist, as a leader of the league. Swabeck also is subjected to personal attack insofar as he has determined his position according to the merits of the actual questions as they arose and has declined to take part in the anti-Cannon movement—a movement, it must be admitted, which has a certain popularity in the New York branch and a far greater popularity in the camp of the enemies of the Left Opposition, who, for some reason or other, now as always are willing to pay a good price for the head of Cannon. But the references to Swabeck in the document are incidental, and so is the window-dressing called "issues." The real purport of the document remains a personal attack against Cannon. For that reason the NC departed from the practice it employs in dealing with the important concrete questions of dispute—the practice of answering them officially in the name of the NC—and assigned the answer to the new Shachtman document to me personally.[48]

I do not like this task. It is a new one for me. In the thirteen years that I have been active in the party—that is, since its foundation—and, I may add, in my activity in the revolutionary movement before the foundation of the party, I never once took the time to reply to personal attacks. There were plenty of them, as all the party veterans know. The struggles in which I took part—or, if you will permit me to say, which I organized and led—in the early disputes with the language federation "leftists" on the trade union question and the legalization of the party, against Pepperism, against Foster and his abominable labor-faker methods, against the petty-bourgeois tendency eventually concentrated around Lovestone, and, above all, in defense of the Russian Opposition—these struggles did not go unpunished in a personal sense. The personal attacks, the slander, the legends directed at me in print and in mimeographed caucus documents would fill several thick books. And if one could collect the oral arguments of this type—the ugly undercover stuff to which no one ventured to sign his name—the bulk would be considerably increased.

To all this I never once replied, because I never construed the party struggles as personal struggles. I never advanced any personal claims, and do not do so now. I can say quite honestly—and there is sufficient material marking the traces of all the disputes to confirm it—that I never took part in a faction struggle without political aims which transcended persons. This course implied and necessitated the frequent breaking of personal relations formed in previous struggles and enterprises and gave rise to not a little personal antagonism to me by the friends of yesterday. I can't help that. Communist politics is not a game of pinochle. The party is not a friendship club. One must expect to have some mud thrown at him. I had plenty. I am proud of that mud. Consider, for a moment, who threw it and where they are now! I do not need to reply to it now, because in the highest degree it has already been answered by the development of events!

But the personal attack of Abern, Glotzer, and Shachtman presents a new angle to the question. It is one thing if the enemies of the Left Opposition concentrate their hatred and their slander on a single person in our ranks. That is a self-evident mark of distinction which, in my case, I always felt was not fully deserved—there are others, the authors of the document included, who are justly entitled to a share of the Stalinist defamations. But it is another thing if the sewage of this Stalinist slander seeps into the league and is scooped up and thrown at the same target. It is quite another thing again if a section of the league, the weakest and most backward in a political sense, the elements who came to the Opposition before they were fully cured of the miseducation they received in the [Communist] party, and others who know nothing of the history of the party or of the part of "Cannon" in the making of it, except what they learned from the gutter gossip of the Stalinists—if such elements bring the Stalinist agitation against Cannon into the league, and if members of the NC base themselves upon these politically backward and as yet unassimilated elements, and form them into an anti-Cannon faction—that is quite another thing.

That, at least in the opinion of the NC, requires an answer and a fight. There is no room for the agitation of the fakers, open or disguised, in the league. They have corrupted the party with their dirty methods. They shall not corrupt the Left Opposition and thereby frustrate its historic regenerating mission.

This is the view of the matter taken by the NC which motivated its instruction to me to write a personal reply to the accusations of Shachtman, Abern, and Glotzer. In carrying out this instruction it is not my purpose to engage the comrades of the league in a discussion of the accusations of a personal nature and the reply to them, and still less of the personal merits of the persons involved on each side. It is my hope, rather, to convince them of the futility of such discussions for the solution of our actual problems. The persons, especially the leaders, must be appraised—that is true. But this appraisal must flow out of the positions they take on the most important problems as they arise, their methods, their conduct from day to day and from year to year, especially in times of crisis. In short, the leaders must be judged by the whole of their political activity which is unfolded before the eyes of the entire membership, and not on the basis of prejudice, gossip, unsupported petty accusations and recriminations, "grievances," etc. Even in this reply to personal attacks I will endeavor to discuss the matter on this plane. To that end I will undertake, insofar as it is possible, to separate the reply into two parts. The first and main part will be devoted to a consideration of those sections of the Shachtman document which discuss political or pseudopolitical issues and differences and the foul methods that have been employed in presenting them. The reply to purely personal accusations, relating to events of three years ago, will be relegated to an appendix so that the comrades may conveniently read it or ignore it accordingly as they find the matters interesting or not.[49]

In replying to the document of Shachtman, Abern, and Glotzer, the arbitrary separation of political and principled questions from the persons will not be easy—in fact in the literal sense of the word it will not be possible. This document is so saturated with the exaggerated self-concern of its authors—with their claims for recognition, for place, for leadership; with their grievances; with their personal merits and the personal faults of others; with snobbish insults regarding their superior education and the ignorance of others; with their ambition to raise themselves higher by pulling others down—all that one must point out, dissect, and discard, even in the discussion of the "political" questions. In doing so, however, I will still endeavor to construe the matter politically. The fight against the odious traits of careerism is in itself a question which towers in importance over any of those raised in the Shachtman document, and all of them together. The league will soon find itself in a blind alley if it does not check these tendencies in their incipiency.

The international question

This question is relegated to eighth place in the document of Abern, Glotzer, and Shachtman. I take it up first not only because, from our point of view, it is the most important question in the conflict and the one around which the whole conflict revolves, but also because the dispute over this issue is the most symptomatic and the most revealing as to the nature of the conflict, the methods of controversy, and the general trend of the disputants. The controversies over the other questions serve to confirm and reinforce the inferences to be drawn from the controversy over the international questions, and in no way contradict them. The approach, the methods, and the errors all have essentially the same root causes.

We approach the international questions from the standpoint of clarifying the position of the NC on them, of putting the entire league on record in support of the progressive and revolutionary elements in the European sections, of educating the league on the meaning of the disputes and arming it for the future, and of removing all doubt and ambiguity as to where we stood. This is shown by everything we wrote and said and did on the subject. If Shachtman had fallen into line with this aim there could not have been any dispute over the question; or, if he had defended his position on this basis, the conflict could have been conducted on a different plane.

But Shachtman's approach to this question was entirely different—one may say, directly opposite. He construed every step we took as part of a plot against him. To the extent that he has been able to influence comrades, especially those elements in the New York branch who have not yet learned to think politically, he has switched the whole issue around from a *political dispute* as to what position we should take on the European conflicts, and (the essence of the matter), to a *personal question*, viz: is Cannon "persecuting" Shachtman or not? (A secondary question, even if it were true.)

As a result of this miserable trick, you have comrades in the New York branch who (by your leave) are members of the vanguard of the vanguard, raising one hand to condemn Cannon for persecuting Shachtman on the international questions, and raising the other hand to vote without any amendment for Cannon's resolution on the subject—a resolution which is aimed in every paragraph against the position taken by Shachtman at the time! Under such circumstances what does or what can the resolution mean to these comrades as a lesson and as a guide for the future? Aside from the political merits of this dispute, which was the determining factor in disrupting the NC, the method employed by Shachtman in shifting the issue from a political to a personal basis, which is by no means a communist method, could not fail to exert a corrupting and demoralizing influence on the inexperienced comrades. Without a condemnation of such methods of controversy, and a ruthless elimination of them from our internal discussions, it will be impossible to prevent the political degeneration of the league and, eventually, a convulsive split. The Bolshevik method—which puts all questions first of all politically—and the petty-bourgeois method—which construes every dispute primarily as a personal one—are mutually exclusive. They cannot live together. Let the "Unity Group," which wants to unite everybody into a happy family, ponder over this question and give a Bolshevik answer to it. That will be far more useful for the cause of real unity than sentimental blubbering on the subject in general.

At the moment when Abern, Glotzer, and Shachtman first presented their document (on the eve of the June plenum) the struggle in the NC revolved around the international position of the league, and the question stood concretely: for or against the resolution of Cannon which had already received a majority of the votes of the NC members and had thereby become the official resolution of the NC. But nowhere in the document do we see an answer to this actual question which stared them in the face. Instead of that we have four closely typewritten pages devoted to argument along the following lines: (1) the conflict in the NC did not begin with the international disputes; (2) Cannon is not sincere in his insistence on a clear international stand, he is not really interested in these questions and does not know anything about them; (3) Shachtman never supported Landau, Naville, and Company *before the national conference;* (4) the NC as a whole was behind-hand on the Landau affair, etc. But to the actual question of the day—where do you stand *now* and *why?*—no answer. That only came out at the plenum after three full days of pounding by the majority for a clear yes-or-no position. The answer finally given—their vote for the official resolution—was welcomed by the plenum as a termination of the controversy without any compromise in principle. We are not people who run after a streetcar that has already been caught, and we saw no point in continuing a controversy over a question upon which agreement had been reached. But when Shachtman now tries to reconcile his new position with his old one, when he insists on sending out in the discussion the document that was doubly discredited at the plenum by his own acts—his vote for the official resolution and the *withdrawal of the document from the records*—he will please excuse us if we retain a certain skepticism as to the actual significance of his vote at the plenum, and return to a more thorough analysis of the arguments presented in his document before the plenum.

What is the primary purpose of a discussion in a communist organization? It is not to discredit one another, not to exalt some and push others down, not to present matters as prosecution on the one side and defense on the other. No, the primary purpose is to clarify the principled questions, to educate the comrades on the meaning of the dispute of the moment, to teach them to penetrate the essence of a question and draw their inferences accordingly, so that the lessons are firmly gained and remembered for the future, when similar problems will arise in different forms. In other words, the primary aim of a discussion conducted by communist leaders is to teach the comrades to think and to fight politically, to grasp the main aspects of a question, to go by principle and not to be sidetracked by incidental matters. The acquisition of this method is the condition *sine qua non* for our comrades to fulfill their mission as the vanguard of the vanguard, not only in future disputes within the ranks of the Left Opposition, but also, and especially, in conflicts with the other party factions, and beyond that in the broad class struggle and in the general labor movement, where they will encounter all kinds of demagogues who are masters of all kinds of tricks.

In what way does the Shachtman document serve this aim? In no way whatever, for it deals exclusively with secondary questions and leaves the heart of the problem untouched. He is *defending himself* against an alleged attack, but he has no time to enlighten the comrades on the question of vital importance: What stand should we take on the international questions, and why? And what evil consequences have already resulted from this method of debate! His partisans—almost exclusively the inexperienced comrades who have yet to be educated or *miseducated*—one after another take the floor in the New York branch to discuss the international question from a defensive standpoint. "Shachtman did not support Landau and Naville. He is falsely accused, etc." Such is the pitiful burden of their discussion. As to the far more important question—what do Landau, Naville, and Company signify and why would it be wrong to support them?—they haven't got that far yet. That is to say, they haven't got anywhere. One of the leaders of the anti-NC bloc (Carter) stated in the New York branch discussion that the comrades were "terrorized" on the French question and were afraid to speak on it concretely lest they be accused of sympathy for Naville or the leaders of the Jewish group. Well, in any case, they were not terrorized by Shachtman on this question.

The whole of the discussion *against* Landau, Naville, Mill-Felix, and the whole combination of careerist intriguants, beginning with my speech at the national conference, up to the present moment, has come from us and from the comrades who consciously support our position. This is no accident. The significance of the division in the leadership is written in this single fact.

Grant for the moment all the contentions on the international questions in the Shachtman document, and how much nearer does it bring us to an understanding and a solution and a firm conviction on the international disputes? Not one inch. Admit, for the moment, that the conflict in the NC antedated the international dispute; agree that Cannon is a scoundrel, as every scoundrel in the party says; take it for granted that Cannon knows nothing about international questions and cares less, as the Stalinists said when he raised the banner of the Russian Opposition; believe that Shachtman did not support Landau, Naville, and Company before the national conference; say that the NC as a whole was to blame for the delay in acting against Landau—grant all of these contentions, and what is thereby understood and learned about the core of the problem, its principled aspect? Nothing at all.

But even these trivial and secondary arguments, brought up to divert attention from the main questions, are false. If we leave the real issue—the position of the league on the European disputes—for a brief period and follow Shachtman on these bypaths, it will not be difficult to prove it. Pardon me if I go too much into detail, but while I am at it, I may as well do the thing thoroughly and answer this section of the document paragraph by paragraph.

1. The conflict "has existed for years in our leading committee" and cannot be explained by "reference to 'international questions' exclusively." Nobody tried to explain the history of previous disputes. The aim of our document of March 28 [22] (Bulletin no. 3) was to explain the concrete disputes of the day, which have no direct connection with

the disputes of two or three years ago. The remnants of these old disputes and the friction engendered in them did not prevent a political collaboration and unity for nearly two years after the first plenum. They did not disrupt the committee. The present disputes over international questions and the New York branch did. Therefore they are the ones which have to be discussed and decided. The old, outlived disputes had a certain importance. There is no doubt that they had profound causes. In a sense they were symptomatic. From this point of view I will refer to them in the appendix to the present statement. But we refuse to accept such a discussion of old disputes as a substitute for the discussion of the concrete disputes of the present.

2. If Cannon and Swabeck say the international question is the decisive one and do not claim any serious differences with Abern and Glotzer, but only with Shachtman, then Cannon and Swabeck have to explain why Abern and Glotzer support Shachtman. A more comical argument than this is not imaginable. Why must *we* explain why people who claim to agree with us in principle on the most important question and disagree with Shachtman, nevertheless support him in a factional grouping against us? *Let Abern and Glotzer explain!* If you insist on our explanation, however, you can have it in plain, blunt words: we understand such contradictory actions as unprincipled clique politics, which puts chumminess above principled considerations.

3. "Cannon's interest in international questions in general, and in internal disputes of the Opposition abroad in particular, has never been a deep and ardent one, except for the last few months when such an 'interest' was required in the pursuit of factional aims. . . ." In other words—to translate journalistic implication into forthright language—Cannon is a provincial faker who makes

use, now and then, of international questions for hometown politics and has no real concern for them otherwise. This is no doubt a very profound observation, but in justice to others, it must be said that here, as is so often the case, Shachtman betrays a sad lack of originality. He reveals himself here once again as a popularizer of the ideas of others rather than a creator, as a propagandist rather than a politician.

The author of this perspicacious character analysis is the unfortunate Gomez. He devised it in 1928 at the time I was first endeavoring to convince the authors of this document that the international questions raised by the Russian Opposition had to determine the whole course of our group in the future. Gomez first advanced it in personal conversation with Shachtman—since Shachtman was his friend, and he wanted to save him from the evil influences of Cannon. But Shachtman at that time was also my friend, and he told me about it, laughing at the foolish arguments of the foolish Gomez.

The years that followed 1928 have not been kind to Gomez. Even his exploit in leading a mob of Stalinists to break up our meeting at the Labor Temple failed to sustain his political career in the party. He died, so to speak, but his one great idea lived its own life and survived him.

In the lynching campaign against us the idea became a battle-cry of the Stalinists, who sought to avoid a discussion of the platform of the Left Opposition by personal attacks on Cannon and his "motives." Weisbord brought the idea of Gomez to the fringes of the Left Opposition. Bleeker whispered it in the ranks after a friendly talk with Foster. Now Shachtman, Abern, and even Glotzer solemnly advance it as a new thought of their own. That is unjust. If I protest against it, it is not for myself but for Gomez, for I believe in fair play, even to a dead enemy.

Shachtman, Abern, and Glotzer cannot plead ignorance of the fact. They cannot be held guiltless of intent to do wrong. They are literary people and they know that plagiarism is a literary crime. Therefore I insist: when you use this argument make acknowledgment to Gomez. Give the poor devil his due.

However, if there are comrades in the league who do not know the history of the party and who seriously and honestly want to be enlightened on my attitude toward internationalism, I will not refuse to answer their questions. Records exist on the subject. The question can be studied and verified on the firmest possible basis—on a basis of established facts.

I was not a patriot during the war. I was a supporter of the Russian revolution since 1917. I was a founding member of the Communist Party, which came into existence as a result of the split over international questions. I was not the last one of the American party leaders to come out in support of the Russian Opposition and its international platform, and I think I have been loyal to that platform.

There is a record of fifteen consecutive years during which the mainspring of my political work has been internationalism. In that record one can distinguish four decisive occasions when allegiance to the principle of internationalism was tested—1917, 1919, 1928, and 1932. On each occasion I took the international question of the hour as my point of departure and subordinated everything else to it. This is precisely what I have meant during the past year in continually insisting that our position on the international questions had to take precedence over all others, and certainly over the picayune quarrel of three years ago.

The international resolution of the NC today is no less significant to me than our declaration of 1928, just as my support of the Russian Opposition in 1928, after I had finally grasped the essence of the question, was for me as compulsory as was my support of the Communist International in 1919. Real internationalism is tested by its consistent manifestations at every turn of events and under all sorts of changing conditions, by the indissoluble connections of one action with another, by the decisive prominence one gives to internationalism in all of his activity.

By this I do not maintain that I have been free from fault or error on international questions in the past. My reference is to the fact that international questions have always been paramount for me *insofar as I have clearly grasped them.*

On the other hand I am far from denying a tendency toward provincialism, which is inseparable from all Americans who came by the same road that I traveled—that is, by the road of direct participation first in the native American labor movement without international orientation or guidance. I had to acquire internationalism. It took a long time. The process was a painful and difficult one, and very probably remains uncompleted. In this field I am still a seeker, a learner. It is very hard for an American to be a thoroughgoing internationalist in the genuine, not superficial, sense of the word. He is not born with this gift. The difficulties of distance, plus language handicaps, determined, and yet determine for me a slowness of orientation and a difficulty in quickly understanding international questions. (Example: The first stages of the struggle in the Russian party.) Even then I cannot say that I succeed in grasping more than their general and fundamental aspects. That is one reason why I do not venture to write very often on these subjects.

I do not recommend this slowness of orientation to others. But I wish to warn comrades—especially the young comrades—against a far more serious fault. That is, superficiality and glib facility of expression on the complex questions of other countries and of the world at large. I am willing to grant one contention which Shachtman makes in his document—that the NC as a whole, myself included, delayed as much as he did in taking a position on the disputes in Europe. I will go further and admit that in most cases he was ahead of us, for that is the fact. (When he acted for delay it was to delay the action of the NC against the position he had already taken.)

The ease with which he gains impressions, and the extraordinary facility with which he formulates and expresses them, gave him an advantage in this respect. His Paris letter to Trotsky (Bulletin no. 2), in which he pronounced judgment with a pompous self-assurance on the most acute conflicts in the International Left Opposition, was written before we had even considered the new developments.[50] There is no doubt that he reacted quickly. But, very probably just because of that, his judgment was superficial and false through and through, and not simply on one episode or another but on the whole process involved in the struggle. It is a fault, I admit, to be slow on the international questions and to write infrequently about them. But it is far worse to be too quick and to write too much on international questions, or any other questions, without really knowing what you are writing about.

To write an article—or a score of them—on international questions is not in itself a difficult task. Any journalist—and I am also a journalist—can do it and make it look very learned too. All that is needed, for an experienced writer, is a general formula, a few facts and figures, a sprinkling of standard Marxist expressions, a few hours' labor—and the job is done. The ill-fated Gomez, for example, wrote scores of articles about China, and the ill-fated Bill Dunne did likewise. I wrote none at all—and for the simple reason that I didn't think I knew enough about it, as indeed I didn't. But when it comes to a question of choosing between a Marxist and a Menshevik line on the Chinese revolution, on the basis of the documents in the controversy, it was not Gomez and Dunne—who by that time had established a reputation as "experts" on China—who showed the way. Their journalistic horseplay around the question added nothing and took nothing away from the problem of *thinking out* the questions of the Chinese revolution and their decisive import for the proletariat of the entire world. The test of internationalism is not the number of journalistic contributions to the subject but the *position* one takes when the facts are at hand.

There is a tendency in the league—which I consider one of the worst tendencies—to talk lengthily and loftily about the great faraway problems—China, Russia, Spain, or anything you want—and to stumble all over the simplest and most elementary local problems of the league. If the great questions of international scope are the decisive criterion to which one's domestic policy has to be related, then it must be understood as a rule that works both ways. The test of one's understanding of the international problems and lessons is his ability to apply it to the concrete problems at home. To those experts on international problems who complain about the fact that I devote the limited spare time at my disposal too much to articles about the simple and prosaic problems of trade unionism, etc., I have to explain that I do this not so much from choice as from necessity. These questions have to be answered by someone promptly, as they arise. And the most complacent pretenders to "theoretical" education show a surprising wariness in answering them, especially if they appear to present new aspects which haven't been answered before and require independent thought.

4. The seriousness of a leader's attitude toward internationalism is further tested not only by his own information on the decisive international questions of the day, but also, and even more so, by the efforts he makes to put the necessary information at the disposal of his organization as a whole. I wouldn't give a fig for the revolutionary qualities of an organization in America whose international knowledge and understanding is monopolized by a few experts more or less. The thing is to educate the entire membership on these questions, to realize a collective understanding and participation in the international questions by all the members of the league. Thus, and thus only, can the *movement* become truly internationalist.

Shachtman, as the document under consideration shows, and as his whole conduct has shown, has never seen the problem this way. He is not enough of an organization man, he thinks too much in terms of persons, he is too much of an individualist, to see it this way. That is why he could conduct the office of international representative of the league in such a loose manner, as though it were an affair between him and other individuals in France, in Germany, in Spain, and in Turkey. That is why the initiative and the constant pressure for the issuance of the International Bulletin in English never came from him, and why, despite Shachtman's great facility in foreign languages, the league owes the translation of all this material exclusively to the unobtrusive and anonymous work of Comrade Gordon.

It was from this point of view—the education of the entire league membership on the international disputes—that I spoke at the conference on the necessity of translating and sending out in bulletin form all the material, from both sides, on the highly significant disputes with the Italian Bordigists.[51] How otherwise can the league members really know about them and learn from them? Is it sufficient for Shachtman—and possibly also Cannon—to understand this matter?

But my remarks at the conference on the laxity of the NC in translating and sending out the polemics with the Bordigists—for which I held and still hold myself partly responsible as a member of the NC—were taken by Shachtman in a characteristic, that is, in a purely personal, way. It is really amazing to read his explanation of this incident. Cannon's remarks were made, he says, "In order to leave the impression that Shachtman was 'concealing' some material on the Italian situation from the membership." How pitiful! How shallow and absurd! And, at the same time, how revealing! Would the proposition lose an iota of its validity if there were no Shachtman and no Cannon, and no sinister "campaign" of the latter against the former?

It is not true, either, that I "promptly forgot" about this matter of educating the league on the disputes with the Bordigists "right after the conference." I haven't forgotten about it yet. And I am not going to forget it, for I hold it vitally necessary for our membership to know for themselves these concrete manifestations of ultraleft sectarianism and the Marxist answer to them, in order that they may be armed for the future and not have to learn in painful experiences of their own what has been realized for them in advance in the experiences of others. It is only due to the fact that Comrade Gordon, upon whom we had to rely for this work of translation, has had his hands more than full that the matter has been so long delayed. I hope it will not be delayed much longer, and my feeling in the matter has nothing whatever to do with the personality of Shachtman one way or another. I am not aware of any differences between us on the disputes with the Bordigists.

5. Our basic differences in approach to serious questions are again illuminated in that paragraph of his document where he takes me to task for failing to express myself on the French trade union dispute in my introduction to *Communism and Syndicalism*.[52] Did he expect that of me then? I do not think so, or, at any rate, if he did he kept it a secret from me. I understood my task to be an *American interpretation* of the pamphlet, especially in relation to the IWW, and so constructed my introduction. That was a year and a half ago, and nobody found fault with the introduction then or afterward. I learn of Shachtman's criticism now for the first time.

But that is a small matter which can be charged off under the heading of polemical "method." If an expression on the French trade union disputes and the persons involved had been in order in that introduction, on what grounds does Shachtman demand that I should have made it? On the sole ground that Shachtman "furnished Comrade Cannon with detailed information about the then situation in the French trade unions, the various tendencies and groups, and particularly the internal situation in the league which had evoked the criticism of Comrade Trotsky." He did this, he says, "for the specific purpose of having it included in the introduction."

Permit me to say in all candor that such information is not sufficient for me to form a conclusive judgment on a trade union question in another country, and still less to put the judgment in writing. I did not know that he expected me to do so. He did not inform me of it. But I wouldn't have done it anyway.

In the first place I know very little about the French trade union movement, and the sketchy information of Shachtman—which is all too often sufficient for him—is not sufficient for me. Trotsky's article appeared to me to enunciate principles on the question of party and trade union that are *universally applicable*. But he directed his polemic against unnamed persons. Why should I, without a single document other than Trotsky's article at my disposal, undertake to supplement him?

I couldn't conscientiously do it then. And, furthermore, I cannot do it now, for the simple reason that I do not know to this day how the various groups and individuals in the French league formulated their positions in the dispute. For that I need their documents, resolutions, motions, etc., which, up to the present, I have not seen. I am inclined to think that Shachtman's criticism of me for failing to express myself a year and a half ago on the French trade union dispute is an afterthought. But if he wishes to insist upon it he can improve the criticism and bring it up to date: I haven't expressed myself yet.

And in the same paragraph there is another accusation that also strikes me as an afterthought. "We have no doubt," he says, "that precisely in this matter did Cannon allow political considerations to be outweighed by 'personal consideration' of the case of Rosmer—whose fate in the French league Cannon continued to bemoan to Shachtman for months afterward." That part of the quotation which contains a truth in reality understates the matter. I not only bemoaned the fate of Rosmer for "months afterward," but I still bemoan it. I do not by any means put Rosmer in the same category with the careerist chaff of the type of Landau and Naville. Rosmer had a great past. He represented a gigantic moral capital for the French league and the entire International Left Opposition. His loss is not to be taken lightly. I am firmly against him now because I think he failed badly in the test put upon him and has become a center of obstruction to our movement. I came to this position with great reluctance and only after I was thoroughly convinced by his own actions that any form of support to him, direct or indirect, would be damaging to the Left Opposition.

But what does Shachtman mean by "personal consideration"? I saw Rosmer on only one occasion that I remember—at the Fourth Congress of the Comintern [in 1922]. I never spoke to him in my life, and in the personal sense of the word I do not know the man. He was not my "chum." I was under no obligation to "protect" him. I formed my impressions of Rosmer by the positive role he played in the movement in the past. I changed my impressions on the basis of the negative role he is playing now. Where are the "personal considerations"?

To make a distinction between an "old revolutionist" and a parvenu who just arrived from nowhere is not a "personal consideration." It is a sense of discrimination which characterizes every serious revolutionist. If Shachtman could understand this it would aid him in correcting some of the crudest mistakes he made in Europe, and is repeating in the [American] league, in his estimations of the people concerned.

6. The document of Abern, Glotzer, and Shachtman devotes much space to prove that the NC records show no *formulated* differences on the international questions prior to the national conference. This is quite unnecessary and is beside the point, for such a contention was not made by us. In our statement of March 28 [22] (Internal Bulletin no. 3) we said in reference to that period: "While we still had apparently 'general' agreement there was to be noted a decided difference in *emphasis* and *definiteness*." The fact that we came to the conference with a common resolution is proof enough in itself that we had no formulated differences at the time.

The formal records of that period, which Shachtman

is at such pains to cite, do not illuminate, but rather conceal, the process of differentiation which was taking place within the framework of unanimous motions. This was the heart of the matter as *subsequent developments* abundantly demonstrated.

In the NC discussions which preceded the formulation of the motions, the emphasis and insistence on an attitude of outspoken opposition, especially to Naville, came not from Shachtman but from us. Shachtman gave us the impression already then of a desire to shield Naville. His delay of more than two months in drafting the international resolution for the conference—which had been assigned to him as the one most familiar with the question—was, in part, the expression of an attitude. His omission of the specific condemnation of Naville in the draft was not an oversight. And, finally, his report at the conference, devoid of any analysis or serious conclusions, called forth my speech on the subject which took up the subject where he left off, and filled in the vital omissions.

This is the only way to explain the trend of developments on the international question before the conference, if the aim is to clarify and not to confuse the issue. It is not to refer to the absence of formulated differences in order to refute a contention that was never made, but rather to explain the differences in emphasis and precision in the committee discussions which *preceded* the formulations and the differences in interpretation put upon them *afterward*. We described this process of differentiation in the NC before the conference, which broke out into an open conflict later, with precise accuracy in our document of March 28 [22]. We referred to it not as a *clearly defined difference of position*, but as a "slowly, but steadily developing *divergence*." We spoke, as has been said, of a "decided difference in emphasis and definiteness."

In that fact, of itself, there is nothing fatal, and it would not be worth discussing if matters had stopped there and the lines had converged again as, at that time, we still hoped and expected. It cannot be demanded that every member of the NC come to the same final estimate of a problem at the same time. If a really firm, not diplomatic, agreement is eventually reached within a reasonable time, there is no point in rehashing the outlived debates which preceded the agreement. But that is not what happened. Just the contrary. Instead of merging into a real agreement, the "divergences" on emphasis and definiteness of the pre-conference period developed into real and formulated differences which played the decisive role in the disruption of the NC. (Compare the Paris letter of Shachtman with the international resolution of the NC which he opposed and obstructed for five months.)

Shachtman's document skips over this period entirely. He substitutes for an explanation of the question which had actuality at the moment, a series of references to formal records of a period before the differences became clear and concrete, and which have a significance only in the light of the open conflict which developed later. To disconnect them from the later conflict in the NC, to direct the attention of the comrades to these formal records of the past and away from the living issues which divided Shachtman from us at the time the document was written means to stultify the whole discussion.

The comrades who want to become real political fighters, able to fight for principle in the league, in the party, and in the broad labor movement, must learn to be on guard against these tricks of debate. Do not let anyone switch the issue. Do not let anyone divert you from consideration of a clearly defined difference of the present by references to the formal records of a time when the difference remained in a nebulous form and was concealed within unanimous resolutions. You will encounter these polemical twistings in multifarious forms in all your activity in the labor movement. Until you learn how to put your finger on them you have not learned the ABC of communist politics.

No, the essence of the problem posed by the international position of the league, as it stands today, is not to be discovered in a search of the records to establish priority of action on one side or the other in one case or another. Even the fact that Shachtman delayed five months before he registered his agreement with us at the plenum, and during that time maintained a contrary position, would have only episodic significance if it were demonstrated that he really sees the issue correctly now. He distorts, or in any case he misunderstands, our attitude when he represents it as a continued prosecution for an error made and corrected. Such a procedure on our part would be a completely sterile one and would soon develop decidedly negative aspects.

Priority in coming to a position in the past does not by itself prove anything for the present or provide any guarantee for the future. The decisive question is how one arrives at the position and what it signifies to him from the point of view of method. Trotsky, who "came to Lenin fighting" and after many years, demonstrated that he understood the *method* of Lenin far better than those old disciples who had always repeated everything after him.

It is from this standpoint that we have to consider the international question now, and to ask why it is that after a unanimous vote at the plenum on the question that had divided us, the factional struggle flares up with fiercer intensity. The explanation of this phenomenon lies in the fact that the formal "general agreement" conceals a difference—a difference, it appears to us, of a serious and probably fundamental character. The international resolution does not mean the same thing to Shachtman that it means to us as a conception of the developments in Europe from the point of view of method and process *and as a guiding line for our internal policy in the American league.*

That is the real meaning of the factional aggressions of Shachtman and his friends since the plenum. That is why he slipped back into the bloc with the Carter group after renouncing it at the plenum. That is why he again brings forward the document, with its personal attack and dubious "issues," which he withdrew from the records at the plenum "in the interests of unity and collaboration."

After this, Shachtman and his friends protested in the New York branch against any further discussion of the dispute with him on the international question on the ground that he had corrected his error. Let us see what that correction really consists of. The statement he introduced at the plenum coincides with the line of the NC resolution—which he had opposed—and even contains an admission of error on the French situation; and on top of that, he cast his vote for the NC resolution.[53]

But to look closely into these actions, as we are obliged to do in the light of what has transpired since, we have to say that they establish a unanimity with us only in the formal, not in the real sense of the word. The admission of error did not appear in his statement when it was first presented to the plenum—it was inserted later, after the absurdity of adopting the standpoint of the NC after a long struggle against it, without a word of explanation for the change of position, was pointed out to him.

But, from our point of view, that acknowledgement of error does not strengthen the statement, if the matter is considered fundamentally. In reality it weakens it, for it represents the conflict as a mere episode of the French league, while we see it as a process involving the entire International Left Opposition, of which the French events are only a part.

Shachtman's error on the European affairs did not consist in expressing a false "casual, episodic opinion" on the French situation, as he represents it in his statement. Such an isolated error might easily be made by anyone, corrected, and forgiven without convulsing the league and alarming the progressive elements of the international movement as Shachtman did. *His error consisted in the fact that his position on the conflict in the French league fitted into a general estimate of the situation throughout Europe which directly contradicted the consistent struggle of the progressive elements all along the line.*

One can really support this struggle only if he sees it as a *process* which is constantly changing in its external forms and in which the *persons* involved sometimes change places. It is not the persons but what they signify at the given moment that must determine one's position. Otherwise the whole process of struggle of the past three years becomes meaningless, no lessons are firmly acquired, and the whole thing has to be gone over again and again.

This is precisely the history of Shachtman's intervention in the international questions. The experience with Landau taught him nothing about Naville. The experience with Naville taught him nothing about Mill-Felix. And the experience with all these disintegrating elements helped him not the least in estimating the fearfully dangerous course of the Spanish leadership.

I do not know too much about the leadership of the French league, and have been obliged to form my impressions to a considerable extent by the nature of the attacks made upon it and the people responsible for them. Sometimes this is not a bad way of judging people—"tell me who your enemies are and I'll tell you who you are." It has been clear to me, as it should be clear to anyone with half an eye, that the rabid personal campaign against Molinier was becoming the rallying cry of all the elements of obstruction and disintegration inside and outside the International Left Opposition, and that this campaign was in reality only a thin disguise for the struggle against the intransigent policy and leadership of Trotsky. And the most dangerous aspect of the whole matter developed when the Spanish leaders, who enjoy an exceptional prestige and influence in the international movement, began to lend their influence to this campaign.

It was at this critical pass that matters stood when Shachtman began his personal excursion through Europe. Read over again his Paris letter and try to locate beneath all the absurd self-assurance the slightest conception of what was involved, of what was really going on. He nibbled at every dispute and at every conflict between persons as though each were a *separate* question. The *essence* of the matter, the *process of struggle* which was coming to a climax, escaped his sage observation altogether.

He wandered around Europe with a scorecard in his hand, marking down a point here for one, a point there for another, expressed a general wish to reconcile everybody, overlooked the fundamental conflict of tendencies, and ended, as with such an approach he could not fail to do, in giving indirect support to the disintegrating tendency. That is what his Paris letter signifies.

If he had understood the problem as it was dealt with in the National Committee resolution he would have been obliged to proceed in an entirely different manner. He would have had to start out from *fundamental considerations,* and not only in France, but also in Germany and especially in Spain.

Instead of encouraging the Spanish comrades in their antagonism to Molinier he would have told them straight out that they were lending aid unconsciously to the Landau-Rosmer bloc and that their grievances against Molinier, whether justified or not, had to be subordinated to the fight against this bloc and its agents inside the Left Opposition.

Instead of advocating a "concentration" leadership in the French league, which would put the present leadership in the minority, he would have found it necessary to support the present leadership and come out squarely against Mill-Felix, whom he criticizes so tenderly in his letter, and against Naville, whom he doesn't criticize at all.

He would have found it necessary to demonstrate a warm solidarity with the German leadership, which is the symbol of the fight against Landau, instead of belittling the German comrades with patronizing insults about their lack of "organizing ability."

And, finally, if he had had any understanding or sympathy for the viewpoint expressed in that section of the NC resolution where it speaks of the necessity to "firmly organize a collective participation" in the international affairs of the Left Opposition, he would have promptly reported his information and his findings to his own National Committee instead of ignoring it entirely. He would have asked for its official endorsement and received it, and thus brought to bear the influence of an organization, not the mere personal opinion of an individual.

Can anyone seriously maintain that such a line of conduct, which is indicated in the resolution of the NC, has anything in common with the course Shachtman pursued in Europe? Does the vote for the NC resolution with the five-line acknowledgment of a "casual, episodic" error on the *French situation alone* reconcile them? Allow us to express our doubts.

By this I do not intend to maintain that Shachtman at the present time is supporting the French intriguants or that he is apt to give them any support in the next period. The purely formal nature of his support for the NC resolution, and the lack of real understanding and conviction of its import will very probably be manifested—it should be said, is already being manifested—in other ways.

But not in France, and most likely not in Europe at all. Having burned his fingers on the European disputes, and having aroused the alarm and vigilance of Comrade Trotsky, he has come to the conclusion—this is my personal opinion—to retire from that field and transfer his operations exclusively for the present to the American league.

In the time that has elapsed since the plenum we have had a full opportunity to see the beginnings of this shift of operations and to observe that his course in the league, and particularly in the New York branch, is no less false and damaging than it was in Europe, and to trace this fact to the same basic causes.

If we follow Shachtman and his friends from the plenum into the New York branch we will be able to judge more concretely and more accurately just how much their fundamental agreement with us, which they registered by formal vote at the plenum, really means to them in practice.[54]

Stalinist-pacifist collaboration

August 9, 1932

The following letter was written to Roger Baldwin in New York. It was published in the *Militant* of August 13, 1932.

My Dear Baldwin:

You left the antiwar conference at the Labor Temple last night after your opening speech as the representative of the American Committee for the World Congress Against War.[55] Allow me to inform you of what transpired after your departure and to put some questions to you.

Two resolutions were presented for consideration—the official (pacifist) resolution presented in the name of your committee, and a different resolution, outlining the Leninist program for the fight against war, presented by the delegation of the Communist Left Opposition (Bolshevik-Leninists).[56]

The floor was then given to a number of speakers who defended the official resolution and attacked the resolution of the Left Opposition. Pacifists, "left" Socialists, official

Communists, and others spoke. The leader of the attack on the Leninist resolution, appropriately enough, was Olgin—the same Olgin whom you will remember as the ardent patriot who attacked the Lenin program in 1917–18 from the standpoint of Wilson's "14 points." *Our request for the floor to defend our resolution and answer the attacks made against it was refused by the chairman.*

Was it a prearranged plan on your part to leave the meeting and thus give tacit support to the steamrolling of the Bolshevik-Leninists? Or did you have other engagements more important and more pressing at the moment than the question of the fight against war and the principle of free speech in a movement under your leadership?

I am inclined to the first assumption. And, from a political point of view, your indirect support of the suppression of the Left Opposition at the conference is quite comprehensible. You, and the tendency you represent—pacifism—were indubitably the victors at the conference. In the united front between the Stalinists and the pacifists in the antiwar movement, the Stalinists have yielded the principal positions all along the line, from Paris to New York. The program, the character of the preparatory propaganda, and the leadership are pacifist. In return for these concessions you allow the Stalinists to manipulate the movement organizationally and to suppress the voice of the Left Opposition, which they fear more than anything else. That is what your united front looks like to us.

It must be admitted, again from a political point of view, that you and your fellow-thinkers have made an excellent bargain. We cannot condemn it on those grounds, for we have never put the question of free speech and democracy as the fundamental question. We have stated more than once that we could reconcile ourselves even to bureaucracy if it could be demonstrated that it serves a revolutionary end. It is precisely because the Stalinist bureaucracy works in an opposite direction, because it serves as a blind instrument of reaction, that we oppose it so intransigently.

But some clarification is needed as to your position. Hitherto you have defended free speech as a principle, even to the extent of demanding it for the Mensheviks in Russia and the Ku Klux Klan in America. That was your right, of course. But if you have modified your standpoint; if you have decided to sacrifice the principle of free speech where we are concerned, in a movement under the direction of your national committee, in return for the truly enormous concessions in principle made by the Stalinists, then you ought to make a frank public explanation of your change of position and the reason for it.

Frankness and clarity are of special importance in every aspect of the struggle against war, which incorporates at the present moment all the interests of the USSR and the world proletariat. In the struggle against war, nothing is more dangerous and disarming than ambiguity and deception. Let the position of every group be made clear in every respect! The faction to which I belong—the Bolshevik-Leninist faction—devotes itself especially to this work of clarification, not only of its own position but also of others.

In putting these questions to you, I trust you will understand that they are not meant invidiously in a personal sense. I do not doubt the sincerity of your intentions in the antiwar movement. It is your program that we oppose. It is the ambiguity as to your attitude toward the right of the Left Opposition to participate and defend its viewpoint in the conferences organized under the auspices of your national committee that we seek to clear up.

The Left Opposition is not against the participation of sincere pacifists in the antiwar conferences. It is against the pacifist program and the pacifist leadership, aided by the treacherous sanction of the Stalinist bureaucrats. To that we will always counterpose the Lenin program and the revolutionary leadership. This aim motivated our appearance at the conference last night and our request from the floor there. It will be the same in the future.

The specific question to which we desire an answer now stands: do you and the American Committee for the World Congress Against War, of which you are a prominent member, recognize our right to participate in the conferences and meetings under its direction and to defend our views there, or have you come to a tacit agreement with the Stalinists to exclude us? We will find the way to popularize the Lenin program in any case. We ask no favors. The sole object of this inquiry is clarification of your position.[57]

Yours,

James P. Cannon

Organizing in the Illinois mine fields

September 23, 1932

The following letter was written to George Clarke in Springfield, Illinois.

Dear George:

I received your letter yesterday morning. It was surely great to hear of your success in Chicago, which made possible your return to the field.[58] The real fault for the extraordinary difficulties which brought about your departure from Springfield lies here, in my opinion, and I shall tell that to Carmody and Angelo, as I have already told it to the comrades here. There has to be some sense of proportion in the hardships and sacrifices. The movement must be educated one way or another to a more serious sense of responsibility toward the functionaries and field workers. I don't see much sense in starving comrades out just to see how tough they will be. Especially when the bulk of our members are taking good care to suffer no bellyaches for the cause.

A week ago, at the branch meeting, we reported on the work in Illinois and raised eight or nine dollars in cash. Then at the NC meeting Thursday night we adopted a detailed program which you will probably hear from Arne. The gist of it is that we undertake to raise an immediate fund of at least fifty dollars to promote a tour through the mine fields for you, Carmody, and Angelo, with Goldberg of St. Louis acting as the transportation company. Following that, a little later, Arne is to go on a national tour and to make Illinois his starting point and spend a couple of weeks there following up what you comrades have started.

We want to do this job systematically. No fly-by-night and no putsches. Out of it we must get several branches of the league. That is the supreme task. It will not be accomplished in a day, and I think you and Jack should settle down to a protracted stay in the field until the branches are established and functioning. You have a right to demand that the organization supply the minimum financial aid. Next time, instead of taking it for granted that nothing can be forthcoming, you should burn up the mails and if necessary the wires with demands for the support that is due you. All talk about the movement not being able to finance this work on such an economical basis as you comrades are willing to operate on is sheer poppycock. The response you got in Chicago is an indication of how the comrades are capable of responding to such work as you are doing, if it is brought home to them with sufficient enthusiasm and energy.

In regard to your difficulties with Jack and Angelo, I think you ought to go at the thing more patiently and make sure that you are looking at all sides of the problem, especially taking care to avoid sharp clashes over questions which are really not fundamental, and even in that case, you must remember that there is a possibility of correcting any serious errors by presenting the disputes to the NC.

On the personal side, try to look at things from their point of view, or at least to understand it. They are both older and more experienced. Jack has been through some fights. Angelo is an old-time militant in the miners' union, and besides that is a well-educated communist. You should not be surprised if they do not put a proper estimation on your opinions at first. It will probably take some time for you to convince them that your ideas are worth considering as you want them to be. If they are human, as no doubt they are, they will strongly resent anything which they construe as a superior or supervising attitude on your part. If you keep these psychological factors in mind and are as reasonable and tactful as possible, I think you will soon get over the present difficulties. You will do it all the sooner if, along with the tactfulness and reasonableness in your relations with the comrades, you stand firmly by your opinions on questions which really matter and clearly establish your right to do so. I am sure that if you follow this line, you will soon find Jack and Angelo just as reasonable as you. I am going to take occasion to write to Jack and Angelo both very soon, without saying anything about your letter. You need not be afraid of this complicating matters. The NC has a vital interest in everything that is going on and I think my letters to them will help to establish the proper perspective all the way around.

You are right in the suggestion that the committee make a more thorough analysis of the situation and the perspectives of the movement there. Our laxity in this respect, as can be seen from your letter, has given ground for needless argument and friction. I can't see any basis for the idea that this strike is revolutionary in any conscious sense, and I am even far to the right of the amendment which you suggested to Jack's formulation.[59] On what ground can anyone say that this is a strike for an offensive movement or the harbinger of one? It is not a demand for better conditions, but a protest against drastic worsening which is being imposed upon the miners. We will be in the soup entirely if we don't begin everything in connection with the strike from a fundamental analysis of its real character.

The new union is going to have a hard road to hoe—there can't be any doubt of this. What the outcome of this first great endeavor will be remains an open question yet, so far as I can see; but we have to go along with the movement with all our strength and enthusiasm in any case, even if the chances for success are not so bright. It is not those who associate themselves with a heroic undertaking of the workers that ends in failure who discredit themselves, but those who stand aside.

I have to leave now for the committee meeting (dictated Thurs. night). I will write you more later. Don't delay with your articles. One suggestion I want to make. The main line of everything you write should be a warm, partisan defense of the new movement as such. Then the critical remarks will have the proper place and effectiveness. Don't be too thesislike in your writing. Try to make all the articles a light, reportorial character, emphasizing the dramatic and human elements, just giving a general political trend to everything, without weighting the articles down too much with sermonizing. I intend to write a series of articles on the mining situation with special reference to Illinois very soon. These will be of a different character. The matter from the field, while proceeding from the same premise, should have quite a different character and be in the form of reports and interpretations of the struggle, direct from the field.

Everything is going well here and all the comrades send you best wishes for a successful outcome.

Fraternally yours,

[Jim]

P.S.—It would be well if you three comrades would work out right away your proposals for the NC statement on the mine situation in Illinois. Don't make it too big a political literary job, but enumerate the important points and give your opinions on them. If you can't agree on everything, send in separate estimates on the points of difference. Besides being a big help to the committee, a preoccupation with this task will also help to straighten out the minor frictions there and relegate them to the background.

On relations with B.J. Field

October 6, 1932

The following letter, drafted by Cannon but signed by Swabeck as national secretary, was addressed to Trotsky and the International Secretariat.[60]

Dear Comrades:

We have received the circular proposing an international discussion of the perspectives of the economic crisis. The National Committee will prepare a contribution to the discussion. This will be printed in the *Militant*, and a copy will be sent to you for transmission to the other national sections for publication in their press as they see fit.

We have noted with surprise and astonishment the proposal to open this discussion in the international organization with the articles of B.J. Field, who was recently expelled from the New York branch of the American league. The fact that Comrade Field now writes from a point of view directly opposite to that with which he began his criticisms of our conference thesis and the first Gourov letter on the subject of a possible upturn of capitalist economy, is not sufficient to convince us of the wisdom of assigning this role to him.

Certainly the National Committee cannot ignore the action of the New York branch in this case and proceed as if nothing had happened, without bringing disorganization into the league. We are in no way disposed to do this. On an international scale such a procedure seems to us to be all the more irregular and to contradict the tendency—which we have always supported—toward the formation of the International Left Opposition into a definite organization regulated by uniform organizational principles, and with the rights as well as the duties of the national sections clearly defined and universally applied.

Perhaps a discussion of organizational questions will also be in order in preparation for the international conference. The actions in the present case, following the Weisbord affair, cause us some concern. If the whole matter is a misunderstanding it can be cleared up. If there is a real difference of viewpoint on the organizational question it should be squarely put. We hope it is only a misunderstanding. If so we will do all we can to dispose of it in short order.

We do not object to an intervention of the international organization in any question concerning the policy and activity of the league. The advice we have received on important questions has always been welcomed and has aided us in correcting errors and strengthening our political position.

We recognize the right of the international organization also to review organizational decisions of national sections, including expulsions. But such interventions ought to proceed according to certain formal rules. Appeal should be taken in regular order, full information secured, etc. In the absence of such a formal intervention based on full information, political collaboration of one section with persons expelled from other sections can only lead to confusion and demoralization.

We do not of course call into question here the right of Comrade Trotsky to engage in a personal collaboration with Field to the extent that he may be able to assist him in his work. But we find most objectionable in the present proceedings regarding Comrade Field what amounts to an informal disregard of the decision taken in the American league. When Comrade Trotsky protested against the publication of an article by Landau in the French magazine *La Lutte de Classes* we fully agreed with him—on organizational as well as on political grounds. Again when he criticizes the Spanish section for allowing the name of one expelled from the French section to appear as a collaborator in its paper, when he asked how they would react if the French league were to print articles from the expelled Gorkin, we thought the right and the logic were all on Trotsky's side. In these fundamental questions of organizational principle also, we do not see any ground for the well-known "American exceptionalism."

Like nearly all the other sections, we have taken a position against the proposal to allow the various expelled groups and individuals to participate in the international conference.[61] But, if we take this point of view in regard to the conference itself, how can a leading role—or any serious role whatever, for that matter—in the preparation of one of the important questions of the conference be assigned to an expelled member of the American league, which has been in existence for four years and has some solid accomplishments to its credit?

We hope you will understand that it is not a matter of narrow-minded fanaticism on our part which regards all members and expelled members as renegades, and excludes every form of collaboration with them. As a matter of fact it was suggested to Comrade Field, who—like many others who do not fit in a communist organization—undoubtedly has some special knowledge and talents which would be useful, that he remain a sympathizer of the league for the time being and enter into a limited collaboration with us in that capacity. His refusal to do this; his failure to make a formal appeal to the plenum of the National Committee against the action of the New York branch; his attempt to circumvent the league by a personal excursion to Europe—in all this is to be seen only added illustrations of the petty-bourgeois freelance spirit which was at the bottom of his hopeless conflict with the league.

In New York as well as in Paris, there are sufficiently numerous casual elements in and around the league who are inclined to play with questions of organization, with political ideas, with the problems of "leadership," and everything. Such people would like to disregard everything that has been done up till now in America and begin all over again. To allow even a small concession in the Field case would only strengthen such elements and tendencies in the league and thereby hamper its development as a proletarian organization. We are pulling in the opposite direction. That is the way we understand the progressive and revolutionary standpoint in the internal conflicts in Europe and interpret it at home. In this we believe we are fully entitled to the support of the international organization of the Left Opposition.

National Committee
Communist League of America (Opposition)

[Arne Swabeck]
Secretary

P.S.—About the Weisbord matter we will write separately.

Minority maneuvers and problems with Trotsky

October 1932

The following letter was written to Vincent R. Dunne in Minneapolis.

Dear Vincent:

As you know, our hopes for an improvement of the situation in the league after the plenum were disappointed. The minority did not keep their word and by that they taught us not to trust them anymore. I don't think they intended to play a deliberate and calculated double game at the plenum. Their intention no doubt was to take advantage of the opportunity we gave them there to retreat gracefully from their untenable position. But the caucus organization they have formed turned out to be a Frankenstein and pushed them back on the slippery path which they left for the moment at the plenum with our assistance.

You will remember they promised not to make a factional opposition to the cooptations on the basis of which we refrained from the alternative measure of reorganizing the resident committee so as to reflect the plenum majority in it. They fooled us there and concentrated their whole campaign after the plenum against the cooptations. This was the most vulnerable point since the procedure is a little bit irregular. The coopted comrades are young and not so well known. Jealousies and all sorts of noncommunist prejudices could be appealed to, etc. The Shachtman-Abern caucus did this to the limit. I have had an opportunity to see a great variety of factionalism in my time, but I must say quite coldly that I have never seen a dirtier, more dishonest, more demagogic and non-communistic campaign than the one which has been waged by Shachtman-Abern-Glotzer, etc., since the plenum. In all this there is a warning for the future, and we will not be true to the movement if we forget it. Every backward, prejudiced, and politically defective element has been appealed to by whatever kind of an argument that seemed necessary to the occasion or to the person. The result of this is the inevitable and already noticeable beginnings of a real political degeneration in the ranks of the comrades who have fallen victim to this caucus, which is in reality an unprincipled clique. We who have the sad experience of witnessing the political decomposition of the Foster group in the party after their split with us, must observe the same kind of a process going on now in a section of the league. But with this difference: the class composition of the Foster group was more proletarian and it took longer to corrupt them.

Do you remember Shachtman swearing with tears in his voice at the plenum that they had nothing to do with the Carter group of petty-bourgeois scholastics, and that all the talk of a bloc with them was a frame-up on our part? Well, nearly four months have gone by since then, during which time every meeting of the New York branch and of the branch executive has been a scene of factional struggle. During that whole time there has not been a single question, great or small, in which those two groups have not been lined up together against us. The bloc of these two groups, plus such demoralized and politically backward elements as they can pick up by an appeal to one kind of prejudice or another, is what constitutes the "majority" at present in the New York branch. An idea of how completely dependent the National Committee minority is upon the Carterites can be gained from the voting on the plenum resolutions. The minority resolution on the Carter group received eight votes; our resolution will have about twenty-two votes when some comrades who are now out of town are registered. *Both resolutions were voted down.* How does that square with the contention that the Carterite tendency has no real influence in the branch? It shows that the National Committee minority cannot influence the caucus to vote against the Carter group, or did not try to. It shows also that we put our finger on the real sore spot when we confronted the minority with the demand that they join us in a fight against these high school quibblers.

To make the question plainer and clearer, I introduced a resolution in the last National Committee meeting which pointed out that both groups at the plenum had condemned the Carter group as representing a harmful tendency in the league and that the action of the leading comrades of this group in abstaining from voting on the international resolution of the plenum separated them still further from the political position of the National Committee as a whole. On that ground, my resolution proposed that the two groups in the resident committee should come to an agreement on the recommendation of a slate for the branch EC in the elections now pending.

They refused to accept this proposal; then they went right ahead and made up a slate with the support of the Carterites in which they allowed three places out of eleven to actual supporters of the National Committee. What is the principle of a faction that proceeds in this way? Can any kind of personal diplomacy lift the league out of the hole they are digging for it?

I suppose you know that they have been flooding the country with caucus agents since the plenum, spreading all kinds of old wives' tales to catch the unwary. Along with this they have devoted themselves to all the familiar high-pressure caucus work that comes naturally to people who are more interested in votes than in the reasons which motivate them. You may have thought it negligence on our part that we have not bothered with this side of the question and have not even kept up any communication since the plenum. But that was a more-or-less deliberate policy on our part. We thought it best to let the documentary matter sent out in the internal bulletins speak for itself. The essence of the question is there, and we wanted to see first how many comrades would be able to find their own way and to know the reason for it. This procedure, which was employed also in 1928, will prove to be the best in the long run. The whole discussion has been for us a sort of political census of the league membership. The results are not very flattering, but at least we know now far better than we were able to know before just what the league membership, as it is at present constituted, consists of, from a political point of view. It is clear that the decisive cadre is with the National Committee. Not a few have proven incapable of a political motivation of their position and can be disoriented by any demagogue who comes along. More skillful demagogues, who can be depended upon to come along later, will be able to take them away from Shachtman-Abern, etc., by the same kind of tricks, more cleverly employed. A considerable section of the league membership remain undecided. Education is the problem there. That is the next task.

The whole situation created by the unprincipledness of the Shachtman clique should not in itself present a very serious problem to experienced people who know what they want and how to fight for it. If that were the only problem, the league would probably surmount it in a reasonable time and be all the stronger for the experience, even if it had to leave behind some illusions about a few people who looked good until they were put to a test or two.

But our situation now appears to have a new complication which is disturbing us very much. The action of Comrade Trotsky in dealing independently with Weisbord—and I must say in misjudging and inflating the importance of this mountebank—created a new problem, or rather revived one that had been well disposed of. Weisbord, as was to be expected, only used the recommendation given him by Comrade Trotsky to bolster up his side against the league and create more confusion. I think we deal adequately with the question in the *Militant*. Further than that we cannot and will not go, and it is hoped that Comrade Trotsky will not demand it.

On top of this there is a still further aggravation in the case of Field. Field is an intellectual, about forty years old, who discovered communism and the Left Opposition simultaneously a year or so ago, after living a peaceful life without being disturbed by any of the problems, labors, and sacrifices that have occupied us for twenty years or more. After he had been in the league for seven or eight months, we had to throw him out. Arne and I did not agree entirely in the procedure in the case taken by the branch, but we were fully convinced of the petty-bourgeois nature of Field and of his unfitness in a communist organization.

After that, Field, following the custom, made an excursion to Prinkipo. In informing us of his impending arrival, Comrade Trotsky wrote us that he would not discuss with Field in any way the question of his difficulties with the league. I have no doubt that he stuck to this assurance. But Field, who is a statistician and has a vast amount of concrete information about capitalist economy, was able to supply Comrade Trotsky with a great deal of data, which will enable him, as he wrote to us, to finish his book about America. So far, so good. No one could possibly object to that.

But matters did not end there. Field wrote a couple of articles about the perspective of the world economic crisis in which the possibility of an upturn in capitalist economy is discussed. Comrade Trotsky has written an introduction to these articles and they have been sent out to all the sections with his proposal that a discussion begin in preparation for a consideration of the question by the international conference. We understand that some of these articles have already been printed in some of the European Opposition papers. Thus we have the spectacle of a man who has been expelled from the American league—either rightly or wrongly, it does not matter, although we think rightly—leading a discussion in the International Opposition on one of the important questions on the agenda of the international conference. Copies of this material have even been sent to us.

What can the league do about a problem like that? Is it possible to maintain an organization in America, or an international organization for that matter, if there is not some more precise regulation and understanding of the rights and duties of the sections and some consideration for their decisions. How could we expect any intelligent worker to have the least respect for the league if it expels a man one day and then allows the other sections of the Opposition to collaborate with him as though nothing had happened, and without protest. It is true that both Comrade Trotsky and the International Secretariat have assured us that they do not in any way seek to interfere or revise the decision in the case of Field. But the fact is—at least the way we see it—that the decision is flaunted by these actions. It seems to us to be a heavier blow to the prestige and authority of the league than an outright interference on the question of his expulsion. We cannot object to a review of our decisions, including an organizational action, by the international organization, but in that case a formal appeal would have to be taken. We would supply the information upon which our action was based, and at least have the satisfaction of knowing that the proceeding is a regular one. But the informal disregard in effect of the action, raises in our minds some very serious misgivings, not only in regard to our relations with the International Secretariat, and with Comrade Trotsky, but also in regard to the whole question of the functioning of the Left Opposition as a real organization.

We have written a letter on the subject to Comrade Trotsky and the International Secretariat in which we state our point of view and record our objection to the procedure. You will receive a copy of this letter from Swabeck in a few days. We all hope that the matter will be straightened out satisfactorily. This will surely be the case if it is merely a misunderstanding and if the infringement of the league's decision is not an intentional one. On the other hand, if it turns out differently, if as some people are already speculating, the Field affair on top of the Weisbord affair indicates some kind of a conscious attempt to undermine or check up the leadership of the league, there is no doubt that we will be in for big complications. For our part—and all the comrades of our group here are agreed on it—we are firmly convinced that the movement in America and in every other country will get nowhere without a leadership that has grown up out of the movement organically and stands firmly on its own feet. Leaders who hold office by appointment or certificate directly or indirectly and depend on that for their authority are not worth a fig, and neither will be the movement that depends on such a leadership. I am not going to move an inch from this principle, no matter what happens.

Endless labors, worries, difficulties, hardships—slow, at times almost imperceptible progress—new complications—this is the road marked out for those who strive to assemble a cadre for the coming day. Patience, confidence, dogged endurance, and a firm will to prevail in spite of everything—these are the qualities which the time calls out and puts to the test. The Minneapolis group has been a tower of strength to us in the difficult years we have been battling, and we are confident it will be the case also in the future. I will write more again, soon. Meantime I would like to hear from you.

Fraternally yours,

[Jim]

For more field organizing

November 5, 1932

The following letter was written to Sam Gordon in Pittsburgh.

Dear Sam:

I am enthusiastic about your work and prospects in Pittsburgh, and am not inclined to make much of a discount for "optimism" in your reports. The developments in Des Moines and also in Davenport—along with what is happening in Pittsburgh—seem to me to give a clue to the process of disintegration which is overtaking the Stalinist apparatus.[62] It looks as though it is cracking first and most noticeably at the periphery. It is reasonable to expect that it should begin this way, since the pressure of the bureaucracy is not and cannot be as heavy in the provinces as at the center, where all the institutions, forces, and material means of compulsion are concentrated.

From this we ought to take a tip to follow the line of least resistance for a while and concentrate more of our forces on these weak spots. To this end, I am urging now that we put as our next step a far more substantial allocation of revenue to the work of field organization and that we make a special campaign to this end. This requires that we take some deliberate steps to break ourselves out of the straitjacket imposed upon us up till now both by conditions and necessities involved in maintaining the central propaganda plant, as well as by the weight of the routine which has probably pressed us into a rut in this regard without our fully realizing it.

When, as seen by your reports—which have been supplemented and confirmed by Comrade Hollander, who was in the other day—that the intervention of a field organizer in Pittsburgh for only a brief time yielded new contacts and the prospects of a branch, it is rather shocking to realize that an appropriation of five to eight dollars has so far been devoted to this—that is, about 1 percent of the monthly expenditure. We have to stand back from the whole problem for a minute and see the thing with a clearer perspective and a better sense of proportion. It was indubitably correct for us to concentrate in the beginning on the formal work of propaganda, and even on the literary side of that. But we must know when to take another step. The time is surely here, and it is possible that we have even overstepped ourselves a little.

We created a good central propaganda machine, but we must see to it that we direct the machine and that the machine does not direct us and keep us in a vicious circle. As the problem now presents itself, we cannot broaden our activities and develop the organizational side of our work as it must be developed now, without more resources. And we cannot create more resources without broadening the activities. It will be very bad for us if we do not recognize the second contradiction and devote ourselves to the solution of it. The temptation and the weight of immediate circumstances impels us to keep on the treadmill where the energies and the worries are all absorbed in the current problems of the day. But the politically correct and necessary thing is to surmount this situation by a decisive course which puts the field organization work as the first, or one of the first obligations to be met, instead of leaving it to the last, where it's never reached.

A decisive new orientation in conformity with the needs and opportunities of the moment will also soon introduce a qualitative change in the composition of the league. If you ask my opinion, I will tell you frankly that I think we have a hell of a lot of dead wood in the league, too many purely literary recruits. This is one of the penalties we have had to pay for our preoccupation with the fundamental work of propaganda. Besides that, this stage of our development gave an abnormal preponderance to purely literary activity in the leadership. It was to be expected that this would result in the convergence of an abnormal and necessarily transitory grouping in the league. That in my opinion is the real meaning of the Shachtman faction. A further development of the league in the normal process of a class-struggle organization will be of itself a great help in the restoration of a healthy balance all the way around.

I don't think I am personally acquainted with Comrade Sifakis. What you say about him is very interesting. I wonder if there are not a considerable number of such proletarian elements developing obscurely in our ranks, who will have their word to say when the windbags begin to get a little hoarse? I hope so. The latter are having their field day now.

I think you ought to give Sifakis the internal bulletins to read and then talk to him about the fight after he has digested them.

You ask about the international developments. Well,

here is the latest. Mill has gone over to the Stalinists, and is selling them the secrets of the International Left Opposition, especially of the Russian section. If Shachtman had some of the qualities of a man, don't you think that instead of blackguarding us for our intervention on the international question, he would be grateful for the fact that we knocked him loose from Mill before it was too late?

The international delegate question

December 20, 1932

The following letter was written to Sam Gordon.

Dear Sam:

The news of your activities in New Castle and Youngstown, which has come in letters from the secretaries at these points, after your fruitful work in Pittsburgh, fills me with joy and strengthens me in the opinion that one of the main lines of our strategy at the present time should be to attack the weak links in the Stalinist chain in the provinces through field organizers. I might say also that it does not grieve me to see that the demagogy which accomplished the defeat of your cooptation to the NC and pushed you out of the center is bringing about a demonstration of your abilities in another field. Many a cat thrown out through the door returns through the window. People would make fewer mistakes in this respect if they would stop to make sure what kind of a cat they are throwing out.

I noticed the minutes of the Youngstown branch on the question of the international delegate at the office today, and also saw a letter from Koehler explaining his attitude.[63] He says he is "in principle" opposed to sending an international delegate while "a factional struggle is going on in the organization." One could hardly find a cruder illustration than this statement provides of the way in which the minds of inexperienced comrades are debauched by the criminal demagogy of the Shachtman-Carter clique. If Koehler had said that he is "in principle" opposed to the league being *without* an international representative *at any time* when material circumstances make it in any way possible, and that it is *especially necessary* to have this international representation during an internal crisis, one could say that Koehler, despite his inexperience, is thinking like an internationalist and therefore has one of the first prerequisites for development into a vanguard communist. In this case, as in so many others we have seen, the clique politicians turn the simplest questions upside down and muddle and miseducate the unschooled people who came into the league to learn something.

I am somewhat in disagreement with the qualified motion you presented at the Youngstown branch meeting, as also with a similar action of the Minneapolis comrades which resulted in a "unanimous" decision which masks the differences on the question. It is quite probable in each case that the tactic was prompted by local circumstances and the desire to bring wavering elements along. But I do not think this consideration justifies the tactic. At any rate it is not the one we follow here. Just the contrary. We force every issue to a clear decision and draw a line which excludes the support of those who do not really understand and agree with us. That is the only way to build a firm group. Compromises with wavering elements can be taken up for consideration later—there is time enough for that if it becomes necessary—but to build on this kind of a foundation now can mean only to introduce contradiction into our own group and delude us with a sense of false political strength. I am sending a copy of this letter to Minneapolis, and the criticism is directed more to the comrades there than to you. When I see them adopting "unanimous" and therefore completely meaningless resolutions with Cowl on a question which the Cowl clique is making a factional issue against us throughout the league, I begin to fear that the Minneapolis branch will present us with some delegates at the conference who cannot be fully relied upon. Cowl is a perfect prototype of those here in New York who are demonstrating at a critical moment in the life of the league that they are incapable of subordinating personal interests and aims to the interests and aims of the movement. It is not by accident that he is in the general combination which is fighting the NC without being able to advance any political reasons for it. We have to make it our aim to shake up the league, to see what it really consists of, to put everybody in his proper place. This can be done only if we put all questions sharply and clearly and leave no middle ground for neutrals and similar half-and-half elements.

For it is not enough for us to raise the league out of the crisis or to gain a victory for the moment. Our fight will really justify itself only if it enables the league to *learn some lessons* that will fortify it against petty-bourgeois politics in the future.

I did not understand your letter of December 5. And although I sympathized with you fully in your financial straits I could not agree with your decision to leave the field and return to New York without a precise understanding to that effect with the center. I saw Arne the next day and induced him to take five dollars from some fund—I frankly told him I didn't give a damn which—and wire it to you. According to the rough calculations I have made, you have received about one dollar a week from the National Office to sustain you in your field work. An abominable showing, a shameful abuse of the good will of a professional functionary! And, worst of all, it is the sort of thing that is taken as a matter of course by too many people in the league who have yet to suffer their first bellyache for the movement. I will support with all my strength the just demands of a functionary for more considerate treatment. If these demands are put in ultimative form—all the better. The issue will be more clearly presented.

What I object to is the practice we have fallen into of letting an organizer starve in the field until he reaches the end of his tether—a crime of the National Committee—and then having him walk off from the field and turn up in New York without previous notice and agreement of the NC—a mistake of the organizer. This happened in the case of Carmody and Clarke. I hope it will not be repeated in your case. One can, and in the case of field organizers especially one should, present certain conditions for remaining at the assigned task: it has been proved many times that a certain minimum of food is necessary to maintain human life, even the life of an organizer. A demand for the means to provide this minimum is not unreasonable. But the NC should be given the opportunity of deciding the question formally and compelled to take the responsibility for the withdrawal of an organizer who is doing fruitful work in the field. The organizer should not make this decision himself in a moment of desperation.

I wish you would write more explicitly about the situation

in Pittsburgh. Did Sifakis receive the internal bulletin? Did you talk with him and others about the internal situation, and what was their reaction? You speak of the harm done by the Petras letter to Vomvas.[64] In what way? Did you get a copy of the letter? I do wish you would write me fully about this matter, as it disturbs me very much, especially since I can't understand the nature of the dissatisfaction.

I should have mentioned above that on the international delegate question in the New York branch meeting we rejected all ambiguities and put the issue sharply and aggressively. The opposition made a sorry showing and were very much on the defensive throughout the discussion. For the first time on an important question we broke the ranks of the combination. Six or seven of the independents—the conscientious, not the fake independents—abstained from voting. I have had long talks with several of them recently. Don't be surprised if you learn in the near future of a group of them issuing a declaration against the unprincipled opposition and for support of the NC.

We are pushing ahead the preparation for Arne's departure. Hope it will not be delayed much longer. The minority supporters and allies of all shades and colors have put a boycott on the funds for this purpose. That means we'll have to raise it ourselves. That's pretty hard, but we'll find the way to do it. As my old friend Bill Dunne used to say, to console us during periods of rough sailing in the party fights: it gets tough for a while and then it gets worse.

We are getting ready to send out a statement to the membership on the results of the postplenum discussion and referendum. I am writing the draft and am nearly finished with it. The document will take the offensive all along the line, and will summon the Oppositionists to an unrelenting struggle against clique combinations and petty-bourgeois politics.

I am going to take over Arne's duties when he leaves. My attention will be particularly directed to field organization work. Do not under any circumstances leave the field without our agreement beforehand (which you won't get). I have no objection if you demand categorical demands for financial maintenance on a minimum basis. If you put these demands concretely, it will help me to put the necessary pressure in the proper place here.

Write often and fully.

Yours fraternally,

[Jim]

Financing the international delegate

December 20, 1932

The following letter was written to Vincent R. Dunne in Minneapolis.

Dear Vincent:

I enclose a copy of a letter to Gordon, which saves me the time of duplication on the same points. You'll notice a little bouquet directed to Minneapolis—my tribute to the Christian Christmas spirit which seemed to be written into the Minneapolis resolution on the international delegate. I myself quit the church a long time ago.

Here is a little piece of news which will cheer you up. Our friends have put a boycott on the fund to finance the international delegate. That practically leaves the groups in New York and Minneapolis—and, still narrower, the few members of each group who retain jobs of some sort—to say whether Arne shall go or not. We need $150 on top of some of the preliminary expenses which have already been met for visas, etc. We will take care of half of it here through a loan which a few of us will pay out personally. Can the Minneapolis group do the same? If so, get busy on it right away and let us know.

We think it high time now to let the Old Man know what is going on here so that he won't be surprised when we begin to deal a few real wallops, and so that he can contribute his advice at the opportune moment.

Big developments are also going on in the European sections, concerning which we need first-hand information in order to profit by the experiences there. Up to date the Old Man has got his impressions of the American movement from Shachtman, Glotzer, Weisbord, Field, and a special delegate of New York intellectuals who are sympathetic to Trotskyism but disinclined to work up a perspiration about it. Do you think it would be amiss if we should send someone over now to chip in a word or two about the American labor and communist movements and the perspectives and tasks as we see them?

In a previous letter I mentioned that we had a very satisfactory adjustment of our misunderstandings and differences with the Old Man on the Weisbord and Field questions. It seemed to us that he went out of his way to meet our objections and to concede all that we were entitled to, if not a bit more.[65] You know how greatly we were disturbed about this matter, and I am sure you share our satisfaction at its adjustment. You will receive all the material on this.

My warmest greetings to all the Minneapolis Roundheads. The Roundheads, as you know, were the soldiers of Cromwell's army who didn't have sense enough to know when to quit, and for that reason couldn't be conquered.

Fraternally yours,

[Jim]

Results of discussion and voting on the plenum resolutions

Published December 29, 1932

The following report was drafted by Cannon and adopted by the NC. It was published in Internal Bulletin no. 5.

The membership referendum on the decisions of the plenum showed the following results:

1. The *international resolution* received general approval, with none voting against and 9 abstaining (all abstentions being in the New York branch).

2. The *resolution of the majority on the situation in the New York branch* received 65 votes with 29 voting against and 12 abstentions. The minority resolution on the same question received 27 votes in favor with 25 against and 24 abstaining. The votes cast against both resolutions as well as the abstentions were all in the New York branch.

3. The *resolution on the Toronto branch* received a majority of the votes, with 30 abstentions in the New York branch and some members of other branches not recording

themselves specifically.

4. The *proposal of the plenum to coopt Comrades Basky, Gordon, and Clarke to the National Committee* received 59 votes in favor, 65 against, and 10 abstaining. The Chicago branch, which recorded itself against the cooptations by a vote of 9 to 4, with 2 abstaining, declared in favor of the formation of a Political Committee of five members, to be composed of Cannon, Swabeck, Oehler, Shachtman, and Abern or Glotzer. The voting on this proposal was 9 in favor, 1 against, and 5 abstaining.

The membership discussion and referendum on the plenum decisions revealed a number of salient features which give the key to an understanding of the present internal crisis of the league, which, instead of moderating, has become more aggravated since the plenum. These features may be summarized as follows:

1. The decisive majority of the members supported the standpoint of the National Committee on all the resolutions of the plenum—all these resolutions, without exception, were endorsed.

2. The cooptations to the National Committee, which were proposed by the plenum majority as an alternative to the formation of a Political Committee which would reflect the majority of the plenum, failed of a majority by 6 votes. The Carter group in the New York branch, which was condemned by both groups of the NC at the plenum, cast the deciding votes against the cooptations. Other comrades who are in conflict with the NC on important political questions (Boston branch) also voted against the cooptations.

3. A group of nine comrades in the New York branch, following the lead of Comrades Carter and Stone, abstained from voting on the international resolution on the ground of "insufficient information"—the only members in the

entire league who required more "information" to take a positive stand against the disintegrating elements in the European sections. Since then, Comrade Carter has openly attacked the international resolution at branch meetings.

4. This failure of the Carter group to support the most important resolution of the plenum did not draw the minority of the NC closer to the majority in the struggle against the influence of this group, as political seriousness and consistency would dictate. On the contrary, ever since the plenum the minority has combined forces with the Carter group and other elements in the New York branch who are out of line with the basic policy of the league, to fight the National Committee. Outside of New York the minority of the NC forms a close factional unity with comrades of the Boston branch who are in conflict with the NC as a whole on questions which have a principled character, and utilizes this branch for the adoption of factional resolutions against the NC.

It is this disregard of all *principled considerations* which intensifies the internal crisis, poisons the atmosphere, and paralyzes the external work of the league. It can be said now with certainty, in the light of what has transpired since the plenum, that the chief obstacle in the way of a real development of the external work of the league at the present time is the factional struggle against the NC, in which no semblance of a separate platform, or even of a serious difference on a single important question of external policy, has been brought forward.

Not only is the practical work of the league (especially in New York) hampered and disrupted by this state of affairs, but the internal work of assimilating inexperienced comrades and training them in the understanding and the spirit of communism has to make its way slowly and with the greatest difficulty through a veritable fog of demagogy, poisonous personal accusations, and political cynicism. But, on the other hand, the elementary communist education—the training of comrades to motivate themselves by fundamental political considerations—which is achieved in the face of the present obstacles, is all the more firmly grounded and sinks all the deeper into the consciousness of the comrades, and arms them for the future. Lessons learned in struggle are not easily forgotten.

5. The New York branch remains as before the focal point of the internal crisis, although it must not be denied that the postplenum discussion has uncovered a number of the same basic weaknesses and contradictions throughout the league as a whole. In this is reflected the fact that between the formal acceptance of the platform of the Left Opposition and a genuine assimilation of it there is a long way to go. The international experience of the Left Opposition all goes to show that this distance is not to be traveled without difficulty, especially when some of those who are regarded as leaders set obstacles in the path. It is in the New York branch, in which the resident members of the NC directly participate, that the results of this conduct manifest themselves most clearly. For that reason the situation in the New York branch brings out the real essence of the conflict and requires now the closest attention of the entire league membership, and of the international organization of the Left Opposition as well.

The heterogeneous composition of the New York branch, and the lack of political experience and party tradition, would make its development into a genuine vanguard communist organization a protracted process in any case. But for all that, a united leadership, working consciously to this end and cooperating loyally in a consistent and unyielding struggle against mistaken conceptions and false tendencies, could educate and consolidate the branch in a normal atmosphere and without serious convulsions.

The refusal of the minority of the NC to cooperate in this imperative and unpostponable task, despite the political agreement with us which they proclaimed at the plenum, complicates the problem in the highest degree and counteracts the struggle at every step.

This conduct is leading the branch onto a dangerous path which brings its majority more and more into conflict with the National Committee and undermines the basis for a common approach to the political tasks of the league and effective collaboration in the daily work. Rejecting collaboration with the majority of the NC on the basis of the plenum resolutions, the minority is compelled by the logic of the situation to base itself on precisely those elements who stand in opposition to these resolutions as well as to other parts of our common platform. It forms factional combinations with all those elements, not excluding even those individuals whose unbridled agitation against the NC bears an ugly taint, alien to communism and in reality directed against its most elementary conceptions.

The factional campaign of the minority against the National Committee boasts of a "majority" in the New York branch. But the voting in the branch on the plenum resolutions and some subsequent political tasks, shows plainly what this "majority" looks like from a political standpoint. On the resolutions devoted to the situation in the New York branch the voting showed the following: for the resolution of the NC, 19; for the resolution of the minority, 11; against both resolutions, 18; abstaining, 12. Here is revealed a sufficient diversity of opinion to show how sadly the "majority" is divided on one of the most important decisions of the plenum. Against the Carter group, which the minority condemned by resolution at the plenum, it could not unite more than 11 votes. But against the NC majority, with which it recorded its agreement at the plenum, it could unite its own 11 votes, plus the 18 who voted against any criticism of the Carter group, plus the 12 (with 2 or 3 incidental exceptions) who abstained from voting one way or another.

At the plenum the minority joined with the majority in support of the international resolution. In the branch voting, nine comrades abstained on this decisive question. But in the branch meeting, on practically every question—including the elections—this unity of the NC is nowhere registered. On the contrary, these nine abstentionists are systematically included in the "majority" which makes sport of "condemning" the National Committee.

In the recent exchange with Weisbord, the National Committee stood united in its policy, as indeed it has been from the inception of this issue. In the branch, a conciliationist attitude toward the views of Weisbord made its appearance on the part of a few comrades who came to the league rather recently. One of them went so far as to violate discipline in the struggle of the league against the disruptive maneuvers of Weisbord. Does the minority join with the majority of the NC to correct his numerous misconceptions, of which the conciliationist attitude toward Weisbord and the violation of discipline were merely reflections? By no means. He is included in the branch "majority" and was rewarded, despite his short time in the league, by election to the executive committee—a body of eleven members out of which the supporters of the NC were allowed only *two places*.

With such displays of political inconsistency on the part of those who should be teachers, with the branch in the control of a majority that is "against the NC" but which has never yet been able to counterpose a different policy against that of the NC on a single important question, it is not surprising that the political level of the branch is low, that the atmosphere is poisoned with quarrels where personal insults take the place of political arguments, and that all kinds of factional excesses are committed.

It could not be otherwise. Communists have never yet been educated in the school of petty-bourgeois politics. And with the same certitude it can be said that the branch cannot emerge from the crisis without a catastrophe until a majority is constituted within it that is united in its political aims and governed in its actions by fundamental political considerations. The NC will not relent in its struggle to raise the branch, and with it the league, out of the crisis on this, the only principled path. In this we are fully entitled to the support of the membership of the league and of the international organization of the Left Opposition, for we are fighting for the preservation of the league and for its future.

Our delegate will be on the boat

January 1, 1933

The following letter was written to Vincent R. Dunne in Minneapolis.

Dear Vincent:

I received your letter of December 26, in which you enclosed the big half of your rather heavy installment on the expenses of the international delegate. Thanks to the prompt and resolute action at Minneapolis and a similar one here in New York, we can say now that Arne's departure is assured, and that it will not be delayed. The boycott of the Shachtman clique on this project up to date has been complete—not one of them has contributed a cent. But in spite of that our delegate will be on the boat in the very near future. You see, it does look as though some of the boys are getting mad and are not only taking off their coats but also their shirts. That's a bad sign for the people who started the trouble. Your letter, with the enclosure, made a stirring impression here. We know well enough that the money you are digging up is like so much skin peeled off your own frames. It makes a fellow feel like doing a little better than his best with this kind of support.

The confirmation of our judgment in the question of the international delegate, and of the complete falsity of the attempt first to defeat it and then to sabotage it, has come with a suddenness that is rather terrific. We have just received a circular from the International Secretariat to the effect that the *Copenhagen delegation* (i.e., the Old Man and those who were there with him) had proposed a *preliminary international conference* for the purpose of preparing for the formal international conference which is scheduled.[66] The secretariat, with the European sections assenting, unanimously agreed to the proposal. The preliminary conference is called *and we are called on to send our delegate right away!* It is perfectly obvious that the conference was originally intended for Copenhagen and that, falling through by the cutting short of the visit there, it is transferred to another place. From the minutes of the secretariat which we have received, it can be seen that a sort of conference was already at work in Copenhagen, for there is a reference to the "Italian Commission at Copenhagen," which adopted some recommendations in regard to the Bordigists. In other words, the decision of the NC on the whole matter *anticipated* just what was done or attempted to be done at Copenhagen, and that our action paralleled the action taken abroad. This gives us the option of being ready, and of having the funds available or nearly so, to participate in the preliminary conference, the date of which is *very near.* But what becomes of the whole campaign against the decision of the NC? Those who represented our proposal for a preliminary conference as some kind of a bureaucratic outrage against the membership will now have to explain why the whole international organization has acted on the same lines *as a matter of course.* Well, these Minneapolis Shachtmans and these New York Cowls will learn in good time that it is not sufficient for a faction to be noisy and venomous; it is necessary once in a while to be right.

In view of the crisis in the organization, and of the necessity now for everyone to put everything he has into the scale, I have decided to return to full-time work for the league when Arne leaves. As soon as I am through some preliminary work in the office I intend to take to the road again, and you can expect to see me in Minneapolis before the winter is over. It isn't exactly a propitious time for a man to take a chance—or rather, to compel his family to take a chance—on economic survival as a professional worker for the league. The *Militant* is on the rocks, we are in the worst financial straits we have been in for a long time, the work is disorganized by the worst kind of an internal fight, and most of our members are out of work and unable to contribute. But in spite of that, or rather just because of that, I have come to the conclusion, after careful deliberation, that it has to be done in order to accelerate the solution of the crisis and point the league toward its really great tasks and opportunities. I mean the decision seriously and will not turn back. All that I ask is that those who also mean things seriously go along with me and do their part in their own way.

The last time I gave up private employment and went to work for the movement was in the spring of 1919 at the height of the postwar anti-Red hysteria. The period of professional work for the movement commenced then lasted for ten straight years and a few months over. Let us hope that the present enlistment will not be shorter.

You will probably be hearing about the Morgenstern case, if you have not heard already. Morgenstern's statement and the statement of the NC will be sent out shortly. The night Morgie got out of prison, his family induced him to go through a marriage ceremony with a rabbi officiating, at the home of his father. Morgie was present at the last meeting of the NC and presented a statement on the matter. He said he had done it in a moment of sentimental weakness to gratify his parents, who never had much joy out of him; that he recognized the seriousness of the mistake; that he did not intend in the slightest way any reconciliation with bourgeois ideology and religious superstitions; that he considered the act as a contradiction to everything he had done since he joined the movement at the age of seventeen; that he recognized that he had compromised his position as a leading comrade and wanted to resign from the NC in order not to compromise it; that he was willing to accept any decision the NC would make in his case and that he wanted a chance to make good the mistake by his future work in the ranks.

Strangely enough, this manly and straightforward statement did not please Shachtman and Abern. They appeared to be not in the least interested in helping a comrade with a really splendid record in the movement to make good an error. They want to kill Morgenstern and, through him, to strike at others—so one must judge their statements that, in spite of his record and his statement, which meets every reasonable demand the NC could make, he should be expelled from the league. In any case they demanded that he be suspended for one year. This we refused, and they say our refusal is prompted by "factional protection," which "will be so much the worse" for us. The decision of the NC is a statement condemning the action of Morgenstern and explaining the principal reasons therefore; an acceptance of his resignation as an alternate member of the NC; and a declaration that Morgenstern's past record and his present stand entitle him to the opportunity to make good the error as a member of the league. We will have to pay for this decision, for the case of a comrade being married by a rabbi is a case made to order for demagogy.[67] On such an issue they will muster the votes of those people whose chief recommendation is that they were not married by a rabbi and were married instead by a police magistrate.

But for all that, our decision is an honest decision and the only one an honest committee could make. In a normal atmosphere nobody would think anything of demanding more. They will make a campaign against us on the ground that we are "protecting" Morgenstern for "factional advantage." But in reality it is just the opposite. The expedient thing in this case would have been to expel Morgenstern in order to prove that we are more radical than our opponents and to take away an issue from them. But this is the Left Opposition, not the Foster group, and we do not play politics that way. Morgie was in a helpless and, worse than that, in a ridiculous position. It would have been easy to victimize him and to howl down anybody who protested. But we do not intend to make any concessions to such a lynching spirit in this case or in any other case. The height of a faction fight is just as good a time as any to teach the new members by example that leaders worthy of the name must not only be politically minded, but must also be honest and not afraid of demagogy.

One might ask why the derelictions of Morgenstern, which are purely individual and isolated, can be grabbed up so eagerly as an issue, and why people who maintained an unruffled indifference to such overshadowing questions as the international resolution can work up such a lather about it. The explanation, of course, lies in the inescapable logic of a faction that is not grounded on principle. Having no principled political differences, or not daring to bring them forward and defend them, they must resort to all kinds of personal issues. Hence the campaigns against Cannon, against Gordon, against Swabeck, etc., with all kinds of accusations that are true or false, mostly false, but in any case personal and not fundamentally political. They grabbed the Morgenstern-rabbi issue because they *need* such an issue and need it badly. What they need on top of that is a good case of "white chauvinism" around which they can conduct a campaign and demand a mass trial of the culprit (provided of course that he does not belong to their clique).[68]

At the last meeting, S. and A. presented a motion for a national conference for May 1. They think, on the basis of the vote against the cooptations and the resolutions against the sending of an international delegate, that they can count on a majority. Their usual superficiality is playing them another trick here. They will find that quite a few comrades who voted against the cooptations for one reason or another do not mean by that to turn the league over to Shachtman and Abern to play with. I could give them the names of several such here in New York alone, and I have no doubt that there will be many others. We are for a conference, as before, and so decided, but we specified that the date be set only after the conference documents are ready, so that there will be adequate time for the discussion both here and in the other sections. That will probably require at least three months after the adoption of the documents. Therefore the conference will hardly be possible by May 1—probably a month or two later. The July 4 week looks most feasible. This will also give time for the return of the international delegate. Wouldn't it be absurd for an organization that prides itself on internationalism first of all and above all, to rush through a conference, after all that has happened since the plenum, without waiting for the report of its international delegate and without giving the other sections a chance to express their opinions?

I don't think we will have any cause to regret our action in sending an international delegate at this time, nor our selection of the person. Among all those who have been pushing and crowding forward on international missions of various kinds, both before our expulsion from the party and since, there is hardly one that has a better claim to the honor than Swabeck. A founder of the party, a prominent worker for communism from the inception of the movement in America, an outstanding militant in the trade union movement—how many who sit in the international conference, outside the Russian delegation, will be able to show a longer or better record? Not many, if any, and I venture to say that the international comrades will get a far more serious impression of our league through him than they have had before.

The league as a whole ought to be proud of the opportunity to send a representative and to make an extra sacrifice for it. Just consider the showing he has made as a revolutionist especially during the past two years. A mechanic accustomed to a wage of fifteen dollars a day, and he was able to make it steadily for he is an especially good mechanic, he came to work for the league for less than that much a week. Do you know—I wonder how many of the comrades know—that since the plenum he hasn't drawn any wages at all? And that for months before that he drew as little as three to five dollars per week—and still held on all this time. To make that possible he had to go into debt in all directions up to his ears, to rent out the best room in his house and turn the kitchen into a bedroom, to send his wife out to work as a servant in other people's houses to provide the food minimum while he does the housework and cooking for the boy.

Yes, it wouldn't be out of order for the league members, and especially the young ones, to take a moment's notice of little things like that, even if they don't hear about it from Swabeck. For that is just one of the things that should be considered when honors are passed around and the selection of leaders is on the agenda. It is remarkable how little this sterling example of responsibility and capacity for sacrifice impresses some of the people, especially in New York, who have yet to learn by experience what it means to be a revolutionist in the way of sacrifice. They talk about Swabeck as though Swabecks grew on bushes for any fool with a stick to knock down. Shachtman is the inspirer of this thoroughly rotten tendency. It was he who set in motion the theory about the "degeneration" of the old guard and blinded the young comrades to the importance of past records and present performances on the part of those who had passed the "age limit." Well, we can be sure this diseased sentiment will not have any lasting influence. And when we overcome it, let us make sure that we have set up some barriers against its reappearance.

I was glad to learn that my criticism of the Minneapolis resolution was somewhat misdirected; and from your letter to the NC, I can see that it is really so.[69] Still, the fulmination was perhaps not entirely wasted. At the present moment it is better, in my opinion, to err on this side than on the other. The Red Army sings the "Internationale" sometimes when it is not absolutely necessary, or so it seemed to me when I was visiting the army camps.

It keeps up the spirit. The spirit which must animate the vanguard now is the spirit of unrelenting struggle to raise the league out of the crisis and set it on the road to the fulfillment of its great historic mission.

As ever,

[Jim]

On the 'money' question

January 10, 1933

The following statement was made for the minutes of the resident National Committee.

I agree fully with the main point of view outlined in the statement of Comrades Swabeck and Oehler, insofar as the fundamental questions are concerned, and think this is the direction the league must take.[70] And I am ready, as I said at the previous meeting, to take the responsibility and all that it involves on my part in accepting the office of national secretary, not simply as a temporary measure. My aim and desire is to devote my time exclusively from now on to professional work for the movement as long as the movement finds my services acceptable.

Together with Comrades Swabeck and Oehler I am in favor of a Bolshevik fight on the fundamental issues involved and will do my part in it in any case. But I doubt the wisdom of allowing myself to become the center of a "money argument" as is now indicated. It is hardly compatible with the dignity of a revolutionist. Besides that, a dispute on these grounds would undoubtedly have a strong tendency to obscure the really important and fundamental questions in dispute, add to the demoralization, and also militate against the solution of the financial crisis.

For these reasons I think it best to remove the "money question" insofar as it relates to me personally and to accept the post of national secretary on a voluntary basis. I will give all the time I can; as long as my personal resources and credit hold out I will give my whole time. The conference will have to decide the fundamental disputes concerning the character, the tasks, and the perspectives of the league as an organization. The disposition of my services will follow logically from that, one way or the other. On this point I will neither present demands nor refuse responsibilities. It is a matter for the league to decide.

The new party turn

Published January 21, 1933

The following article was published in the *Militant*.

The new turn, or half turn, of the party in the unemployment movement opens up the possibility for a broad development of the unemployment struggle, which hitherto has owed its stagnation and ineffectiveness, in no small degree, to the absurdly narrow and sectarian policy of the Stalinists.[71]

To the extent that it creates the conditions for the free participation of all workers' organizations, whose members have a good cause and a genuine will to react against the fearful pressure of unemployment, the new policy of the party creates the primary conditions for the transformation of the isolated vanguard actions of the Communist militants into a united movement embracing masses of workers. Such a movement, driven forward by the appalling mass misery and discontent and putting all parties and leaders to the test of action, can lead to a stormy development of working-class struggle and a rapid expansion of Communist influence. From this point of view the Left Opposition is bound to greet the new turn, to support it with full strength, and to penetrate into the very heart of the unfolding movement.

At the same time, the new turn puts the Left Opposition before new opportunities and tasks. By releasing their monopolistic stranglehold on the emaciated movement and inviting all workers' organizations "irrespective of political opinions or affiliations," the Stalinists are perforce required to leave a crack open for the feared and hated "Trotskyists." We must and we will make our way through that crack, spread it wider, and establish direct contact with the workers, including the Communists who are assembling for struggle under the banner of the united front.

Up to now the strength of the Marxist wing of the movement has been chiefly in its criticism. The opportunity to participate in a movement of struggle against the plague of unemployment places us also before the test of action. The Left Opposition will grow in numbers and influence to the extent that it makes good in this test—to the extent that it demonstrates its qualities as a fighting political organization, not a mere propaganda circle.

But this direct participation in actions can be really effective for the unemployment movement and for communism only if it supplements and reinforces the criticism of all harmful and retarding currents and tendencies, including the tendency of bureaucratic centrism. In no case and under no circumstances can this criticism be submerged in a general sentiment of "unity."

First of all, we have to see things as they really are and to talk out loud about them. Not a few party members, discouraged and demoralized by the devastation of the "third period," will hail the new turn uncritically, as a way of salvation. Is it possible that a Left Oppositionist here and there, chafing for action and wearied of the drawn-out struggle of our small faction for the principled foundations, can fall into the same error? Hardly. But such things have happened before. Every zigzag of Stalinism, the whole course of which is a series of zigzags to the left and to the right, has claimed its credulous victims. For this reason also a critical appraisal of the new united front policy at the beginning, and at every turn, must go along with and condition our support.

In initiating the new tactic, the Stalinists have been true to themselves—to the vacillating, cowardly, half-measure character of centrism. In the first place, the turn from the "social fascist" theory is not a complete one: The *branches* of the Socialist Party and the local AFL unions are invited to the united front. But what of the *central bodies* of these organizations? What of the *leaders?* Can you convince any Socialist worker or AFL unionist that these leaders are unwilling to participate in a real struggle for the unemployed if they are not even invited to do so?

Secondly, the turn of policy is carried out not in the direct, straightforward manner of Bolsheviks, but in the indirect and shamefaced manner of Stalinists. The party does not proclaim the policy, issue the call, and take the lead. That is all left to the "Trade Union Committee" controlled by the party.

Thirdly, there is no frank acknowledgment of the ruinous errors of the "third period," and no explanation of the reasons for the change. Thus the door is left open for a retreat—also without explanation.

Yet another—and the most dangerous—of all the weaknesses of the new step of the Stalinists has already been pointed out in last week's *Militant*. That is the parliamentary reformist trend of the proposals. The time to warn against such a trend is now. Having concocted their policy of ultraleft adventurism in an artificial atmosphere of revolutionary upsurge, the Stalinists can now be expected to swing to the other extreme and transform the party militants into petitioners for picayune reforms.

The Amsterdam Congress Against War heralded this swing to the right on an international scale.[72] The watering down of policy in every field is on the order of the day. The overemphasis on purely parliamentary action in the call for the unemployment conference becomes all the more menacing in the light of this general shift of policy to the right.

Having failed to conquer American capitalism in frontal attack, the Stalinist generals have now given the signal to go after a little at a time; to tone down the talk about the final goal of the struggle. A highly amusing but nonetheless significant incident is reported from Des Moines. A functionary responding to a critical speech by Comrade Lewit explained that he had been instructed "not to talk about revolution in the West." In this crude remark of the naive field worker is embodied the essence of the new Stalinist strategy: "We couldn't get the workers by command; now let us fool them in." By this maneuver they can fool the workers and themselves into a swamp of reformism, but never into a revolutionary struggle.

The Left Opposition, and only the Left Opposition, can sound the alarm against this element of the new turn in united front policy and lead the struggle against it. But this cannot be done effectively by a negative or standing-aside attitude toward the united front movement. On the contrary. Such an attitude can only alienate the Left Opposition from the Communist workers and doom its criticism to futility. An active participation in the movement, in the work and in the fight, is the only way to make the revolutionary influence of the Left Opposition count in the new turn of events.

The New York unemployed conference

January 22, 1933

The following speech was given by Cannon as the CLA's official delegate to the New York City conference.[73] It was published in the January 28 *Militant*.

Comrades and fellow-workers:

In the limited time allotted for speeches from the floor it is naturally impossible to deal adequately with the whole problem which has brought us into conference here today. I will therefore confine myself to some of the most salient points which must be considered in connection with our next steps on the road to a broader movement and a more effective struggle. Permit me to refer you to the mimeographed copies of the statement and resolutions of the Communist Left Opposition which have been distributed to the delegates. In this material you will find a more thorough elaboration of the program and tactics which the Bolshevik-Leninists advocate than I will be able to present orally in my limited time.

The conference here today represents a step forward in the direction of a united struggle of the workers against the unbearable burdens of the crisis. The tendency toward such a union of forces in the fight constitutes, from our point of view, the progressive feature of this conference. For it is only when the workers of various organizations and political trends are welded together in a common front that real blows can be directed against the class enemy on the great class issue of unemployment. When this union of forces is lacking, when the comparatively small groups of the workers' vanguard take the field alone and fight as isolated detachments, the blows fall heaviest on them, the class enemy remains unshaken, and the masses of the workers gain no advantages.

To the extent that the present conference signifies a progressive step toward the united front struggles of the workers, we of the Left Opposition declare our readiness to give hearty support to the movement and to work loyally for its advancement.

The invitation which the committee extended to the branches of the Socialist Party, to the trade union locals of the AFL, and similar conservative organizations, means in itself and can only mean a recognition of the fact that the unemployed issue is not an issue of any party, tendency, or group, but rather an issue of the class. This is the only way to present the question and to lay the groundwork for a real struggle. But this step in itself remains uncompleted. The roll call of the delegation bears eloquent testimony to this fact.

Between the aspirations of the committee which called the conference and the workers' organizations actually represented, there is an enormous gap. From this we do not conclude that the calculations of the committee were wrong, or that the aspirations to draw the reformist and even the reactionary organizations into the joint struggle are without foundation. No. We only have to conclude that the step taken toward this end must be followed by others.

The tactics of the united front, as Lenin laid them down and as they have been verified by experience on an international scale, must be unfolded in their full scope. It is not sufficient to invite the branches of the Socialist Party and the local unions of the AFL to join us in a common fight. To be sure, that is something. By such an invitation we recognize the fact that the workers in these organizations also suffer from the plague of unemployment and that it is quite possible for them to join in a fight for a program of immediate demands even while they remain reformist and conservative in their political views—even while they retain membership in organizations representing these political currents. That is the beginning of wisdom on the question of the united front.

But it is by no means the whole of it. The fact remains that these workers in the reformist and reactionary organizations, who have good cause and very probably feel a real will to fight against the scourge of unemployment, are not ready to break with their organizations and are not convinced that their leaders, who talk against the evils of unemployment no less than we do, do not mean what they say. They are not ready to break with their leaders at the present moment and to respond to appeals over the heads of their official leadership and their respective central organizations. This is the situation as it exists in reality, and not in somebody's imagination. The problem is to base ourselves on this reality, and to find the way to draw these workers into the common struggle with us in spite of that. For this we must have recourse to the genuine tactics of the united front.

The appeal to the Socialist Party branches of Greater

New York brought a response from one single branch, which is represented here alone—and even that branch is located outside the metropolitan territory. The appeal to the AFL locals brought a mere handful of delegates; and even these, in almost every case, come from locals already under the influence of the left wing. Do not shut your eyes to these facts, comrades. Let us not delude ourselves with the idea that we have a united working-class front. For that, we must have a large section of the workers who are absent here today.

If we proceed from the point of view of the committee, that the workers generally, regardless of their political views and their affiliations, want to struggle against unemployment—and I think this is the correct point of view—then we ought to ask ourselves why they have not responded to the call. And if we face the problem clearly, we will have to say that the fault lies not with the workers but rather with the manner in which they were approached. By ignoring the central organizations, by ignoring the official leadership of the reformist and conservative organizations, the committee unfortunately gave these treacherous leaders all the ground they needed to excuse themselves before their own membership for their own failure to participate.

Moreover, it put the locals and branches of these organizations before the problem of acting over the heads of their official leadership and their official central bodies. If you understand something of the mechanics of organization you will recognize that this is an untimely demand. The workers take their organizations seriously, no less perhaps than we do. They do not act over the head of their official institutions and leadership until they are ready to break with the central organization. Do we act otherwise? And cannot we find our way to the reformist workers more effectively if we attribute to them something of the same sense of organizational loyalty that we ourselves manifest?

In the resolutions of the Communist Left Opposition, which I have introduced here, there is a proposal to call a second conference within two weeks and to invite to this conference not only the locals and branches of the AFL, the Socialist Party, the Workmen's Circles, and similar organizations, but also their respective central bodies. I will be answered to the effect that the leaders of these organizations obstruct and sabotage the movement and do not want to engage in any real struggle with the employers and the state. We are quite convinced that this is true. But the AFL and Socialist Party workers are by no means convinced and will not be convinced merely by our denunciations.

The way to convince them is to put their leaders to the test in action. That is the meaning of our proposal to invite also the leaders to join in the common struggle. It puts the conscientious workers in these organizations—those who really want to fight—in a position to demand of their leaders that they translate their words into deeds without in any way, at the beginning, involving a break with their organization. It puts them in a position to bring pressure on their leaders by normal organizational means, to force some of them, if only for a short time, to participate in the united movement and to convince themselves by this test, by this experience, that their leaders have been deceiving them with phrases.

Only in this way, in this process, can we separate the masses of the conscientious workers in the reformist organizations from their treacherous leaders and draw them into a common struggle without those leaders and against them. This is not a revelation of the Left Opposition. This, comrades and fellow-workers, is the ABC of the united front tactic of Lenin.

This is the way we must move. This is the way the movement is tending under the enormous pressure of conditions on the one side, and the bankruptcy of all other tactics on the other. The united front tactic, as we have laid it down in our resolution, is a means for the mobilization of a genuine workers' mass movement for the struggle against the class enemy. It is, at the same time, a means for the separation of the reformist workers from the influence of their treacherous, phrase mongering leaders.

The tactic that has been employed up till now, despite all the good intention, has served opposite ends. Here in the fourth year of the crisis, the capitalists remain secure and arrogant. The reformist and reactionary labor bureaucracy, in the political as well as in the trade union field, remains unshaken in its position. The vanguard workers' movement remains comparatively weak, isolated, and ineffective. All the objective conditions point to a different state of affairs. The fearful mass misery, the appalling hunger, destitution, and discontent of the millions is a powerful force to change the whole situation in a comparatively short time. It is to aid this process that the Left Opposition has come to this conference and submitted its resolutions for your consideration.

Breaking out of the narrow groove

January 24, 1933

The following letter was written to Carl Skoglund in Minneapolis.

Dear Skoglund:
Special for Skoglund and Dunne:
   Shortly before Arne left, he asked you and Vincent to send in your vote on the proposal to constitute a Political Committee composed of three—Oehler, Cannon, and Shachtman—during his absence from New York. Up to date your vote has not been received. Consequently we have now a committee of four, which is hardly workable. For example: at the meeting yesterday we had two and two votes on conflicting motions regarding the student antiwar conference held at Chicago—no small matter; the policy in certain respects remains undetermined.[74] I wish you would send in this vote by airmail and so put an end to this.
Dear Skogy:
   Things have been happening and moving so fast here

since Arne left January 11 that I have not had time to write. I have been on the job fulltime and overtime ever since. Here in New York the Left Opposition is rapidly breaking out of the narrow groove in which it has been confined so long. We scored a big success at the unemployment conference about which you have already been informed. I was formally admitted as a delegate of the LO and took the floor as the first speaker in the discussion. It was quite a moment for us—the first time in four and a half years that I have had the opportunity to speak directly to a conference composed primarily of party people. Two weeks ago, as you will have noted in the *Militant*, I spoke at the Lovestone forum by invitation. We intend to bring out the stenographic report of this speech in a pamphlet. At the united front conference we had five bona fide trade union delegates supporting the resolutions of the LO. From this you will see that we are making headway in spite of everything.

You have seen Internal Bulletin no. 6, which contains the circular of the International Secretariat on the preliminary international conference. It makes interesting reading in contrast with the factional campaign against the sending of our international delegate. Did you ever see a political position refuted more completely and more quickly than this? Also I hope you read the Gourov letter on Mill.[75] What a lesson and what a warning for people who disregard political considerations in the internal politics of the organization!

Here is another matter of the utmost importance which all comrades should weigh fully: *A new capitulation movement* has broken out in the German section. The group of Roman Well, which has been fighting the German leadership for a period of time on apparently secondary and incidental questions, has now come out with a position which amounts to capitulation to Stalinism. We have a lot of material on the matter, including several articles and letters by Trotsky and Gourov which are now being mimeographed for a special Internal Bulletin which will be sent out to all members.

Things are developing rapidly in Europe. On the one hand, the selection of the central cadre is proceeding rapidly; on the other hand, elements who cannot keep step are being sloughed off. The lesson of principled politics in the internal life of the league and the selection of its basic cadres is becoming the outstanding lesson of the experience of the last three years. We have sent our delegate across just at the right time, thanks to the prompt and sacrificial responses of the Bolsheviks, who know what they want and do what is necessary to get it, pushing aside the oppositions and the opposers.

We have set the date for the national conference for June 30–weekend of July 4. This is to give three full months' discussion in order to give the International Secretariat a real opportunity to participate and to express their opinions. A circular is going out to the branches on this matter. (I guess you saw it already—R[ose] K[arsner])

Tomorrow morning I am leaving here for Gillespie to attend a conference of progressive trade unions, sponsored by the Progressive Miners of America. According to our view of things, the turn of the league toward a more direct class-struggle activity has to mean first of all a development of serious trade union work, and this kind of work has to be done to a large extent in the field, on the spot where things are happening, and not merely in the editorial office.

Can anyone seriously maintain that this work can be developed and organized in any systematic way without a staff, without at least one experienced person devoting his full time and energies to the political and organizing work and getting out in the field where things are happening, at the moment when they are happening? Who talks about mass work without this is a phrasemonger. Yet this is precisely the current strategy we encounter at this important conjuncture in the life of the league. I returned to full-time work just at the moment when all the circumstances point to such a necessity. But I have to do it without the agreement of the Shachtman-Abern-Carter combination, and with their insistence that no provisions of any kind be made to maintain me in this work. If you have a stomach for ironic jests, consider this one: Up till now there has always been a motion on the books that the national secretary shall receive wages. It is true he did not get them, but at any rate there was a promise to that effect, and by that the declaration of intentions. But when Cannon comes into the office he is confronted with a specific motion that he shall not even have the promise of any means to maintain his family, and more than that there is a campaign in the ranks against it. Swabeck and Oehler have put a statement into the records on this little matter. We shall see.

I have to break off now. More later. Write often and fully.

Fraternally yours,

[Jim]

The Left Opposition at Gillespie

Published February 11, 1933

The following article was published in the *Militant*.

One hundred and seventy delegates, more than half of whom came from the locals of the Progressive Miners of America, assembled at the conference in Gillespie, Illinois, on January 29 in response to the call of the Gillespie Trades and Labor Council, to discuss the project of a new federation of labor. The representation at the conference and the sentiments expressed by the great majority of the delegates gave a most emphatic confirmation to the estimate which the *Militant* had made of the new movement and of the proposal to organize a new trade union center. The conference revealed most convincingly that the organizational basis for a new general labor movement is by no means sufficient at the present time, and the project was taken off the agenda. Instead of that, a realistic program of agitation to coordinate the work of militants inside and outside the AFL was adopted.

This outcome of the conference should be a matter of great satisfaction to the militants throughout the country, who warmly support the new rise of the Progressive Miners movement and who feared that it might handicap itself at the beginning by a dangerous mistake. At the same time, both by its size and by its spirit, the conference refuted those conservative and sterile formalists, such as the right-wing Communists, who look upon the Progressive Miners organization as simply another unfortunate split. The conception of the Stalinists that the Progressive Miners of America is just another edition of the Lewis type of union could likewise find nothing to nourish it at the Gillespie conference.

The PMA, whose locals furnished the driving force and the bulk of the delegates at the Gillespie conference, is a movement pulsing with life. It is calling out new resources of proletarian energy and militancy, new hope and vision. In the course of epic struggles it is throwing up a cadre of new leaders from among the young miners who, if they still lack experience and ease of orientation in complicated problems, are by that uncorrupted and unspoiled by the deadening routine, conservatism, and treachery of the old bureaucracy. Behind them is a surging, militant rank and file. From all these aspects, one who looks at the Gillespie conference with a clear eye can see that although it could not constitute the basis for a new labor federation, it did nevertheless represent a significant step on the path of a regenerated labor movement, and contained forces which are destined to be a dynamic factor in advancing that movement.

The program adopted by the conference tallied very closely with that of the advanced left-wing labor elements nearly everywhere. Industrial unionism, shorter workday, unemployment insurance, trade union democracy, abolition of high wages for officials, class-struggle policies, relentless fight against labor fakers—all of these and similar demands, which are becoming the fighting program of insurgent workers in every section of the labor movement in all parts of the country, found their place also in the program of the Gillespie conference. In this fact is to be seen the best basis for the eventual fusion of the Illinois movement with similar movements in other parts of the country into a single national formation.

For various reasons this necessary unification of the scattered insurgent elements on a national scale remains to be realized. An organization, or a group of organizations, with sufficient stability and influence to attract the other scattered movements around it is one of the elements still lacking for this national concentration. The Gillespie conference and the forces represented in it could not yet serve this purpose. It could only contribute to the process. But the dynamic potentialities of a great role are there. The developments of the Progressive Miners in Illinois in the coming months may have a decisive bearing not only on the mining situation but also upon the whole left-wing and progressive labor movement of the entire country.

The importance and significance of the Gillespie conference derives primarily from the participation of the Progressive Miners of America. Not only from the top but also from the bottom, from the local unions, the fighting Illinois miners came to rub shoulders with delegates of other trades and take counsel with them. Here is a heartening sign, one of many signs, that the PMA stands higher and sees further than the previous district formation of insurgent miners. Still going through its own birth pangs as a union, the PMA already looks beyond the borders of its own industry and seeks alliance with the workers of other trades. And the participation of the rank and file, through delegates from the local unions, shows very clearly the genuine mass impulse behind the movement.

But if the domination of the conference by the Progressive Miners was the strength of the conference, then, in another sense of the word, it was also its weakness. The other delegations came from the small local craft unions and central bodies in the Illinois mining towns, and from left-wing groups which are still in the stage of propaganda rather than stable union organization. Such a combination can and should work out a common program of agitation. But on such a basis there can be no serious talk of a new labor federation.

The prospects of the new union represented at Gillespie are the prospects, first and foremost, of the Progressive Miners of America. If this new union survives the test of fire in the coming months and consolidates its organization more firmly in the struggle against the operators and the UMWA, it will by that fact lay a big section of the foundations of the new unionism. If the PMA goes down in the fight and loses its organizational base, the new union movement will receive the heaviest blow.

In other articles the specific tasks and problems of the PMA and its prospects for expansion into a wider field will be considered. In our opinion, the Progressive Miners movement in Illinois occupies at the present moment the key position in the unfolding of a new progressive sweep in the labor movement on a national scale. For that reason it deserves the closest attention of all those elements and tendencies which strive, or pretend to strive, in one way or another, to break the labor movement out of the paralyzing grip of the AFL bureaucrats. And by the same token, the worth of these various tendencies in the field of trade unionism can be judged most concretely by their attitude toward the activities and problems of the PMA, and especially by the answers they give to the questions which haven't been answered yet.

From this point of view it is interesting to note the position taken on the Gillespie conference by the various political groups. The Socialists, the CPLA, the Lovestoneites, the Stalinists, and the Left Opposition—all of them reacted to the Gillespie conference. But the only group that gave a clear and definite answer beforehand, and had its position confirmed to the letter by the experience of the conference itself, was the Communist Left Opposition.

That wing of the SP which trails along with the Progressive Miners and fattens itself parasitically on the blunders and crimes of the leadership of the official Communist Party, had nothing to say, and no advice to offer, about the project of a new federation of labor before the conference. As with the formation of the PMA itself, these parasites wait to see what luck the miners have with their ventures. If a given undertaking fails, they wash their hands of it; if it succeeds and sweeps a mass movement with it, they trail along and exploit it. And all the time they maintain a solidarity within one party with the Hillquits, who support Lewis and all the other black reactionaries.

The CPLA, which recommends itself as the center and leader of the progressive labor movement, also showed the quality of its leadership in the matter of the Gillespie conference. The recent issue of *Labor Age* printed the call for the Gillespie conference with its announced intention of "formulating a new federation of labor," without saying definitely what it thought about the project. Were the Musteites in favor of the proposal? Or against it? Or neutral? You will look in vain for a categoric answer in their publication before the event. And it is on just such questions that clear and categorical answers are required.

The comment of *Labor Age* implies a certain support for

the idea of a new federation of labor to be formed at the Gillespie conference. But the door is left open to face the other way, if things go wrong and the miners involve themselves in a serious mistake. In this attitude the Musteites ran true to form. In all their dabbling with the Illinois miners situation they have never failed to show this policy of halfwayness, by which they blunt the sharp edge of all the issues and muddle up the progressive movement from within. It is in the highest degree thanks to them that the Farrington-Howat betrayal was put over on the miners and the liberation movement against the Lewis bureaucracy was so long arrested and disoriented.[76] Let the Illinois miners who retain some confidence in these pseudoprogressives, after all their experience, ask themselves why the CPLA did not take a clear position and warn them against premature and dangerous experiments with a new federation of labor. By what right can they claim to be leaders if they can't answer such questions, and answer them at the right time?

The position of the Stalinist delegates in the Gillespie conference was indeed a spectacle for gods and men. A half a dozen or so delegates from TUUL groups in Chicago came to the Gillespie conference and gave the miners another occasion to scratch their heads in wonderment at this queer melange of contradiction and inconsistency, this combination of adventurous leaps and panicky retreats, which goes by the name of the trade union policy of Stalinism. The conduct of the Stalinist delegates at the conference was indeed a humiliating confession of bankruptcy and a complete repudiation of everything that they have done on the trade union field in the disastrous years of the "third period."

If the trade union policy of a political group is any good, it should reveal its strength precisely on such an occasion as the Gillespie conference, where workers' organizations are seeking an answer to new questions. Isn't that a fair test? The Left Opposition thought so, and that is why its representatives at the conference expounded there its trade union policy, not in a new edition but in the old one. Nothing that we said or did there stood in contradiction to the standpoint we have taken in the whole course of the development of the progressive labor movement in recent years. We are quite willing for the militant miners to judge the trade union policy of the Left Opposition not only in the light of what we said at the conference, but also in the light of what we said before the conference.

The Stalinists came to the conference under a heavy handicap. The best militants in the miners' organization were antagonistic to them, and for very good reasons. The Stalinists fought the opposition movement in the UMWA which laid the ground for the formation of the PMA. They fought the PMA, which represented a mass movement, and set up against it the National Miners Union, which did not exist in Illinois. They set up the TUUL as a new labor center in 1929, and since that time have been characterizing all unions that did not affiliate with it as "company unions." If these policies had been confirmed as correct by the development of the movement itself, the Gillespie conference was just the place to defend them and to make further proposals along the same lines. But there was the rub. The policies had been completely discredited in life and did not in any way fit the problem of the hour.

How did the Stalinist delegates get out of this contradiction between the whole policy of the recent years and the concrete needs of the moment? Very simply. They made a complete right-about-face on everything. And they did this without previous announcement or warning in the party press, without any acknowledgment of previous error; and they even kept, or tried to keep, straight faces through this bizarre performance. In the conference there were not a few conscious militants who follow all developments closely and take careful note of what each group and tendency stands for. But even these seasoned people, who were glad enough to see the old, ruinous policies discarded bag and baggage, regarded the spectacle with a certain amount of amusement and incredulity, as one watches a circus performer going through flip-flops and wonders how he does it.

If the party stands for the formation of a new labor movement, and if the TUUL is in fact the new labor center, as they have maintained since 1929, then why not urge the Gillespie conference to join the TUUL? That is certainly a logical conclusion—if the policy was a correct one. But the Stalinist delegates did not even mention the TUUL. More than that, they appeared there as the most vociferous opponents of any idea of the formation of a new general labor movement at the present time. They repeated all the arguments which the Left Opposition has been making on this question, the arguments which up to yesterday had been denounced as counterrevolutionary.

They went further than that. In their disorderly retreat from the discredited policy of yesterday, they arrived at such a conservative position, they argued so passionately against the danger of premature splits in the AFL unions, that they found themselves a number of times in alliance with the extreme right wing of the conference, with those who wanted only to let well enough alone and take no further progressive steps of any kind.

If the National Miners Union is the only organization of the progressive miners, and if the PMA is only an imitation of the Lewis union—as was maintained up till yesterday—then the Gillespie conference should have been made a forum for the advancement of this idea. But this policy had likewise gone to pieces on the rocks of reality. So . . . the National Miners Union was not mentioned by a single word. It is by such contradictions and zigzags that the Stalinists have succeeded in discrediting the Communist Party in the Illinois coal field and facilitating the revival of the Socialist organization.

The Left Oppositionists, who, by a consistently correct policy over a period of years and by a loyal participation in the struggles, have gained a certain influence and prestige in the Progressive Miners movement of Illinois, have great and unique tasks before them. They have to lift up the banner of communism, which has been trampled in the mire, and make the miners understand that the monstrous blunders and crimes of the recent years are not an expression of communism but of the Stalinist perversion of it. In view of the annihilation of the party organization in southern Illinois, they are obliged to fulfill the natural functions of the party: to conduct the direct struggle against the reformist elements for the decisive influence in the movement. They have to take upon themselves directly the initiative and the leading role in the organization of a strong left wing which will steer the new movement firmly on the path of a class-struggle policy.

The destiny of the Progressive Miners movement of Illinois depends on this. And conversely, the chances of an early revival of the communist movement and organization among the miners, under the direct leadership of the Left Opposition, depends upon the complete identity of its own interests with the fundamental interests of the miners' movement. The Left Oppositionists at the Gillespie conference were animated by this fundamental conception and made it the starting point of new plans and new endeavors. Great things can follow.

Above, Gerry Allard, Vincent R. Dunne; below, Max Shachtman, Albert Weisbord.

Show by concrete example what we can do

February 11, 1933

The following letter was written to Gerry Allard.

Dear Comrade Allard,

The new German situation burst over our heads and swamped us so that I didn't get an opportunity to write you before.[77] I still hold to the plan we worked out there, but it will probably be some weeks before it will be possible for me to get away from the National Office. Meantime, we are sending Comrade Oehler on a tour which will bring him to Gillespie on March 6. The decision is that he is to remain there for organizing work in the coal field. I hope to be able to come soon afterward and to carry out the plan we agreed on with full force.

Oehler, as you know, is an experienced organizer and will be a big help to us in this work. In addition to that, he can be very useful in conducting classes to educate the young miners in the principles of Marxism if we can succeed in organizing classes in the various towns.

Our general plan is to hook the mining campaign of the league onto the present campaign we are making on Germany and gradually to bring it forward as the one big campaign of the league in the field of mass work. Up till now, it has been acknowledged that the league is a good critical group and is strong in questions of policy. But many people believe that we are not good for practical work in the class struggle. And now we have to show by concrete example what we can do in this field, and the Illinois mine field is the best place to begin.

I was greatly enthused and inspired by my visit there, and I feel sure that we will be able to work together and do great things for the miners' movement and our own political group at the same time.

I have some good news for you. We are in touch with a comrade who can supply some excellent material in the way of an economic analysis of the coal industry, of the profits made, of the effects of the new machinery on the profit rate, of the interlocking ownership of the various mines and companies, of the difference in the profit rate between the organized and unorganized fields, etc. Now this is Comrade B.J. Field. I spoke to him today and he said he would be glad to send you material regularly for the *Progressive Miner*. What he wants first of all is some concrete information about the names of the mining companies in the Illinois field—union and nonunion. He worked for years on Wall Street financial journals and if he has the names of the companies, he will trace down their Wall Street connections and show who they are and who is back of them. Send this information along, and you will soon receive some articles from him on this and other points.

I am somewhat disturbed about the problems which are going to arise for the PMA in connection with the renewal of the contract. Here it is necessary to gauge very accurately the strength of the organization and the general conditions when the demands are formulated. "Radicalism" is not proved by making more extreme demands than others, but by formulating demands which are realistic and realizable in a concrete situation, taking the relation of forces as it is. I think you and your closest coworkers should give some serious thought to this question and be ready with some proposals which you can stand on. We will be glad to hear from you about this and to contribute our opinion.

Give my warmest regards to all the comrades and tell them I hope to be with them again, and for a protracted period, before very long.

Yours fraternally,

[James P. Cannon]
Secretary

External advances, internal turmoil

February 11, 1933

The following letter was written to Arne Swabeck in Europe.

Dear Arne:

The developments here since your departure necessitate a supplement to your report on the activities of the league. The conditions for the rapid expansion of the league are breaking favorably in all directions and we are doing our best to keep step with the opportunities. In doing so we confront an internal contradiction which can endanger, and even negate altogether, the gains that are ours to grasp.

On the one side, thanks to the favorable developments of external conditions and our previous work of preparation, the decisive turn of our main activity from propaganda to agitation is well under way. On the other side, this transformation has not resulted—as many comrades hoped—in a moderation of our internal crisis. On the contrary. It has intensified and accentuated it in the highest degree. The moment in which the NC, taking advantage of the external situation, points the league toward a most energetic intervention in the general class struggle, is the moment which has called forth the most violent factional struggle against it.

The successes and the widespread effects of the new activities we have unfolded are indubitable, and have been registered on three fronts—in the unemployment movement, in the Illinois miners' movement, and in the German campaign—and have had widespread general effect. The turn of the party toward a broader policy in the unemployment movement found us prepared, and we took full advantage of the democratic rights granted to us for the first time in four and a half years. The Left Opposition appeared at two of the united front conferences in New York, and on each occasion the conference discussion revolved almost entirely around our resolutions and speeches. In the same period, in connection with the trade union conference at Gillespie, Illinois, we decided to take a bold step toward a real and direct participation in the trade union movement. The decision of the National Committee to send me to this conference—a distance of 1,200 miles from New York—signified in itself a big advance from the purely literary intervention in the trade union movement. The results fully justified the step from every standpoint. I was given the opportunity to speak at the conference and also at a mass meeting of miners which took place in connection with it. My visit there was also the occasion for lengthy discussions with a number of selected left-wing militants in regard to the policy of the new miners' union and the problem of organizing a firm left wing within it. We came to an agreement for a plan of work over a period of some months, which centers around the proposal of the miners that I should return to the field to lead and organize the campaign. About this project I will write separately. But here I wish to remark that the project has aroused great enthusiasm among the left-wing miners and a pledge on their part to work with me in a disciplined formation to build a left-wing movement and a network of branches of the league within it.

From the *Militant* you will learn of the great campaign we are unfolding on the German situation and the decision to publish the *Militant* in a half-size edition three times a week. This involves a tremendous strain on us, as you can imagine. All the more so since it is combined with a broad program of mass meetings and a national tour of Comrade Oehler. The results are astounding. Our bold steps have thrown the Stalinists into a panic and the LO is on the offensive everywhere. Our mass meeting in the Bronx last Sunday, the first indoor meeting we ever held there, was packed to the doors. Close to 500 were present— the majority of them party members and sympathizers of the party. The answering of questions lasted until one o'clock in the morning. The whole affair was a political triumph for us. Similarly with my meeting in Philadelphia last week—the largest meeting the LO has ever held there. Tomorrow night we invade Brooklyn with a mass meeting.

The three recent advances—in the unemployment movement, in the Illinois miners' situation, and in the German campaign—have had a remarkable effect on our sympathizers and half sympathizers, and this is reflected in a considerable improvement in our financial crisis. We are still under a heavy strain in this respect, but it is due entirely to the new expenses and obligations we have incurred in the expanded activities. The crisis on the old basis that confronted us at the turn of the year appears now to have been solved. If we do not suffer a letdown or reaction as a result of our internal contradictions, we will soon be on the highroad.

But this is just the danger that must be considered. The

faction struggle against the National Committee has flared up again more fiercely than ever and has taken on even more venomous personal forms even than you were able to witness before your departure. And this takes place under conditions when nobody finds anything wrong with the policy of the committee or brings forward any "political differences" with regard to our course in general or the specific campaign in particular.

Example: The announcement of my delegation to the Gillespie conference, formally agreed to by unanimous vote in the National Committee, called forth a furious agitation against the "flying trip" and a sabotage of the special fund to finance it. At that branch meeting in New York, Weber, Bleeker, and others attempted to shift the discussion to the alleged neglect of the mining situation last summer and to the vilest personal attacks on Swabeck and Cannon. Up to the last moment I lacked the bus fare to make the trip, and finally managed to get away only by securing the personal loan of a comrade's house rent money for one week.

The success of the trip, the enthusiasm which it aroused among the miners and in Chicago, Cleveland, and Buffalo, where I stopped off on my return journey (at Buffalo I succeeded in organizing a new branch of the league with eleven members), did not in the least moderate the internal antagonisms. The New York branch meeting which followed our great mass meeting on Germany and the announcement to bring out the *Militant* three times a week was the scene of such venomous factionalism as neither you nor I ever witnessed in our party experience. Hermann, for example, took that occasion to accuse Cannon of "practicing Stalinism." Several times during this meeting it was on the verge of breaking out in fist fights among the comrades; and yet, I repeat, nobody challenged the correctness of the general policy of the NC, of its policies in the special campaign under way, nor its method of conducting them. The occasion for this display was the discussion of the resolution on proletarianization, which finally came up on the agenda after such a long delay. The single proposal to take in no petty-bourgeois elements for the period of six months called forth an attack against the NC which sponsored the proposal, and against us personally, that cannot be described in words. All the militancy that has been so painfully lacking in the struggle against the Stalinists, especially in the needle trades, was supplied with double measure against us. Is that because we have faltered in the struggle against the Stalinists and thereby justify such a hostility within our own ranks? On the contrary. The bureaucrats of Stalinism have found it necessary to intensify their own attacks on us, and especially on me personally. In their own way, Browder, Hathaway, and Company have intervened in our internal struggle. And not on our side. In the *Daily Worker* of January 27 (city edition) there was a fulmination, primarily against the "demagogic" Cannon, in connection with our appearance at the united front unemployment conference. I had to hear the same accusations, in almost the same words, at the branch meeting.

Hathaway summed up his long article as follows: "The Chicago experience manifests the need of watchfulness to prevent the Socialist and renegade leaders, especially Cannon himself, from disrupting the workers' fighting front."

And to that there is a still more interesting sequel. At the second meeting of the united front conference, where I again appeared as the leader of our delegates, the Stalinist steering committee nominated Comrade Bleeker as a member of the permanent executive committee of fifteen. I also stood as a candidate, with the following result:

I received twelve votes—the same twelve votes that were cast for our resolution; Bleeker received the unanimous vote of the conference, following the lead of the Stalinist steering committee. What does such an incident signify from a political point of view?

The aggravation of the internal crisis since your departure, in the midst of new campaigns, will very probably be no surprise to you, since it does not contradict but rather confirms the estimate we made before. Those comrades who wanted to construe the internal struggle as a mere misunderstanding or personal quarrel which should be altogether liquidated by the immersion of the league in mass agitation, are proving to be poor analysts and prophets. I do believe that the new course of our work will be a powerful factor in the solution of the crisis, but that solution will not come of itself and independent of the internal struggle. The mass activity, it is to be hoped, will bring an influx of new proletarian elements into the league, which will strengthen the position of the politically principled group, just as the internal struggle against unprincipledness and clique formations creates the necessary conditions for a real development of the league in the class struggle.

I am convinced more than ever, as we have repeated many times, that our internal dispute cannot be resolved in debate alone. The debates and the debaters must be put to a test, and we are bent on shifting the issue to this ground. We plan to make the Illinois mine situation the central campaign of the league in the field of direct mass work. Hugo is going out there, and later, if it appears feasible for me to leave the office for a while, I will go also. All of our close friends are in favor of such a step, with the perspective of moving our center to Chicago and putting a firm proletarian base under the National Committee. On this point I will write you in more detail later.

Resolution on the Red Army and the German revolution[78]

March 1, 1933

The following resolution was submitted to the National Committee and later published in the Internal Bulletin.

The Left Opposition takes the following position on the question of the Red Army and the German situation:

The Red Army exists to defend the conquests of the October revolution and to aid in extending this revolution to other countries. The Red Army is not only the arm of the Soviet Union as it exists at the present time within the territorial limits of old Russia (and not even the whole of that), but it is in the fullest sense of the word the arm of the international proletariat.

In the international class struggle the bourgeoisie in every country threatened by a revolution of the proletariat counts on and receives international support—economic, financial, political, and, in case of need, military. This is particularly true of the countries contiguous to the present Soviet Union, such as Poland, Romania, Finland, etc.

It is true also of Germany. The German proletariat, in the impending civil war, is entitled to, and must receive, the same international support from the international working class.

Included in the international working class is the Soviet Union and its Red Army. The method by which this international working-class support is extended to the German proletariat in its revolutionary struggle—moral, political, economic, military—and the *nature* and the *time* of the specific actions, or combination of actions—is determined exclusively by practical, strategic, and tactical considerations, which flow out of the circumstances of the moment, the relation of international class forces, etc. Military action, which is nothing but the extension of politics, is not only not excluded, but in case of need and at a certain conjuncture, must be definitely and positively included in the genuine international concept of the question of the Red Army and the German revolution. Moreover, the role of the Red Army cannot be exclusively a *defensive* one with respect to the present territorial limits of the Soviet Union, but under certain conditions can and must be an *offensive* one.

These fundamental internationalist considerations—concerning which there can be no two opinions in our ranks—determine our attitude toward the problem of the Red Army and the German revolution as it would be posed concretely in the event of a fascist victory in Germany. For the Red Army to remain passive while the German working class is crushed under the heel of fascism, its organizations annihilated, and its capacity for resistance destroyed for a number of years, would not only create the conditions for a world imperialist assault against the Soviet Union, led by German fascism, and endanger the existence of the former. It would signify in no small degree a colossal betrayal of the German and consequently of the whole international proletariat, on the part of the Stalinist leadership. For the Left Opposition to keep silent in the face of a policy that leads objectively in this direction, for it to retreat to a presentation of the question from the point of view simply of the *self-defense* of the present Soviet Union, would be to make itself a party to this historical betrayal.

Theoretical considerations, and the Polish experience of 1920, show that the Red Army cannot *make the revolution* in an important capitalist country.[79] For it to intervene successfully there must be a conjuncture of the rising of the proletariat and such a relation of the class forces locked in mortal combat that the Red Army appears on the scene as the reinforcement of the rising proletariat, its ally against the murderous violence of the armed class enemy at home and its protector against the armed intervention of foreign imperialist forces. This conjuncture does not exist as yet in Germany, and for that reason the International Left Opposition concentrates its present policy in the main on the internal action of the German proletariat and makes no demand for the immediate intervention of the Red Army. At the same time it explains openly and fearlessly the inevitable part the Red Army must play in a further development of events. By this it warns the Soviet Union to get ready and it encourages the German proletariat by reminding it of its own international resources and allies.

The agitation of the American Stalinists to the effect that "the Red Army is international in the sense that the workers of other countries will eventually join it"; of Wicks, that the German workers must complete their own revolution and organize their own Red Army without the direct aid of the existing Red Army of the Soviet Union, and that the elucidation of the true international role of the Red Army by the Left Opposition is "provocation for a war on the Soviet Union"—in all this agitation of the Stalinists there are contained the most reactionary national socialist conceptions and an ideological preparation to sanction a colossal betrayal. The spirit of this agitation is, in essence, the spirit of August 4, 1914.[80] This the Left Opposition must say out loud.

The motion on policy "with regard to the present situation in Germany and the role of the Red Army" introduced by Comrade Shachtman at the NC meeting on February 24 is a capitulatory retreat before the pogrom agitation of the Stalinists around this question. The document of Comrade Shachtman is made all the worse by the introductory acknowledgments of the international role of the Red Army in "principle." The question is *concrete* and *specific*. It is not now a problem of the right and duty of the Red Army to be ready to "carry out revolutionary tasks" in some indefinite place beyond the "frontiers" of the present Soviet republic. The place is Germany. And the question is: the revolutionary tasks of the Red Army in the German revolution.

Likewise must be rejected in the present situation the negative and defensive approach to the question contained in such apologetic formulas as "The communists cannot entertain any objections in principle" and "The Communist International in the Leninist epoch *did not consider it wrong* in principle." The Left Opposition does not fulfill its duty in the given situation with general explanation to the effect that it has no "objection" and that it does not "consider it wrong" for the Red Army to cross the artificial national boundary lines established by the relationship of international class forces at a certain period. It is specifically the German revolution that is involved in the present instance. Not what we "have no objections" to, not what we "do not consider wrong," but what we consider *right*, what we consider *necessary* at a certain stage in the developments of the German civil war—this is the way the Left Opposition must approach the question.

Comrade Trotsky has explained with sufficient lucidity the direct menace to the Soviet Union that would follow inevitably from a fascist victory and consolidation in Germany, and the necessity of mobilizing the Red Army at the first news of a fascist state revolution. But he did not stop, as Comrade Shachtman's motion does, with the *self-defense* side of the question. The quotation cited from Trotsky is not complete—and therefore it is false—when it leaves out the sentences which followed it in reference to the offensive side of the same question: "The Red Army is not only the Red Army. It is the arm of the proletarian world revolution" *(Germany—The Key to the International Situation.)*[81] Our dispute with the Stalinists over the Red Army hinges precisely on this aspect of the question. They shall not drive us away from it.

Comrade Shachtman declares: "The International Left Opposition has not, however, and does not now raise the demand that *at the present time*, in the situation as it is *today*, with the *present* relationship of forces, the Red Army is to be mobilized for the purpose of 'marching on Germany' now." That is quite true. And it could not be otherwise as long as the Left Opposition retains its conception that the role of the existing Red Army is to *help* the workers in revolution in other countries, and not to make their revolution for them.

But who has raised the demand for a "march on Germany" "*at the present time*" "in the situation as it is *today*," etc.? Moreover, who of any serious consequence in the league, who in its leadership, which—it is assumed—is composed of grown-up people who do not lose their heads at every turn in the situation—who among these could raise such a demand? If nobody has done so—and we know of nobody—then what is the necessity for such a solemn denunciation of the idea? Why is it necessary to protest that we regard the "propagation" of this slogan as "out of harmony with the tactical line of the International Left Opposition on Germany today"? Why is it necessary to make this the central point of our policy?

We know that the Stalinists have *imputed* this slogan to us. They are inciting a pogrom against us on this ground—on the ground that we are "provoking a war on the Soviet Union." But the Stalinists are liars, and the way to answer them is to say they are liars, to show how *by this very agitation* they cover their own national socialism, and to explain fully, clearly, and boldly what the internationalist standpoint of the Left Opposition on the question of the Red Army and the German revolution really is. To react to the Stalinist slander by denouncing the viewpoint they falsely impute to us is not the best way to meet the reactionary incitement of our opponents. More precisely, it is the worst way.

The concessions which Comrade Shachtman makes to the pogrom agitation of the Stalinists increase progressively in every paragraph of his motions on policy. Beginning with a defensive general premise about our lack of "objections" (instead of a positive statement of our principal views), he glides, in the next paragraph, to the denunciation of the slogan for an immediate "march on Germany" (which nobody proposed), and then draws nearer to the position of the Stalinists in the next paragraph with the more direct statement that "the premature advancing of such a slogan, before civil war in Germany has appeared unmistakably, means laying the ILO open to the charge, on the part of the official CP of provocation to precipitate a war on the Soviet Union." (Nothing less!)

Already, we are not only accused by the Stalinists of provoking war on the Soviet Union, but we (or someone among us, name unknown!) are "laying ourselves open" to this monstrous accusation. Perhaps that is why, in his motions on policy "with regard to the present situation," as well as in his journalistic comments in the *Militant*, Comrade Shachtman has not devoted a single word to the slander of the Stalinists, has not answered it, has not called it slander, and has not seen fit to print my article on the subject. What he has written in the document under consideration is not an answer to this slander. It is a supplement to it. But what the members of the Left Opposition require from an NC motion which is "to be sent to all branches as a guiding line of the league for the work of all its members and spokesmen" (Who are these mysterious spokesmen?), is advice on how to meet the pogrom agitation of the Stalinists, *how to refute it*, and, above all, *how to explain its fundamentally reactionary content.*

Comrade Shachtman's motion in no way serves this purpose. And in the next paragraph of his document, following after that referred to above, Comrade Shachtman expounds a view which has nothing in common with ours and has very little to distinguish it from the standpoint of the Stalinists. It is possible that Comrade Shachtman has written it hastily and will clarify his position and formulate it in a different—that is, in an opposite—sense. It is to be hoped that he will do so. But as the formulation stands now, we can under no circumstances accept it "as the guiding line of the league" and "all its members," not overlooking its "spokesmen."

"This slogan," he says (immediate mobilization of the Red Army), "clearly aims to warn the Soviet Union to prepare in good time to defend itself." The necessity of preparation for such self-defense is of course correct, self-evident, and obvious, and there is not a Stalinist from Stalin's cabinet to Browder's private office who will object to the Soviet Union "defending itself." But this slogan (for the immediate mobilization of the Red Army) aims to do more than that. And when Comrade Shachtman concludes: "War in that case comes not on the basis of a Red Army marching into Germany, but because the international Brown Shirts are marching on the Soviets," he stops precisely at that point where the difference between internationalism and national socialism on this particular question begins.

The *essence* of Comrade Trotsky's warnings on the inevitable war between the Soviet Union and a victorious German fascism consists precisely in this, that the Soviet Union *must not wait* until the fascists "are marching on the Soviets" but must strike them down before they are ready. The *"self-defense" of the Soviet Union* in this case merges completely into the *offensive struggle against German fascism* and the *defense of the German revolution*. The schematic separation of these three aspects of one and the same question is the heart of the falsity in the policy, dangerous and even treacherous in its implications, which is expounded by the American Stalinists. Comrade Shachtman, retreating before the Stalinist incitement and "looking for deviations" in his own camp, offers a formula "as the guiding line of the league" which would make it follow the Stalinists as a captive on this fundamental issue.

The discussion of the role of the Red Army in the German revolution must take into account, at the present time, diplomatic and military considerations which dictate a certain tact in public utterances. But for all that, the internationalists must speak in such a way as not to confuse and mislead the proletariat but to inform it and put it on guard. Trotsky, writing in the bourgeois press (the *Forum* magazine article reprinted in *Militant* of July

16, 1932) showed how to do this even within the restricted limits of this medium.[82] Contrary to Shachtman, who counterposes the "march on Germany" to the march on the Soviets, Trotsky wrote:

> When you have a mortal enemy before you, and when war flows with necessity from the logic of the objective situation, it would be unpardonable light-mindedness to give that enemy time to establish and fortify himself, conclude the necessary alliances, receive the necessary help, work out a plan of concentric military actions, not only from the west but from the east, and thus grow up to the dimensions of a colossal danger.
>
> Hitler's shock troops are already singing all over Germany a marching song against the Soviets, composed by a certain Doctor Hans Buchner. It would be imprudent to let the fascists drawl this martial air. *If they are destined to sing it, let them sing staccato.* [Our emphasis]

Between this estimate of the problem, which makes its meaning clear even through the screen of the capitalist press, and the estimate of Comrade Shachtman, written with all the frankness that is possible in a document for internal circulation in the league, there is a wide abyss. The NC can do no other than categorically reject the whole presentation of the question by Comrade Shachtman. The present resolution is submitted from this point of view—as a statement of policy different from that expounded by Comrade Shachtman and against it.

The gross perversion of principle in Comrade Shachtman's motion can be fully understood only in its setting in the present internal crisis of the league. Comrade

Shachtman is not a Stalinist. We are convinced that he is no less hostile to their policies in general than we are, and that he has no more intention of capitulating to them than we have. If he retreats before them in this particular issue, and expounds a position that is nearer to their standpoint than to ours—and that is indubitably the case in the single question at issue—it is the result primarily of the indefensible and hopeless position he has taken in the internal faction struggle.

Embarking on a fight against the NC without any "political differences" and organizing a faction without a political platform, he inevitably gathered around himself all those elements in the league who are in conflict with the NC. In this unprincipled faction struggle Comrade Shachtman attracted and became the rallying center for the confused, politically backward, and casual elements, for those who resist all organizational restraint and discipline, and also those elements who have not completely broken their ideological bonds with Stalinism, who are impressed by the agitation of the Stalinist bureaucrats, and transmit, in one form or another, their ideas and their slander into the league.

These latter elements, who register the pressure of the Stalinist agitation against us outside the league by the volume and intensity of their unbridled agitation against the NC inside the league—as a seismograph records earthquake shocks—are beginning to exert an increasing influence on the policy of the Shachtman faction, which is compelled by the logic of its position to yield more and more to these dubious political elements within it, who really disagree with the NC on more than one question. Among these, the elements who differ with us in the direction of Stalinism are naturally the most aggressive, because behind them and their half-thought-out and half-spoken ideas is the weight and pressure of the Stalinist campaign. Their influence on the policy of the Shachtman faction is recorded in the present instance—and not for the first time.

A persistence with the present unprincipled faction combination cannot fail to bring further divergences and sharper conflicts with the NC and all those in the league who are firm in their convictions and united on the basis of them. The Shachtman faction began—and still remains—without a separate platform. On this basis it is impossible to continue for any length of time, and this fact is evidently becoming clear to the leaders of the faction. They are beginning to look for "differences," to exaggerate them, and to manufacture them where they do not exist. The experiment "with regard to the present situation in Germany and the question of the role of the Red Army" is a shocking revelation of the dangers which bestrew this path. It gives the comrades who have been supporting the unprincipled struggle against the NC—as well as the leader—an occasion to pause and reflect on its logic and its inevitable consequences, and to turn back in due time.

THE MILITANT

Official Organ of The Communist League of America (Opposition)

DURING THE GERMAN CRISIS THE MILITANT APPEARS 3 TIMES A WEEK!

WORKERS OF THE WORLD, UNITE

VOLUME VI, NO. 8 [WHOLE NO. 155]   NEW YORK, WEDNESDAY, FEBRUARY 15, 1933   PRICE 1 CENT

Hitler Is Consolidating the Power of Fascism In Germany! Whoever Blocks the Workers' United Front Is a Traitor!

Scottsb'ro Frame-Up Laid Bare

CHARGE OF "RAPE" PROVED TO BE UNFOUNDED; LETTER OF GIRL NOW PUBLISHED

Hitler Threat to Soviet Union

ANALYSIS SHOWS THAT CONTRADICTIONS IN POLITICS OF HITLERISM DRIVES IT TO AN ALLIANCE WITH THE OTHER IMPERIALISTS FOR AN ASSAULT UPON SOVIET UNION

Nazis Murder 11 Workers

Fascism: Italian and German

COMPARISON BETWEEN ITALIAN FASCISM OF 1922 AND THE HITLERITE MOVEMENT OF TODAY SHOWS POSSIBILITIES FOR SUCCESSFUL COUNTER MOVEMENT OF PROLETARIAT

Millions to Be Jobless Perman'tly

ARMY OF UNEMPLOYED SWELLS; ASSERTS HEAD OF A. F. OF L., WM. GREEN

Test of Ruhr Letter

OPEN FORUM

"WHY MUST THE NEEDLE TRADES"

SOCIETY DEVELOPMENTS IN THE PARTY AND LEFT UNIONS
The Policy of the Left Opposition
By J. P. CANNON
Friday, F'by 17th, PIERRE 8 PM
138 East 14th Street
AUSPICES:
N. Y. Br. Communist League of America (Opposition)

Oehler Tour this Week

Suspend 19 C.C.N.Y. Students

B'KLYN MASS MEETING   **"The CRISIS IN GERMANY"**   James P. Cannon   Max Shachtman   **Labor Lyceum**

The conflict sharpens

March 2, 1933

The following letter was written to the International Secretariat and Leon Trotsky.

Dear Comrades:

Enclosed herewith you will find the copies of NC minutes nos. 134, 135, and 136.

Your attention is especially directed to the motion by Comrade Shachtman attached to minutes no. 135 regarding our policy on the Red Army and the German revolution, and the resolution on the same subject by Cannon attached to minutes no. 136. Also to the decision in minutes no. 136 to discuss this question in the Internal Bulletin.

In minutes no. 135 you will note the attached motion by Comrade Shachtman on the question of our policy in the Illinois mining campaign, and the statement by Cannon that he will submit a counterproposal. This counterresolution will be forwarded without much delay—as soon as I find time to draft it.[83]

In other parts of the enclosed minutes you will see that the conflict in the NC of the American league is becoming sharper, and that it is beginning to take a political form. These official records reflect, in a somewhat moderated form, the still more violent antagonisms brought out especially in the verbal discussion in the New York branch meetings.

The statements on the differences which were requested from each group in the leadership by the international preconference are to be prepared and forwarded in the near future.

With communist greetings,

[James P. Cannon]
Secretary

Speech at Albany unemployed conference[84]

March 6, 1933

The following speech was published in the March 10, 1933, *Militant*.

Comrades and fellow-workers:

We meet here in the fourth year of the crisis which has brought the most appalling misery and privation to the masses and which is profoundly affecting the entire working class. The terrible and unprecedented conditions are undermining the workers' accustomed standards of life. They are destroying all their security of existence, such as it was, and are putting before them, in ever more categorical terms, the necessity of seeking a way out by new methods and means. In such a situation this conference of 346 delegates from 248 workers' organizations can serve as a starting point in a significant movement of working-class resistance, or it can remain a mere episode soon passed over and forgotten. It is for us to decide which it shall be. It depends in the highest degree on the success we achieve in pointing out the way to the impoverished masses, and in working out the methods and means of uniting with them in the struggle.

In order for us to give the right answer to this question, which is of such crucial importance, we must first see the situation as it really is. And at the very beginning we must discard any illusions about the real nature and composition of our conference. To talk as though the conference represented the unemployed millions of New York State, or even a numerically significant section of them, is a sure way of condemning all the deliberations of the conference to futility. The real class movement of the workers against the scourge of unemployment does not yet exist on any wide scale.

The movement which is on its feet and attempting to struggle against conditions of the crisis remains, in the fourth year of the crisis, primarily and almost exclusively a movement of the class-conscious vanguard. The composition of this conference, called together after the most extensive preparation and agitation, is the most eloquent testimony to this fact. In this there is nothing fatal if we recognize the fact; if we do not deceive ourselves with illusions about a united front movement which does not as yet exist in reality.

The composition of the conference determines its specific tasks. To me it is quite obvious that general agitation against the evils of unemployment is unnecessary here, since everybody is already convinced. There has been enough, if not too much, of this already. There is very little doubt that the conference is ready now, without any further discussion, to endorse the most radical demands, and the social revolution too. If someone should move a resolution for the dictatorship of the proletariat, in order to test the sentiments of the conference, there is no doubt that the overwhelming majority, if not every single delegate here, would vote for it with both hands. In its composition it is a conference of the vanguard.

The important and decisive questions for such a conference are the questions of program, perspectives, and tactics. From this point of view I shall undertake to analyze the situation as the Left Opposition sees it, and from which our proposals flow. The crisis is preparing the ground for a great resurgence of the American working class. The cynical indifference of the capitalist rulers to the plight of the hungry masses, the paltry relief doled out as charity, the savage wage cuts and other aggressions on the one hand, and the bankruptcy of all the capitalist panaceas for overcoming the crisis on the other—all this is producing in the depths of the working and unemployed masses the most profound resentment and dissatisfaction. The necessary conditions for the transformation of the psychology of the working class, for its political awakening and its emergence as a class on the road of the class struggle, are maturing rapidly; to a certain extent they have already matured.

The furious resentment of the workers is accumulating to the breaking point, preparing the way for a great explosion of working-class protest. Of decisive importance to facilitate this are the program, the tactics, and the perspective. The present conference has to be conceived not as the culmination but rather as a point of departure in the struggle to get a real class movement of the working and unemployed masses on foot.

The hesitation of the masses to express their profound resentment at the terrible conditions imposed upon them in the crisis in aggressive struggles on a broad scale, which up to now has been one of the most outstanding characteristics of the situation, has certain causes. The mass unemployment overwhelmed the employed workers with a sense of insecurity and helplessness, and served as a deterrent to actions on their part. In addition to that, the absence of any organized movement of the unemployed on a sufficiently large scale, and the disunity in such movements as have existed, have operated to paralyze the development of a real class movement. All this does not preclude the possibility of a change in the attitude of the workers, and that in comparatively short time.

The program for the translation of the mass discontent and resentment of the employed and unemployed workers into class actions on a broad scale and for the fusion of their interests and their actions in a common struggle, centers around the following main demands:

1. Immediate relief.

2. Unemployment insurance, to be paid for by the employers and the government.

3. The six-hour day and the five-day week without reduction in pay.

4. Long-term, large-scale credits to the Soviet Union, as a means of unemployment relief for the American workers and the cementing of fraternal bonds between the American and Russian workers. This implies the demand for the recognition of the Soviet government and the establishment of trade relations with it.

The tactic by means of which the scattered, separate movements can be welded into one, and the still inactive masses can be drawn into the struggle, is the tactic of the united front. The united front tactic aims to bring about common action of various workers' organizations, trade unions, and parties. It proposes their joint action in a common movement for immediate aims. It is addressed to the official organizations as well as to the rank-and-file members, and puts the leaders to the concrete test of struggle.

Without this tactic, the reformist leaders who disrupt and sabotage the movement escape unpunished, they continue to deceive large masses of workers with empty phrases and to thwart their desire for united struggle. On the other side, without the tactic of the united front, the actions organized under the leadership of the revolutionary workers remain isolated vanguard actions; they do not succeed in reaching the less awakened workers and drawing them into the fight; and, consequently, they fail to exert the necessary class pressure on the capitalists and their government.

The present composition of the Albany conference (almost exclusively Communist and left-wing delegates) is the most striking illustration and warning on this question. A decisive turn to the genuine tactic of the united front is the most imperative need now for the further development of the movement. The actions of the impoverished and hunger-driven masses, which can follow with accelerated speed and accumulating force from the program and tactic laid down above, must now primarily take the form of demonstrations which really unite wide masses in struggle. The appearance at the state legislature must not be conceived as an end in itself, but as a means of popularizing and stimulating these mass demonstrations.

Such demonstrations, in the next stage of the movement—to the extent that they really involve broad masses and bring a class force to bear—can put upon the capitalist rulers a pressure which they have not felt up till now. These demonstrations can force concessions from the capitalists and compel them to pause before further onslaughts on the workers out of fear of giving a further stimulus to the movement. Moreover, such united demonstrations, increasing in size and militancy and gaining visible results in the concrete cases (as, for example, in Chicago), will enormously strengthen the morale of the masses, increase their self-confidence, and lead, in turn, to broader, bolder, and stormier demonstrations.

On this road, the hesitating mood of the masses and their more or less passive discontent can be rapidly transformed into the impulse for active resistance all along the line. The moment this decisive turn in the situation is clearly recorded, new and vast perspectives will be opened up. The increased self-confidence that will follow from the first successes in the demonstrations of the unemployed, can be rapidly reflected among the employed workers in the industries in the impulse to resist further aggressions on their already unbearable standards. This can lead to economic actions of the employed workers, to local strikes on the basis of concrete local grievances, to the combination of these economic actions with the political demonstrations of the unemployed masses, and to the reciprocal influence of these movements upon each other. In face of continued wage cuts, which raise the workers' resentment to the explosive point, the multiplication of such strike actions is quite possible. In such an event, and on the basis of a stormily developing strike movement, a demonstrative general strike of short duration is not excluded.

The general strike, however, is not an agitational slogan for the present.[85] An adventurous playing with the slogan of the general strike at the present time can only operate to prevent the development of the elemental workers' movement on the basis of those demands and actions which are appropriate to the present situation and the present stage. The general-strike formula cannot be substituted for the preliminary partial actions necessary to prepare the conditions for it. We must not attempt to compensate for the failure or the inability to organize a broad movement on the most elementary basis with big talk about a general strike.

The Left Opposition in Springfield

March 15, 1933

The following letter was written to Joe Angelo in Springfield, Illinois.

Dear Joe:

We are overjoyed at the formation of a branch of the Left Opposition in Springfield. I hope it signalizes the beginning of a transformation of the work of the Left Opposition in the coal fields. The building up of this branch and others like it is the absolute, indispensable condition for us to play any serious role in the mining situation. The Left Opposition does not function at all until it begins to function in an organized way. . . . Under separate cover I am sending you a mimeographed copy of the outline for a study class in communist fundamentals.

I received your letter of March 13 regarding the Webb case today.[86] Isn't this a good issue to begin some pressure inside the PMA? It seems to me it would be a mistake to start an independent movement outside the union, since he was arrested on the picket line. From a tactical point of view, this pressure on the union is preferable to appealing to the ILD. I would suggest that you write an article for the *Progressive Miner*, and also that you ask Allard to write a short editorial on the case. Better still, write the article yourself and ask Gerry if he will run it on the editorial page.

I noticed with considerable apprehension the statement on policy by the Taylorville Defense Committee in a recent issue of the *Progressive Miner*.[87] The half-and-half reformist elements seem to dominate the policy. That would not be so bad if there were any signs of a class-struggle opposition. We must become articulate in the union and especially in the paper. It would be a good idea for the new Springfield branch of the Left Opposition to adopt a resolution of solidarity with the Taylorville prisoners and in favor of a big demonstrative protest movement of the miners and other workers before the trial, not after it. It also would have the highest value if contributions from you representing a communist class point of view began to appear regularly in the paper. Every kind of reformist muddlehead seems to have free access to air his views there. It is high time for the communists to be heard from. As I have written you before, it will be far better if the voice of communist criticism is heard inside union ranks and in the paper. If it can't be done there, we will have to do it in the *Militant*.

I intend to write you at considerable length on the question of policy in the PMA. In the meantime, I would appreciate a line from you in regard to the above.

With communist greetings,

[James P. Cannon]
Secretary

Albany: Three years of party policy

Published March 18, 1933

The following article was published in the *Militant*.

The Albany State Conference for Labor Legislation represented a culminating point in the endeavors of the party, over a period of nearly three and a half years of the crisis, to organize and develop a movement of the workers on the issue of unemployment. In all that time the heavy burdens of unemployment have been accumulating and growing more and more intolerable, and the situation has therefore become increasingly favorable for the work of the revolutionary party. There has been no lack of effort; agitation, slogans, conferences, demonstrations and marches, organized and directed by the party in these past years, have centered chiefly around the burning question of unemployment.

The Albany conference itself was conceived and prepared as a major demonstration. It was preceded by months of preparatory work, including two conferences in New York City. On top of that, it should be added, the Albany conference came after the recent half turn in the policy of the party and provided a means of measuring its value. Socialist Party branches and local unions of the AFL were invited to participate—the well-known "united front from below."

And what was the net result of three and a half years of the "third period" frenzy, capped with the latest half turn? Out of 348 delegates, seven local unions of the AFL—and all left-wing locals—and one branch of the Socialist Party were represented from the entire state of New York! Crushing and irrefutable testimony to the utter falsity of the policy of the party leadership!

The shadow of the catastrophic failure to create even the semblance of a united front movement outside the sphere of direct party influence hung over the conference on the first day. The attempt of the leadership of the conference—Hathaway, Winter, and lesser bureaucrats of the Stalinist apparatus—to compensate for the failure to attract the non-party workers—who, according to their own thesis, are eager to struggle against unemployment—with windy soap-box agitation, could not banish from the minds of the delegates the haunting question: why are these workers not represented here?

A delegate from the bakers' local union gave a truer expression to the unspoken sentiment of the great majority than all the official speeches when he said: "I read in the *Daily Worker* that only seven AFL unions are represented here. As a trade union man I would like to see this hall packed with union delegates." But such delegates were not there. The question of why they were absent and how to attract them in the future—to these questions, which were uppermost in the minds of those who want to see a broad class movement on the class issue of unemployment, the

Hathaways have no answer. They could only put a cross over the bankruptcy of all their previous maneuvers and leave the future blank.

To all that has gone before, to the great detriment of the movement, the official leaders added new blunders and stupidities at Albany. The conference was obviously not a united front affair in the real sense of the word. It was a gathering of the vanguard—of the Communist Party and its auxiliaries and sympathetic organizations. Besides that, it had very little of a statewide complexion. The roster of delegates could have served, with a few alterations, for a roll call of the second- and third-line functionaries of the party and left-wing organizations in New York City.

Even such a representation, after a united front conference of workers' organizations in the whole of New York State has been aimed at, might have been turned to advantage. If the conference had been led by halfway competent politicians, they would have sized up the situation, charged off the expenses of transportation to profit and loss, and devoted themselves to a discussion of ways and means of transforming the Albany conference of the vanguard into a conference of the class another time.

Instead of that, they tried to solve the contradictions by a characteristic exhibition of Stalinist self-deception. The thing that was, became transformed—in their minds—into the thing that had been desired. The conference of the party members and sympathizers was declared to be a united front conference of workers' organizations, political parties, and trade unions. Their speeches to the conference were predicated on this fictitious assumption.

The conference needed the concise, businesslike elaboration of a program for changing the situation and uniting the vanguard with the masses—a single bullet aimed at a real target. It got, from the official leaders, the thunder of agitation in the name of the masses who were not represented in the conference—blank cartridges fired in the air. Worse, they not only talked; the actions of the conference under their control were the same caricature. Comedy, in the speeches of the leaders, alternated with tragedy in the misguided "legislative" deliberations of the delegates.

As sad and pitiful a spectacle as one could expect to see in the revolutionary movement was the session of the conference devoted to the report of the "Bills Committee." (This was the committee that had been charged with the task of drawing up legislative bills for presentation to the state legislature.) As if transported to another world, the delegates—Communists almost to a man—who had expressed their real sentiments shortly before in cheers for the overthrow of capitalism, were put through the ridiculous and futile business, for many wearisome hours, of discussing and debating line by line the legal phraseology of proposed legislative measures.

What, for example, is the precise legal residence of a seaman under the terms of the bill for unemployment insurance? And how shall the different rates of wages for various categories of labor employed on proposed public works at some future time be decided in the meticulous details? With just such questions the conference of the workers' vanguard was occupied, solemnly and seriously, for hours on end. Pitiful!

Here was a picture of the double face of bureaucratic centrism. Poised on a half turn in policy under the pressure of events, and of our criticism, the futile bureaucrats at the Albany conference stood with one foot in the mud of ultraleft sectarianism and the other foot in the mire of parliamentary cretinism. The conference was dedicated to a melange of both, and thus it was confused and muddled and demoralized.

Among all the "leaders" there was not one to explain to the worker delegates that the fight for a legislative program does not require, and is in no way advanced by, trying to transform a conference of several hundred worker delegates into so many amateur lawyers. The task of the vanguard workers is to formulate a program of demands clearly and concisely, and then to mobilize the power of a mass movement behind the program. The task of the leaders is to show the vanguard how to do this. As for the drafting of the bills for presentation to the legislature, a small committee with the aid of a jack-leg lawyer is sufficient. It is a shame to let conscientious worker militants go through the rigamarole of solemn debate about the wording of legislative bills.

More than that, it is a crime, for it sows illusions as to the real nature of the struggle for labor legislation. This was to be noted already in the session of the conference devoted to this tragicomedy. The bold note of militancy in the remarks from the floor in the earlier sessions was muted down, became more "practical" and restrained. And, even more significant, a different type of delegate became conspicuous in the discussion. The militants, imbued with the spirit of the class struggle, gave place to the legal-minded elements, who took the wording of bills very seriously and read them carefully, lest a comma be out of place and the law fail on that account.

In both sides of their policy the Stalinist miseducators worked against a fruitful outcome of the conference. With their sectarian "left" tactic they shunted the conference off the broad highway of the united front which could lead to a broader movement; with the vulgar opportunist comedy of the bills they put brakes on the future development of the narrow vanguard movement.

The hope for the emergence of a broad workers' front

of struggle against unemployment was in Albany, in spite of all its limitations, just because the pick of the vanguard militants, the indispensable dynamic force for the creation of a broad class movement, were there. But the leaders, not all of whom are as stupid as the policy they expounded under orders, did all they could to frustrate this hope.

They gave no review and summary of the experiences of the movement in these years of the terrible crisis—for this would require the examination of missed opportunities and multiplied mistakes which have left the movement weaker than it began three years ago, despite all the powerful social forces propelling the movement forward. They laid out no perspectives and offered no real measures to get the vanguard out of the straitjacket of isolation—because this would require a sharp turn in policy which they are not permitted to make.

It remained for the delegates of the Left Opposition, a small minority in the conference, to analyze the situation realistically and to point out the way to improve it radically. We did this to the best of our ability within the short time allotted to speeches from the floor. In the formal sense of the word, our views did not prevail. The Stalinists entrenched in the apparatus scored another victory which, like their old victories over the Marxist wing, was a defeat for the party and for the whole movement.

For this victory had a certain Pyrrhic quality, filled with ominous forebodings for the victors. One fact stood out above all others at the Albany conference: *the delegates wanted to hear the Left Opposition.* Our speeches were heard in a tense silence, without a single interruption from the floor, and received closer attention than any others. Our statement was distributed to all the delegates without interference, and was read attentively by them. The closest fraternization between the Left Oppositionists and other delegates, comradely discussion with large groups of party members and sympathizers, went on continuously throughout the conference.

While still remaining within the framework of the bureaucratic discipline and voting as they were required to vote, the conference delegates, nevertheless, expressed in all these actions a different attitude. In substance, after four and a half years of falsification, slander, incitement, and violence against the Left Opposition, the rank-and-file delegates, by their attitude, said to the bureaucrats: We don't believe it; we want to find out for ourselves!

Armed with the invincible ideas of Marxism, that is all the Left Opposition needs. Given such a hearing, as was the case at Albany to a far greater extent than ever before, our eventual victory is assured.

Open letter to the Central Committee of the Communist Party

Published March 18, 1933

The following letter was published in the *Militant*.[88]

Comrades:

Events in Germany are moving with breakneck speed. There is very little time left. The German proletariat, facing the bloody avalanche of fascism, stands in desperate need of international aid. In the first place, it needs the aid of the Communist International in guiding it to a correct policy. A tremendous responsibility rests on the Comintern in this fateful hour. As a section of the Comintern, the American party bears a full share of this great historic responsibility. The Left Opposition, which is a faction of the party and the Comintern, turns to you now once more with concrete proposals for a line of action which in our opinion must be followed without delay.

Our proposals are the following:

1. That the American party openly demand of the Comintern and the German CP that they adopt completely

and unambiguously and carry out in practice the policy of the united front.

2. That the American party demand the convening of the Seventh Congress of the Comintern immediately, with the participation of the International Left Opposition, and that Trotsky and Rakovsky be especially summoned to Moscow to take part in the congress.

3. That the German question be put as the most important question before the party, that systematic discussion on it be organized in every unit of the party from top to bottom, and that it be the first point on the agenda of the forthcoming party convention.

4. That the Left Opposition be readmitted to the party on the basis of party democracy; that the American CP support in the Comintern the readmission of the Left Opposition on an international scale, and the release and return of the imprisoned Bolshevik-Leninists in the Soviet Union.

5. That the party call for a united front conference of all workers' organizations, including the Socialist Party and the AFL, to formulate a concrete program for united front demonstrations in solidarity with the German workers. This action to begin on a national scale, and proceed from that to local actions along the same line.

For several years now, week in and week out, the Left Opposition has been warning of the very things that are happening now in Germany as the consequence of a false policy. It has predicted and its predictions are literally verified. The Left Opposition has pointed out the way and the events have confirmed its prognosis. It is time now to turn the helm. There is very little time left.

We hope you will realize it, and do your part to help the Comintern and the German party to realize it, before it is too late. The way to do this has been outlined above. The

Left Opposition, for its part, stands ready, now as always, to help the party find its way on the path of international duty. Our agitation, our criticism, and our warnings are all directed loyally to this end. And in any actions which will be undertaken to rouse the American working class and form a united front of international support with the German proletariat, all the members of the Left Opposition will put themselves at the disposal of the party for any services required of them.

With communist greetings,
National Committee
Communist League
of America (Opposition)

J.P. Cannon
Secretary

Errors of the majority

March 27, 1933

The following letter was written to Hugo Oehler, Vincent R. Dunne, and Carl Skoglund.

Dear Comrades:

I am sending you copies of the letter from Arne and two other documents received from him—one, the criticisms of Comrade Trotsky, and the other, Arne's reply.[89] In studying this criticism it should be remembered that it is addressed to us, as stated, "totally independent from the evaluation of the attitude of the minority."

We have talked the thing over here and are all pretty much of the opinion that we will have to give this criticism very serious consideration on its merits and make some gestures and modifications in our organizational policy. Not, however, out of political conciliation toward the corrupt, petty-bourgeois political methods of the Shachtman clique, but in order to wage a more effective struggle against them.

I am very anxious to hear from you immediately and to have your opinions before answering Arne.

I don't doubt that we have made some errors. But we have made some errors of a secondary character in a fight that has been fundamentally correct and necessary. It seems to me the Old Man is leaning over backward to find points of criticism because he is afraid we are driving to a split too soon. It is to be noted, however, that his criticism of us is restricted entirely to the question of organizational policy.

Please let me know right away if you will agree for me to make a few motions in the NC respecting organizational concessions along the lines specified by the old man. As for political concessions, I propose that we give nothing.

Fraternally yours,

Jim Cannon

P.S.—I am having a hell of a time here with financial problems at the office and double ones at home.

JPC

NC motions on Gillespie conference

March 29, 1933

The following motions prepared by Cannon were adopted by the National Committee. The third part of the motion was not voted on, but was sent out together with a countermotion by Shachtman. They are taken from the minutes.

I. From a trade union standpoint, the conference at Gillespie on April 1 will consist basically of units of the PMA plus a few scattered local craft unions in the mining area. The nondescript organizations that may be there in addition will add no serious trade union weight to the conference. This applies also to the paper local organizations of the TUUL which may be present.

With such a composition there is not the slightest ground for the conference to aim at the creation of a new federation of labor. The attempt can only result in dismal failure and discredit to its initiators. We must resolutely oppose this utopian idea and every tendency to give the conference such a direction. In view of the persistent efforts of some of the official elements in the movement to push toward the formal organization of a new paper federation, it is necessary to take a firmer stand against it and put the conference on record *specifically against such a plan*.

The *most* the conference could do is to create a center for propaganda, and partly also for organizing progressive groups in the unions. But even in this it can play only a limited role. Both the composition and the leadership of the conference preclude the idea that it can become the national organizing center of the left and progressive forces in the labor movement.

Such a formation requires a further development of the left-wing movement, which will lead toward the coming together of the various organizations, formations, and currents for a common struggle. The Gillespie conference can only be regarded as a single factor in this development, but it cannot replace it. This must be frankly stated and explained. The whole idea that a few sectional organizations—in reality only the Progressive Miners—whose stability is yet to be established, and with a leadership that has yet to clarify its aims and establish a national prestige, can take over the direction of a national movement by means of a conference, is unsound and foredoomed to disastrous failure.

Therefore, we are of the opinion that the constitution of a permanent organization at the Gillespie conference would be incorrect. The right thing for the conference to do would be to say openly:

1. That the response to the initiative of the Gillespie Trades and Labor Council, as indicated by the conference representation, shows that a sufficient basis for the creation of a new federation of labor is lacking, and therefore this project is definitely put aside.

2. That the representation at the conference, because

of its limited and sectional character, shows that it cannot take upon itself at the present time the formation of a permanent organization. Such an organization of the left and progressive forces on a national scale is a perspective to be aimed at, but it cannot be realized now through the medium of the Gillespie conference. The three conferences at Gillespie have made a contribution to this end. They helped to prepare the ground for an eventual national movement on a broader basis. That is all that can be done at the present time.

3. The conference recommends the program adopted at the January 29 session to the consideration of the workers who are struggling for the regeneration of the labor movement and its liberation from reactionary policies and leadership. It decides on the continuation of a committee to keep in touch with sympathetic trade union bodies and be ready to act jointly with them in the preparation of a broader conference at some future time when conditions will be more propitious for success.

Our delegates should oppose the formation of a permanent organization, the adoption of a specific name, or the calling of a national conference at this time. Our delegates should point out the necessity of drawing these conclusions and the danger of playing with illusions and paper organizations which do not advance, but rather retard their declared aims.

II. On the new wage contract, from such information as we have, it appears to the NC that big concessions have been made to the operators and that the leaders of the union (Percy and Keck) are minimizing these concessions and justifying them with class-collaborationist reasoning. There cannot be any doubt that the *two-year* contract works greatly to the advantage of the operators and will reduce the real wages of the miners when prices rise as a result of an economic upturn, or inflation, or both. The left wing ought to take a sharply critical attitude on this question and warn against every tendency to reconcile the interests of the workers with the exploiters. If a suitable occasion offers itself in the Gillespie conference, one of our delegates should speak on this theme and point out that a union can be really *progressive* only if it approaches every conflict from the point of view of the class struggle and entertains no illusions about the fact that the employers are class enemies in every case.

In the Gillespie conference our delegates should take occasion to bring out—in a careful, planned way—a distinction between their position and that of the PMA official leadership on the most appropriate concrete questions.

1. They should bring in a resolution on the Taylorville cases, which refers to the resolution adopted at the January 29 conference. This January 29 resolution called for a class policy in the defense and a program of mass demonstrations. Instead of that the defense committee, under pressure of the lawyers, came out for a legalistic policy and dampened down the mass movement. We have to come out openly against this policy and the dangerous illusions it creates, counterposing to it the class-struggle concept of the nature of capitalist justice, and citing the experience of Sacco-Vanzetti, Mooney, etc.

III. If political organizations are admitted to the conference, Comrade Oehler should present a credential as fraternal delegate of the league. Since the call for the conference does not provide for this it will be best if Comrade Allard raises the question specifically in the Executive Committee for a general ruling—not in regard to the league, but in regard to political organizations as such. If the Executive Committee decides adversely, our steering committee can decide whether to take the general issue to the floor.

It would be tactically incorrect to allow this question to become the center of the conflict. It would give the right-wing elements the best chance to carry the conference on formal trade union grounds. At the same time, they would be in the most advantageous position under the present conditions if they can center their fight on communism as such rather than on the concrete issues.[90]

For a realistic policy at Gillespie

March 30, 1933

The following letter was written to Hugo Oehler in Gillespie, Illinois.

Dear Comrade Oehler:

I sent you yesterday by airmail the motions we adopted here in regard to the Gillespie conference. They are very largely self-explanatory. You will note that they are different from the proposals contained in your letter of March 24.[91] In our opinion it is necessary to explain to the miners in very plain words now the complete falsity of the idea that a new federation of labor can originate in Gillespie, and to close the doors to any further moves along this line. Our delegates at least have the duty to explode this whole conception. Any further temporizing or diplomacy on this point is absolutely unwarranted.

You are very probably correct when you say the present official leaders of the conference "will continue to call conferences until they get what they want." They probably think they will slip the program through somehow or other. Just for that reason we have to knock the idea on the head at the April 1 conference. Such people are capable of doing the greatest harm and bringing discredit on the movement. We will be partly responsible if we do not make a sharp break with their theories on April 1.

That brings us to the second point: the idea of a national conference sponsored by the movement at Gillespie. We are also irreconcilably against this project. Granting that the idea of smuggling in a new federation of labor can be excluded from the program, how can anyone conceive of the forces and the leadership represented at Gillespie actually constituting a serious left-wing movement on a national scale? If we had the forces and were in a position to take over the leadership of the movement, there might be something in the idea. But even then, it can be undertaken only from the standpoint of strengthening the position of the Left Opposition in the fight for national unification of left and progressive forces. Can anybody in his right mind imagine that a national left-wing movement can be created without the participation of the party forces, the CPLA, and other serious tendencies on a national scale? If they do not come to the national conference sponsored at Gillespie, said conference would have no real significance. On the other hand, if they should come, it would only be with full forces in order to capture the movement, which would be a comparatively simple task, as one can readily see when he measures the forces of the party on a national scale with the forces leading the Gillespie movement.

The whole conception, both of a new federation of labor and of the expansion of the Gillespie conference into a national movement at this time, is false and artificial through and through. The first duty of the Left

Oppositionists at Gillespie is to deflate these unfounded pretensions, to make the assembled delegates understand precisely what they have and especially what is lacking for such ambitious programs.

Our motions, as you will note, restrict the organizational program of the conference to the election of a committee to keep in touch with other progressive trade union elements and be ready to participate in a big movement in the future. We expect our comrades to fight intransigently on this point, and to puncture any illusions regarding a more ambitious program at the present time.

If the present conference continues along its present line calling one conference after another, it is going to drag the Progressive Miners into all kinds of disastrous adventures. On the trade union side it will draw them into organizational relationships with scattered secessionist bodies which have no real significance and which, moreover, represent no progressive tendency and can only compromise the progressive aims of the Gillespie movement. The calculations of McFarlane on such bodies as the Independent Chicago Teamsters is a case in point. Such organizations, which are at loggerheads with the AFL bureaucracy over some jurisdictional squabble or other, are no new phenomenon. They have always existed and always will exist, but they represent no progressive tendency whatsoever, and their adherence will only pull the movement backward, not forward. Of course it is possible to gather a few of these scattered independent unions together, but this will only give such organizations pseudoprogressive cover and a prestige of national affiliations, which they need. But it will not in the least advance the cause of the progressive labor movement. On the contrary, it would serve to discredit it and draw it backward.

By the way, the idea of gathering such organizations

together and collecting enough per capita tax to keep a new set of offices going can only serve the shortsighted aims of individual officeholders. In the long run, if not from the very beginning, such motivations will exercise a conservative and not a progressive influence.

Now the political side of the present trend of the Gillespie movement has possibly even more dangerous implications. The invitation to farmer organizations shows a tendency to undermine the class basis of the movement in the interest of numbers—to create something new at any cost. In this there are all the germs of a caricatured farmer-labor movement. In our opinion the Left Opposition has the imperative duty at the April 1 conference of puncturing these illusions and bringing the movement back to a basis of reality.

What is important and significant there at the present time is the organization of the PMA. The rest is fictitious organizationally, and falsely motivated politically. The April 1 conference should be the occasion for the clear separation of the one from the other, and should get down to business with the real task at hand—the organization of a genuine left-wing movement in the PMA. The future of the PMA, including the possibility of it playing an influential role in the national left-wing movement, depends directly on this.

You will note two motions referring to the question of official delegates of the league at the conference. The decision on this point is left to the steering committee on the basis of conditions as they find them. I am enclosing herewith a credential for possible use if the steering committee decides matters that way, but speaking for myself I strongly urge the comrades not to sacrifice substance for form and not to make a decision in this case which gains a momentary advertisement of the Left Opposition at the expense of future effective work. Our aim is to make the Left Opposition a power in the miners' movement. We have a long way to go, and we must not act at the beginning as though we represent the power which we expect to be later on.

One word more in reply to your letter of January 26. Under the present conditions in the left-wing and progressive labor movement, the creation of a new national center in addition to the TUUL and the CPLA would have a certain justification if it represented a real force and if it were led by a group representing a firm tendency and capable of maneuvering and dealing with all the other forces. For example, if the Left Opposition had a group of unions and opposition groups in other unions under its influence, it would be justified in organizing them into a sort of TUUL on its own; but that could be justified only as a stage in the process of struggle for the national unification of all the left and progressive forces. Such a conference under our direction would draw up its program and would immediately begin to force the other formations—TUUL, CPLA—with the issue of united action. It would not in any case undertake to supplant them entirely, and certainly it would not deceive itself with the illusion that it can simply call a conference and solve the problem.

In our hands such a national organization would be a weapon in the struggle for unity and an extension of our own influence and prestige. But to play such a role, strong leadership based on a consistent tendency is a prerequisite, to say nothing of a considerable organizational basis. All this is lacking in the Gillespie movement, as has already been amply demonstrated. The leadership of this movement is empirical and confused. Its organizational support outside of the PMA amounts to virtually nothing from a trade union standpoint. We do not yet have the strength or the forces to gain the leadership of the movement. Under these circumstances any project which assigns to the Gillespie movement an influential national role at the present time is foredoomed to catastrophe. We will bear a heavy responsibility if we let the movement drift by its own momentum to this culmination.

It all comes back to the same point. The real important constituent of the Gillespie conference is the PMA. The left wing must entrench itself there and quit chasing rainbows. Once a firm left wing is consolidated in the PMA that is able to exercise a direct influence on the policy of the organization and its leadership or else to bring in a different leadership, it will be possible for the PMA to play a big part in the left labor movement on a national scale. To a certain extent it can play the leading part, but that requires some time and further development of the left-wing influence within it.

Allard, Angelo, Oehler, and Glotzer have been designated as the steering committee to work together and make all practical decisions at the conference in line with the resolutions sent from here. We will await full reports of the conference with the greatest interest. Please bring all the material including this letter to the attention of all the comrades of the steering committee.

About work in the PMA I am going to write at considerable length in a separate letter.

Yours fraternally,

[James P. Cannon]
Secretary

Deadlock in the National Committee

April 7, 1933

The following letter was written to Arne Swabeck in Prinkipo, Turkey.

Dear Arne:

Enclosed herewith you will find NC minutes nos. 145 and 146. These are for Comrade Trotsky's records. Please hand them over to him after reading. Your own copies of the minutes are being addressed now to your home as you requested. From the motions by me and the reaction to them in the motions of Abern and Shachtman you will be able to form a judgment of the first results of the organizational concessions.[92] At the moment when the situation has matured and the ground has been prepared by the preliminary work of Comrade Oehler for my going into the coal field, the project is tied up by a deadlock in the committee. We are sending the motions out for referendum vote. But there is very little hope that it will yield anything except a tie vote. The action of Abern and Shachtman in this matter is a real blow at our mining campaign. Now is just the time to strike there with full force.

Henceforth, until you return, with the restoration of Abern's vote in the resident committee, the "majority" will constitute a minority in the functioning center and will be unable to carry through anything. I will retain of course the full and complete right to carry on the financial responsibilities without any interference or assistance, as hitherto. This brings up the question of the funds for your return. I did succeed in making a loan of seventy-five dollars for this purpose, but was compelled to use it right away for the most pressing current obligations and have not been able to get it out again. You know the minority has yet to contribute one cent to this fund. I am doing my best in this regard and hope to cable you enough money to get to Paris and send the balance there. Meantime please compose yourself and cultivate the Lutheran virtues of patience, moderation, conciliation, and humility. By the way, have you noticed what Hitler is doing to your church in Germany?

I have dictated a longer letter in reply to those received from you, but Rose has not transcribed it yet. As soon as it is ready, I will send it along—in a day.

Yours in the fight,

[Jim]

P.S.—Regarding your suggestion of a postponement of the conference date. That will be feasible only if the initiative comes from there. As matters stand now we are scheduled to go through with it on June 30. I will not make any proposal to postpone the conference longer.

Turkey, February–March 1933. Standing: Leon Trotsky, Arne Swabeck, Pierre Frank. Seated: Jean van Heijenoort, Rudolf Klement.

Concessions to the minority

April 1933

The following is a draft of a letter to Arne Swabeck in Prinkipo.

I have delayed the answer to your letters pending a consultation with other comrades. Your letters in full and all the material have been brought to the attention of all the comrades of our group—first with the leading comrades here, then with all the comrades together. I sent copies of the material to Oehler, Dunne, and Skoglund, and have conducted a correspondence with them in regard to it. Our discussion of the whole matter has been quite extensive and thoroughgoing, and the conclusions we have arrived at are common ones.

In a previous letter I sent you a copy of the motions I introduced in the NC. From these motions it will be clear that our group is ready to do everything to ensure a democratically organized conference and to establish safeguards against organizational split. The action should also convince Comrade Trotsky that we are by no means so uncivilized as he seems to fear. The motions, taken together, are obviously in the nature of concessions to the minority. They are directly prompted by the criticisms of Comrade Trotsky. If they result in a certain easing up of the internal tension, the credit will belong in the first place to him, and to us only in a secondary place, insofar as our action shows that we are willing to learn, to improve our manners, and to allay suspicions about our cannibalistic propensities.

A slackening of the tempo of the internal struggle and a normalizing of the process of bringing out the more or less hidden differences to the surface, is undoubtedly desirable and necessary. We ourselves, as you will remember, have often discussed this, without however discovering the way to do it on our own resources. Our aims in the internal struggle have been indubitably correct, and the future of the movement is bound up with their achievement. On this point there is not a shadow of a doubt in our ranks. But particularly since the plenum, it must be admitted that we allowed ourselves to a considerable extent to give way to impatience, to be caught in the logic of a factional situation and to assist thereby the efforts of others to confuse and muddle the important and essential issues.

But we are not inclined to agree with the concrete criticisms in a sweeping, one-sided manner. On every point specified by Comrade Trotsky there is more to be said. Each action, and all of them together, have to be considered in their setting and with a number of qualifications. I will return to this later. But before doing so I want to deal with the more important implications of Comrade Trotsky's criticisms.

There is little doubt that bigger prospects are opening up for the expansion of the league. If there is one country outside of Germany where the Stalinist machine has the least ground under its feet and can come to the quickest catastrophe, it should be here. We may be confronted in a shorter time than elsewhere with the responsibility not merely of a propagandist faction, but of the movement itself. The problems of such transformation are already to a certain extent foreshadowed in the transition from propaganda to agitation—a process that can be said to have begun in the life of the league, although this should not be taken too sweepingly. We are yet in the early stages of this transition.

Now the prospect of new forces coming toward us from various directions puts some new problems before the leadership. Can the same group which stood up in the long period of isolation as a propaganda circle by virtue of its endurance and its firmness in principle, cope with the new tasks and the problems? Above all, can it assimilate new forces, make room for them, allow them to live in the movement in the process of their assimilation without on the other hand turning the movement over to them? These are the questions which it seems to us are implicit in the critical remarks and questionings of Comrade Trotsky regarding our inflexibility in organizational policy.

This side of the question occupied the major part of our discussion, because it seemed to us to be the most fundamental. On the whole, we do not think it can be justly said that the faults we have shown in this respect proceeded from a systematic narrowness of conception. That is why errors can be acknowledged and corrected all the easier. In addition, there is just as much or more to show on the other side of the picture. In the case of Field, as an example, every reasonable provision has been taken to facilitate first his collaboration and finally his reentry into the league. Similarly with Weisbord, with whom we have now concluded an agreement for collaboration leading toward a fusion.[93] In each of these cases we have proceeded with an eye toward the future, with the conscious purpose of demonstrating to the league membership and to a broader circle of the communist workers that the LO pursues a genuinely political course and always leaves the door open for others, once the principled basis for common work is established. Even if our dealings with Weisbord and Field were not free from errors, the course on the whole—the conflict as well as the conciliation—always had a deliberate political motivation. Right now we are watching the development of the Gitlow-Lovestone split very attentively from the same point of view, with the idea of facilitating the development of any trend in the direction of the LO that may develop out of this split. (The orientation of the Gitlow group appears to be toward the right, but this may be more formal than real. Having disentangled himself at all costs from the net of the Lovestone clique, Gitlow may experience a political rebirth. He is already talking in a very friendly and respectful way about the LO and denouncing the Lovestone claptrap about "Thermidor.") I mention these examples because I think they are also important in the estimation of the organization policy of our group. They show that we think in terms of a movement, not of a clique, and that our organization policy, fundamentally considered, and despite the errors and distortions, is not committed to the fetish of intransigence. At any rate, the critical observations of Comrade Trotsky have stimulated us to a new consideration and evaluation of the problem and put us on our guard.[94]

Our work in the PMA

April 10, 1933

The following letter was written to Gerry Allard in Gillespie, Illinois.

Dear Comrade Allard:

At the last regular meeting of the National Committee, we had a discussion of the mining situation in Illinois and various questions connected with it, including the *Progressive Miner*.

It was decided to publish an article in the *Militant* "polemicizing in a comradely tone and spirit with the reformist views expressed in the columns of the *Progressive Miner* and the false or ambiguous ideas conflicting with the Left Opposition standpoint, voiced in the personal column of Comrade Allard (Conveyor)." It was also decided to notify you to this effect.

We have also received the reports of the April 2 conference at Gillespie, to the effect that you and other members of the league were unable to work together as a unit and took different positions on some questions in the conference.

The differences are not entirely clear to us and we can reserve our opinions until we hear fully from you. What appears to us as most important in the affair is the inability of our steering committee to work as a unit. This is hardly a credit to a communist organization, and we should like to hear from you and to learn your point of view about the whole matter.

We have had many discussions here regarding the Illinois situation since I returned from Gillespie. The great opportunities, and also the dangers confronting the Progressive Miners of America, and its significance for the whole national progressive labor movement make it of necessity a major concern of the Left Opposition. And this concern is multiplied by the responsibility which the Left Opposition carries, especially by virtue of your position and prestige in the PMA on the one side, and your membership in the LO on the other. Under these conditions, it must be perfectly clear to you that the LO bears a direct public responsibility for everything done by you, for your achievements as well as for your mistakes. Therefore, as a communist, we are sure you will not take any offense at the questions we raise with complete communist frankness. The interest of the cause demands it, and the object now, as before, is to come to an understanding with you and work together in all respects, as communists, above all as Left Oppositionists, should and must.

Your merits as a militant in the class struggle and your loyalty to the cause of the workers are sufficiently appreciated by us. The calumny which has been directed against you by the Stalinists is beneath contempt. Your sterling work on the firing line of the class struggle, which has brought you to such a prominent position in the miners' movement, has also redounded to the credit of the Left Opposition, with which your name is linked in the minds of the class-conscious workers throughout the country.

But there is another side of the question, regarding which I have written you before and which has been discussed in personal conversation with you at various times by members of the National Committee; that is the responsibility which the Left Opposition bears for your work and for the ideas you express in it, especially in the columns of the *Progressive Miner*. That much of this is not in accord with our views, you already know; and in our opinion, the problem is reaching the point where a solution must be found. This is the meaning of the National Committee decision to subject the *Progressive Miner* to a certain criticism in the *Militant*. But it will be obvious to you that the matter cannot rest there. What is necessary and indisputable, it seems to us, is a thorough discussion with the object of coming to an agreement for common work and a common policy. We are ready to give the fullest consideration to anything you have to say, and to take into account all the difficulties and complications of your position. That goes without saying. But nevertheless we must move more deliberately now toward a solution. The only road toward that is a frank discussion.

This letter, which is sent by direction of the National Committee, should be taken in that sense. It is to be hoped that your reply will be prompt and that it will be actuated by a full realization of what is involved: the work of the Left Opposition in the Illinois miners' movement and your relationship to it in the future.

We are of the opinion that the leaders of the PMA are steering the union in a conservative direction. Their public pronouncements, their proposals to Governor Horner, the renunciation of the class-struggle policy in the Taylorville defense and the attempt to soft-pedal the mass demonstrations, and the statement issued to the union members on the new wage contract—in all this, the official leaders of the union departed from the policy of the class struggle and made unjustified concessions to the pressure of the class enemy and of bourgeois public opinion generally. The result of such a course, if it does not meet a militant and organized resistance, will be the downfall of the PMA, its transformation into a domesticated and conservative union, or even its reintegration into the Lewis organization. The Left Opposition is duty bound to warn the miners against such a course and to do all it can to organize the fight against it. Do you agree with us in this conception, and will you take part openly in this fight, regardless of consequences? That means concretely: are you ready to give full assistance to the work of organizing the most advanced and classconscious miners into branches of the league and to organize a broader left wing which will take up an organized fight in the union against its reformist degeneration?

In the *Progressive Miner* the reformists and confusionists have free play to attack and ridicule the communist movement. Up to now there has been no reply to their attacks. It is understood that different views cannot be excluded from the columns of the paper. But why cannot the communist view find expression also? Specifically, is it not feasible for you to write a column under your name, giving your personal views, making clear that your justified hostility to the policy and actions of the Communist Party is directed not at communism but at Stalinism; pointing out how communism as represented by the LO has served the interests of the miners, sided with them with its suggestions regarding policies and in the daily work of its members, and that you personally belong to and support this political tendency.

Do you consider this suggestion in any way unreasonable? You can be assured that such an action on your part will begin to bring clarity into the situation right away. It will not weaken your position, but strengthen it. And if you accompany it with an outspoken personal criticism of the tendencies to conservatize the union, you will immediately begin to rally the genuinely militant forces more closely around you, and the union itself will gain thereby by the beginning of a genuine left-wing organization under your leadership.

The policy of ambiguity does not in the least shield the union from the class enemy. It only disarms it before their attacks.

We are not speaking here for an ill-considered outburst, but for a carefully planned movement to put the miners on guard and to begin the real crystallization of the left wing, at a signal from you. If you fail to do this, or if you wait too long, you will bear the heavy share of the responsibility for a possible catastrophe later on, and compromise yourself for a long time to come. Don't forget the experience of the Howat movement and of the Rank and File movement.[95]

The foregoing does not of course exhaust the question. These remarks are meant to serve as the points of departure in our discussion. We trust that you will give them the most serious consideration and transmit a prompt reply. Despite all the differences and the criticisms, we hold fast to the hope that a thorough discussion with you will result in a strengthening of our solidarity and an agreement for common work on the basis of a common policy.

The interests of the miners and of the LO, the nucleus of the future of American communism, will be served in the highest degree by such an outcome.

With communist greetings,

James P. Cannon
Secretary

On collaboration with Allard

April 10, 1933

The following letter was written to Hugo Oehler.

Dear Hugo:

We received your report of the Gillespie conference. On the whole it appears that we made some headway and that we can proceed from that to another step forward. The main aspect of this of course is the PMA. The crux of the question of the new venture entering the left-wing labor movement on a national scale is the PMA itself. The rest of the Gillespie conference is mainly froth. To base oneself for a moment on this is to lead inevitably to big blunders. As far as the Left Opposition is concerned, it represents so far merely an idea in the left-wing labor movement. In order for it to become a real force, it has to get some ground under its feet somewhere in the labor movement. The PMA at present offers the best possibility. We must continue a concentration on this sector until we get some real results.

It appears to me that the results of the conference tended to confirm the prior estimate made here. Doesn't it look this way to you? A national conference engineered by the forces in charge of the Gillespie affair would be a comedy. This movement, as an independent movement on a national scale, is by no means ripe. For that two things are necessary: first, a real consolidation of the PMA itself; and second, the crystallization of a genuine left wing with a firm and consistent ideology which will find an adequate representation in its leadership. Both of these are possible music of the future. Let us hope that this tune will be played in good time.

We are not inclined to agree entirely with the attitude you and Glotzer took regarding the Washington conference.[96] It would probably have been better to favor the sending of delegates with definite instructions. As far as I can make out, it appeared that Gerry's difference with you on this question derived from a difference in attitude toward the conference. Does he really think we ought to support this conference? That is surely wrong through and through. We will try to get him to stop off in New York if he goes to the conference, and have a talk with him about this and other questions.

I am enclosing a copy of a letter sent to Gerry. Show it to Glotzer and Edwards. Your reports about his lack of cooperation, or at any rate, his half-hearted assistance to you in the work there, and his actions at the conference, are very disturbing. It is absolutely necessary to come to a more definite understanding with him and to help him, by pressure as well as by persuasion, to clarify his position. I retain my optimistic hopes that things will turn out this way in regard to Gerry, and am opposed to his expulsion from the league before a real effort has been made to bring him our way. This is in large part a matter of education, for it is obvious that much of Gerry's weakness comes from a lack of understanding of the political way to cope with his extremely difficult situation. We must have patience and take time. The PMA is a big proposition, and Gerry is to a large extent the key to our further penetration of it. An abrupt and ill-considered break with him, before every possibility of an agreement for common work has been exhausted, would be light-minded folly. At the same time, we can't let matters drift any longer. The next time you see Gerry, and in any letters that are sent him from Chicago, the necessity of clarifying his relations to the Left Opposition and his responsibility to it as a prominent member must be stressed.

I feel very sorry that financial difficulties forced you out of the field, and doubly so, that more help could not be sent to you from here. The financial situation here is extremely difficult and critical and we are keeping the machine going this week by means of rubber checks that are fated to bounce back in a few days. In spite of that, I firmly intend to send you some money to enable you to return to the field at the very first opportunity. I hope that in the meantime you will have succeeded in raising a few dollars in Chicago for this purpose. I will never be convinced that the Illinois situation is not ripe for an organization of the left wing and an expansion of the Left Opposition there until it has been tried out thoroughly with all possible forces. I am especially anxious to spend a period of time myself in the Illinois field. It is now proposed that I remain here. I sent out the motions on this question to a referendum vote. Yours was addressed to Springfield. Please see Glotzer or Edwards right away to get a copy of the minutes and record your vote on the various disputed motions.

I am drafting a resolution which embodies my estimation of the PMA movement and the tasks of the Left Opposition in connection with it. I will send you a copy of the resolution as soon as it is finished.

Yours,

[James P. Cannon]
Secretary

Allard at the turning point

April 20, 1933

The following letter was written to Hugo Oehler.

Dear Hugo:
   Your letter received. We agree with your remarks about Allard and your proposals, as you will see from the resolution and letter enclosed. You are requested to take this matter up personally with Comrade Allard. Strive in every way to convince him of the necessity of the steps outlined in the resolution. Make it clear to him that there can be no further temporizing. It is absolutely imperative now to start a counterstruggle against the communist scare, which is only a preparation for a campaign to hound them out of the union and then deliver the union to the bosses, and very possibly to Lewis also.
   Allard is the one to lead this fight. It is his duty as a Left Oppositionist to do so. If he refuses, we have to part company with him. This must be made clear to Allard right away. What we consider necessary is a statement from him in the paper correcting his statement of April 14 and declaring his position as a communist and as a supporter of the Left Opposition as outlined in the resolution.[97] If he

agrees with this, you should work with him in the drafting of the statement. Make Gerry understand that he is at the turning point right now and must make up his mind which way he is going to go. Furthermore, he must make up his mind right away, within one week.

We expect to hear from you not later than a week from today. On the basis of your report we will take the next step. If Allard refuses to accept the resolution of the NC, we will break relations with him and come out against him in the *Militant*. Bring all possible pressure to bear on him. Work on all the bona fide left-wing militants and make them understand that this "red scare" has got to be met face to face. This is not a question of the Lewis union, where communists have to hide. It is a progressive union based on a miners' revolt. It cannot be a real progressive movement without communists functioning in it freely and openly.

We are very much gratified by your initiative in going to Gillespie. I will try at all costs to wire you a few dollars to keep you going. At the moment we are flat broke and I don't know whether we will be able to get out the paper this week or not. But you can expect a few dollars anyway no matter where it comes from.

The question of Allard has, of course, an enormous importance for us. He has a great future in the miners' movement if he knows how to prepare for it. It will be a real blow to the league to lose him, and we should not leave anything undone to help him find his way together with us. But it will be a hundred times bigger blow to the league to condone the policy he has been following, especially in this last statement of his.[98]

Yours fraternally,

[James P. Cannon]
Secretary

Red-baiting in the Illinois mine fields

Published April 29, 1933

The following article was published in the *Militant*.

In recent days, the reactionary press in Illinois has attempted to work up a "red scare" in the Progressive Miners union. Having failed to break the magnificent movement of the progressive miners by frontal attack, the coal operators have decided to supplement the physical terror of the state forces and the Lewis gangsters with a campaign of ideological terror within the union. They have developed a great solicitude about the political opinions of some of the leading miners in the union—especially Gerry Allard. And with their well-known concern for the welfare of the miners, they are warning them to get rid of him and all others whom they identify as communists or class-struggle militants.

They are saying, in effect, to the miners: "We have nothing against you as coal diggers. As a matter of fact, in that capacity you are necessary for the production of our profits. What we object to is the fact that you have broken with the Lewis unionism, which suited us to perfection, and have begun to fight for your rights. If you will give up this idea and stop listening to people who stir up the spirit of class militancy and resistance, we will be satisfied. In other words, if you will transform yourselves into sheep, we will eat you up and then we will have peace together."

The attack on Allard as a communist, conducted in sensational articles in the *Taylorville Breeze* and other organs of the big interests, is obviously a part of the general campaign of reaction against the Progressive Miners. The object of the red scare is to discredit the union before public opinion and thus to prepare the ground for more terroristic aggression; to intimidate the membership and consolidate the conservative right wing in the union (the concealed agents of Lewisism); and to drive the official leadership of the union at a faster pace on the path of conservatizing the organization.

If they can succeed with this campaign of demoralizing the union from within, then the Progressive Miners organization, as a center of resistance to the capitalists and an inspiration to the miners throughout the country as well as to the working class generally, will have become a thing of the past.

The game of the operators and their agents is an old one. And there is only one way to meet it, as all experience has shown. That is to assert the independence of the union—to reject all advice offered to it by the class enemy. The union will not thrive and grow by conciliating the bosses, by capitulating to their ideology, by domesticating the union and making it acceptable to the bosses. This is what the bosses want. This is what they are aiming at with the new communist hunt. To understand this and to fight against it is the elementary duty of the leading elements in the union, including Allard and the other individuals under attack.

But the response made to the attack in the *Progressive Miner* up till now does not in the least indicate an understanding of this strength of the enemy. Underestimating the inner resources of the Progressive Miners' movement, as is always the case with "progressives" of all hues, they are trying to counter the brutal offensive of the class enemy with a "clever" strategy of camouflage and capitulation. They seek to ward off the attack by denying the charges of any communistic influence in the union. Thus, by implication, they disavow any tendency toward class-struggle militancy, which is what the bosses really mean when they talk of communism. Thus they lay the ground for the proscription not only of communists but of all class-struggle militants inside the union. And by that they concede the main demands of the bosses. Allard too, who should know better, allowed himself to fall in with this worthless strategy.

The class-conscious members in the Progressive Miners' movement have to recognize the real purpose of this new attack of the class enemy on the ideological front. The operators and their tools have been unable to smash the movement in open struggle. Now they are trying to demoralize it from within; to rob it of the militancy which called it into life and sustained it in struggle; to purge it of those very qualities which have distinguished it from the corrupt unionism of Lewis and, eventually, to drive it back into the Lewis camp.

Now is the time to call to mind the tragic fate of the previous insurgent movements which were disorganized and defeated by those very methods. Now is the time for the real militants, who have carried the new movement on their shoulders in struggle and sacrifice, to remember the bitter experiences with Walker, Howat, and Edmondson and to say to all the leading forces in the new movement: "Nobody can lead us again onto this slippery path which leads to demoralization and defeat."

The present trend, however, is in this direction. The course of the official leadership over a considerable period now has been to seek a "stabilization" of the union at the expense of its class-struggle character. The negotiations and proposed agreement with Governor Horner, the ban on the demonstrations for the Taylorville prisoners, the new wage contract—in all these, and in a number of other important questions, the course of the official policy has tended to narrow down the differences between the Progressive Miners and the type of unionism against which the rank and file rose in revolt.

Since the inception of the new movement the Left Opposition has warned against a repetition of the cruel experiences of the past, and urged the militant elements to consolidate their forces in a firm left wing on a policy of class struggle. This warning must be repeated again now when the demoralizing agitation of the bosses is reaching into the union and finding direct and indirect supporters there. The left wing must rally its forces for a resolute counterattack. In the circumstances the strategy of the militant forces cannot reconcile itself with that of the leading circles in the union.

The Progressive Miners of America is the product of a miners' revolt. Its preservation and further development depends on a sustained militant policy, which is impossible without a free participation of communists in the union.

The progressive character of the union, which has distinguished it from the Lewis organization, cannot be maintained if it permits the hounding of communists. At the present stage this is precisely the crux of the problem of the PMA. What is a progressive union for if it allows the operators to dictate the opinions of its membership? An open fight for the right of workers of all political opinions—including communists—to participate freely in the life of the union is the only way to reply to the attack of the reactionary press.

The resolutions of the local unions and of the Ladies' Auxiliary, printed in the *Progressive Miner*, show that the rank and file can be mobilized to fight on these lines. What is needed is an organization of the fight and leaders who are equal to it.

For a united front to defend Mooney

May 2, 1933

The following motions were introduced by Cannon on behalf of the CLA to the Free Tom Mooney Congress held in Chicago.[99] They were published in the May 20, 1933, *Militant*.

1. This congress is conceived not as the culmination but rather as the starting point of a new movement to rally a powerful united front of the working class in the struggle for the liberation of Mooney and Billings.

2. The next steps along this line shall be a series of local and district united front conferences which have the aim of broadening the movement in setting ever wider masses of the working class into motion, drawing in new forces not yet in the united front, and cementing the solidarity of those already participating.

3. This work shall lead in the next stage of the struggle to a *national and international Mooney Day*, at which the attention of the working class of the entire world shall be concentrated on the Mooney case.

4. All the agitation and activity in the next period shall be connected with the perspective of a second national Mooney congress with a goal of at least 10,000 delegates.

5. The policy for all this work that shall govern the activity of the leading committee on a national scale and all the local organizations is the policy of the united front of workers' organizations. Only in this way is it possible to unite the masses of workers of varying political opinions and tendencies into a single fighting unity in the interests of Tom Mooney and the cause which he symbolizes. The failure of the leaders of some working-class organizations to participate in the movement up to now, and their persistent attempts to sabotage the struggle, must not in any case lead to an abandonment of the united front policy with respect to their organizations. On the contrary, the leading organs of the Mooney movement must make it clear at every turn that all organizations and their leaders are invited to participate in the movement and that the door is left open to them even if they have previously refused. Only in this way will it be possible to really rally the masses of workers within the various organizations and give them proper ground upon which to fight every attempt of the leadership to sabotage unity.

Financial factionalism

May 29, 1933

The following letter was written from Minneapolis to Rose Karsner in Connecticut.

Dear Rose:

I received your letters and material sent here. I was greatly surprised and upset to learn that the financial situation remains acute and that the difficulties are increased and complicated by dishonest and disloyal agitation over the German funds. The motive for this rotten campaign, this nauseating fakeristic "defense of the German Opposition against the NC," is obviously to sabotage and hold up the sending of funds to Swabeck as long as possible. Why didn't they raise the question of the German funds when Shachtman was grabbing all the money in sight for his personal expenses to Europe?[100]

Support for a Fourth International

September 11, 1933

The following letter was written to the International Secretariat in Paris, with a copy for Trotsky.

Dear Comrades:

We have received the Gourov letters regarding the decisive break with the Stalinist organizations and have sent all the material out to the membership in an internal bulletin.[101] The National Committee has *unanimously* adopted a resolution in support of this proposal. The material is now before the branches for discussion. The New York branch has already voted unanimously for the Gourov proposals. We expect a virtually unanimous agreement, as the members have already more or less been prepared for this step. Enclosed herewith you will also find a copy of our resolution and our program for action.[102] We are driving hard now with full force, and expect to put the whole project, including the removal to Chicago, into effect within two months.

We notice that *Unser Wort* prints the first Gourov article in the current issue. This procedure seems to us to be incorrect. Our plan is to confine the matter to internal discussion until the official position of the National Committee is ratified by the membership. Then we will launch the matter publicly in an official manifesto of the league.

Fraternally yours,

J.P. Cannon
Secretary

Membership discussion of the new turn

September 16, 1933

The following letter was sent to all branches of the CLA.

Dear Comrades:

Since the first bulletin you received on this subject, we received reports from: Minneapolis, New Castle, New Haven, Newark, Kansas City, and Chicago. In each case, the branch members reported themselves unanimously for the Gourov proposals and the resolution of the National Committee. The Chicago branch expressed itself in favor of the decision being made by a conference of the league after a broad preconference discussion of the question.

Since events are moving very rapidly and time is a very important factor, the National Committee had previously decided to make the decision on the turn public if the branches expressed themselves in support of it through a referendum. Since the expression of the membership has been so unanimous, we felt it is necessary to make the turn without delay. This prompt action is made all the more necessary by the developments of events in Europe. For example, at the Conference of the Left Socialists and Independent Communist Parties, the delegation was to declare where it stood on the question of the International.[103] They declared themselves in favor of a new International, but explained that their final decision rested with the national sections of the league. From all indications, it is almost certain that we will have to act openly on an international scale before a conference of the league could pass finally on the matter. For these reasons, we believe the league membership will endorse the action of the National Committee in publishing the manifesto in the forthcoming issue of the *Militant*, or, at the latest, the following week.

Fraternally yours,

James P. Cannon

The left wing needs a new policy and a new leadership

Published September 16, 1933

The following article was published in the *Militant*.

The American workers, stirring again on the trade union field after a long passivity and confronting a formidable and well-organized class enemy, need their own plan of battle.[104] The class enemy has organization and a plan. That, in essence, is what the NRA really is. In the unified and comprehensive program of American imperialism against the world, the NRA is that section of the program aimed against the enemy at home, the American working class. The strike movement of the workers, on the other hand, has been elemental and spontaneous, lacking a conscious direction.

Who will assist the workers to formulate their own battle plan in their own interests? Certainly not the present leaders of the AFL and kindred labor organizations. These in reality belong to the capitalist board of strategy. In the machinery of the NRA they are filling to perfection their long-established role of labor lieutenants of the capitalist class. A plan and program for the workers in the trade unions, by means of which their struggle could be organized on a national scale, can come only from the left wing, that is, from the class-conscious section of the movement.

But in the present situation, which has witnessed the beginning of a colossal wave of strike struggles, the left wing failed completely in its function. The new events, which should have been foreseen and anticipated, found it unprepared and impotent. The domination of Stalinism deprived the left wing of the possibility of influencing the new movement of the masses and of drawing new life and strength from it. The dogmatic program which had been imposed upon it was refuted in life. The leadership of bureaucratic usurpers showed itself to be bankrupt and helpless. The necessary conclusions from these happenings must be drawn without delay. The problem of reestablishing the left wing, correcting its program, and renovating its leadership is the most immediate and burning problem of the labor movement.

This is a new situation in the labor movement, which the left wing must take as the point of departure. The wave of strike struggles did not fall from the skies, nor were Roosevelt and the labor fakers the creators of it. The fearful sufferings inflicted on the masses during three and one-half crisis years; the starvation rations of the unemployed; the multiplied wage cuts and unprecedented speedup which goaded the employed workers to desperation—these were the real authors of the present strike movement. The workers' resentment and dissatisfaction was due for an explosion, and it was reasonable to assume that it would coincide with the first signs of an economic upturn.

This was foreseen by the most perspicacious representatives of capitalism. The NRA was devised as a means of coordinating the efforts of the employers and their labor lieutenants with the government in a single scheme to arrest this movement at its first stages and to keep it within safe bounds. It is possible that the inauguration of the NRA precipitated the strike movement. But at bottom it was caused by the discontent of the workers with their unbearable conditions, and their aspirations to improve them at the first opportunity.

These causes will remain and will evoke increasingly powerful movements of the masses after the ballyhoo of the Roosevelt program has spent itself, leaving conditions substantially unchanged except insofar as they are improved by organized struggle. Bitter experience will work rapidly and mightily to free the workers from their present illusions about the purposes of the NRA. The capitalists will not voluntarily improve the lot of the slaves under the beneficent influence of the Blue Eagle. The workers will gain nothing they do not fight for. The labor agents of imperialism will not become leaders and organizers of militant struggles, but on the contrary will do all they can, now and in the future, as in the past, to sabotage and defeat them.

The left wing cannot depart for a moment from these self-evident ABC propositions. What has been happening in the way of working-class activity in the recent months is only an anticipation of things to come. It is possible, of course, and even probable, that the NRA swindle will succeed in harnessing the new movement for a time. The illusions of the masses are very great. But the higher the hopes, the more certain the disappointment and the expression of this disappointment in more resolute and determined class action. The first magnificent upsurge of the workers is, after all, only a tentative beginning, a preliminary testing of their collective strength and solidarity. It is implicit with the certainty of another movement, deeper, wider, and more militant.

The left wing must base itself on this perspective and be ready for it. That means to begin now to re-form its ranks and begin to assert its influence in the mass movement. Can this be done on the basis of the trade union policy of Stalinism? No, that is absolutely impossible. Those who try it will be deprived of all influence. On this question the decision has already been rendered by the actual developments in the labor movement. The trade union left wing which eventually rises to the magnitude of the new tasks, coordinates the militant forces on a national scale, and organizes the real struggle against the capitalists and the labor fakers will consist of those who make a complete break with the bankrupt and discredited trade union policy of Stalinism.

The tactical line which the left wing must take is clearly marked out by the actual course of the movement, and no arbitrary scheme which contradicts this course is worth a cent. The left wing must put itself in line with the main trend of the workers, assist and encourage their impulse for organization, and become itself a force to bring the workers into the unions—into the real unions, not the paper unions. And the left wing must go with them and organize the fight inside the unions against the capitalist agents in the ranks.

The left wing—that is, the real left wing, which remains true to principle and to the interests of the workers—will enter the mass unions and urge other workers to do likewise, without any illusions about the reactionary leaders and without the least AFL fetishism. Communists do not make a fetish of any trade union organizational form. In the future, as in the past, a rise of militancy in the unions will be apt to bring wholesale expulsions and splits. It is quite likely that many of the greatest battles will have to be waged independently, as "outlaw" organizations. The resurgent left wing—again, the real left wing, not sycophants and traitors masquerading as such—will remain with the masses under such conditions and not flinch from the formation of independent mass organizations.

That, however, is more a prospect of the future than a present problem. We will keep it in mind and let no labor fakers' cry of "dual unionism" bluff us out of it. But, just as firmly, we must refuse to accept the paper unions of the Stalinists as substitutes for genuine mass organizations. Independent unions have a very slim chance in the present situation. That is not because there is any law to this effect—as the Lovestone opportunists imply—but because a force capable of organizing them is lacking and because the trend of the masses toward the conservative unions cannot and should not be counteracted. (For Marxists, independent unions are not a dogma or a fetish any more than AFL unions are.)

But not the least, and very probably the greatest, factor in the situation which excludes any widespread development of independent unions at the present time is the fact that the Stalinists, who have made a dogma of independent "class struggle" unions, have succeeded in discrediting the idea and alienating the workers who might have cooperated in building them in those industries where their existence had a certain justification and necessity. By their fictitious new trade union center, their stupid tactics, their arrogant bureaucratism, their hooligan abuse and expulsions of critics and political opponents, their subordination of the unions to the narrow clique interest of the Stalin faction, and the conversion of the decimated organizations into mere appendages of the Stalinist party—by their whole policy and regime, they have covered the idea of an independent union movement with their own disgrace.

The verdict of doom has already been pronounced on the so-called unions under their domination. As for the organized workers, they are passing them by, and the non-Stalinist members who have not been expelled are leaving them. Make no mistake about it. Unions that cannot grow now, when new strata of workers are surging forward and seeking organization, are dead beyond the possibility of resurrection. The left-wing militants who want to play a part in the new situation in the labor movement must turn their backs on the Stalinist paper unions and put a cross over the whole experiment.

To see the present strike wave as only the first stage of a resurgent class activity of the American workers and prepare to influence its further development; to call the workers to enter the trade unions and to go with them on this path; to struggle increasingly within the unions against the policy and leadership of the reactionaries; to break resolutely and completely with the Stalinist sectarian paper unions—these, in our opinion, are the main points of the new trade union thesis which the left wing requires.

But the new program, by itself, is not enough. The left wing also requires a new leadership. Up till now the Stalinists have dominated the movement, disorganizing and disrupting everything they could not control and silencing all critical voices with threats and expulsions. They had a monopoly in the leadership. Consequently, the responsibility for the results is also their monopoly. In the light of what happened in the past three months, on top of all that went before, it is possible now—it is absolutely necessary!—to draw the final balance of their trade union policy.

The beginning of the strike wave was the great opportunity of the test of the left wing and its leadership. Given a correct policy and a competent leadership, the left wing in the labor movement could not fail to bound forward, to expand in influence and organization at the expense of the reactionaries. It happened differently, as everybody knows. In the trade union movement in America, as in every vital problem of the working class throughout the world, Stalinism remained true to its mission as the great organizer of defeats. The conclusion which the revolutionary workers throughout the world are drawing must also be drawn here.

In the trade union question, the necessity for a complete break with the Stalinist leadership is especially obvious and imperative. And their disastrous leadership in this field is only a particularly illuminating illustration of their leadership in general.

The question brooks no delay. The liberation of the left wing of the labor movement from the strangulating grip of Stalinism is the key to the problem of planning and organizing the struggles of the American workers, of raising the elemental movement to new heights. This is today the crux of the trade union question.

Initial discussions on forming the new party

September 25, 1933

The following letter was written to the International Secretariat with a copy to Trotsky.

Dear Comrades:

In the recent minutes of the secretariat that we have seen, there was a reference to a section of the Left Opposition in Cuba. Up until now we have not been able to establish any direct connection with them. Since in the present development this is very important,[105] we request that you send us this information if you have it. And also ask the Cuban comrades to get in touch with us. We should be able to give them some assistance.

In the latest issue, the *Communist*, the Stalinist magazine here, makes an attack on the Opposition group in Cuba. We lack material with which to reply to them.

A few days ago we informed you of the resolution adopted by the resident National Committee in support of the Gourov proposals regarding the new International. Since then a discussion has been proceeding in the branches and a referendum vote taken. Nearly all the branches have reported and in each case the decision was unanimous in support of the proposals. We had a test meeting the other night here with sympathizers who came to the meeting by invitation, without a public notice. Over 150 were present and the response was very enthusiastic. We opened the floor for discussion and asked for dissenting opinions, but there were no objections. The one question troubling many comrades both in our ranks and among the sympathizers was the question of the Soviet Union. The previous articles of Comrade Gourov have clarified this question to a considerable extent. But a still further and more elaborate exposition of the question would be timely.[106]

The Gitlow group here has also come out in favor of a new party and a new International. This is a split-off from the Lovestone faction. The split occurred some months ago, ostensibly over the Russian question, on which the Gitlow group appeared to take a Bukharinist position. They also emphasize very strongly the question of a labor party. While from a formal point of view the orientation of this group would appear to be to the right of the Lovestone faction, we have considered from the first that the dynamics of its development would bring it around toward our direction. It consists of workers who constituted in many respects the healthiest section of the Lovestone faction. Gitlow also is a very prominent figure, both a founder of the party here and a popular militant in the left-wing trade union movement. He went to Europe to present his position before the recent congress of the Brandlerites but was refused admission on the formal ground that the meeting was to be confined only to members of the International Bureau. He is in contact with the Kilbom people in Sweden and is working with them, so it appears, toward a rapprochement with us. One of the demands which he proposed to the Brandlerists' "International" was that it come out for a new International which would include the "Trotskyists." Since his return to America he has announced his break with the Brandlerists' organization, condemning its policy in Germany and its attitude toward the CI.

We have had some informal discussions with members of this group and already are working in close cooperation with them in the hotel workers' union, where they have some forces. We know that a number of the workers in its ranks are already now prepared for a fusion with us, and that they will put increasing pressure on Gitlow in this direction. Our next step with them will be to send them a copy of the "Declaration of the Four" and ask them to take a position on it. In the event of a favorable action on their part in this regard, the next big stumbling block will be the question of a labor party.[107] Their proposal will probably be the coming together of the organizations on a basis which permits differences of opinion and discussion on such questions. Our course will probably be to propose a public discussion both in the press and at meetings on such questions before any formal relations between the organizations are established.

There are several other groups here who could be expected to take a favorable standpoint toward the new International but who are separated from us on important questions, some of them of a principled character. Is it advisable to establish some kind of a loose federation with such groups as a transitory step during which some joint work could be undertaken while the disputed questions are subjected to a clarifying discussion? We should like advice at every step we take.

There is no need for us to hurry with such formations in America. Our organization is strongest and best equipped from the standpoint of press and forces, of all the forces now visible which might be assimilated into the new party, and there is no doubt that our preponderance will increase in the coming months. There is every reason to believe that our direct recruiting work will bring good results in the next period as a result of the turn. As this process goes on, our position in relation to the other little groups will naturally become stronger.

Fraternally yours,

James P. Cannon
Secretary

The British section and the ILP

September 27, 1933

The following letter was written to Reg Groves in London, with copies to the International Secretariat and to Trotsky.

Dear Comrade Groves:

We received a copy of Comrade Gourov's letter to you under date of September 16, in which he deals with the question of the entry of our British section into the ILP.[108] We gave serious consideration to this letter. Prior to its arrival we had discussed the question a number of times, as we have an especially deep interest in the development of the British movement, and have been following the evolution of the ILP as closely as study of the press makes possible. We are of the opinion that the proposals of Comrade Gourov are correct in the situation, and had arrived at a somewhat similar point of view before receiving his letter. The complete hopelessness of the British section of Stalinism, its ideological stagnation and small membership isolated from the labor movement, contrasted with the convulsive movement taking place within the ILP, which represents evidence of life as well as of decomposition, seem to us to indicate the need of pointing the efforts of our British section toward the ILP.

The ideological confusion of the leadership of the ILP, and its tendency to drift back and forth before the pressure from one side or another, a circumstance which renders the ILP organization as a whole especially susceptible to the influence of a determined group which knows what it wants, seems to us to open up exceptional possibilities for a fruitful penetration of this movement by the Left Oppositionists. The fact that we already have cadre united on clearly defined principles, even though as yet numerically small, ought to give us exceptional advantages in the free, fluid situation. That is, if we connect ourselves with the flowing movement wherever possible and do not permit an isolation from it.

The situation in America is somewhat different. Our league has five years of preparatory work behind it, and already represents an organization of considerable independent weight and influence in proportion to other groups which are moving toward the left. This creates the possibility for the Left Opposition here to become the main rallying center of the new party. The left movement in the SP as yet is very weak, and the Conference for Progressive Labor Action, a centrist independent organization somewhat similar to the ILP, does not represent a movement any larger than ours numerically. Therefore our tactics have to be somewhat different than the one we favor for England. Nevertheless, if we were confronted with the possibility of penetrating any of these centrist groups we would consider it necessary to take advantage of it.

It seems to us that another factor which will facilitate your work within the ILP is the step taken by the four organizations of Paris and the influence which this action is bound to exert within the ILP. If the Left Opposition is able to synchronize and direct activity among the members of the ILP with the forces exerted from the outside by this independent development, we ought to be able to save the ILP or a considerable section of it from the blind alley of Stalinism. The circumstance that the influence of Stalinism is declining at a fearful pace while ours is ascending and acquiring new organizational strength, is a factor of enormous importance. We are very strongly of the opinion that it should be for you a deciding element in the decision to put the British forces of the Left Opposition inside the ILP now.

In a previous letter we informed you of our wish to give you direct material help through supplies of the literature and bundles of the *Militant* without charge.[109] Granting the correctness of our policy and tactic in England, the speeding up of our direct agitational and propagandistic work in the ranks of the ILP membership has a vast importance even though our material means are very slight, measured against the Stalinist cash box. We ought to mobilize everything we have and bring its weight to bear on those points where motion is in progress, before a crystallization on a false basis takes place. The ILP at the present moment is surely such a point, and one of great world importance. We will do all we can to help you with this task of direct propaganda in the ILP ranks. We suggested before that if you can get the names of local secretaries or other key members of the ILP we will put them on the free list of the *Militant* for a while.

We would be very glad to hear from you and to exchange opinions and advice on this and other questions.

With warmest greetings to all the British comrades,

Fraternally yours,

James P. Cannon
Secretary

For a new party and a new international

Published September 30, 1933

The following declaration of the CLA National Committee was published in the *Militant*.

After the ignominious collapse of both the Social Democracy and the Communist International in Germany, and the subsequent inability of both these organizations to draw any lessons from this historical catastrophe, it is impossible any longer to conceal the fact that a revolutionary organization of the proletariat capable of leading it to victory does not exist. It must be created anew.

The National Committee of the Communist League of America (Opposition) is in complete agreement with the declaration issued to the Paris conference by the delegation of the International Left Opposition and approves its actions there. The NC likewise endorses the steps taken by the four organizations at the Paris conference toward the formation of a new communist International, and will devote its efforts henceforth, in cooperation with all other revolutionary groups and organizations willing to participate, to the task of directly assembling the forces for the creation of a new party, as the American section of the new (Fourth) International.

The entire membership of the league has unanimously endorsed this course after a thorough internal discussion of the question, and has empowered the National Committee to proclaim its complete break with the Stalinist Comintern and its American section, and to renounce the struggle to reform them. From this time onward the Communist League ceases to regard itself as a faction of the official Stalinist party, which has become a direct brake on the development of the workers' movement, and invites the cooperation of all revolutionary workers, regardless of their present affiliation or nonaffiliation, in common efforts leading to the construction of a genuine communist party in America.

Taking the necessity to create a new party as the point of departure, the Communist League proposes a frank and comradely discussion with other individuals, groups, and organizations aiming toward the same goal, and submits for their consideration the following points:

American perspectives

Under the terrific pressure of the crisis years, the conditions have been rapidly maturing for the class awakening of the American workers and for an enormous acceleration of the class struggle. In the next period the social contradictions will explode in a series of gigantic class battles, in the course of which the workers can assimilate the revolutionary lessons in an abridged form and rapidly leap forward on the path toward revolutionary action. To assist and guide this process, a new party, wresting the banner of communism from the sabotaging bureaucratic clique of Stalinism, must be created. And, under the given conditions, this new party will have before it the possibility and prospect of expansion into a powerful mass organization within a comparatively short time.

Fundamental principles

The new communist party, the necessity for which arises from the complete bankruptcy of reformism on the one side and of bureaucratic centrism (Stalinism) on the other, cannot consist of an indiscriminate combination of reformist and centrist elements. On the contrary, the new party can come into existence, take shape, and grow up to the requirements of its colossal historic task, only if it stands on a firm programmatic foundation and tolerates no conciliation toward reformist and centrist currents. For this program no new revelation is needed. The revolutionary teachings of Marx and Engels, cleansed once again of the reformist and centrist distortion and falsifications, are the fundamental principled guide for the new party.

The first four congresses of the Comintern, conducted under the leadership of Lenin and Trotsky, have concretized these teachings and applied them, in a series of unsurpassed theses and resolutions, to the basic problems of our epoch. The ten-year struggle of the International Left Opposition (Bolshevik-Leninist), during which the guiding ideas of the first four congresses of the Comintern were carried forward and counterposed on each and every important question of the living movement to the degenerating course of Stalinism, have been summarized in the eleven points adopted by the International Preconference of the Left Opposition.[110] All these documents referred to above retain their fundamental validity and constitute, in our opinion, the programmatic basis for the new party.

For revolutionary internationalism—
Against the theory of socialism in one country

The theoretical source of the degeneration and final downfall of the Communist International and its national sections, including the American, was the rejection of the Marxist principle of revolutionary internationalism and its substitution by the theory of socialism in one country. The Communist movement, which has been destroyed by this reactionary nationalist theory, cannot arise again without a clear and categoric rejection of it.

Defense of the Soviet Union

The ten-year regime of Stalinism has strangled the party and the workers' organizations in the Soviet Union and has facilitated enormously the danger of a counterrevolutionary capitalist overthrow. The Stalinist regime has undermined the foundations of the Soviet state and is leading it toward destruction. The social content of the October revolution, however, is still alive and, by its property character, which is a decisive criterion, the Soviet Union remains, even with the monstrous bureaucratic distortions, a workers' state.

The defense of the Soviet Union, encircled by a world of class enemies and systematically weakened from within by the Stalinist regime, is the unconditional duty of the international proletariat. The formation of new parties and a new International does not contradict this task but is necessitated by it. The *reform* of the Soviet workers' state in the USSR and its defense against capitalist intervention and *counterrevolution*, now depend upon the formation of strong revolutionary organizations in the capitalist countries, which will be capable of putting up a revolutionary resistance at home to capitalistic military ventures, and of exerting pressure on the internal regime in the USSR and influencing the Soviet proletariat.

Under the theory of socialism in one country the role of Communist parties has been debased to the task of the pacifist "defense of the Soviet Union," and for this all kinds of dubious "friends of the Soviet Union" have been recruited and hired while the tested revolutionary militants have been persecuted, slandered, and expelled.

But it is precisely in the task of defending the Soviet Union at the moment of danger that the present Stalinist parties are most completely impotent. The *strongest* party of the Comintern, the German CP, capitulated without a sign of resistance to the fascist bands, before the latter were armed with state power. The possibility that the weakest of such parties can offer any resistance whatever to the military designs of the capitalist states, must be dismissed altogether as the most dangerous fantasy. The internal reform and regeneration of the Soviet state and its defense against world imperialism, is the joint task of the new parties in the capitalist countries and in the Soviet Union.

The united front

From its inception, and also in the process of its formation, which may be more or less prolonged, the new party will naturally take part in the living movement of the working class and employ therein the tactic of the united front. This tactic, which presupposes temporary agreements with reformist organizations for specific actions, requires a categorical rejection of the theory of "social fascism" and the "united front from below only." On the one hand, the new party should conduct negotiations and make temporary agreements with the official representatives of reformist organizations when they take a step forward under the pressure of the masses—a tactic which the Stalinists have rejected "in principle." And on the other hand, it will reject any proposals for a "nonaggression pact" excluding criticism—which the Stalinists have accepted.

Trade union policy

The new party will find its road to the masses and gain influence over their movement only on the condition that it follows a Marxist policy on the trade union question, that is, the most important question of the American movement. Such a policy requires a penetration of the workers' mass organizations as they exist in reality, regardless of their form, and at the same time an irreconcilable struggle against the capitalist agents within them. The Stalinist dogma of "red" paper unions and the opportunist policy of "adaptation" to the reactionary leadership in the trade union movement are equally pernicious.

Against the right-wing apologists of Stalinism

The new party cannot represent a mechanical combination of "opposition" groups, but will be obliged to take a precise attitude toward each of them with respect to its platform and, especially, with respect to the *general direction* of its development. The Brandlerist clique (Lovestone, Wolfe, and Company), which effected a formal separation from the Stalinists with the dissolution of the right-center bloc in 1929, devotes itself to servile attempts to reestablish this bloc. It remains in fundamental unity with Stalinism on all the principled questions and shamefully justifies and apologizes for its systematic errors and crimes. The irreconcilable struggle of the new party against Stalinism presupposes and requires an equally unrelenting hostility to the right-wing camp followers of Stalinism.

Party democracy

The new party must establish within its ranks a regime of democratic centralism, which permits freedom of discussion and criticism on the one hand and unity of action on the other. The free election of officials from top to bottom, the control of the officials by the rank and file, and the right of every member to express his opinions in an atmosphere free from baiting and threats of expulsion, must be combined with a clearly defined principled foundation for party membership and a disciplined unity of the entire organization in action before the outside world.

Forces for the new party

The Communist League, as it is at present constituted, does not consider itself a party and has no intention of anticipating the real establishment of the new party by proclaiming itself as such. The task now is to recognize firmly that our role as a faction striving to reform the party of official Stalinism is exhausted, to strike out on a completely independent path, and to prepare, in cooperation with all other groups and organizations moving in the same direction, for the formation of a new party.

In the course of its struggle to reform the official party, as a faction of it, the Left Opposition worked out a program, consolidated a cadre of principled militants, and formed the skeleton of a national organization. These accomplishments can be regarded now as part of the capital of the new movement—not all that is necessary for the formation of the party, but contributions to it.

What is needed now is the coming together of the various groups of revolutionary workers who have broken, or who are in the process of breaking, with reformism and centrism, as well as those dispersed individual revolutionists who have been repelled by the Stalinist bureaucracy and remain without affiliation. It is self-evident that the working out of a common program, and the eventual concentration of these forces in a single party, must be preceded by an exchange of opinion and discussion and, very probably, will involve a transition period of cooperation before the final fusion.

Whatever form the next development may take, the Left Opposition is ready now to enter into open and comradely negotiations and discussions with other groups which seriously set for themselves the same goal. After its long and unrelenting struggle against the arrogant bureaucratism and ultimatistic methods of Stalinism, the Left Opposition least of all can seek to *impose* anything on others or to demand the acceptance in advance of its proposals, its program, or its "leadership." Submitting the foregoing points for discussion, we on our part are ready to give attentive and comradely consideration to any different proposals and to bring them to the attention of our members and supporters by publication in the *Militant*, together with our comments on them.

With this object in view, the columns of the *Militant* will be open for a discussion of the question of a new party and a new International.

Negotiations with the Gitlow group

October 11, 1933

The following letter was addressed to branches of the Communist League.

Dear Comrades:

A few weeks ago the official paper of the Gitlow group, the *Voice of Labor*, carried an article by Gitlow declaring for a new communist party. In this article he sharply attacked the Stalinists and recorded a complete break with the Lovestone faction. He especially attacked the position of the Lovestoneites on Germany and expressed a point of view very much in harmony with that of the Left Opposition on German perspectives. We addressed a letter to the Gitlow group, enclosing a copy of the "Declaration of the Four" at Paris, and asked them to take a position on it. They didn't reply directly but instead proposed a formal meeting of the two groups to discuss matters.

On Monday, October 9, a subcommittee of the National Committee and a similar committee of the Gitlow group had a discussion that lasted several hours. The representatives of the Gitlow group expressed themselves very definitely in favor of collaborating with us for the building of a new communist party. They seem to show a firm will to work with us and expressed great confidence in our joint appeal to initiate the movement that will culminate in the formation of a new party in six months to a year.

It was our aim to clarify some of the programmatic questions which remain in dispute between the groups. That, of course, will be necessary before any public steps can be taken. The Gitlow group appears to be somewhat evasive in this respect. This attitude on their part of course is understandable. The group that has to come from the Lovestone faction to a fusion with the Left Opposition—that is, from one polar extreme of the communist movement to another—can be expected to take some time to go over a number of contradictions. Nevertheless the general direction of this group appears to be very definitely toward us. And this is the most important question. It is our task, as we understand it, to facilitate the development of the Gitlow group to the point where joint work and even actual fusion with us will be based on a firm programmatic basis. This will have to be recorded as a process in the course of which it is quite probable that we will establish some kind of a working agreement with this group before a complete fusion takes place.

Next Monday the joint committee holds another meeting. This meeting will take up the question of the contents of a proposed joint statement to be issued by the two groups. It is to be expected that certain difficulties will be encountered there. The program which we will propose of course is embodied in the eleven points, the Declaration of the Four, and the manifesto of our NC. At this meeting we will record it as a step forward if we succeed in clearly defining the points of agreement and the points of difference between the two groups. On that basis we can well decide whether a public action is possible or whether a period of discussion is necessary. The branches will be informed fully of every step in the negotiations.[111]

Fraternally,

James P. Cannon
Secretary

The AFL, the strike wave, and trade union perspectives

Published October 14, 1933

The following editorial was published in the *Militant*.

The Fifty-third Annual Convention of the American Federation of Labor convened at a turning point in the life of the labor movement, when the resurgent forces of new life, thrust forward by the powerful impulsion of the class struggle, are beginning to push their way through the dry crust and restraining forms of conservative trade unionism.[112]

The new masses who are sweeping into the trade union movement, heralding their arrival by tumultuous struggles, are without any direct representation at the convention. The strike wave, the great, new, vital, and determining factor in the labor movement, lacks an authentic spokesman there. But this dread specter is present all the time and dominates the proceedings. The strike wave is the unofficial delegate which disturbs the dead calm of self-satisfied conservatism so familiar at all AFL gatherings in recent years. All the important speeches and deliberations were made as if in reply to the thunderous arguments of this new force which is speaking in terms of class battles, of strikes and picket lines.

The forces of resurgent life, represented by the strike wave, which have not yet found formal expression in official representation, did not record their real strength in the convention proceedings. They only recorded their presence in the situation and served notice of a future participation. That alone was sufficient—so ominous is the new power—to make it the axis around which all the proceedings and discussion revolved. The stormy and irrepressible forces of the new labor militancy, clamoring their demands in the nationwide strike movement, evoked the terrified concern of the labor lieutenants of capital gathered in solemn convention, and of the political spokesmen of capital, including the president of the U.S. and his general, Johnson, who addressed them.

The real design behind the benevolence of the Roosevelt administration toward union organization was brought out more sharply and clearly at the convention. They want a trade union movement that will be an instrument to restrain the workers, to prevent strikes and to suppress and outlaw the strikes that do occur. Only a few months have gone by since the NRA was hailed as the liberator of the workers, and already the iron fist is coming out of the velvet glove. Roosevelt's threat to put the recalcitrant horses in a corral; General Johnson's blunter declaration, "You cannot tolerate the strike," and his appeal to public opinion "to destroy every subversive influence"; the glorification of Gompers and the reminder of his role in dragooning the American workers into the war—in these expressions of the authentic spokesmen of the capitalist exploiters the Roosevelt program was given a plainer and more easily read translation than before.

The appearance of Green in a Washington church pulpit, with his pitiful appeal in biblical language to the "masters" to be good to their "servants," unspeakably contemptible and servile as it was, only served to demonstrate how neatly the AFL leaders have fitted themselves into the NRA scheme to harness the insurgent movement of the American workers through the official trade union movement. There is no doubt where they stand, nor where the convention which they dominate stands.

But the outward manifestations at Washington are by no means an accurate reflection of the situation within the AFL, and still less of the present-day labor movement in its broader aspects. Against the policy and intentions of the capitalist politicians and their labor allies, as revealed at the Washington convention, the new outstanding developments must be considered—the influx of hundreds of thousands of new workers into the unions, the formation within a few months' time of 500 new federal unions, the insistent demand for the industrial union form of organization to meet the needs of the newly organized masses. These factors, counterbalanced to the formal official decisions and pronouncements, require consideration in a rounded view of the actual situation.

They are an essential part of the "proceedings" of the fifty-third convention of the AFL. And in addition to that, the thunder of the strike wave outside the door also belongs in the record. An appreciation of the present situation in the trade union movement, and of the AFL convention as a distorted reflection of it, is possible only if these factors are taken into account and given due weight and importance. In that case the one-sided picture of the Washington gathering, as just another expression of hidebound conservatism, fades away and we see the actual movement as it is in reality, fermenting with new life and on the verge of great convulsions which will upset all the schemes and plans.

Nothing was firmly settled or decided for the labor movement at the Washington convention. The new elements at work in the trade unions registered themselves and served notice, so to speak, of a further participation later on. The contending forces in the trade union movement, which will clash with increasing fury from this time forward, met in a preliminary skirmish at Washington. From there the conflict will be transferred back to the field of class struggle—to the strikes, the picket lines, the battles with the state forces and armed thugs, and the forthcoming internal struggles within the trade union organizations.

All of this is projected on the basis of a strike wave of such dimensions as has not been seen in recent times and which, in our judgment, is only a curtain raiser of what is to follow. The bosses and their political and trade union agents apparently have the same opinion. They have enunciated their program at the AFL convention. The labor movement itself, that is, the real movement of the masses, has not yet worked out an estimation of the perspective and a program of its own. This is the big task and need of the present time. Its solution devolves naturally on the class-conscious elements.

The strike wave is the first reply that the American workers have made to the frightful conditions and standards imposed upon them during the crisis and which the NRA mechanism is seeking to stabilize and make permanent. The present scope and insurgent militancy of the strike wave are especially portentous as to what is to follow if the workers fail to get satisfaction of their demands.

And this, in our opinion, is precisely what is going to

happen. The attempt of the Roosevelt administration to "plan" industry on a basis of capitalist private ownership is inevitably doomed to a resounding collapse, and that very probably in the near future. With that, and with the failure also to satisfy the expectations of the workers which were aroused by the ballyhoo campaign of the NRA, will come a tremendous disillusionment of the workers and a rapidly increasing tendency on their part to resort to more aggressive struggles; to rely on their own strength and organization. Trade unionism, which was held out to them in the first stages of the NRA as a device to restrain their independent movement, will become for the workers the medium for its expression on a colossal scale. The workers will turn to trade unionism in real earnest, and they will be bent on making the unions serve as instruments of struggle against the exploiters.

Then, as has already been clearly intimated in the threatening speeches of Roosevelt and Johnson at the Washington convention, the benevolent mask of the Roosevelt administration will be taken off. The unions they encouraged, and even coddled, as long as they thought they could serve as "harness" will meet open opposition from the government. All the forces at its command, from systematic antiunion and antistrike propaganda to police and military force, will be brought to bear. The unions, insofar as they really fight—and that is the function which the conditions of the times impose upon them—will have to fight for their existence against the government itself.

The capitalist attack against the trade unions as organs of struggle will be carried inside the unions. Green, Lewis, and Company will be called upon to purge the organizations of their militant elements and restore the unions to conservative and respectable docility. The prompt response of these treacherous agents of capital to this demand is assured in advance; their attitude at Washington, in harmony with all their previous conduct, signifies this first of all.

The trade unions, swelling into larger proportions by the influx of new members on one side, will witness wholesale expulsions and splits, engendered by the reactionary bureaucracy on the other. Insurgent workers who insist on striking—the "horses" that "refuse to work in harness"—will meet the condemnation of the labor bureaucracy. Their strikes will be outlawed and denounced as communistic plots. A campaign of red-baiting will be inaugurated against revolutionaries and communists. Where these do not exist they will be invented. Every worker who wants to fight for his rights and wants to make the union fight for them will be branded as a "red." The next developments of the trade union movement will unfold in a seething tide of labor rebellion—of "outlaw" strikes, clashes with the authorities, fierce internal struggles in the unions, expulsions, and splits.

The fact that already today hundreds of thousands of workers are streaming into the trade unions is in itself a fact of incalculable significance. The workers are on the move. That is what is new; that is what is important in the situation. The trade union is the first and most elementary form of working-class organization, for which no substitute has ever been invented. The workers take their first steps on the path of class development through that door. Hundreds of thousands are taking this step already today, a large percentage of them for the first time. Millions of others will follow them tomorrow. No matter how conservative the unions may be, no matter how reactionary their present leadership, and regardless of what the real purposes of the Roosevelt administration were in giving a certain encouragement and impetus to this trade union revival—in spite of all of this, the movement itself represents an elemental force, a power which properly influenced at the right time by the class-conscious vanguard, can break through all the absolute forms and frustrate all the reactionary schemes.

This movement of the masses into the trade unions can be seriously influenced only from within. From this it follows: Get into the unions. Stay there. Work within.

Before any serious development of a revolutionary organization can be expected in America this penetration of the trade unions must begin in earnest. The militants who undertake this task now, after all the discredit brought to the name of communism by the Stalinists, will labor under a double handicap. The complete and unchallenged supremacy of the reactionaries in the trade union leadership; the weight of the government and of all capitalist propaganda and repressive forces on their side; the popular hostility to communism and the relationship of forces in general—these circumstances alone will constitute huge obstacles at the beginning. Besides that, the new left-wing movement will have to pay for the sins and failures of the old.

The labor fakers will start new expulsion campaigns against the radicals the moment their influence is felt again in the mass movement. It is folly to think that the task of penetrating the mass trade unions, under the given conditions, and of reconstituting a vigorous left wing within them can be accomplished with brass bands playing and banners flying. Quiet and persistent work, and loyal cooperation with all progressive-minded workers who want to build fighting unions—this simple prescription stands first in order. The rest will follow.

We give no pledge to refrain from revolutionary activity in the unions or to turn our backs on "outlaw" strikes.

We leave such trade union tactics to opportunists and traitors. It is our aim, on the contrary, to be with the masses, especially at the moment of their sharpest collisions with the capitalists, whatever form these collisions may take. In order that this association with the revolting masses can have a fruitful revolutionary influence, it has to begin now by an entrenchment of the militant and class-conscious elements in the AFL unions and the formation of a left wing within them.

CLA activity among Jewish workers

October 17, 1933

The following letter was addressed to branches of the Communist League.

Dear Comrades:

At its last meeting the National Committee considered the work of the league in the Jewish field with the participation of a representative of the Jewish committee.

The comrade of the Jewish committee reported on the achievements in this field of work since they first started the publication of our Jewish organ, *Unser Kamf*. Altogether twenty-four issues of the paper have appeared in this period, having an average distribution of two thousand copies per issue (300 individual subscribers, 800 in bundle orders, the rest in sales and distribution of single copies). The paper is distributed in about fifteen cities in the U.S. and Canada. Aside from this *Unser Kamf* has been used as the spokesman by Opposition groups in six foreign countries (France, Belgium, South Africa, Argentina, Uruguay, and

Brazil). In the same period the Jewish comrades published one pamphlet, which was distributed in more than 2,000 copies. Since August 1 no issue of the paper appeared due to a financial crisis that paralyzed the work.

The principal weakness of the work lies in the organizational field. The *Unser Kamf* clubs that have been started as the organizational base for the paper have not been functioning, with the exception of the Toronto club, which has had a fair measure of success.

Our turn in the direction of a new party and a Fourth International places upon us the obligation of intensified work in this field. The Jewish working masses are today the principal props of the SP as well as of the Stalinists. The only Socialist daily in this country is in the Jewish language (the *Forward*), and the Stalinist *Freiheit* is by far the most circulated party daily. Even the Lovestoneites have recently made some headway in this field by commencing the publication of a Jewish monthly.

The National Committee adopted several decisions:

1. That the Jewish committee publish immediately a special issue of *Unser Kamf* devoted to the new turn so as to bring to the attention of the Jewish workers our present orientation.

2. That henceforth *Unser Kamf* is to appear *monthly* and is to be stabilized on this basis for several months until the conditions will warrant a more frequent appearance.

3. That the Jewish workers' clubs are to be organized on a broad basis, in line with our general new policy in this respect.

4. Every branch having Jewish-speaking members is to organize them into fractions, directly responsible to the branch executive committee and to the NC for Jewish work. The branches are to guide and assist the Jewish fractions in its work, for the proper distribution of *Unser Kamf*, and

in the building of clubs wherever possible, in the work in Jewish fraternal and mass organizations, etc.

5. The reorganized National Committee for the Jewish work consists of Comrades Lewit, Eckshtat, Kling, Orland, and Dryer.

Please give careful consideration to this communication and inform us of the number of Jewish comrades you have organized in your branch into a fraction and the steps taken regarding future work.

Comradely,

James P. Cannon
Secretary

Relations with the United Workers Party

December 6, 1933

The following letter was written to Albert Glotzer in Chicago.

Dear Comrade Glotzer:

Our resident NC has taken up the question of negotiations with the United Workers Party, and as you know, I wrote informing Comrade Satir of our invitation to them to state their views for publication in the *Militant*, as part of the discussion of the issues before us.[113] That time we did not yet have a summary of the further discussions in regard to the practical collaboration. We have since considered this side as well, and the following are the conclusions we have arrived at:

1. We endorse in general the proposals for practical collaboration in the Workers League. We accept joint responsibility for the leadership and activities of the league and for the paper, but in respect to the latter, we want to make sure that we take no responsibility for the views represented by the Mattick group. To make this more specific,

we propose an arrangement as follows: We take responsibility only for our own views, and propose to advance as a condition for editorial collaboration the appearance of a standing declaration in the paper, that the authors of signed articles bear responsibility for them, that unsigned articles are to represent the opinions of the joint editorial board.

2. We agree to collaborate to extend the Workers League on a national scale, especially in such cities where the possibilities are at hand, and where it is feasible to organize the league. But that shall not be construed as meaning that our policy in every city is to localize the unemployment movement into the at-present narrow framework of the essentially Chicago Workers League, but rather that in every city the organizational form of the movement be dealt with concretely in accordance with the local conditions and possibilities. In other words, this basis allows for some flexibility; however, with the emphasis put on extension of the Workers League and activity of our comrades within it, wherever this does not mean conflict because of particular existing local conditions.

3. We propose to hold in abeyance the matter of the creation of a national committee of the Workers League until such time as the organization is further extended. This point naturally presupposes that we are ready right now to collaborate jointly in the Chicago leadership with them with the full cooperation of our local comrades, and from that as a basis proceed to extend the organization as above proposed.

From this of course follows that the *Militant* will also signify its support of this movement. But, as we feel sure the Chicago comrades will readily understand, the complete formation on a national scale of such a movement in the sense of also having a national committee, etc., etc., will involve a number of problems; for example, in regard to actually existing unemployment organizations, united front possibilities of federation, as well as, in several cities, specifically existing local conditions. These aspects we have to discuss a little further, and at any rate, it should seem reasonable to await the formal consideration of a national committee until there are some actual organizations to unite nationally.

In regard to the question raised by the Cook County federation, we have no particular comment to make.[114] We feel quite satisfied that you comrades can start working out a solution of this problem, but should some serious question arise, that you take it up with us first. To the extent that this involves further developments of unemployed federations on a national scale, naturally that is also a matter for further discussion, and we shall be able to inform you in regard to this very shortly.

It is our view that the understanding we had amongst us prior to my leaving Chicago is correct. That is, the attempt to draw the section of Sinclair and Dixon closer to us and to aid the course toward a split in the United Workers Party, but in the process to collaborate in the practical work and to get all our unemployed comrades actively engaged within the Workers League. We note what you say about Oscar Peterson. Please send us his address, and we'll stick him on the mailing list. We will do the same for other similar types when we get the addresses.

What you propose in regard to the workers' school in Chicago is entirely agreeable, and the comrades should go ahead completing the arrangements. We should particularly bear in mind, however, that since now the class becomes a more directly LO institution, it is necessary that we take up the question of its further strengthening, bringing in workers to take part in that class much more energetically, and that we are also having class activities properly coordinated with the other work at hand. I hope you will make sure to stress this matter before the branch.

In regard to the Friends of the *Militant* Club, there is hardly any comment to make. I have reported to the comrades here that I consider your views in general to be correct.[115] It would be the best policy, however, to maintain a friendly attitude to encourage the club as much as can be done to get it to stand on its own feet, to maintain as little formal relations as possible, but to also make sure that we show an attitude of giving the club the support it is entitled to. If we maintain this attitude we should be able to know just what the intentions of these comrades are, whether they will let the club function as a support for the *Militant*. We will communicate with them from here in the sense of suggesting various courses of activity for them, without, however, going into the question of the controversy. We want to wait and see if this controversy can be liquidated by itself in this fashion, or else if the group will leave the basis of its original purpose. Further action can then be taken later.

The International Youth Conference has been postponed until the end of January.[116] Please make sure to hold yourself as a delegate.

With very best regards to all the Chicago comrades,

Fraternally yours,

[James P. Cannon]
Secretary

The lynching wave and American fascism

Published December 9, 1933

The following editorial was published in the *Militant*.

In the outbreak of lynchings that swept the country, striking at three widely separated sections with the fury of a hurricane, an old American custom was repeated with some new and distinctive features which are of exceptional significance. In the present situation such orgies of mob violence as those in California, Maryland, and Missouri do not fit into the old pattern.[117]

Mob murder in itself is no novelty in the United States. In the South, as everybody knows, it is an established institution for the repression of the Negroes, operating all the time as an extralegal supplement to the regular court procedure. In the North, also, lynching has been known before, but it is not "recognized" here as it is in the South and, except in isolated instances, has appeared only in connection with social disturbance.

The frenzied lynching bees of the recent days, however,

had their scene in the northern part of the country, or on its border; white men as well as Negroes were victims; there was not one single lynching but three, and those in rapid succession; and the happenings precipitated a hysterical public controversy over the issue, with Governor Rolph of California and other prominent people, including—God save the mark!—a New York preacher (who later recanted), openly condoning the bestial actions of the mob. It is clear that last week's lynchings had special features of their own; they represent a new and somewhat different phenomenon, and they arose from a special combination of causes.

The three lynchings did not occur merely because of popular revulsion at some crime of a particularly shocking nature. The California kidnapping was the match that set off the explosions of unrestrained moronic hysteria and violence, but the explosive material itself for some kind of an eruption was already there. It consists of the unrest, and dissatisfaction of the people, primarily the ruined petty-bourgeois elements, their uncertainty and their sense of frustration, which charge the social atmosphere like a Leyden jar.

All of this has been accumulating during the crisis years. It presses for outlet and may readily find it in strange, irrational, and violent ways. The lynching hysteria which has swept the country derives from the same source as the fanatical million-headed following of Father Coughlin, the demagogue priest. The real author is the social devastation wrought by the crisis.

The material out of which fascist gangs, anti-Semitism, religious frenzies, and moronic lynching mobs all may be set in motion is at hand in the social tension which produced three lynchings within a week. The material for the rapid development of a revolutionary labor movement is there also in the bitter discontent of the workers, but a leading force capable of organizing it is so far lacking. The disintegration of the communist movement aids the one-sided expression of the general mass of social discontent in a fascist direction.

The popular support received by Governor Rolph, in his stand as the champion of the mob, is a significant indication of the extent to which public imagination was stirred by the San Jose lynching, and even of the widespread vicarious participation in it. Rolph, a demagogue of the first water, appears in this instance more as the reflector of petty-bourgeois mass prejudice and hysteria than as the authentic spokesman of the decisive sections of the ruling class. There is no foundation for the contention (*Daily Worker*, November 30) that the mob violence was deliberately unleashed at the command of the big capitalists and that Rolph speaks in their name. They will come to such a policy in time, of this there is no room for doubt, but it is no part of their design at the present moment. Just the contrary, as an examination of the facts will show.

The inflammatory utterances of Governor Rolph aroused a storm of controversy and revealed a division of opinion. This division, and its nature, must be perceived and understood, not ignored. The lynching governor was "showered with telegrams of approval." But, on the other hand, the capitalist press, led by the big New York dailies, and an imposing committee of "citizens" headed by ex-President Hoover, condemned him. The real present sentiment of the big capitalists was indubitably expressed by them. And for good reasons.

Unrestrained mob action is a dangerous fire to play with under the present conditions. The leading exploiters will not lightly instigate it. They do not feel the need of it yet. Mob hysteria might easily express itself in a different direction under the slightest incitement. As long as the rulers feel themselves secured by the legal processes of repression they will not deliberately encourage extralegal mob actions. That is why the most authoritative representatives of capital frowned on Rolph's condonement of them.

The psychological factors for a rapid transformation of the social conflict out of the realm of legality and parliamentarism into that of open mass violence, and for the lightninglike emergence of a revolutionary movement on the one side and a fascist movement on the other, have an exceptional strength in America; they are rooted in the tradition of the country as well as in the conditions of the present. The American people of all classes, by and large, have very little regard for "law and order" when it stands in the way of something they really want to do. (The almost universal disregard for the prohibition law is an interesting illustration of this attitude on a wide scale.)

American labor history has been written in struggle, violent and bloody. Many a strike took the form of armed conflict; few pass without violent clashes. On the other hand, the American capitalists never hesitated to go outside the bounds of their own legality when the exigencies of the class struggle required it. Frank Little was killed by lynchers. So also was Wesley Everest and many other labor militants. The radical workers were dragooned into support of the war or bludgeoned into silence by unofficial lynching mobs which supplemented the legal compulsion of the state authority. A good half or more of the brutal violence against the workers in strikes is the work of unofficial thugs and gunmen. When the two main classes in this country get ready to settle accounts, and long before they come to the final account, the "legal" framework of the struggle will have been shattered to bits.

The reservoir of mass violence in America is a huge one,

and the events of the past week have demonstrated how easily it can be tapped, and with what unbridled fury it can rage. The mob of humans turned into wild beasts who mutilated and killed the two helpless prisoners at San Jose, and that far bigger mob of vicarious participants who applauded them from afar, have presented a spectacle of menacing implications to the labor movement.

The same mobs can be directed against the workers. They are the material out of which the murderous bands of fascism can be organized when the big exploiters feel the need of them. The working class had every reason to take alarm at the spread of lynching and to raise a mighty protest against every official condonement of it. But the bare appeal from mob violence to ordered legal processes—the sum and substance of liberal and Socialist agitation—does not touch the heart of the issue. The problem is rooted in the social conditions of class society just as the whole oppressive system of class justice is. The same class forces which administer the "law" need only to sense the danger to their rule in order to organize and bribe the dregs of society and hurl them against the workers with unrestrained violence. To rely solely on capitalist legal procedure in the struggle against lynching and other forms of illegal mass violence is to clear the way for the latter. Under different circumstances the force behind each is the same.

The movement of fascism does not come into existence at the command of the capitalists. It arises out of the conditions created by capitalism at a certain stage of its disintegration as a social and economic system. Its troops, for the greater part, are the petty-bourgeois elements, ruined and driven to frenzy by the crisis. The movement is aimed, at its inception, against big capital as well as against the labor movement. The former take over the movement and hurl it against the workers if the latter do not show sufficient strength to crush the movement of fascism and gain the support of the petty-bourgeois masses for their revolutionary program.

These fundamental considerations should be kept in mind in connection with the various manifestations of incipient fascism in America. The revolutionary labor movement and the movement of fascism both grow out of the same social conditions. The devastating crisis of American capitalism has prepared the soil for both. What is most alarming in the present developments is the increasing number of signs that the restless and dissatisfied petty-bourgeois elements are finding expression in various ways which, taken together, lead in the direction of a fascist movement. The lynching orgy of the past week was undoubtedly such a sign—one of many. Of the revolutionary countermovement among the masses there is hardly a trace.

For this one-sided development, which is fraught with so much danger to the working class, the conditions themselves are not to blame. All the objective requisites for the speedy development of a revolutionary movement in the working class have been maturing under the enormous pressure of the crisis. What is lacking to organize it and set it on its feet is a revolutionary communist party. The disintegration brought into the movement by Stalinism has taken a fearful toll. *Stalinism has destroyed the Communist Party.* We must build a new one without delay. This is the imperative warning sounded again in the events of the past week.

Striking out on an independent path

Published December 23, 1933

The following editorial was published in the *Militant*.

In breaking finally with the Stalinist party and the Comintern, and in striking out on an independent path toward the building of a new party, the Communist League has taken a step which flows with irrefutable logic from the realities of the situation; it corresponds completely to the burning needs of the working class and the political movement of its conscious vanguard section. The political wisdom of this decision will be verified in life, as in a certain measure it has already been verified, to the extent that we steer a resolute course on the new path.

Our break with Stalinism, its organizations and its treacherous policy, is irrevocable; there is no turning back. The time when the faction struggle within the ranks of the Comintern occupied the center of our attention is behind us. The main weight of our activity has to be shifted now directly into the broad class struggle. Delay or hesitation with this radical transformation of our work can only militate against the movement and our own influence in it.

It is not enough to recognize the logic of this decisive turn and to accept it formally. The next problem—and it is a crucial one now—is to assimilate the idea with all its implications to the very end, into our blood. A complete break with narrow factional activity and the psychology engendered by it is an imperative necessity. Only then will we be able to translate our decision into action. A checkup of our activity and its results since the publication of our resolution on the question of the new party, which is in order now, will convince us of this.

One of the most conspicuous examples of the fruitful results of the new orientation of the league is to be found in the experience of the Minneapolis comrades in the unemployment movement. For a long time there, as elsewhere, while we maintained our position as a faction of the Stalinist party and of its peripheral organizations, the league members and other revolutionary workers attempted to participate in the Unemployment Councils of the Stalinists. A futile task and a waste of time, as experience demonstrated. These Unemployment Councils, like all other Stalinist "mass organizations" are narrowly constructed family affairs, isolated from the actual movement of the masses and serving the special interests of the bureaucratic machine. They were far more concerned to keep "Trotskyites" out than to get workers in. The attempt to work in the unemployment movement under such auspices became a monotonous process of squeezing into the so-called Unemployment Councils and being thrown out again. The more the burden of mass unemployment pressed the workers toward action the more the Stalinist clique blocked the way. A resolute break out of this vicious circle became the condition for a real activity among the masses on the issue of unemployment.

An independent course of action was commenced by the internationalists in this field. The sterile "councils" were left to stew in their own juice. Unemployed workers and workers' organizations were approached with a program of united action. This tactic brought gratifying results in a comparatively short time. The will of the workers generally to get together in the fight against the scourge of unemployment was shown in the widespread response to the initiative of our comrades. The relative insignificance of the Stalinist clique in the broad movement, and the absurdity of their claim to a "monopoly" of leadership, were likewise revealed with striking force.

Several conferences, embracing the bulk of the workers' organizations, have already been held; a big mass meeting on the unemployment question has taken place; the movement is growing and broadening in scope and the decks are being cleared for a real demonstration of working-class unity and discontent that will wrest concessions from the masters. The developments to be seen in Minneapolis already are a heartening sign of the moving power that resides in the slogans of struggle against unemployment once they are taken out of the closed circle of a clique and made an issue of the class.

In the broad united front of the real workers' movement in Minneapolis the Stalinists appear only as a small minority of disrupters. The workers turned against them. Before the workers, who are concerned vitally with the united fight to make the conditions of their lives more bearable, the Stalinists appeared as enemies of the movement, resentful of its success and bent on disrupting and disorganizing it. In this way they convince the workers, on the basis of their own experience, that the Stalinist party, which serves the special interests of a bureaucratic clique, is a sabotaging obstacle to the development of the workers movement.

These lessons derived from experience are not the least of the benefits accruing to the general movement from the wide-scale unemployment activity which is being unfolded in Minneapolis. The members of the Communist League, while proceeding with their constructive work in the forefront of the movement, are true to its interests in exposing the fundamental meaning of the Stalinist tactics and aiding the workers to draw the necessary conclusions. Nevertheless, it appears to us that too much time and effort should not be devoted to this aspect of the problem. In the broad movement of the working class it is most important to see things in their true proportions. We should be careful not to carry with us too many relics of the internal faction struggle that dominated our activity for so long a time.

The completely independent course in the class struggle, which our preparations for the new party enjoin upon us, gives us at the same time the opportunity to contrast our policy to that of the Stalinists before the workers in actual practice. This is the most effective way now to complete the task of annihilating Stalinism and liberating the vanguard labor movement from its disruptive influence. Our strength in the broad workers' movement will grow most rapidly if we appear there, in relation to the Stalinists, not as one faction fighting another, but rather as the representatives of the fundamental interests of the class opposing a policy of sabotage and disruption based on interests alien to those of the class. That, in fact, is how the conflict stands in reality. It is up to us to make it clear, in practice, in the whole course of our activity, as well as in words.

That is the way to ensure success in our aim to establish

a new and genuine party of communism without too much delay and to line up the forces for a great forward leap of the revolutionary movement in America. We have not yet set our feet firmly on this path—this we must acknowledge. Our long years of existence as a small faction fighting to restore the line of Marxist principle—a position inseparable from a certain tendency toward sectarianism—have left marks in our habits of thought as well as in our method of work. We have broken with the old position as a faction. Now we must break with the psychology of a faction and appear in all our work as the banner-bearers of an independent party.

Strike the hotels!

Published December 30, 1933

The following editorial was published in the *Militant*.

One of the bright spots in the rising labor movement is the sensational rise of the Amalgamated Food Workers and its militant challenge to the big New York hotels, which have been completely unorganized and immune to "labor troubles" for many years. Within the space of a few months' time, thanks to the strong sentiment for organization in the ranks of the fiercely exploited workers and a competent leadership in the union, the Amalgamated has bounded forward to a commanding position in the situation and is the indicated medium for the organization of a general strike to smash the infamous NRA code and enforce the workers' demands.[118]

The action of the union in putting the preparation of the general strike now definitely on the agenda, after the arduous preliminary work in spreading the message of unionism and gathering the forces of the workers together, raises the prospect of a battle that can mean much for the labor movement in general as well as for the workers directly involved. Shut off from unionism for so many years, the biggest industry in New York—for that is what the hotel and restaurant business is—remained a stronghold of superexploitation which helped to depress the standards and undermine the organizations of all the other workers.

In invading this field and establishing the firm basis of a union there the Amalgamated Food Workers has rendered a signal service to the whole movement of organized labor. In the projected strike it will be entitled to solidarity and support, which are needed to ensure success.

To wrest concessions from the big New York hotels is no small undertaking. It cannot be accomplished without a real battle, and the battle cannot get a good start without serious preparation and a fair basis of organization beforehand. In proceeding from this point of view, and in moving step by step along a consistent line—gathering forces, building up the union, popularizing the idea of general strike action instead of reliance on the NRA—the Amalgamated has already stamped itself in the minds of thousands of discontented hotel slaves as an organization that means business, not bluff and ballyhoo. The steady stream of new recruits into the union bears testimony to this. These demonstrations of confidence in the union presage a widespread response to the strike call when it goes out.

The challenge to the NRA code and the hotel magnates in whose interest it was drawn up leads with iron necessity to a strike. There is no other way but by a show of strength to convince these people who refuse to hear or heed the bitter grievances of the workers. The demands gained and the organization established in this way will be all the more secure. There will be no ground for the illusion that anybody gave the workers anything. It will be clear that everything gained is the result of organized struggle and it will not be easy to take the gains away again.

The general strike of the New York hotels will be an undisguised fight between capital and labor under modern conditions. The New York hotels are not one-horse concerns—they represent a huge concentration of capital closely tied up with the banks, and in some cases directly controlled by them. This policy is antiunion from start to finish. The Amalgamated union, on the other hand, is a modern type of labor organization, industrial in form to include all workers in the industry, militant in policy and relying on its own strength.

The AFL unions in the industry have never tackled the big hotels; they have confined themselves to smaller units—little cafes, cafeterias, and night clubs—leaving the big and powerful concerns and the workers enslaved by them pretty much alone. Antiquated craft unionism demonstrates its inadequacy and the whole theory of the "partnership of capital and labor" goes to pieces when large-scale aggregations of capital are confronted.

The Amalgamated Food Workers arose as an independent industrial union in a field that was deserted and unoccupied, just as similar organizations must and will take shape in other big industries which the craft unions are unable or unwilling to organize. It is not a "dual" union but the legitimate organization to serve the needs of the workers. The foremost and fundamental task in preparation for the general strike is to build and strengthen the Amalgamated Food Workers.

Concentration on this fundamental task of organizing the workers into the Amalgamated does not, of course, prevent cooperation with other unions in the industry and, in our opinion, the Executive Board of the Amalgamated was right in declaring its readiness to engage in joint actions with the AFL unions in case the latter are really prepared to act, that is, to call a strike of the workers under their jurisdiction. Such a proposition can very well remain as a standing attitude provided it does not lead to illusions among the members that some nebulous combination or instrument outside the hotel and restaurant workers' branch of the Amalgamated can be the driving force of a real strike. The Amalgamated itself is the driving force! It would be fatally wrong to shift attention from the fundamental task of organizing the unorganized hotel workers into the union to the field of negotiations, discussions, and recriminations with other organizations which have no basis in the hotels. The mechanism for a strike is first of all membership in a *union*. A hundred "joint committees" and "united front conferences" cannot be substituted for it.

As the hotel and restaurant workers move toward a showdown with the rapacious exploiters who coin their lives into dollars, one warning cannot be repeated too often. That is: Put no faith in the NRA, distrust every move it makes, rely on your organized strength and the solidarity of your fellow workers alone!

There is no doubt that many hotel and restaurant workers believed in the NRA at first and expected that Roosevelt would really do something for them. They have reason to know better now. After the approval by the NRA of the shameless hotel and restaurant code—one of the very worst of all, with its fifty-four-hour week and similar odious provisions in favor of the bosses—it should be clear to every thinking worker that no help can be expected from this quarter. Just the contrary. The whole NRA scheme was hatched to head off the independent action of the workers, fill them with false hopes, dampen down their militancy, and harness them for a long time to the old conditions. The proof of this, which has been amply

Above, New York hotel strike, January 1934. Below, Minneapolis Teamsters Local 574 strikers battle police and special deputies, May 1934.

provided already in the experience of the hotel and restaurant workers, is driving them to unionization and to concrete preparations for a strike. That is the only way to success in the struggle to improve conditions and make life more bearable for the cruelly exploited workers of the hotel and restaurant industry of New York.

Field's policy in the hotel strike[119]

February 15, 1934

The following motions by Cannon were adopted by the National Committee of the CLA. They are taken from the minutes of the NC.

1. A union of newly organized workers confronting a powerful aggregation of capital represented by the Hotel Owners Association was up against tremendous odds to begin with. A complete victory in the first battle is hardly to be expected.

2. The outstanding negative factors in the strike from the beginning were:

a. Disruptive splitting policy and actions of the Stalinists who set the sectarian interests of their own clique above the interests of the mass movement, spread slander, sowed confusion and disorganization, and did everything they could to demoralize the fighting power of the workers.

b. The conservative, bureaucratic policy and methods of the Field-Caldis-Costas leadership, its clique methods, which separate it from the living movement, its cowardly, capitulatory attitude before the offensive of the bosses and the NRA and bourgeois public opinion, by their break with the league, their factional maneuvers and intrigues against it.

3. As a result of the whole situation the union was compelled to make a retreat and to accept a settlement which leaves the main objective of the struggle unattained, at least for the time being. The methods of the leadership in negotiating the settlement and bringing it before the union are responsible to a high degree for the failure to extract a better settlement out of the situation.

4. The great task now is to preserve the union insofar as it is possible and to lay the groundwork for rebuilding it on a sounder basis. An essential element of struggle for this end is an uncompromising struggle against Stalinist disruption, who will seek to exploit the difficulties of the union for disruptive purposes; against every element of anarchist demoralization and against the conservative bureaucratic clique of Field and Company and the right-wing elements on which it bases itself.

5. On this basis steps must begin at once for the constitution of a genuine left wing under the leadership of the Left Opposition, which will wage a struggle to preserve and rebuild the union and provide it with qualified leadership.

Steps toward fusion with the American Workers Party

February 26, 1934

The following motions by Cannon were adopted by the National Committee.[120] They are taken from the minutes.

1. On the basis of discussions already held with the committee of the CPLA (AWP) in which important principled concessions have already been made by the latter, we consider that there is a possibility of eventual agreement on a program in harmony with the fundamental standpoint of the LO and a correct attitude toward the Fourth International.

2. The CPLA is the most important single organization besides the league standing for a new party, an agreement with whom would make the actual launching of the new party possible.

3. On this ground we adopt as our orientation the aim of uniting forces with the CPLA for the formation of the new party if agreement on the program can be reached.

4. As a step on this path we will strive to enter at once

into close cooperation with the CPLA in practical work in the class struggle, particularly in the fields of the unemployed movement, trade unions, and labor defense.

5. Complete reports of the negotiations and the proposals of the NC in regard to this question are to be made at once to the league membership and to the international organization. If the orientation and proposals of the NC are supported, further steps toward clarifying the principal questions, drafting a program for the new party, and preparing the joint organizational steps for its formation are to be taken without delay.

6. The league convention, which is to be held as soon as possible and before any final steps are taken for a merger of the organizations, shall put the question of the new party, and our relations to the CPLA concretely in connection therewith, as the main point on the agenda.

7. Negotiations with communistic groups are to be continued with the aim of drawing them into a close bloc with the league in preparation for the new party.

Internationalism and the new party

Published March 10, 1934

The following article was published in the *Militant*.

As has already been reported, the National Committee of the Communist League is conducting negotiations with the Provisional Organizational Committee of the American Workers Party. We hope for fruitful results from these negotiations and for the eventual fusion of the two organizations in the great task of launching the new party. Such an outcome of the negotiations would undoubtedly give a tremendous impetus to the reorganization of the proletarian vanguard in America and could not be without effect internationally.

And since, in our conviction, this can be realized only if there is firm agreement on the fundamental questions of principle—an agreement, moreover, which extends into the ranks of both organizations—we are bringing out, in a series of articles in the *Militant*, the point of view which we are advancing in the discussions within the joint committee of the two organizations. The more openly and clearly the points of disagreement are discussed, the firmer will be the foundation for eventual fusion if agreement is arrived at.

For us, the question of internationalism is a paramount question, as it has always been for revolutionary Marxists. Marx and Engels began with an international program—the Communist Manifesto. After all that has happened since, after the collapse of the Second International along the line of social patriotism and the downfall of the Comintern along the line of "socialism in one country" (national reformism), there is less ground than ever to think the problems of the proletarian revolution can be approached from a national standpoint. It is from this point of view that we raise the question of the Fourth International as a fundamental consideration in the discussion of a new party in America. We take part in the discussion of a new party in America not merely as American revolutionists but as internationalists, as adherents of the Fourth International.

The programmatic statement of the American Workers Party ("Toward an American Revolutionary Movement") appears to us to be inadequate and decidedly incorrect in its treatment of the international question and to chart a course which would doom the new party from its inception. The collapse of the Stalinist and Socialist parties in this country, from which the imperative necessity for a new party arises, is not due simply to "national peculiarities" of these parties; it is the expression, rather, of the downfall of the Internationals which they represent. Stalinism and Social Democracy are bankrupt on a world scale. A new party which emerges to challenge them must begin with this principled condemnation and then translate it into criticism of the concrete activities of these parties here at home. An "American" party, hazy about its own international positions, would be obviously incapable of such a struggle.

Without exhausting the question in a single article, the mistakes of the international section of the statement of the AWP may be enumerated as follows:

1. The building of new parties and the new International, which are inseparably bound together in a single task, are *counterposed* as separate tasks, and the building of national parties is put in the first order. The statement speaks of "putting the cart before the horse," and adds: "The primary contribution revolutionary workers in any country can make towards building an effective International is by building an effective revolutionary movement in their own country." Also: "Our absorbing concern is with the colossal job on our own doorsteps, building a revolutionary party in the U.S., rooted in the American soil," etc.

All this has a certain "realistic" sound, but it does not fit the realities which every new party must confront—the realities of world economy and world politics and the world crisis of the labor movement. (American imperialism lives in the world, not in the forty-eight states.) It is impossible to build a revolutionary party or to draw up a revolutionary—that is, a Marxist—program in any single country today without taking the world realities as the point of departure. That means, the new parties must be internationalist from the moment of their inception, and even in the process of their formation, and have a definite international orientation. The international position of any party is today the primary test of its revolutionary character.

To be sure, the new party must live in America, speak the language of the country, "feel" the moods, psychology, and tradition of the masses, etc. In this sense the new party must be "American." It must be a power in the country in order to be a real support of the new International. But that does not mean that it should adapt itself to the backwardness, prejudices, and narrow-mindedness of the masses of American workers. Marxism is not a foreign product; it is the theory of the class struggle in every country; it is "native" to every land of capitalist exploitation. The new party will have the task of making the theory of Marxism understandable to the awakening workers of America and of applying this theory in their struggle. Only on this foundation can a genuine revolutionary party be constructed. Such a party can only be a thoroughgoing party of internationalism.

2. The statement of the AWP tends to limit the concept of internationalism to joint actions of strong national parties. Action, of course, is the highest expression of the international organization of the vanguard, and everything leads to that end. But the role of internationalism is no less weighty in the preparation of the actions and in the development and training of the national party. At the present moment, with the whole international organization of the vanguard in a state of crisis and demoralization, this side of the question acquires exceptional importance.

International cooperation in the work of charting the new parties and the new International, mutual exchange of experiences and ideas, putting the collective experience and theoretical knowledge of the Marxists of all countries at the disposal of each and every national party or group—it is precisely in these fields that the real spirit of internationalism manifests itself most prominently today in preparation for the actions of tomorrow. Herein lies the great historic significance of the work already in progress for the building of the Fourth International.

Can the new parties each develop independently, work

out their own programs, acquire mass proportions and influence—and *then* come together to form the new International? This is the concept that appears to govern the AWP approach to questions. "The AWP stands for one compact revolutionary labor International by actually functioning revolutionary parties of various countries. . . ."

This idea, which is very similar to that expressed by Gitlow, takes active internationalism off the agenda for the present and gives no assurance for the formation of the new International in the future. Just the contrary. The new parties, left to themselves, without international cooperation and assistance, would develop along different lines, adopt contradictory programs on many questions, fall victim of national isolation, and experience repeated internal convulsions and splits.

The program of building the parties first, *then* the International, is utopian, not to say non-Marxist. The genuine revolutionary internationalists in the whole world today, as in the period of the World War, are not too numerous. It is a life-and-death matter for them to get together *now* on an international scale to prepare the program of the new International and to work for the formation of its national sections. The task of building the Fourth International goes hand in hand with the task of forming new national parties in the separate countries. Genuine internationalism today cannot allow separation of these two aspects of the same problem.

Is the Fourth International to imitate the methods of the Stalin Comintern, with everything decided in advance for the national parties, with uniform tactics imposed everywhere, with leaders imposed from above, etc.? This question is asked in some alarm from two different points of view. Some who have learned to despise the methods of degenerate Stalinism in struggle against it want to establish safeguards; others, it must be said, are inclined to raise the bugaboo of Stalinism as an excuse to avoid any kind of centralized organization, discipline, uniformity of principle, and control. We have definite opinions on the subject and will stand up for them in the Fourth International and in the conferences leading to its formation.

The International Left Opposition stands for a world program and for uniformity in fundamental principles. Its concept of the Fourth International is the concept of a world party. But, along with that, we stand for *internal democracy* in the parties and in the International. The parties affiliated to the Fourth International must be real parties, standing on their own feet, living their own life, and *selecting their own leaders*. If we consider it impossible to build revolutionary parties without international cooperation, then we assert no less emphatically that the International can become a power only if its component parts—the national parties—are really functioning organizations in the full sense of the word.

3. The programmatic statement of the AWP leaves its own international orientation undecided. Or, at any rate, its position is not clearly stated. Four currents are to be recognized in the international field: The Second, the Third, the Two-and-a-half (centrist), and the Fourth (revolutionary communist). The AWP is against the Second and the Third, but does not mention the other currents. It declares its readiness to "remain in sympathetic contact and engage in discussions with all who are interested in that problem, and especially with those parties which like ourselves cannot accept either the Second or Third International today."

In the course of discussion, both in the joint committee and in the press, we hope to convince the AWP that it is absolutely necessary to take a precise attitude on this question, to declare *what kind* of a new International is needed and to agree with us that the new party should place itself on the day of its birth under the banner of the Fourth International.

Such an agreement, which would imply a solidarity on other principled questions, could make the launching of the new party in America, by the joint efforts of the AWP and the Left Opposition, a realistic prospect for the not too distant future. There can be no doubt that such a party would be from the start a powerful magnet of attraction for the revolutionary workers in America.

The furriers and the needle-trade unions

Published March 24, 1934

The following article was published in the *Militant*.

In many respects the situation in the fur trade, reported by a correspondent in last week's *Militant*, presents a unique trade union problem.[121] The right of the workers to join an organization of their own choosing, the cardinal principle at stake in many of the labor battles now taking place or impending, is clearly at issue. The fur department of the Needle Trades Industrial Union (TUUL) has the great majority of the workers on its side—but no recognition from the bosses and no agreement with the bosses' associations. The International Fur Workers Union (AFL) has an agreement with the bosses—but only a few hundred members and no real support of the workers.

On the face of it, the attempt to impose the International on the furriers is an attempt to force them to accept an organization chosen for them by the bosses. How can there be two opinions as to the stand the workers should take on such a question? If the bosses are to be allowed to decide which union the workers should belong to, why not let them specify a company union and be done with it? That, in our opinion, is the fundamental issue, although it is somewhat obscured by numerous complicating aspects of the situation.

An analogous case is not to be found anywhere in the American trade union movement. The fur workers, a small section of the needle trades as a whole, constitute the only section where the Stalinist industrial union has the majority of the organized workers. In the other trades the organized masses are in the AFL unions; outside the furriers, the Needle Trades Industrial Union, like all the other Stalinist unions, leads an isolated, sectarian, and futile existence devoid of any future.

Beside that, the leadership and internal regime of the furriers' section do not speak for its future either. The paralyzing bureaucratism—characteristic of all Stalinist organizations—to say nothing of the systematic errors—also characteristic of Stalinism—weigh in the scale against the union and mark it for the same doom that has befallen all the other Stalinist unions. The Stalinist party, which controls the furriers' section of the industrial union, has shown an infinite capacity for disrupting and destroying mass organizations, but no capacity whatever, in any field, to build and maintain them. In supporting the industrial union in the fur trade as long as the majority of the organized workers prefer it to the AFL body, the revolutionary militants in the trade should not close their eyes to all these facts.

The role of the Lovestoneites in this situation is particularly revealing, both as to the ultimate logic of their trade union policy and as to the essentially opportunist political character of this group. The Lovestoneites are betting on the victory of the reactionary combination of the bosses, the NRA, and the AFL, and have taken steps to "get in on the ground floor" of the boss-supported International. They have accepted leading posts in the International. Thus they give a "radical" face to this organization, which has no support except that which it gets from the employers.

The Lovestoneite policy of supporting the AFL at all costs, which led them to an objective support of Lewis against the heroic struggle of the Progressive Miners, has brought them to the shabby role of agents of the fakers in the case of the furriers. *AFL fetishism* as a trade union policy is false to the core. In the present case, as in many others, it serves as a cover for political and *personal* opportunism. The revolutionary militants among the furriers, without deluding themselves in the least about the perspectives of the Stalinist union, must respect the attitude of the majority of the workers who support it and fight in the ranks beside them. The Lovestoneite policy must be rejected with contempt.

Inside the Stalinist union, however, the militants should fight for a realistic policy that would open up the perspectives for success in the struggles, which are not too bright with the present policy and leadership. A head-on fight against the AFL in a comparatively small and isolated sector of the needle trades, reduces the struggle of the furriers to an endurance contest in which the odds are on the other side. A broader and more flexible strategy is necessary.

The heart of such a strategy is the fight for unity not only of the furriers but of all the needle-trades workers. Nobody in his right senses can imagine that such unity is to be realized under the banner of the TUUL. As things stand now, after the reconstitution of the ILGWU and the affiliation of the Amalgamated to the AFL, it should be clear which way the stream is flowing. The furriers ought to aim deliberately to connect themselves with the mainstream and influence its further development.

In order to do so it is necessary for them to overcome prejudice against affiliation to the AFL—prejudices against the course of a mass movement are quite futile anyway. It is likewise necessary to make a sharp break with any sense of obligation or loyalty to the TUUL—this paper pretense of a labor movement is not worth anybody's loyalty. Once this correction in the orientation of the left-wing furriers' union is made, its position in the struggle will be strengthened and the way will be opened for a number of effective moves to get out of the present blind alley.

First, it can demand a charter from the International with only one condition: that the local retain its autonomy and the right to choose its own officials. If that is refused, a proposal can be made to unite the two local organizations into a single body affiliated to the International and, consequently, to the AFL, with officials to be elected in a supervised election of the united organization. Third, the left-wing union can declare its intention to campaign for the amalgamation of all the needle-trades unions into one industrial organization affiliated to the AFL.

If such proposals are made known to all the furriers and combined with a widespread agitation for unity throughout the needle trades, they will awaken a hearty response from the workers, strengthen the sagging morale of the left wing, and put an enormous pressure on the officials of the International, including their Lovestoneite come-ons. Either these officials will be compelled to accede to the demand of the masses for unity, or they will be convicted to the hilt of responsibility for the split, robbed of every plausible argument, and completely isolated from the masses, who want unity more than anything else.

In any case the position of the left-wing union will be strengthened, and if it has to fight alone for another period its members will be fortified with a new conviction. The chances of victory will be multiplied many times.

The Stalinist bureaucracy in charge of the left-wing furriers' union, of course, will oppose such a strategy and will try to suppress any free discussion of it in the union. But these ideas will make their way just the same. They are stronger than the apparatus of the bureaucrats because they correspond to the burning needs of the workers. And, in addition, they indicate the only way to save the furriers' organization from the debacle which overtook all the other sections of the industrial union.

Reaction hounds Trotsky!

Published April 21, 1934

The following article was published in the *Militant*.

With the fury and venom reminiscent of the mad campaigns against the Bolsheviks in 1917—and identical with them in content—the attack of world reaction is concentrated today against Trotsky.[122]

In France, where the forces of fascism on the one side and the working class on the other are speedily moving toward the decisive struggle that will have fateful consequences for the entire world, the reaction is striking with full force against the leader who personifies revolutionary struggle and victory of the proletariat.

The summary order deporting Trotsky from France, the closing of the doors of other European countries, and the rabid incitement against him—in all this there is to be seen not only a reactionary political campaign but also a direct and immediate threat on the life of the organizer of the Russian revolution and the herald of its international extension. World reaction wants the head of Trotsky! Let the workers take heed and raise the alarm!

French fascists, Russian White Guards, and reactionary forces everywhere cry out against Trotsky and the dread specter of communism, rising again on the world arena in the Fourth International. And the Stalinist bureaucracy, which has facilitated the march of fascist reaction throughout Europe, joins in the chorus. This infamous representative and carrier of corruption and treachery in the labor movement reveals its perfidious function once again in the united front of reaction. For the mortal danger to Trotsky's life in the present circumstances, and for whatever may befall him at the hands of a White Guard, a fascist, or a Stalinist assassin, the revolutionary workers, taking stock of all the events which have led to this climax, will not fail to place the responsibility where it belongs.

The accusations against Trotsky, which have been made the basis of the deportation order, have undoubtedly been manufactured by the extreme reactionaries to serve a momentary political interest. But this maneuver is only the superficial expression of powerful motive forces for the reactionary attack. The fascist movement of France, which advanced with seven-league boots after Hitler's effortless victory in Germany—thanks to the shameful capitulation of Stalinism—has taken alarm at later developments and feels impelled to strike quickly.

The heroic resistance of the Austrian Socialist workers, the great French general strike and the united front demonstrations against fascism, and the emergence of a movement for the Fourth International—these three events, each separately and all together, have contributed mightily to the revival of the will and capacity of the workers to fight against fascism.[123] They constitute an assurance that the French workers will take the road of the united front and of struggle to the death against French fascism. The ideas of the International Communists, and of Trotsky in the first place, were expressed and verified in these events. The blows of reaction dealt against the person of Trotsky, and the screams of rage and fear directed against the Fourth International, have, therefore, a logic and a profound significance in the French and international struggle of the classes.

The fact that the Austrian workers were defeated does not suffice to reassure the French reactionaries, nor is the circumstance that the Fourth International is as yet only in the formative stage, and without a broad organizational basis, very consoling to them. They have seen the *spirit* of the Austrian socialist workers mirrored in the menacing demonstrations of the French proletariat and have taken alarm at them, especially at the unity as well as the militancy which the French workers have displayed. And they remember all too well—when they witness the first appearance of the Fourth International—how revolutionary socialism, that is, communism, reduced to a small spark during the war, was rapidly kindled into a gigantic flame in 1917.

They dread the prospect of a combination of the heroic *spirit* of the Austrian workers with the *united front* policy which gains ground every day in the French labor movement, and the fusion of this movement with the revolutionary aims and international organization. This is the specter that haunts them. This is what they strive to exorcise when they strike at Trotsky and the Fourth International.

The authorities, who have no reason to fear a bureaucratized and degenerate "communism" that capitulates without a fight, as in Germany, fly into a panic at the bold manifesto of the Fourth International, summoning the workers to the struggle for power.[124] Charging Trotsky with a plot to set up a dictatorship in France, the authorities quote the demand of the manifesto for the creation of a workers' militia and its clear sharp warning to the workers:

"The two forces have just measured swords. War has begun between them. There is no possible peace but in a fight to the death. In the street, by force, will be decided the future."

The United Press dispatch comments significantly that "there was some indication that the government was anxious to get Trotsky out of France before May Day" and adds:

"Though secret police said that they believed that the Fourth International was largely in the formative stage, European governments seemed to fear it, and were reluctant to give the exiled Communist shelter."

None of the capitalist governments offers a refuge to "the vanguard of the counterrevolutionary bourgeoisie," as Trotsky is described in the precise and felicitous expression of Stalin (who expelled him from the Soviet Union). Says the United Press:

"Flight to Italy, Germany, Poland, Greece, Jugoslavia, Spain or Austria is definitely closed because the governments distrust his activities.

"England has not been approached because it was said at the British Embassy that London would refuse. Turkey will not tolerate his return. France will not permit him to go to Morocco, Algeria, or any other African colony . . . Belgium and Switzerland, because of their sympathy with France, are not believed likely to grant him asylum."

Meanwhile, the incitement to drive him out of France in "the shortest possible time," if not to assassinate him, proceeds with unabated fury. "He reeks with the blood of our soldiers," says *La Liberté*. "His residence in any part of France would be a scandal. He must be driven away like a dog."

How clearly and forcefully the political issues eventually become! How unmistakably, through all the fog of slander and falsification, the essence of the eleven-year struggle of the Bolshevik-Leninists makes its way in the expressions of the bourgeois governments and newspapers! In the above quotations the capitalist spokesmen of Europe testify to their unalterable conviction that Trotsky is the veritable representative of the revolutionary program which they hate and fear.

The treacherous policy of Stalinism, exposed already in a long chain of events, is demonstrated once again before the workers of the entire world in the present case. The false face of Bolshevism is torn aside; the ordinary standard of labor ethics espoused by every simple and decent trade unionist, which dictates an attitude of labor solidarity with a victim of capitalist persecution—even this is lacking in the conduct of the cynical bureaucrats from Moscow to Paris and from Paris to New York.

Not a united front of the working class against the class enemy, but a united front with fascist reaction—this is the essence of the Stalinist practice in the campaign against Trotsky. Frothing at the mouth, every jackal of the apparatus, every corrupt functionary of a regime that is corrupted to the core, barks at the heels of the international revolutionist.

"Drive him away like a dog," demands the fascist newspaper. And the spokesmen of the Soviet embassy in Paris add: "The Soviet government is making no effort to interfere. *We assume the French government is capable of handling him.*" (United Press, April 18.)

"He advocates a revolution by 'an armed workers' militia,'" say the French authorities in announcing his deportation (Associated Press, April 18). *L'Humanité*, organ of French Stalinism, replies: "He is a renegade and a despicable character generally." (*Herald Tribune* correspondent, April 16.)

"During the February clashes between the police and the mobs," the French police charge, "he sent agents to the Socialist and Communist leaders urging a 'monster joint meeting' to prepare for mass action." (Associated Press, April 19.) And the New York *Freiheit*, which is against *that kind* of a united front, explains in an editorial on April 19 that "Trotsky . . . is a man whom the revolutionary workers the world over hate and despise. . . . For class conscious workers the Trotsky matter is no more than an incident among capitalist governments and their servant."

Yes, Stalinist perfidy is revealed once again, and it is not by accident that they direct it against the chief exponent of the revolutionary doctrines which they trample in the mud. They deported him from the Soviet Union; they dickered with the Turkish police to immure him on an island as in a prison; they connived with capitalist governments to keep him out of Europe; under the guise of calling attention to his lack of adequate protection at Prinkipo they incited White Guards (if not Stalinist agents) to assassinate him; they organized demonstrations against his admission to France, and now they salute his deportation by a reactionary government that paves the way for fascism! And all this cynical cooperation with the class enemy is passed off as revolutionary Bolshevism! Revolutionary workers, learn to despise the bureaucratic *canaille* which defiles the very name of Bolshevism!

The advanced workers all over the world in increasing numbers are beginning to see the issues as they really are and to draw the necessary conclusions. They are breaking out of the circle that has been drawn around them—the devil's circle of lies and calumnies, of perversion, fakery, and disorientation.

In the hail of persecution and slander directed at the person of Trotsky, first by warmongers and social patriots during the war; then by the whole camp of reaction in the Kerensky days and in the first period of the Bolshevik revolution; later taken over and magnified by the Stalinist bureaucracy after the death of Lenin; and now unfolding again under the leadership of the blackest forces of capitalist reaction, with the Stalinists in their train—in these campaigns of rage and hate and persecution concentrated on Trotsky the advanced and thinking workers of the world are beginning to see what is really involved: *the struggle of the classes.*

And, more than that, the eleven-year campaign of the Stalinists, sandwiched in between the two great world crusades of the bourgeoisie, and fusing more or less openly with the latest one, stands out now more clearly in the same light. Trotsky, the person, is the target of the attacks of capitalist reaction because he, more ably and consistently than any other, has pointed the way to the revolutionary struggle and victory of the workers.

The campaign of Stalinism against him personally was a campaign against his ideas, and that, in turn, has been at bottom a fulfillment of the commands of alien classes. The whole "anti-Trotsky" course of Stalinism, studded along the path for eleven years with disorganization and defeat of the workers' movement in all countries, is true to itself and more self-revealing than ever now. And the conclusion is clearer and more inescapable than ever: *Stalinism is a reactionary force in the labor movement of the world.*

The accusations brought against Trotsky by the French police reveal the whole essence of the matter in a few compact sentences. They accuse him of working for a united front of Socialists and Communists "to prepare for mass action." They charge him with advocating the formation of "a workers' militia" to repel the fascist attacks and to take the offensive against them. They indict him for his solemn warning to the workers that they must "fight to the death." And they drive him out of France because he summons the workers to reorganize their ranks under the banner of the Fourth International.

That, in brief, is indeed a program to strike terror into the hearts of all exploiters. In those clear, simple words there is the prescription for the workers' struggle and victory. If the workers will heed these words in time, and carry them out in deeds, they can re-form their ranks and halt the march of reaction. They can smash the dread menace of fascism and clear the way for revolutionary victory.

In these issues, so fateful for the future of humanity, capitalist reaction has taken the offensive. Driving with breakneck speed toward the establishment of a fascist regime in France, they scent danger in the program of Trotsky and launch a furious campaign against him. By the same token the workers of France and of all countries ought to rally to his aid without delay. The defense of Trotsky's life at the present moment is a duty enjoined upon the labor movement in order to defend itself.

All out to Madison Square on May Day

Published April 28, 1934

The following article was published in the *Militant*.

On May Day this year New York will witness the most imposing demonstration of the workers and the most tangible advances toward their united struggle against the common enemy that has been seen for many years. The participating workers' organizations will march together in a single parade and hold a common demonstration at Madison Square. The Communist League (International Communists) will march in the parade under its own banner and will be represented by its own speakers at the demonstration.

The idea that the political and economic organizations of the workers, regardless of their differences of principle, must form a united front of action against the class enemy—this idea, which was rejected with such fatal consequences in Germany, has brought a host of organizations together and governs their practice in carrying out all the arrangements of the united front May Day parade and demonstration. The no less important condition—that each organization shall preserve its own identity and march under its own banner—is likewise respected and observed by the participants.

The features of the demonstration signify a victory for the idea of a workers' united front and the beginning of its realization in action. For these reasons alone, the Communist League, which insistently fights for the united front of the workers' organizations, would be duty bound to take part in the work and actions of the May Day Labor Conference which culminate in the parade and demonstrations on May Day. But there are other reasons of no less weight and importance which make the course we have taken mandatory upon us as communists.

The Stalinist party (CP) and the organizations under its control are conducting a separate parade and demonstration at the same hour. Thus, although the preponderant weight of forces is with the Labor Day Conference, a serious element of division remains in the workers' ranks. Such a division is not of our making. We stand for the united front of all the workers' organizations and will continue to fight for it in the future. Nevertheless, the division, and the holding of the demonstrations at the same hour, compel each organization and each individual militant to make a choice.

We have made our choice in this matter with full deliberation, and our decision is not an isolated one, applicable only to a single occasion. It corresponds, rather, to the trend of developments in the labor movement. And this, in turn, determines the tactical course of the revolutionary Marxist.

The Stalinists, who reject the united front with all organizations not under their direct control, demand that the workers demonstrate on May Day only under Stalinist auspices. This ultimatum is repeated by their camp followers of various kinds in varying stages of confusion and demoralization.

The ultimatums of the Stalinists have no interest for us. We reject the "leadership" of these political hooligans and condemn them as a menace to the labor movement. But to the conscientious left-wing workers who may have the mistaken impression that the May Day demonstrations present a choice between communism and reformism, we owe a frank explanation of the course we have taken. Our remarks on the question are addressed especially to them.

It is argued by the Stalinists and their camp followers that the parade and demonstration at Madison Square, organized by the Labor Conference, will be composed predominantly of the Socialist political organizations and reformist trade unions, while the Union Square demonstration represents the revolutionary workers. The workers who want a united front of action and defense are called upon to choose between the Socialist Party and the Communist Party. This ultimatum contains three propositions which have to be dealt with separately.

It is quite true that the Madison Square demonstration will be predominantly Socialist and trade unionist and that these organizations have by far the main weight in the conference. But that is not a reason for communists to stay away from the demonstration. On the contrary, it is the duty of the communists to march with the Socialist workers and the trade unionists and to raise the banner of communism in their midst. As long as the communists are permitted to march with their own banner and to be represented by their own speakers at the demonstration—and these rights have been expressly provided for all the participating organizations by the joint arrangements committee—they have no need and no right to present any other demands as a condition for a united action. March separately, strike together—this is the fundamental basis for the united front of the workers.

We do not demand that the Socialist workers leave their own organizations as a condition for common action with us. We do not demand that they cease to be Socialists in order to make the united front with communists. We do not demand that our leadership be recognized beforehand, and we do not repeat the insane gibberish about the "united front from below." It is such *ultimatums*, which the Stalinist bureaucrats are in the habit of laying down to the workers, which negate the very idea of the united front and make it impossible. We hope to *convince* the workers, *in the course of common action,* of the inadequacy of reformism and the necessity for revolutionary policy and leadership. But we do not demand that they be convinced of this in advance. Therein lies the fundamental difference between the Stalinist and the revolutionary communist conception of the united front.

The second false assumption in the ultimatum of the Stalinists and their ideological captives is the argument that the Union Square demonstration is a demonstration of the "revolutionary workers," that the Stalinist leaders are the representatives of communism. This contention, false to the core, is especially repugnant today in the face of the cynical united front of Stalinism with world reaction in hounding the organizer of the Russian revolution.

Many workers with the impulse to be revolutionists will undoubtedly participate in the Stalinist demonstration. But Stalinism as a political current contributes nothing to the labor movement but ideological disorientation, demoralization, and defeat. The Stalinist hooligans corrupt every principle of communism and defile its very name. They always subordinate the interests of the working class to the special interests of a bureaucratic apparatus. The Stalinists disrupt and sabotage every attempt of the workers to unite their forces for a common fight against the class enemy. Stalinism is a poison in the veins of the labor movement, and its harmful influence derives precisely from the assumption by many workers that it represents communism.

It is necessary to attack this illusion in deed as well as in word and to put the question as it really stands: *Stalinism is a reactionary force in the labor movement of the whole world.*

The Madison Square demonstration will be predominantly reformist, in composition and leadership. That is true. But revolutionary internationalism will be represented there this May Day, *and only there.* Not the banner of Stalinism, splotched with crimes and treacheries, but the banner of the International Communists—this is the banner of communism. Every revolutionary worker ought to march behind it and no other.

The third fallacy in the ultimatum of the Stalinists and their apologists consists in the posing of the question of a united front on May Day as a rivalry and conflict between the Socialist Party and the Communist Party, and the demand that the workers choose between the two parties. "March with the Communist Party, not with the Socialist Party" is the formula of this ultimatum. For our part, if it is a question of party preference, we choose neither the CP nor the SP and follow neither. If the May Day meetings are to be construed simply as meetings of different parties then the revolutionary workers supporting the Communist League would have no choice but to abstain from both demonstrations and to organize their own, however small it might be.

But this is not how the question presents itself to us. Quite the contrary. General political meetings of the parties can be conducted apart from the demonstrations under the auspices of the respective parties—the Communist League, for example, will hold its own meeting in the evening. But the *demonstration and purpose* on May Day ought to represent a *united front* of all the parties and workers' organizations in a single demonstration against war and fascism and for the immediate needs of the workers.

It is precisely the inability of the Stalinists even to comprehend the question in this sense, their shopkeeper's conception of the special interest of their own party apparatus and their fear of "competition," that impelled them to organize the Union Square demonstration as a demonstration for the Communist Party. Their stubborn refusal to merge their party interest for a single occasion, on May Day of all days, with the general class interest, condemns the demonstration to isolation as an affair of the CP and its auxiliaries, despite all the crooked ballyhoo about "unity" and the "united front."

And by the same token this policy of the Stalinists and the whole line of conduct flowing from it, not forgetting the Madison Square Garden affair[125]—this policy and conduct make it easy for the Socialist leaders, who are no more in favor of an all-inclusive fighting united front than the Stalinists, to counteract the pressure of their own members for a single, united demonstration.

The fact that the Socialist leaders felt obliged to agree to joint action with every other group and organization except the Stalinists, to give up their original demand that the May Day Labor Conference be labeled as "Socialist and Labor," their agreement that all the participating organizations be represented with their banners at the head of the parade as well as on the arrangements committee and on the speakers' platform—all this is powerful testimony to the deep-rooted sentiments of the Socialist workers for a genuine united front.

The Communist League fought in the conference and arrangements committee for an invitation to the Stalinists, but without success. We also sent delegates to the Stalinist conference to propose that a direct approach be made to the May Day Labor Conference for a single demonstration. Our proposal was rejected with the usual barrage of epithets and slander. Nevertheless, it can be asserted, so pressing is the need for unity and so powerful the sentiment of the rank-and-file workers for it, that if our proposal had been adopted and carried out honestly and consistently, it would have been extremely difficult, if not impossible, for the Socialist leaders to refuse.

We shall continue to fight for this policy as we have fought consistently for it in the past. For years, as a faction working for the reform of the CP, we continuously advocated the adoption by the party of the policy of the united front in the same sense that we present it today. The victory of fascism in Germany is directly due to the rejection by the Stalinist leadership of the united front with the Social Democracy and the reformist trade unions, which the Left Opposition insistently demanded. The weakness and disorganization of the working-class movement in this country, after four and one-half years of the unprecedented crisis, is in large part also the result of the same fatal mistakes, systematically repeated.

Breaking with the Comintern because of its obvious and irremediable bankruptcy, and taking the path toward new parties and the Fourth International, the International Communists (formerly the Left Opposition) in no way alter or modify the principles, strategy, and tactics with regard to the broad labor movement which they formerly proposed for the adoption of the official Communist parties. The only difference is that we carry out in

Scenes from May 1, 1934, united front demonstration. Left, Lovestonite contingent marching down Fourteenth Street; above, Jay Lovestone addresses rally at Madison Square; below, participants in CLA contingent.

practice now, as a completely independent organization, the tactics which we previously recommended to the CP. This is the meaning of our decision to participate in the Madison Square demonstration and parade with the Socialist Party, the trade unions, and other political groups and tendencies.

The parade and demonstration organized by the May Day Labor Conference, lacking the inclusion of the Stalinist organizations, is obviously not a complete united front and should not be represented as such. But this is not a reason to abstain from participation. After all the divisions and demoralization, it is utopian to expect that the idea of the united front will take hold everywhere with the same force and that it can be realized organizationally overnight.

The building of the united front of the workers is a process. This process involves agitation for the idea, experiments in cooperation, and tests in action. Including all the tendencies of the more or less progressive section of the labor movement, with the single exception of the Stalinists and their satellites, the May Day Labor Conference represents a tremendous step forward. From this point of view it must be hailed and supported by the revolutionary workers. At the same time efforts must be made to broaden out its composition and extend it to other fields of activity in the class struggle.

Needless to say, our participation at Madison Square does not imply in any way the slightest reconciliation with the Socialist Party. The united front of action on concrete questions does not signify political collaboration. No blurring of principled issues. No mixing of banners.

Our principled differences with social reformism remain. We shall fight them out to the end. Not by lies and slanders, not by hooligan violence, but through argument and example we shall endeavor to convince the Socialist workers of the necessity of a revolutionary policy and leadership. In intransigent principled struggle against social reformism we shall work for the new party and the new International.

Meantime, now as always, we shall stand for the united front in concrete struggles of the day with the Socialist workers through the medium of their chosen organization.)[26]

New defense organization needed

Published May 19, 1934

The following editorial was published in the *Militant*.

One of the most promising developments in recent days has been the activity displayed by the Provisional Committee for Non-Partisan Labor Defense and the hearty acclaim which has greeted its initiative in numerous circles of the progressive labor movement. The profound impulse of the militant workers to get together for a common fight against reaction, which was the driving power behind the great May demonstration at Madison Square, is expressing itself also in this response to the movement for a union of forces in the field of labor defense.

There is both a reason and a necessity for these manifestations. With the fearful examples of Europe before them, with the terrible threat of war and fascist reaction menacing the world, the need of solidarity in action becomes ever more imperious. The great idea of the united front is making its way in spite of everything. It can and must be realized on the labor defense front without delay.

A significant aspect of the Provisional Committee is the presence in its composition of a number of people who in the past have been prominently identified with the work of defense organizations in administrative, publicity, and executive capacities. This, taken together with the active cooperation of experienced militants of various organizations, which the initiating group has already enlisted, constitutes a certain assurance that the task, as well as the way to accomplish it, is understood.

This confidence has been further reenforced by the efficient handling of the Bellussi case and the protest movement for the four young German Communists who were handed over to the Hitler police by the Dutch authorities. The work done in these instances is now to be followed by the organization of a movement in behalf of the imprisoned hotel strike pickets, Robins and Gras, who have entrusted their case to the Provisional Committee.[127] The method pursued by the Provisional Committee—directly organizing concrete defense activities while simultaneously negotiating with other organizations to broaden the base of the movement—strikes us as the correct and businesslike way to proceed. Patently, the formation of a real defense organization on a firm foundation is in the making.

It is high time. The strangulation of the ILD by the Stalinist adventurers has long since passed the point where the possibility of reforming this organization could be seriously debated among working-class militants whose eyes are open and whose heads are in working order. After the treacherous sabotage in the cases of Morgenstern and Goodman, Bellussi, the marine workers, and many others; after the miserable bungling and complete disorganization of the Mooney movement; after the cynical prostitution of the ILD to the factional needs of the clique of

Stalinist bureaucrats serving private interests, and not the interests of the class or the class-war prisoners—after all this, the question has become clear beyond all dispute: a new defense organization is an unpostponable necessity.

In our opinion the new organization should not represent a system of committees but a solid organization based on individual members assembled into permanent branches; labor organizations of every kind, sympathetic to the aims and purposes of the movement, should be affiliated collectively. In its attitude toward class-war prisoners and other victims of capitalist persecution, at home and abroad, the new defense body should be honestly nonpartisan, defending them against the class enemy without conditions and providing material aid without any strings attached to it. At the same time, the Non-Partisan Labor Defense organization should be militant in its policy and should proceed in all its activities from the standpoint of the class struggle.

The composition of the new organization, in its leading bodies as well as in its branches, ought to represent a coalition of all the honest, progressive, and militant forces, in the labor movement and sympathetic to it, who are willing and able to cooperate loyally in the fight against reactionary persecution. Communists, Socialists, anarchists, syndicalists, and trade unionists—they all should band together in the defense of the rights of the workers and their organizations. The new defense organization can become the medium for such a united front. At any rate it should strive to do so.

Much depends on it. An honest defense organization, conscientiously carrying out in practice the policy of the united front, will be a support to the labor movement as a whole and a star of hope to the individual victims of reaction. In addition, it can set an example which will stimulate the formation of the united front of the workers in other fields of struggle.

Let us hope that the near future will see the consummation of the program of the Provisional Committee and the definite launching of a new organization for nonpartisan labor defense.

Learn from Minneapolis!

Published May 26, 1934

The following article was published in the *Militant*.

Today the whole country looks to Minneapolis.[128] Great things are happening there which reflect the influence of a strange new force in the labor movement, an influence widening and extending like a spiral wave. Out of the strike of the transport workers of Minneapolis a new voice speaks and a new method proclaims its challenge.

It was seen first in the strike of the coal-yard drivers, which electrified the labor movement of the city a few months ago and firmly established the union after a brief, stormy battle of unprecedented militancy and efficiency. Now we see the same union moving out of this narrow groove and embracing truck drivers in other lines.

Behind this, as was the case with the coal drivers, there are months of hard, patient, and systematic routine work of organization. Everything is prepared. Then an ultimatum to the bosses. A swift, sudden blow. A mass picket line that sweeps everything before it. The building trades come out in sympathy. The combined forces, riding with a mighty wave of moral support from the whole laboring population of the city, take the offensive and drive all the bosses' thugs and hirelings to cover in a memorable battle at the City Market.

The whole country listens to the echoes of the struggle. The exploiters hear them with fear and trepidation. Weaving the net around the automobile workers, with the aid of treacherous labor leaders, they ask themselves in alarm: "If this spirit spreads what will our schemes avail us?"

And the workers in basic industry, vaguely sensing the power of their numbers and strategic position, can hardly help asking themselves: "If we should go the Minneapolis way could anything or anybody stop us?" The striking transport workers are a mighty power in Minneapolis today. But that is only a small fraction of the power of their example for the cheated and betrayed workers in the big industries of the country.

The message of Minneapolis is of first-rate importance to the American working class. A careful examination of the method from all sides ought to be put as point one on the agenda of the labor movement, especially of its most advanced section. A study of this epic struggle, in its various aspects, can be an aid to their application in other fields, and, by that, a rapid change of the position of the American workers.

There is nothing new, of course, in a fight between strikers and police and gunmen. Every strike of any consequence tells the old, familiar story of the hounding, beating, and killing of strikers by the hired thugs of the exploiters, in and out of uniform. What is out of the ordinary in Minneapolis, what is more important in this respect, is that while the Minneapolis strike began with violent assaults on the strikers, it didn't end there.

In pitched battles last Saturday and again on Monday, the strikers fought back and held their own. And on Tuesday they took the offensive, with devastating results. Businessmen, volunteering to put the workers in their place, and college boys out for a lark as special deputies—to say nothing of the uniformed cops—handed over their badges and fled in terror before the mass fury of the aroused workers. And many of them carried away unwelcome souvenirs of the engagement. Here was a demonstration that the American workers are willing and able to fight in their own interests. Nothing is more important than this, for, in the last analysis, everything depends on it.

Here was a stern warning to the bosses and their hirelings, and not only those of Minneapolis. Transfer the example and the spirit of the Minneapolis strikers to the steel and automobile workers, for example, with their mass numbers and power. Let the rulers of America tremble at the prospect. They will see it! That is what the message of Minneapolis means first of all.

A second feature of the fight at the City Market which deserves special attention is the fact that it was not the ordinary encounter between individual strikers and individual scabs or thugs. On the contrary—take note—*the whole union* went into action on the picket line in *mass* formation; thousands of other union men went with them; they took along the necessary means to protect themselves against the murderous thugs, as they had every right to do. This was an example of mass action which points the way for the future victorious struggles of the American workers.

It is not a strike of the men alone, but of the women also. The Minneapolis drivers' union proceeds on the theory that the women have a vital interest in the struggle, no less than the men, and draws them into action through a special organization. The policy, employed so effectively by the Progressive Miners, is bringing rich results also in Minneapolis. To involve the women in the labor struggle is to double the strength of the workers and to infuse it with a spirit and solidarity it could not otherwise have. This applies not only to a single union and a single strike; it holds good for every phase of the struggle up to its revolutionary conclusion. The grand spectacle of labor solidarity in Minneapolis is what it is because it includes also the solidarity of the working-class women.

The strike of the transport workers took an enormous leap forward and underwent a transformation when the building-trades unions declared a sympathy strike last Monday. In this action one of the most progressive and significant features of the entire movement is to be seen. When unions begin to call strikes not for immediate gains of their own but for the sake of solidarity with their struggling brothers in other trades, and when this spirit and attitude becomes general and taken for granted as the proper thing, then the paralyzing divisions in the trade union movement will be near an end and trade unionism will begin to mean unity.

The union of the truck drivers and the building-trades workers is an inspiring sight. It represents a dynamic idea of incalculable power. Let the example spread, let the idea take hold in other cities and other trades, let the idea of sympathy strike action be combined with militancy and the mass method of the Minneapolis fighters—and American labor will be a head taller and immeasurably stronger.

Those who characterize the AFL unions as "company unions" and want to build new unions at any price will derive very little consolation from the Minneapolis strike. We have always maintained that the form of a labor organization, while important, is not decisive. Minneapolis provides another confirmation, and a most convincing one, of this conception. Here is the most militant and, in many respects, the most progressively directed labor struggle that has been seen for a long time. Nevertheless it is all conducted within the framework of the AFL.

The drivers' union is a local of one of the most conservative AFL Internationals, the Teamsters; the building trades, out in sympathy with the drivers, are all AFL unions; and the Central Labor Union, backing the drivers' strike and the possible organizing medium of a general strike, is a subordinate unit of the AFL. The local unions of the AFL provide a wide field for the work of revolutionary militants if they know how to work intelligently. This is especially true when, as in the Minneapolis example, the militants actually initiate the organization and take a leading part in developing it at every stage.

Further development of the union, and perhaps even of the present strike, on the path of militancy may bring the local leadership into conflict with the reactionary bureaucracy of the International and also with conservative forces in the Central Labor Union. This will be all the less apt to take the local leaders of the militant union by surprise, since most of them have already gone through the school of that experience. In spite of that, they did not turn their backs on the trade unions and seek to set up new ones artificially.

Even when it came to organizing a large group of workers hitherto outside the labor movement, they selected an AFL union as the medium. The results of the Minneapolis experience provide some highly important lessons on this tactical question. The miserable role of the Stalinists in the present situation, and their complete isolation from the great mass struggle, is the logical outcome of their policies in general and their trade union policy in particular.

The General Drivers Union, as must be the case with every genuine mass organization, has a broad and representative leadership, freely selected by democratic methods. Among the leaders of the union are a number of Bolshevik militants who never concealed or denied their opinions and never changed them at anybody's order, whether the order came from Green or from Stalin.

The presence of this nucleus in the mass movement is a feature of the exceptional situation in Minneapolis which, in a sense, affects and colors all the other aspects of it. The most important of all prerequisites for the development of a militant labor movement is the leaven of principled communists. When they enter the labor movement and apply their ideas intelligently they are invincible. The labor movement grows as a result of this fusion and their influence grows with it. In this question, also, Minneapolis is showing the way.

Victory in Minneapolis

May 29, 1934

The following article was published in the June 2, 1934, *Militant*.

Minneapolis—The drivers' strike conducted by General Drivers Union No. 574 was settled on the basis of recognition of the union, unconditional reinstatement of all strikers, and agreement to arbitrate the demands for wages and hours. Employers had previously granted substantial wage increases in the attempt to head off the strike and avoid recognizing and dealing with the union. The union is now presenting demands for further increases. Out of the six thousand men involved in the strike, only a few isolated cases of attempted discrimination had been reported to the union since the settlement of the strike three days ago. The majority of these men had already been reinstated on demand of the union.

Last night's general membership meeting was a rousing affair. Thousands of newly organized workers, the majority of whom never belonged to a union before, crowded the big strike headquarters to hear reports on the execution of the settlement and further plans to strengthen and consolidate the union. The speeches of union leaders Brown, Skoglund, and Dunne reflected the spirit of the crowd, and every appeal for continued militancy and vigilance was cheered to the echo.

The spirit of victory and achievement was in the air, although no attempt had been made by the leadership to exaggerate the gains of the first battle. Recognition of the union, which, in the language of the Minneapolis striker, means "protection" of his job, is regarded as a great achievement for a new union. The workers are determined to hold on to this achievement.

And it is quite clear that the bosses, after the experience of the ten-day battle, are not anxious for another fight soon. This has been shown particularly by the readiness of the individual bosses to meet with the union officials and adjust any claims of discrimination in rehiring the strikers. It is further shown in the absence up to date of any threat of prosecution of the union leaders for the casualties that resulted from the strike battles. A stern warning that any such attempt will bring the workers into action again was sounded at last night's meeting and brought a roar of approval from the workers.

The militancy of the drivers' strike is known to the world. The efficiency of its organization and the quality of its leadership—which released this mighty wave of rank-and-file militancy with such telling effect—is also acknowledged on all sides in Minneapolis.

The prestige of General Drivers Union No. 574 and the group of militants at its head, is on the heights. There is little doubt that they will be a force for still greater accomplishments in wider circles of the labor movement. The strike brought a shower of telegrams from workers' organizations and numerous invitations to the men at the head of "574" to come to other localities to lead organizing campaigns.

Minneapolis and its meaning

June 1934

The following article was published in the July *New International*.

Standing by itself, the magnificent strike of the Minneapolis truck drivers would merit recognition as an extraordinary event in modern American labor history. Its connection with the second wave of labor struggles to sweep the country since the inception of the NRA, however, and its indubitable place as the high point of the present strike wave, invest the Minneapolis demonstration with an exceptional importance. Therefore it has come by right to be the subject of serious and attentive study and of heated discussion. This discussion, despite all the partisan prejudice and misrepresentation injected into it, is bound on the whole to have a profitable result. The best approach to the trade union question, the key question of revolutionary politics in the United States, is through the study and discussion of concrete examples.

The second strike wave under the NRA rises higher than

the first and marks a big forward stride of the American working class. The enormous potentialities of future developments are clearly written in this advance. The native militancy of the workers, so impressively demonstrated on every strike front in recent months, needs only to be fused with an authentic leadership which brings organization, consciousness, and the spirit of determined struggle into the movement. Minneapolis was an example of such a fusion. That is what lifted the drivers' strike out above the general run. Therein lies its great significance—as an anticipation, if only on a comparatively small, local scale, of future developments in the labor movement of the country. The determining role of policy and leadership was disclosed with singular emphasis in the Minneapolis battle.

The main features of the present strike wave, on the background of which the Minneapolis example must be considered, are easily distinguishable. Now, as in the labor upsurge of last year, the attitude of the workers toward the NRA occupies a central place. But the attitude is somewhat different than it was before. The messianic faith in the Roosevelt administration which characterized the strike movement of a year ago and which, to a certain extent, provided the initial impulse for the movement, has largely disappeared and given place to skeptical distrust. It is hardly correct, however, to say, as some revolutionary wishful thinkers are saying, that the current strikes are consciously directed *against* the NRA. There is little or no evidence to support such a bald assertion.

It is more in keeping with reality to say that the striking workers now depend primarily on their own organization and fighting capacity and expect little or nothing from the source to which, a short year ago, they looked for everything. Nevertheless they are not yet ready even to ignore the NRA, to say nothing of fighting against it directly. What has actually taken place has been a heavy shift in emphasis from faith in the NRA to reliance on their own strength.

In these great struggles the American workers, in all parts of the country, are displaying the unrestrained militancy of a class that is just beginning to awaken. This is a new generation of a class that has not been defeated. On the contrary, it is only now beginning to find itself and to feel its strength. And in these first, tentative conflicts the proletarian giant gives a glorious promise for the future. The present generation remains true to the tradition of American labor; it is boldly aggressive and violent from the start. The American worker is no Quaker. Further developments of the class struggle will bring plenty of fighting in the USA.

It is also a distinct feature of the second strike wave, and those who want to understand and adjust themselves to the general trend of the movement should mark it well, that the organization drives and the strikes, barring incidental exceptions, are conducted within the framework of the AFL unions. The exceptions are important and should not be disregarded. At any rate, the movement begins there. Only those who foresaw this trend and synchronized their activities with it have been able to play a part in the recent strikes and to influence them from within.

The central aim and aspiration of the workers, that is, of the newly organized workers who are pressing the fight on every front, is to establish their organizations firmly. The first and foremost demand in every struggle is: *recognition of the union*. With unerring instinct the workers seek first of all the protection of an organization.

William S. Brown, president of the Minneapolis union, expressed the sentiment of all the strikers in every industry in his statement: "The union felt that wage agreements are not much protection to a union man unless first there is definite assurance that the union man will be protected in his job." The strike wave sweeping the country in the second year of the NRA is in its very essence a struggle for the right of organization. The outcome of every strike is to be estimated primarily by its success or failure in enforcing the recognition of the union.

And from this point of view the results in general are not so rosy. The workers manifested a mighty impulse for organization, and in many cases they fought heroically. But they have yet to attain their first objective. The auto settlement, which established the recognition of the company union rather than the unions of the workers, weighs heavily on the whole labor situation.[129] The workers everywhere have to pay for the precedent set in this industry of such great strategic importance. From all appearances the steelworkers are going to be caught in the same runaround. The New York hotel strike failed to establish the union. The New York taxi drivers got no union recognition, or anything else. Not a single one of the "red" unions affiliated to the Trade Union Unity League has succeeded in gaining recognition. Even the great battle of Toledo appears to have been concluded without the attainment of this primary demand.[130]

The American workers are on the march. They are organizing by the hundreds of thousands. They are fighting to establish their new unions firmly and compel the bosses to recognize them. But in the overwhelming majority of cases they have yet to win this fundamental demand.

In the light of this general situation the results of the Minneapolis strike stand out preeminent and unique. Judged in comparison with the struggles of the other newly formed unions—and that is the only sensible criterion—the Minneapolis settlement, itself a compromise, has to be recorded as a victory of the first order. In gaining recognition of the union, and in proceeding to enforce it the day following the settlement, General Drivers Union No. 574 has set a pace for all the new unions in the country. The outcome was not accidental either. Policy, method, leadership—these were the determining factors at Minneapolis which the aspiring workers everywhere ought to study and follow.

The medium of organization in Minneapolis was a craft union of the AFL, and one of the most conservative of the AFL Internationals at that. This course was deliberately chosen by the organizers of the fight in conformity with the general trend of the movement, although they are by no means worshippers of the AFL. Despite the obvious limitations of this antiquated form of organization it proved to be sufficient for the occasion, thanks to a liberal construction of the jurisdictional limits of the union.

Affiliation with the AFL afforded other compensating advantages. The new union was thereby placed in direct contact with the general labor movement and was enabled to draw on it for support. This was a decisive element in the outcome. The organized labor movement, and with it practically the entire working class of Minneapolis, was lined up behind the strike. Out of a union with the most conservative tradition and obsolete structure came the most militant and successful strike.

The stormy militancy of the strike, which electrified the whole labor movement, is too well known to need recounting here. The results also are known, among them the not unimportant detail that the serious casualties were suffered by the other side. True enough, the striking workers nearly everywhere have fought with great courage. But here also the Minneapolis strike was marked by certain different and distinct aspects which are of fundamental importance. In other places, as a rule, the strike militancy surged from below and was checked and restrained by the leaders. In Minneapolis it was organized and directed by the leaders. In most of the other strikes the leaders blunted the edge of the fight—where they could not head it off altogether, as in the case of the auto workers—and preached reliance on the NRA, on General Johnson, or the president. In Minneapolis the leaders taught the workers to fight for their rights and fought with them.

This conception of the leadership, that the establishment of the union was to be attained only by struggle, shaped the course of action not only during the ten-day strike but in every step that led to it. That explains why the strike was prepared and organized so thoroughly. Minneapolis never before saw such a well-organized strike, and it is doubtful if its like, from the standpoint of organization, has often been seen anywhere on this continent.

Having no illusions about the reasonableness of the bosses or the beneficence of the NRA, and sowing none in the ranks, the leadership calculated the whole campaign on the certainty of a strike and made everything ready for it. When the hour struck the union was ready, down to the last detail of organization. "If the preparations made by their union for handling it are any indication," wrote the *Minneapolis Tribune* on the eve of the conflict, "the strike of the truck drivers in Minneapolis is going to be a far-reaching affair. . . . Even before the official start of the strike at 11:30 p.m. Tuesday the 'General Headquarters' organization set up at 1900 Chicago Avenue was operating with all the precision of a military organization."

This spirit of determined struggle was combined at the same time with a realistic appraisal of the relation of forces and the limited objectives of the fight. Without this all the preparations and all the militancy of the strikers might well have been wasted and brought the reaction of a crushing defeat. The strike was understood to be a preliminary, partial struggle, with the objective of establishing the union and compelling the bosses to recognize it. When they got that, they stopped and called it a day.

The strong union that has emerged from the strike will be able to fight again and to protect its membership in the meantime. The accomplishment is modest enough. But if we want to play an effective part in the labor movement, we must not allow ourselves to forget that the American working class is just beginning to move on the path of the class struggle and, in its great majority, stands yet before the first task of establishing stable unions. Those who understand the task of the day and accomplish it prepare the future. The others merely chatter.

As in every strike of any consequence, the workers involved in the Minneapolis struggle also had an opportunity to see the government at work and to learn some practical lessons as to its real function. The police force of the city, under the direction of the Republican mayor, supplemented by a horde of "special deputies," were lined up solidly on the side of the bosses. The police and deputies did their best to protect the strikebreakers and keep some trucks moving, although their best was not good enough. The mobilization of the militia by the Farmer-Labor governor was a threat against the strikers, even if the militiamen were not put on the street. The strikers will remember that threat. In a sense it can be said that the political education of a large section of the strikers began with this experience. It is sheer lunacy, however to imagine that it was completed and that the strikers, practically all of whom voted yesterday for Roosevelt and Olson, could have been led into a prolonged strike for purely political aims after the primary demand for the recognition of the union had been won.

Yet this is the premise upon which all the Stalinist criticism of the strike leadership is based. Governor Olson, declared Bill Dunne in the *Daily Worker*, was the "main enemy." And having convinced himself on this point, he continued: "The exposure and defeat of Olson should have been the central political objective of the Minneapolis struggle." Nor did he stop even there. Wound up and going strong by this time, and lacking the friendly advice of a Harpo Marx who would explain the wisdom of keeping the mouth shut when the head is not clear, he decided to go to the limit, so he added: "This [exposure and defeat of Olson] was the basic necessity for winning the economic demands for the Drivers Union and the rest of the working class."

There it is, Mr. Ripley, whether you believe it or not. This is the thesis, the "political line," laid down for the Minneapolis truck drivers in the *Daily Worker*. For the sake of this thesis, it is contended that negotiations for the settlement of the strike should have been rejected unless the state troopers were demobilized, and a general strike should have been proclaimed "over the heads of the Central Labor Council and state federation of labor officials." Dunne only neglected to add: over the heads of the workers also, including the truck drivers.

For the workers of Minneapolis, including the striking drivers, didn't understand the situation in this light at all, and leaders who proceeded on such an assumption would have found themselves without followers. The workers of Minneapolis, like the striking workers all over the country, understand the "central objective" to be the *recognition of the union*. The leaders were in full harmony with them on this question; they stuck to this objective; and when it was attained, they did not attempt to parade the workers through a general strike for the sake of exercise or for "the defeat of Governor Olson." For one reason, it was not the right thing to do. And, for another reason, they couldn't have done it if they had tried.

The arguments of Bill Dunne regarding the Minneapolis "betrayal" could have a logical meaning only to one who construed the situation as revolutionary and aimed at an insurrection. We, of course, are for the revolution. But not today, not in a single city. There is a certain unconscious tribute to the "Trotskyists"—and not an inappropriate one—in the fact that so much was demanded of them in Minneapolis. But Bill Dunne, who is more at home with proverbs than with politics, should recall the one which says, "every vegetable has its season." It was the season for an armed battle in Germany in the early part of 1933. In America in 1934, it is the season for organizing the workers, leading them in strikes, and compelling the bosses to recognize their unions. The mistake of all the Stalinists, Bill Dunne among them, in misjudging the weather in Germany in 1933 was a tragedy. In America in 1934 it is a farce.

The strike wave of last year was only a prelude to the surging movement we witness today. And just as the present movement goes deeper and strikes harder than the first, so does it prepare the way for a third movement which will surpass it in scope, aggressiveness, and militancy. Frustrated in their aspirations for organization by misplaced faith in the Roosevelt administration, and by the black treachery of the official labor bureaucracy, the workers will take the road of struggle again with firmer determination and clearer aims. And they will seek for better leaders.

Then the new left wing of the labor movement can have its day. The revolutionary militants can bound forward in mighty leaps and come to the head of large sections of the movement if they know how to grasp their opportunities and understand their tasks. For this they must be politically organized and work together as a disciplined body; they must forge the new party of the Fourth International without delay. They must get inside the developing movement, regardless of its initial form, stay inside, and shape its course from within.

They must demonstrate a capacity for organization as well as agitation, for responsibility as well as for militancy. They must convince the workers of their ability not only to organize and lead strikes aggressively, but also to settle them advantageously at the right time and consolidate the gains. In a word, the modern militants of the labor movement have the task of gaining the confidence of the workers in their ability to lead the movement all the year round and to advance the interests of the workers all the time.

On this condition the new left wing of the trade unions can take shape and grow with rapid strides. And the left wing, in turn, will be the foundation of the new party, the genuine communist party. On a local scale, in a small sector of the labor movement, the Minneapolis comrades have set an example which shows the way. The International Communists have every right to be proud of this example and hold it up as a model to study and follow.

The Socialist Party convention
June 1934

The following article was published in the July *New International*.

It has been remarked before that the ferment which heralds the struggle to solve the crisis in the international labor movement is now manifested conspicuously in the camp of Social Democracy. The Detroit convention graphically demonstrated that this international trend has struck the Socialist Party of America with full force.[131]

The influence of events impressed itself on the labor movement in peculiar and seemingly contradictory ways. Shut out of the Comintern by the frightful and unprecedented bureaucratization and ideological decay of recent years, the discussion of new paths is breaking out in the Socialist parties. The Comintern stagnates and dies before our eyes. The international organization which arose out of the crisis of the World War and the Russian revolution, having failed in its mission, is passing from the scene amidst incredible corruption and degeneration. No doubt further developments of the crisis will bring cataclysmic eruptions in the Stalinist parties also. But, for the present, new life asserts itself most prominently in the Social Democracy.

In many respects we are witnessing today a repetition of certain peculiarities which marked the first emergence of American Communism. The official Communist Party is reenacting the role of the IWW. This organization, which had stood in advance of the SP, failed to react to the great international events of war and revolution. The new left wing, which was destined to become the Communist Party, took shape in the SP and passed over the head of the IWW, leaving it behind. A striking analogy is to be seen today. There is one important difference, however. An independent body of communists, armed with the program of the future movement, has long since separated itself from decaying Stalinism and is in a position to exert an independent influence on the development of the new movement. Their task is to see where the living movement is and strive to influence its course. This obligates them at the moment to devote special attention to the ferment in the SP. The Detroit convention revealed the depth of this ferment more clearly than before.

The strong sweep of radical sentiment in the ranks of the Socialist Party was officially registered at Detroit. At the same time the inadequacy of all the present radical groupings in the party was cruelly demonstrated. The convention marked the definite official shift of the party from social reformism to centrism, even if it is a diluted form of European centrism. The happenings at Detroit prepared the way for an accelerated development of the genuine left-wing forces. And, finally, the Detroit convention met under the predominating influence of international events. Its whole course, from beginning to end, was decisively affected by the trend of developments in the European movement. Here, once again, the determining role of internationalism in the labor movement was made manifest.

The reaction of the American Socialist Party to international events, and to the devastating crisis at home, revealed several distinct groupings in this once more or less homogenous body of social reformism. The Old Guard, who control all the important and rich institutions and are in the habit of ruling, fought a desperate battle at the convention. They appeared there in struggle for the first time without the leadership of Hillquit, and the loss they have suffered was painfully evident. Hillquit, in such a situation, would have tacked and maneuvered and cheated the convention majority with a compromise. Without the adroit leadership of Hillquit, the Old Guard was able only to bludgeon.

The leaders of the Old Guard, by far the outstanding personalities of the convention, with the exception of Thomas, impressed one as a group of Tories who have learned nothing and forgotten nothing and who are incapable of recognizing the frightful debacle that has been suffered by social reformism in Europe. They are old and aging men, settled in life, well-satisfied with the status quo. They gave the impression of wanting everything to remain as it is in the Socialist Party, and in social life also. They are grey, hard-faced men. "Socialism" is their business, and it has paid. They are getting their socialism now. They are mostly lawyers or officials, with lucrative positions, salaries, fees, and other fat emoluments which cushion their sacrifices for the cause and enable them to live comfortable, middle-class lives. They enjoy honors and run no risks. The prospects of a disruption of this idyllic situation arouses in them sentiments of indignation. This broke out in their voices every time they spoke.

They are ready men on the floor, fluent speakers, skilled debaters, dogged fighters for their own interests. From their die-hard attitude at the convention, to say nothing of the furious offensive they have launched to overthrow its decisions in the party referendum, any grown-up person could understand that the leaders of the Old Guard will never give up their positions, the institutions they control, or their way of living. They will live in the same party with the faltering amateurs of the Militant group, and suffer the pious exhortations of Norman Thomas, only so long as they are left with their positions and their possessions.

The term *Militants* is a very loose and decidedly inappropriate name for the new party majority established at Detroit. If the term *militant* means fighter, the Old Guard deserves it more. The Militants would be better described as combinationists. Horse-trading to line up votes for the National Executive Committee was their principal occupation at the convention. Lacking dynamic personalities and leaders, except for Thomas, and making a miserable showing in the forensic conflicts with the Old Guard, they nevertheless did an effective job of vote-wrangling behind the scenes.

Among the majority which they patched together were delegates of every type and tendency. There were the New York and Chicago Militants—typical centrists. There were the Municipal Socialists from Milwaukee, who were primarily interested, as one delegate expressed it, in "overhead sewers and steam-heated sidewalks." There were trade union bureaucrats such as Krzycki, vice-president of the Amalgamated Clothing Workers, and Graham, president of the Montana Federation of Labor—officials who would risk their positions by getting crossways with Hillman and Green as readily as you would give up your right eye.

There were old "post-office socialists" from the hinterland, smelling faintly of moth balls. There were the Christian pacifists, such as Norman Thomas and Devere Allen. And in this motley assemblage that constituted the convention majority in Detroit, there was included the Revolutionary Policy Committee, which had raised the flag of the dictatorship of the proletariat a short while before.

The RPC was under fire for the first time at Detroit. There it appeared as a weak, amateurish, and ineffective group which was unable to grasp its opportunity or to measure up to the expectations which had been aroused by its manifesto. Twenty-five to thirty delegates, it was reported, were ready to follow the leadership of the RPC in a principled fight. Instead of concentrating on that, they got involved in caucus maneuvers with the Militants for a place on the National Executive Committee a fatal error which ended in a miserable fiasco for the RPC. In the end they got their representative on the NEC. But for that they gave up their independent position and never presented it to the convention. A wonderful bargain—like that of the farmer who traded his farm to a confidence man for a half-interest in the City Hall.

The political instability of the majority of the convention was shown in the fights on the floor over the three main questions: the international report, the trade union question, and the Declaration of Principles. The Militants didn't carry a single one of these fights to victory on the basis of their preconvention program. Their resolution on the international report was cut to pieces by an amendment of Thomas. On the trade union question they capitulated before the offensive of the Old Guard. The famous Declaration of Principles, as it was presented and adopted, was primarily a document of militant pacifism.

An interesting debate developed around the international

report, originally slated for the central place in the convention. The resolution proposed to enforce the report of the majority of the American delegation at Paris—supporting the standpoint of the centrist majority there—and to declare this to be the official policy guiding the work of the American party.[132] The Old Guard attacked the resolution in the name of "democratic socialism" and already began to mutter their threats about a split. Mayor Hoan of Milwaukee, who was to combine with the Militants in the majority bloc, testified to his interest in revolutionary internationalism, as follows: "I don't give a hoot in hell which report is adopted. . . . Only let's not get excited or bitter about it. . . . For my part, I'm in favor of not sending any more international delegates if they come back here and stir up trouble in the party."

As the debate came to a climax, Thomas came forward with his amendment to strike out that paragraph which committed the American party to the policy supported by a majority of its delegation at the Paris conference of the Second International. This amendment was carried by a majority of delegates present. On the roll call according to membership represented, the entire resolution was defeated.

Here, early in the convention, Thomas appeared in the role which he hoped to play at Detroit and afterwards. His aim was to stand somewhat above the factions, to conciliate and compromise and keep peace in the family. But in this attempt he encounters the stubborn intransigence of the Old Guard. They want to mediate between themselves and anything that suggests radicalism. They want "democratic socialism" without any radical frills or phrases. Besides, they hate the pious idealism of Thomas. They envy him his popularity and moral influence and do not wish to add to it.

The debate on the trade union question was a real test

of the SP and especially of the convention majority. The result was a sorry picture of timidity and cowardice. The trade union resolution proper was a routine declaration that did not touch the vital question of attitude to the treacherous officialdom of the AFL. In the resolution on the NRA and socialism, however, one mild paragraph of criticism was smuggled in. It read as follows:

"The NRA has also shown fundamental weaknesses in the American labor movement. It has shown up more clearly than any other event the obsolete ideology of the AFL. The many instances in which leaders have counseled workers against striking or even ordered them back to work in the face of an overwhelming indication by the membership of a desire to strike, has indicated their abandonment of the belief that unions are fighting organizations. It has shown that inadequacy of the AFL structure in organizational work and the positive harm of the craft form of organization."

But even this plaintive bleat at the labor agents of capital was too much. The Old Guard launched a ferocious offensive at this mild criticism of their blood brothers, and in this offensive they were joined by a heavy section of the "allies" of the Militants. "Don't attack the unions," they shouted in chorus, conveniently identifying the unions with the bureaucracy. "What the trade unions want of us," said Vladeck, "is not advice but service. . . . The leaders are often more radical than the rank and file." Judge Panken took off on a flight of oratorical denunciation of the offending paragraph and warned the convention of disaster for the party if it ventured to make faces at the labor skates. Mayor McLevy of Bridgeport declared the SP should "stop telling the trade unions what to do. Let's attend to our own political business and let them attend to theirs," said the mayor.

Krzycki and Graham, part of the majority that voted for the Declaration of Principles, broke over the traces on this question that brought principle too close to home. Krzycki prophesied the doom of the party if this innocuous paragraph was left in the resolution. "I can't speak to the unions any more if you carry this," he said. Most entertaining of all were the fulminations of Graham—later put on the NEC by a deal with the Militants—against the "college professors" and other highbrows who want to violate the independence of the trade unions. "These monkeys don't know what they're talking about," he shouted, in language not too professorial, to the accompaniment of loud applause from the Old Guard and the trade union officials.

It was a field day for trade union conservatives. Thomas, retreating under the barrage, declined to speak on the question except to express agreement with "what has been said and well said." The Militants, who had sponsored the paragraph, made a sorry showing in the debate. They appeared to be as frightened by the ferocity of the attack as a group of boys caught stealing apples in a private orchard. They ran for cover, and the debate ended with the announcement that the resolutions committee had withdrawn the contested paragraph.

It was a miserable and shameful capitulation on the key question of proletarian policy. The real caliber of the Militants was well demonstrated in this skirmish. For the trade union question is precisely the question which puts theories and general declarations to the concrete test and brings immediate repercussions in the class struggle. All the great questions—war, fascism, revolution—converge on this point. Without a real basis in the trade unions, conquered in relentless struggle against the reactionary officialdom, no serious resistance to war and fascism is conceivable, not to speak of the revolutionary overthrow of capitalist society which rests on its supports in the labor movement represented by the conservative bureaucracy.

The feverish internal life of the Socialist Party is centered now on the campaign of the Old Guard to overthrow the Declaration of Principles adopted at Detroit. To a revolutionist who takes formulations seriously, the clamor raging around this declaration seems entirely uncalled for. There is an element of unreality, even of burlesque, in the exaggerated denunciation poured out on this document, which reminds one of the campaign of the super-reactionaries against such "dangerous reds" as the editors of the *New Republic* and the director of the American Civil Liberties Union.

This declaration in reality is pretty thin soup. It is not a document of revolutionary Marxism on the question of war, as has been maintained, but rather of militant pacifism. It is the program of the pacifist preachers, not of the revolutionary workers. The war section under dispute was written by Devere Allen, a prominent worker in the peace movement and an avowed pacifist. In his speech for the declaration he announced himself as "a pacifist and proud to bear the name." As for the other sections of the declaration, they are shot through and through with ambiguous formulations and characteristic centrist bombast.

A bizarre combination was assembled to make up a majority for the declaration as a whole. It extended from the Milwaukee advocates of municipal reform to the Revolutionary Policy Committee. Everybody was for it. Except the Old Guard. They are not even radical pacifists. Thomas made the most eloquent speech for the declaration and ended by committing himself into the hands of his Maker with the invocation, "God give me the grace to live up to it." After that there was no way to stop the stampede to carry the declaration. By the grace of God—and a terrestrial horse-trade for the NEC—the resolution was adopted with a large majority and the SP shook its fist at war and fascism. But there is nothing in the fist. Neither war nor fascism will be impeded by it.

There were left-wing delegates at the convention—quite a few of them. But they were juggled and maneuvered out of their rights by the caucus sharks, railroaded and denied the floor by the chairman of the day, Vladeck, who frankly stated that he was selecting speakers according to the lists prepared by the caucus leaders. One delegate, Peter Fagan of Michigan, managed after a long fight to get the floor to explain his vote and to denounce "the centrist steamroller in the convention which suppressed the voice of the left wing."

The convention took no position on the Soviet Union. On this pivotal question of proletarian policy the centrist majority simply "ducked" and referred the matter to the new NEC. The weakness, confusion, and cowardice which are the soul of centrism were manifested on this question with singular clarity. Does the SP propose to defend the Soviet Union or not? Does it support the Stalin bureaucracy? What is its standpoint on the foreign policy of the Soviet Union? Or, is it indifferent to the position of the workers' fatherland in the sphere of diplomacy? Does the SP demand "freedom of expression" for the counterrevolutionists in the Soviet Union or does it confine its demands to democracy for the loyal defenders of the revolution? Is the SP for "socialism in one country" as the guiding policy of the Soviet Union, or does it take the standpoint of revolutionary internationalism?

The convention gave no answer to any of these fundamental questions; and, sad to relate, there was no other group in the convention to force an answer one way or the other. Delegates were there ready to support such a fight, but there was no one to lead them.

The Revolutionary Policy Committee was confronted at the convention with an exceptional opportunity to show its colors and establish itself firmly as a principled faction in the party. Formed only a short while ago, it rapidly developed a surprising strength. The revolutionary elements in the party took the RPC leaders at their word and were ready to shove them to the front of the genuine left-wing movement. But when the opportunity came, perhaps because it came too soon, they lost their heads completely. They appeared inexperienced, weak, and unsure of themselves, and they made a pitiful showing.

The horse-trade engineered by Matthews—to sacrifice their independent position for a place on the NEC—precipitated a crisis and split in the RPC caucus on the first day of the convention. So great was the demoralization and resentment of the left-wing delegates that the affair became common knowledge. A conciliation later, with the understanding that the position of the RPC would be presented independently after all, turned out to be deceptive. Nothing happened. The RPC didn't even speak. Naturally such procedure fearfully undermined the prestige of the RPC.

The left-wing elements in the party had begun to rally around it for want of another center and, for the same reason, a formal unity of the faction was maintained even after the disgraceful performance at the convention. From all appearances the RPC still has a chance to make good, but it is under a real test now. The leaders, whose not too great authority was seriously weakened at Detroit, will be obliged to lead a principled fight in the near future or make way for others who are more steadfast in their convictions and more able to fight for them.

Since the convention the right wing, led by the New York Old Guard, has taken the offensive and set up an apparatus to conduct a campaign for the defeat of the Declaration of Principles in the party referendum. Their fight is waged with great aggressiveness. Threats of split fly right and left. In this, however, there is a great deal of bluff. The split, in our opinion, will not come immediately. The Old Guard know the weakness and flabbiness of their opponents and count on clubbing them into submission. Thomas has already come forward with an "explanation" of the declaration which opens the door to a complete retreat. On top of that the declaration has been submitted to a committee of Socialist lawyers for an opinion as to its legality. The whole issue is thus switched from the political to the juridical field. This is duck soup for the Old Guard, which is a miniature bar association all by itself.

Agreements or compromises at the top will not be able to stop this development. That is because the real pressure behind the conflict of the groupings at the top comes from below, from the proletarian sections of the party and from the youth. They will continue to push with increasing insistence and clearer aim for a revolutionary policy. The convention appears to us not as the end, but rather as the real beginning of the internal conflict in the party.

In the present situation the RPC is again presented with a great opportunity. As has been shown, it gave little promise at Detroit, but the group still has a chance. The next few months will decide its fate. It will either show itself as a miserable windbreak for reformism and pass from the scene, or become a rallying center of those elements who are moving for a revolutionary party. In order to play the latter role it will be necessary for the leaders of the RPC to clarify their aims and answer the question: "Where are we going?" They must understand clearly that a break with the Second International, politically and organizationally—and that means also its American prototypes—is the indispensable condition to the constitution of a revolutionary party. And this necessary break leads with iron logic to the issue of fusion with revolutionary elements outside the SP.

There also a fight is raging that is no less intransigent and irreconcilable than the fight in the Socialist Party. Will the left Socialists go over to the Stalinists—that is, from one bankrupt International to another? To the Lovestoneites? This is the most miserable prospect of all—to break with one bankrupt organization in order to "reform" another from the outside. To escape such a fate the militants of the RPC might well appeal to Norman Thomas's God for aid. Will the RPC eventually go with the revolutionary Marxists who are coming together from various sources to create a new party of the Fourth International?

These are the life-and-death questions facing the RPC and all the revolutionary elements in the Socialist Party. Only that faction which knows where it is going will be able to lead the revolutionary socialist workers and the youth behind it. We, on our part, watch the left movement in the SP with the greatest interest and sympathy, and aspire to aid it. The best way to do that is to tell the truth and combine loyal cooperation with frank criticism.

In any case, whatever path the different existing factions in the SP take, we can be reasonably sure that a large detachment of the new communist party, perhaps its most important detachment numerically, will come out of the ranks of the SP. For the truly revolutionary elements in the SP and the youth in the first place, there is only one program, one banner: the program and banner of the Fourth International.

Report and motions on SP developments

June 25, 1934

The following report and motions were presented by Cannon to the National Committee and unanimously adopted. They were reprinted from the minutes; motions 6, 10, and 11 were proposed by other NC members and incorporated into the final list of motions.

The RPC appeared in the convention as the weakest section and composed of politically inexperienced elements. All loose radical delegates sided with the RPC, but it became entirely lost in its caucus with the Militants. The RPC caucus split in two because of the deal with the Militants to support them on the basis of obtaining one member on the NEC. (Matthews engineered this deal; he was denounced by the RPC caucus but later reconciliation was effected.) Cannon had proposed to the RPC from the outset to cut loose from the Militant caucus and put forth its own program. This did not materialize.

The RPC, because of its entanglement with the Militants, never appeared as an independent body in the convention.

In addition, most of its leading members were not delegates. In this situation it could give no lead to the left-wing delegates; hence the contest was exclusively between the Militants and the Old Guard with the former capturing the nominal majority. It is not necessary to go into the issues of policy; they have been elaborated in the *Militant*.

The Lovestoneites have a plant in the leading RPC councils. Whatever elements the Stalinists had supporting them in the SP, they are withdrawing just now when the struggle begins in a serious manner. Influential leaders and members of the RPC group are sympathetic to us. It became possible before the close of the convention to gather the RPC forces and to restore it as an independent body. It decided to continue its struggle after the convention and for that purpose set up a national council. We have small forces now in various parts of the country within the SP who can be counted on to work in our direction.

The perspective for the SP is not that of an immediate split. The Old Guard uses the split threat as a club against their opponents and are succeeding in forcing the Militants into a retreat. It appears that the Lovestoneites are driving for a quick split in order to get something out of that for themselves. The prospects for a national fraction working in our direction are good. We should proceed to organize such a fraction centered around the sympathetic elements in Minnesota and Chicago and to work under the direction of our National Committee. We should through this fraction build the RPC, elaborate our program step by step, and gauge the opportune moment to put forward our full position for a new party, etc., this depending upon developments in the SP.

Motions:
1. To concentrate upon the immediate task of forming

a national fraction in the SP and YPSL.

2. It shall be the immediate tactic for this fraction to work in the RPC as its left wing, to begin a concerted struggle, to push it leftward, and to endeavor to isolate Lovestoneite and Stalinist influence. Where no RPC group exists, efforts should be made to form and to organize our fraction within them.

3. For this purpose we develop our program step by step, beginning with issues of trade union policy, next the issues of the proletarian struggle for power leading up to the international question (the Fourth International).

4. The direction of the national fraction is to be centralized in New York under the direction of the National Committee with Cannon as national organizer and Carter as the assistant with particular reference to the YPSL.

5. For general strategy, as a rule, our connection in the SP should not be organizationally connected with the local branches of the league, but have contact only with the branch organizer or a specially designated comrade.

6. In regard to the referendum on the Declaration of Principles, we should tell the comrades to advise the RPC to vote no on the declaration with a statement of the reasons for the same.

7. We should propose to those comrades who are with us to issue their own paper which, regardless of official standing, is controlled exclusively by our fraction.

8. In our press, in the *Militant, New International,* and the *Young Spartacus,* together with this proposed paper, we should launch a systematic and furious campaign against the Militants and feature it prominently.

9. We should start immediately a campaign of publicity and a campaign in the SP for a demand that the SP break with the Second International and come out for a new International. (In this we must make clear that we

mean the Fourth International.)

10. Our comrades should propose immediately in the fight they undertake the expulsion of Waldman as a traitor and of Sharts as a chauvinist and the expulsion of all those supporting their positions.[133] Our comrades should sharply differentiate themselves from the Militants in their opposition to these people.

11. We should endeavor to popularize the conception that there are such traitors and chauvinists in the SP.

The strike wave and the left wing

September 1934

The following article was published in the September–October *New International*.

The wide shift of the American working class to the left, prepared by the ravages of the five-year crisis, found its expression primarily in the two strike waves which swept the country since the inception of the NRA. This shift has been more or less steadily gaining in scope and tempo. All signs point to a deepening of the process of radicalization and stormier manifestations of it in the near future. The fighting energy of the insurgent workers has not been spent, nor have their immediate minimum demands been satisfied. They have not been defeated in a test of strength, but rather tricked and maneuvered out of their first objectives. The net result is that the dissatisfaction and resentment of the workers is multiplied, the antagonism between them and the leaders who thwarted them is sharpened, and their faith in the Roosevelt administration is more violently shaken.

All this speaks for the assumption that a still mightier strike movement is in the offing and that it will clash more directly with the main agencies which have balked the great majority of the strikes—the government and the AFL bureaucracy. Roosevelt's "truce"—to be arranged by conferences "with small groups of those truly representative of large employers of labor and large groups of organized labor"—will have far less prospect of success than the Hoover truce of 1929. The workers were passive then; they are moving now.

The second strike wave under the NRA, climaxed by the general strike of the textile workers, went far beyond the wave of 1933, involved many more workers, and reflected a more earnest mood. State intervention with armed force, supplementing the mediation machinery of the NRA, became the rule rather than the exception. Violent conflicts occurred; many were killed or injured, more arrested. The cold brutality of these police and military attacks, and the courage with which they resisted, cannot have failed to leave a deep mark in the working-class mind. The experiences of these recent months have been important preconditions for a great political awakening.

The open resistance to the conservative labor bureaucracy at Minneapolis and San Francisco, and the disillusionment ensuing from the systematic treacheries in the other situations—in averting strikes that were due and in wrecking those which could not be prevented—presage a widespread revolt against the reactionary officialdom.

A remarkable feature of the 1934 strike wave has been the popular support for the strikes, manifested by the workers not directly involved, as well as by the "little fellows" of the lower middle class who have been squeezed, first by the crisis and again by the monopoly-aiding features of the NRA cure-all for the crisis. At Toledo and Milwaukee this ardent and demonstrative support of the masses played a decisive role. In Minneapolis, also, public sympathy and the solidarity of the trade unionists proved to be a tremendous reservoir of support for the famous strikes of Local 574.

Public sympathy in nearly every instance has taken an active form. The strike sympathizers picketed, paraded, fought with the scabs, police, and militia. This phenomenon undoubtedly has a deep significance. It indicates deep-seated mass dissatisfaction with things as they are and as they have been in recent times. The spontaneous movement of the masses to the side of the striking workers argues for the idea that the workers can find ready allies in the lower middle class when they strike out against capital and lead the way. Fascism begins to make real headway with the aggrieved petty bourgeoisie only when they lose faith in the determination and ability of the workers to lead.

Public sympathy, including the sympathy of other workers, for strikers gave the main impetus to the sentiment for local general strike action in support of the Toledo strike. The general strike became a popular slogan. It was looked upon as the certain way to victory. Finally, for the first time in fifteen years, the general strike was realized in San Francisco in sympathy with the marine workers. The disastrous outcome of this action put the damper on general strike agitation, for the time being at least, and impelled the advanced workers to a more sober and critical examination of the possibilities and limitations of general sympathy strike action. Far from discrediting the idea of the general strike, the 'Frisco struggle revealed that such a radical weapon requires a sure hand to wield it if it is to bite deeply and effectively.

The 'Frisco experience demonstrated with cruel emphasis that the general strike by itself is no magic formula. There, it was a two-edged sword that cut more sharply against the embattled marine workers. The leadership came into the hands of the reactionary officialdom. They transformed it into a weapon against the marine workers and against the "reds." Having shifted the center of gravity and control from the marine unions to the general strike committee which they dominated, the reactionaries then deliberately broke the general strike and pulled the marine strike down with it. A wave of reactionary persecution followed as a matter of course. The Stalinists, who advocated the general strike as a panacea and were among the first victims of its tragic result, have not understood to this day what happened and why.

The 'Frisco debacle does not in the least prove the contention of President Green that the general strike, being a challenge to government, is bound to lose. (These dyed-in-the-wool lackeys of capital never even dream of the workers being victorious in a contest with the capitalist government). From this example, however, it is necessary to conclude that the general strike is not to be played with carelessly or fired into the air to see what will happen. It must be well organized and prepared. Its limitations must be understood and it must aim at definite, limited objectives. Or, if the aim is really to challenge the government, the general strike cannot be confined to one locality. In any case, serious agitation for a general strike should presuppose the possibility of removing the reactionary leadership or, at least, of being able to deprive it of a free hand by means of a well-organized left wing. That was lacking in San Francisco. The general strike revealed in a glaring light the wide disparity between the readiness of the workers for radical and militant action and the organization of the left wing.

The same contradiction was to be seen in the general strike of textile workers which marked the peak of the strike wave and ended too abruptly and ingloriously. This was the greatest strike in American labor history in point of numbers, and the equal of any in militancy. Called into being by the pressure of the rank and file at the convention against the resistance of the leadership, it was frankly aimed at the NRA and the whole devilish circle of governmental machination, trickery, and fraud. The workers, the majority of them new to the trade union movement, fought like lions, only to see the fruits of their struggle snatched from their hands, leaving them bewildered, demoralized, and defeated—they knew not how.

But, for all the tragedy of the outcome, the general textile strike was distinguished by an extraordinary vitality and some distinct features that are fraught with bright promise for the future of the textile workers and the whole working class of the country. Within the framework of one of the most decrepit and reactionary unions, hundreds of thousands of textile workers waged a memorable battle. The "new" proletariat of the South, steeped in age-long backwardness and superstition, came awake, prayed to God, and then went out to fight the scabs, the gunmen, and the militia. From North to South the battle line extended. The mills were shut down. The big push of the bosses to reopen the mills a few days before the strike was called off, came to nothing except a demonstration of the strikers' dominance of the situation.

With their ranks unbroken, with the universal sympathy of the workers throughout the country, with victory in their grasp—the textile workers saw the strike called off by their own officers without a single concession from the bosses, and without having a chance to express their own wishes in the matter. And most significant of all—the key to the fatal weakness of the trade union movement today—this monstrous betrayal could be perpetrated without a sign of organized resistance. *There was no force in the textile workers' ranks to organize such resistance.*

That is the general story of the second strike wave under the NRA, as of its precursor last year. The workers, awakening from a long apathy and ready for the militant struggle to regain their lost standards, have not yet found a leadership of the same temper. Minneapolis is the one magnificent exception. There a group of determined militants, armed with the most advanced political conceptions, organized the workers in the trucking industry, led them through three strikes within six months, and remain today at the head of the union. It was this fusion of the native militancy of the American workers, common to practically all of the strikes of this year, with a leadership equal to its task, that made the strikes of a few thousand workers of a single local union events of a national, and even international, prominence; a shining example for the whole labor movement.

The resources of the workers, restricted and constrained in the other strikes, were freely released and deliberately stimulated by the leadership in Minneapolis. One example, of many: the textile workers, half a million strong, had to depend on the capitalist press for information: Local 574 of Minneapolis published *a daily paper of its own!* What miracles will the workers in the great industries be capable of when they forge a leadership of the Minneapolis caliber!

The year, approaching its last quarter, has been rich in experience which can and will be transformed into capital for the future. The lessons, once assimilated, will ensure that the future struggles will take place on higher ground and with brighter prospects. The striking workers and great masses, seething with strike sentiment but restrained and out-maneuvered by the leaders and the politicians of the Roosevelt administration, have for the most part failed to gain their objectives. But they have not been really defeated; they have not been overwhelmed. The struggles, despite their severity, were only tentative. The real tests are yet to come, and the workers will face them stronger as the result of the experiences of the first nine months of 1934.

Five years of crisis have done their work. The workers, half-starved on the job, are no longer afraid of risking the job in a strike. It has been demonstrated on a nationwide scale that the unemployed will not scab if the trade unions establish a proper connection with them. On the contrary, the unemployed can be organized as a powerful ally of the strikers.

At Toledo this was first demonstrated effectively by the initiative of the American Workers Party in organizing the unemployed for mass picketing. Taking a leaf from this experience, the Communist League members, the dynamic force in the leadership of the Minneapolis strike, adopted the same policy in regard to the unemployed, with no less telling effect. The members of the MCCW (the Minneapolis organization of the unemployed) played a big part on the heroic picket line of the strike of Local 574. One of them, John Belor, paid for it with his life. The necessity of a close union of the employed and unemployed is one of the big lessons in strike strategy to be derived from the experiences of the recent months.

The political parties and groups have been tested. The advanced, thinking workers can appraise them more accurately now on the basis of their performance in the strike wave. The balance sheet of the Stalinists is zero, symbolized by the abject capitulation of their bankrupt "red" textile union to the UTW on the eve of the general strike.

They wrought a great work of destruction; they strangled the left wing that had been under their leadership for a decade and left the reactionaries a free field to strangle the strikes. The Socialist Militants displayed a considerable activity in the strike movement, offset by a complete silence in the face of the greatest treacheries of the labor bureaucracy. They have not even begun to criticize the labor traitors, to say nothing of organizing a determined struggle against them.

The Communist League and the American Workers Party, despite the limited forces at their disposal, took advantage of such opportunities as they had and demonstrated in practice, notably in Minneapolis and Toledo, that they are the bearers of trade union policies and methods around which the left wing of tomorrow will crystallize. The fatal weakness in the labor movement today is precisely the lack of a genuine left wing. This left wing can come to life only on a new basis, with a new policy that is free from every taint of reformist cowardice and degenerate Stalinism.

The mainspring of the new left wing can only be a revolutionary Marxian party. Its creation is our foremost task.

For fusion with the AWP!

Published September 15, 1934

The following article was published in the *Militant*.

The most important political news of the day is the report about the decisive steps taken during the past week to facilitate and hasten the fusion of the American Workers Party and the Communist League.[134]

The news is of paramount importance because it spells definite progress toward the forging of the sharpest and most indispensable weapon of the working class—a revolutionary party. By itself, the merger of these two organizations, of entirely different origins but moving toward the same goal, would signify the actual *beginning* of the new party and make its formal proclamation possible.

Armed with the program of Marxism, the new political center thus created would speedily attract the scattered revolutionary militants as a magnet attracts steel particles. The adhesion of thousands of awakening workers could be expected. The expanded political organization would be in a position to connect itself with the stormy movement of the working masses and give that movement a conscious direction.

The native militancy of the American workers, surpassed by none as our labor history shows, and again brilliantly demonstrated in the present strike wave—in Toledo, Minneapolis, San Francisco, Kohler, the textile fields—would be fused, through such a vanguard party, with that decisive element which has been lacking in all past periods of labor resurgence: scientific doctrine, political clarity, leadership.

It has been the lack of precisely this element, which only a Marxist party can supply, that condemned the insurgent labor movement of the past to futility and defeat. Lacking a class theory of its own, which can come into the labor movement in no other way than through the Marxist party, the American workers, with all their militancy and capacity for sacrifice, fell victim to all kinds of quackery and treason and landed in a blind alley every time.

Capitalism itself creates the conditions for the elemental movement of the workers, as the far-flung general strike of the textile workers proves once again. But the Marxist party, which alone can shape and guide this elemental movement to the goal of emancipation, must be made by the deliberate work of the conscious vanguard. Since such a party does not exist today—and experience on a national and international scale testify to that bitter fact— it must be created anew. This is the first and foremost task of all revolutionists.

Every serious step in this direction is important. The progress that has been recorded in the past week toward the fusion of the two most important groups standing outside the poisoned swamps of Stalinism and Social Democracy, and dedicated to the aim of building a new party and a new International, cannot fail to inspire all revolutionary workers with enthusiasm and hope as it inspires us. It opens up the prospect of saving time in the execution of our great historic task, and time is a weighty factor now. Events move with lightning speed. We must move with them.

On an international scale the political organizations of the working class have suffered a collapse no less devastating, and no less irremediable, than that of 1914. Germany and Austria tell the story of the bankruptcy of the Second and Third Internationals in letters of fire.

During the five years of the crisis we have witnessed the paralyzing influence of this international debacle on the American movement. Even after five years of the crisis, during which the insoluble contradictions of the capitalist system did their best to prepare the soil for revolutionary political development, the great strike movement of the awakening workers, with a few exceptions such as Minneapolis, is controlled and throttled by the old reactionary leadership. A real challenge to this leadership, which represents the influence of the exploiters in the labor movement, has not yet been made for the simple reason that there was no force able to offer the challenge and make the challenge good.

For that, and for all that logically follows after, a party is needed. An International is needed.

Revolutionary internationalism is the heart and core of the system of ideas which binds us together and unites us indissolubly with our comrades in other countries. This conception, which is expressed in the struggle for the Fourth International, animates and guides us in every phase of activity in our own country, whether it be the holding of a public meeting, the organization of a strike, or participation in the formation of a new party.

We have said at many times, and we underscore it here once more, that the organization of an American party cannot be separated in any way from the struggle to form a new International, but on the contrary is an inseparable part of that struggle. The new party will be able to solve the national problems and find its way into the mass movement of the American workers only if it approaches them from the international point of view; the new party can become a national power only on the condition that the banner it raises is the banner of internationalism.

This is the cardinal lesson of all the great events of our time; this is the wisdom of the great teachers. This unshakable conviction has entered into the marrow of our bones. Whatever we do and wherever we go, it goes with us. We seek allies and co-workers first of all among those who hold similar views.

The decision of the active workers' conference of the AWP in favor of hastening the fusion and the joint launching of the new party, coincided with a similar decision of the New York membership meeting of the league. These actions gave expression to the fact that the two organizations have drawn closer together in the course of practical cooperation in various fields of activity, and comradely discussion devoted to clarification of questions of the program.

It appears to us that the revised draft program of the AWP formulated a position on the question of the new International that is nearer to our viewpoint than the formulation of the first draft. We, on our part, venture to say that the work of the league in the Minneapolis strikes helped convince the members of the AWP that we also are able to "speak American"; that our internationalism is not an abstraction but a guide to action on the national field. Joint work of the two organizations in practical work, limited though it has been, has demonstrated in practice an ability to work out a common policy and to cooperate loyally in advancing it. These are all factors which have strengthened the will for organic unity and the hope that it may be expedited.

Our National Committee has not yet had the time and opportunity to make a critical analysis of the revised draft program of the AWP. Progress has undoubtedly been made toward working out a common standpoint on some of the most important questions. Further discussion and clarification will yet be needed to assure a firm principled basis for the unification. Other obstacles may arise. But it is our firm conviction that all difficulties standing in the way can be overcome if there is a determined will to overcome them, if there is an understanding, on both sides, of the overshadowing importance of finding a common path and launching the new party without the needless loss of a single day. All our efforts will be directed to this end.

Textile strike debacle

Published September 29, 1934

The following article was published in the *Militant*.

The great general strike of the textile workers, which raised the whole insurgent movement of labor to a new height and stirred the workers everywhere with its mighty sweep and militancy, has come to an inglorious end—defeated and shamefully betrayed by the leadership of the UTW and the upper crust of the AFL.

In the history of the American labor movement it would be difficult to find a more cruel example of the evil role of the labor lieutenants of the capitalist class and the heavy price the workers must pay for allowing them to hold the leadership of the unions. Incompetence, cowardice, and, at the crucial moment, outright treachery—these are the contributions which McMahon and Gorman, pushed from behind by Green and Company, made to the strike from the vantage point of the leading staff.

To call the ending of the strike a settlement is to rob

the word of any meaning. The whole report of the Winant board, stripped to its essence, was nothing more than a promise to look into the grievances of the workers.[135] And not even that was accepted by the bosses. Without that, without even an agreement to reinstate the strikers, the leaders called off the strike at the peak of its strength and abandoned the workers to the savage reprisals of the mill owners.

Tens of thousands of workers, unionized for the first time and staking everything on the struggle, have been left in the lurch by their leaders and locked out of the mills by the bosses. A terrible introduction to the trade union movement for them; a terrible warning for all of what the present leading staff of the labor movement will be capable of in the greater tests to come if they are not thrown overboard in time.

The executive council of the AFL cold-bloodedly isolated the textile workers, refused to move a finger to provide funds to feed them—millions could have been raised in the trade unions at the scratch of a pen by Green—and devoted themselves exclusively to machinations to get the strike ended at any cost. These scoundrels fear the mass struggles of the workers no less than the bosses fear them. A militant labor movement, drawing great masses into action, is incompatible with their role. They aim to crush this movement, and restore "peace" in the relations between labor and capital, even if it is the peace of the breadline and the graveyard for the workers.

What is most remarkable and outstanding in this tragic situation is the proof on every side that the rank and file of the textile workers were without any means of resistance to the perfidy of the leadership; that the millions of other trade unionists who were inspired by the magnificent struggle and wished to aid, were powerless to make a move. Black reaction and cynical treachery are enthroned in the labor union machine. The mass discontent at the bottom, generating enough energy in these years of crisis to blow the bureaucratic machine to bits, and the whole system of exploitation along with it, remains without organization, without program, without leadership. The Greens and Gormans rule the movement and ruin the most heroic struggles because there are none to challenge them.

The fearful textile strike debacle follows the tragic experiences of the auto workers, the steelworkers, the San Francisco general strike, and other movements of insurgent labor in 1934 which have been turned into bitter defeat. They all cry out the same warning: The insurgent movement must be organized; it must work out its program and find its authentic leadership. The heart of this program must be an unrelenting struggle against the labor agents of the masters who sit on top of the trade union movement. The insurgent leadership must be dedicated to this struggle as a part of the struggle against the bosses and the National Run Around.

Forces for a mighty left-wing and progressive movement in the trade unions are not lacking. The crisis years have created the conditions for its emergence on a wide scale. Every new treachery of the bureaucracy prepares new recruits. What is lacking is a conscious, unifying, and guiding nucleus which alone can organize the movement and provide it with a program. What is lacking is a revolutionary party.

The Stalinists perform all the functions of a party in reverse order. Where organization of the vanguard is needed, they disorganize. Where clarity is required, they sow confusion. Even the weapon of denunciation—the sword of Lenin against traitors—is blunted in their hands. They crack their voices in slandering honest opponents; when they try to screech against real betrayers their stock of epithets is exhausted and they are too hoarse to be heard. As for the Socialist Militants, they belie their name by their silence in the face of the black betrayal of the textile workers. They have not yet learned to criticize the traitors. Will such people lead a fight against them?

No! The workers need a new revolutionary party. Even a vanguard organization of a few thousand, if it understands the trade union question and penetrates deeply into the mass movement, can become the crystallizing agent for a colossal progressive movement in a short time. The times are favorable for the launching of such a party. Its program has been worked out in the years of principled struggle against revisionism and reaction. Sufficient forces are at hand to make a beginning.

As the two most important independent groups, the American Workers Party and the Communist League bear a heavy responsibility. It is their duty to get together and set the new movement into motion. The tragedy of the textile workers is another warning against delay.

Report on situation in the French section[136]

October 31, 1934

The following letter was written to the International Secretariat. A copy of the original letter has not been located, and it is printed here retranslated from *Bulletin Interieur, Groupe Bolchevique-Leniniste dans la SFIO, No. 3,* November 1934.

Dear Comrades:

As a member of the commission assigned to apply the decision of the plenum in regard to the dissident groups, I had many meetings with the various comrades concerned. Therefore I am submitting a report to you on the discussions and their results.

1. *The Central Committee of the French section.* The Central Committee accepted the resolution of the plenum despite the fact that it contains a criticism of the majority on the international struggle that preceded the plenum. The CC and its leading members, Molinier and Frank, agreed, on the commission's request, to coopt Naville to the CC if he and his group accepted the plenum resolution. In a

general way, the CC cooperated with us and facilitated the execution of the IS policy on this question, that is: conciliation and unification with the dissident groups on the basis of the plenum resolution.

2. *The Naville group.* This group having already entered the SFIO, it appears that the differences between it and the majority are limited and that unification with the majority can take place. As stated above, the majority accepted the position of the IS and stated that it was ready to accept the Naville group and give it representation in its leadership.

Preliminary discussions with Comrades Naville and Blasco [Pietro Tresso] established that the differences with the majority were not of a principled political character. The real obstacles to unification concern the question of the internal regime and memories of old conflicts which may have arisen in the isolated propaganda-circle existence of the [French Communist] League.

Comrade Naville maintained that the internal regime of the French section is bad and that his group's return to the league now would only result in new expulsions and another split. He believed that a certain period should elapse and that new forces should be recruited before the unification. He proposed to maintain a separate group, for the present period, with the aim, however, of establishing friendly collaboration with the French section and establishing the organization's unity later. In no less than six meetings with Comrade Naville, I tried my best to convince him of the danger that maintaining a separate group would lead to new conflicts which could compromise our work in the SFIO, just getting under way, and tend to perpetuate the split rather than heal it. I maintained that new and favorable conditions for unification of the French league, and certain guarantees for normalization of its internal life, already existed. These were: (1) the new field of mass activity opened by the entry into the SFIO; (2) a continuing increase in the influence of our youth [among the Socialist youth]; (3) the intervention of the international organization. I tried to convince Comrade N. that it was decidedly an error to reject unification in these new conditions *in advance;* that a conscientious effort should be made in all these cases and that the international organization should be given another opportunity to examine and supervise the collaboration of the French comrades in a common organization as the plenum resolution recommended.

These efforts were unsuccessful. Finally, the commission addressed a formal letter to Naville asking him and his group to accept the plenum resolution in a disciplined way and stating that special measures would be recommended by the IS to assure a normal regime after unification.

This proposal too was rejected by the N. group. Their resolution will be sent to the IS. As far as I was able to understand, it stipulates that they are in favor of maintaining a separate group, but it states that they agree to collaborate with the official French section under the IS's supervision, and that the aim is unification within a short period of time.

That is where things stand now. The members of the plenum and the national sections can form an opinion on the situation and prospects. In my opinion, the IS, while holding exactly to the plenum resolution and giving its full support to the French section in all its work on this basis, should seize on even the limited possibilities offered by the resolution of the Naville group in order to secure its collaboration with the majority and ease conflicts between them.

The French section now needs a period of freedom

from the brand of factionalism and survivals from the past. It needs free rein to concentrate all energies on the concrete tasks inside the SFIO. *It needs a chance to recruit a substantial number of workers from the SFIO.* That will be the fundamental solution to the problem. The plenum resolution furnished the political bases for this development. The international organization should give all possible aid for its early realization.

3. *The Bauer-Lhuillier group.* I also had five or six meetings with Comrades Bauer and Lhuillier. Politically, reconciliation with these comrades is impossible at present, considering their statement that the plenum resolution is false from a principled standpoint and unacceptable.

This group seems disoriented by the international turn of events and contradictory in its positions. This is shown, for example, by Bauer's tendency to go to the SAP with his group (a split-off) and his reproach that we should have joined the London-Amsterdam Bureau. From a political standpoint, these positions appear to be in direct contradiction with his opposition to entry in the SFIO for principled reasons.

I proposed to Bauer that he not yet take steps further away from us but that he wait until the international outlook becomes clear and perhaps come to the next IS plenum after the French experience in the SFIO can be concretely assessed. His group adopted a resolution in which it offered to stay within the international organization, but our "conditions" were obviously unacceptable.

Following that, I had a final conversation with Bauer, whom I once again pressed to reflect further on these questions and to wait for further developments before closing the door on possible reconciliation with our international organization.

The same with Lhuillier. He promised, while maintaining

his separate group, to keep friendly relations with our French section and to abstain from any attacks which might tend to compromise it as a fraction of the SFIO.

In general, a certain lapse of time and experience with work in the SFIO are necessary before reconciliation with these groups will become possible. Already several facts confirm the political line of the majority for entry in the SFIO and refute the arguments of the dissidents. Undoubtedly the coming months will bring stronger proof. That will turn some, if not all, of the dissidents back toward us. It is necessary to keep the door open to them, especially those who have not compromised themselves by hostile acts against us or by going into the camp of centrist opponents.

Fraternally,

J.P. Cannon

For a new revolutionary party

Published November 17, 1934

The following article was published in the *Militant*.

We celebrate the sixth anniversary of the *Militant* on the eve of our national conference, which has to pass final decision on the proposal to unite forces with the AWP and launch a new, independent, revolutionary party.[137]

From all present indications the conference of both organizations, meeting simultaneously, will approve the recommendations of their respective national committees and conclude the fusion in a joint convention. If this turns out to be the case, as we are confident it will, our sixth anniversary will mark the conclusion of the first phase of our historic struggle, first as a faction then as a separate independent group, and will open up a new chapter of joint struggle with other progressive forces on a broader basis. The time is ripe for such a decisive turn, and we are ready for it.

The prospect of fusion between the CLA and the AWP

has become the center of interest in the radical labor movement. It has already produced sharp reactions in all circles, ranging from panic in the camp of Stalinism and hysterical appeals to the "rank and file" of both organizations to hold back, to hasty maneuvers of the pseudo-Militants in the SP to open the doors to penitent ex-communists in the hope that they will provide the SP with a left covering to halt the movement toward the new party. As for the numerous small, independent groups, which have expressed by the fact of their existence the confusion and disintegration of the movement, the question of our fusion has thrown them into internal crises which herald splits or liquidation in practically every case.

The actual accomplishment of the fusion will produce far deeper repercussions. It will mark the opening of a new stage in the process of differentiation and regroupment in the general movement of the advanced workers. If the participants on both sides prove equal to their task and their opportunity, the fusion will decisively influence the future developments of the political labor movement in the U.S. And it will begin to assert this decisive influence from the very start. The twofold significance of the move will not be lost on those who observe political developments, especially on those who want to take a part in shaping their course.

First, the fusion will represent the first step toward *unification* of the revolutionary forces that has been seen for thirteen years! Since the merger of the CP with the left Socialists (Workers' Council group) at the end of 1921 there has been no such thing as any two or more groups getting together. The CP expelled the left wing (the "Trotskyites") in 1928. Less than a year later the right wing (Lovestoneites) who had officiated in this expulsion were themselves expelled. The Proletarian Party, itself a small sect, suffered two splits. A multiplicity of little grouplets appeared on the scene and they in turn split among themselves and moved in opposite directions (the ill-starred Gitlow-Field group, for example).[138]

The general picture of the whole post-Lenin period in the United States has been a picture of disintegration. The masses of workers awakening to class consciousness were repelled by it. They left the parties, or passed through them, or stood aside from all organizations, waiting for a sign of unity and order in the general chaos. The fusion of the CLA and the AWP, that is, of the two largest and strongest of the independent groups, is bound to signify for such workers the opening of a contrary process, the process of the *unification* of the revolutionary forces. By that fact alone our fusion will stir the deepest interest and attention of the nonparty radical workers and help to break their passivity with regard to organization.

On the other hand, and this is no less important, the formal proclamation of a new party will bring all speculation about a return to the CP, on the part of those who have broken with it on principled grounds, to a definite conclusion. This will leave no more room for those who have occupied a halfway position. They will have to choose. At the same time the launching of the new party, irreconcilably hostile to Social Democracy in all colors and variations, slams the door in the faces of those weaklings and deserters of the revolutionary cause who want to "unite" everybody in the Socialist Party and closes the debate with them.

The new party thus deepens the *split* in the political movement with the reformist and centrist parties, and gives the split a clearer meaning and more definite, finished form, while it heralds the *unity* of the revolutionary elements in the struggle against them. The chaos and disintegration will give place to a clear line-up of parties: Social Democratic, Stalinist (centrist), and the party of revolutionary Marxism. Small groups and individuals will find their place in one or the other, and in making their selection they will disclose their real tendency unfailingly. The issue will be clear.

The process of clarification, unification, and split, in a word, the process of regroupment on party lines and the liquidation of separate groups, has not been invented or set into motion by the groups or parties, all of which, without exception, are caught in it. The process in the radical political movement is taking place under the impact of momentous developments in the working class of the country. International events have played their part, especially in the fundamental ideological regroupment, but it is the rising mass movement of the American workers which is putting all the organizations and groups to the test, shaking them out of the old ruts and driving them to seek a new point of departure.

Fundamentally, the parties and groups find it necessary to *adapt* themselves to the rising mass movement in one way or another. The CP discards the whole idiotic rigamarole of the "third period" ("red" unions, "united front from below," theory of "social fascism," etc.) like a dirty shirt, liquidates its separate unions pell-mell, and knocks at the back door of the SP with the offer of a non-aggression pact. The SP pushes its "left" wing forward, and decorates itself with the red feathers of a few wretched "captured" communists. Meanwhile the small propaganda groups, which came into existence in the period of stagnation and reaction, are confronted by events with a veritable command to break out of their propaganda circle and connect themselves with the mass movement or suffer annihilation. Those groups which do not heed this command in time are doomed.

Our organization, on the whole, has understood this. Such is the explanation of the course we have followed during the past year. The definitive break with the Stalinist party and Comintern, the course toward trade union work and effective participation in strikes, the approach to the AWP the moment it declared for an independent political party—all this has been inspired and motivated on our part by a conscious determination to get out of the propaganda circle into the broader movement. The actual fusion with the AWP, now on the order of the day, is, in our understanding, a more decisive step on the same path; by no means a solution of the problem, for the combined forces of the two organizations are modest enough, but a real move in this direction.

In turning deliberately toward a broader mass activity through the medium of a new party, we do not thereby contradict our past existence as a propaganda group, and still less do we renounce it. There was a time when the propaganda circle, as a result of the general stagnation and theoretical degeneration, was the only existence possible for those who retained allegiance to principle. The situation of the time determined the progressive nature of the propaganda circle. We understood it better than others and tenaciously stuck to our task, rejecting all magic prescriptions for short cuts to mass work. In that we were absolutely right, as subsequent experience demonstrated.

Those who built on firm foundations of principle proved to be most effective in mass work directly, and in establishing relations and uniting with other progressive elements which, in the nature of the case, broadens the prospective mass activity in the future. The others, who did so much talking about "mass work" and condemned our preoccupation with propaganda as "sectarianism" (Weisbord,

Field, etc.), made miserable failures with mass work, with propaganda, with organization, and everything else. It is an ironic commentary on these grouplets of professional "mass workers," plunged into internal crisis by their total isolation from the mass movement on the one hand, the fusion of the CLA and the AWP on the other, that they are compelled to seek some kind of a "principled" basis to maintain their "independence." They will not find it.

The propaganda circle must give way now to the political party tied up with the movement of the masses. Under the impact of the rising activity of the general labor movement thousands upon thousands of workers are beginning to awaken to political life; others, who have fallen away in the period of reaction and stagnation, are being roused out of their passivity. These new forces will not go to little groups. They will seek political expression through the medium of one of the parties. This is understood, more or less, by all the political-minded people in all the groups. They are moving to adjust their activities accordingly, and, by the direction they take, they reveal their real colors.

Lovestone moves desperately to reattach himself to the Stalinist party, in its swing to the right, before his group falls to pieces before his eyes. Gitlow-Zam-Goldman crawl back into the Socialist Party to make good the "mistake" of 1919.[139] We, who are neither Stalinists nor Social Democrats, move to unite with other forces to form an independent party opposed to both. Each, according to his opinion and his inner tendency, will find his place; except those who want to continue to "clarify" themselves in a small circle. For such there is no salvation and no political life in the period unfolding now.

Degeneration is the fate of all propaganda groups which are not able to transform the nature of their activity and connect themselves with the broad movement when the hour strikes for such a transformation. We are prepared by our past for a great leap forward; but we ourselves must take the leap. We fought a good fight. It was historically necessary and progressive. Against the stream for six years, against unparalleled difficulties, against slander, isolation, and poverty of resources, we held tenaciously to our course.

The history of the American movement does not know another example of a group that was put to such severe tests and stood up under them so firmly. We survived. We have a right to be proud of our six-year struggle for principle; but it would be a tragedy if we should fail to understand that this struggle was not an end in itself but a period of preparation for new opportunities and new tasks which stand before us now.

We must acknowledge that we are not immune from such a danger. A certain element of "sectarianism" is inseparable from the life of a group which lives a long time in isolation and is compelled by the needs of the movement, as we were, to preoccupy itself almost exclusively with theoretical work, with the intransigent struggle to clarify questions of principle. It is possible that we will have to face the decisive turn in our work with some "sectarian" hangovers in our ranks, some hesitations and fears of the new tasks and the broader stream. Such a tendency could have only a negative influence now. We must face the problem squarely at the national conference and solve it. That means: we must not yield an inch to any kind of sectarian considerations in regard to the fusion and the launching of the new party.

Sectarianism can be a great danger in the present period of flux and change in the movement, when vast new perspectives open up before us; when new opportunities to extend the basis and broaden the influence of revolutionary

Marxism are ours to grasp. We shall oppose every manifestation of such a tendency with all our strength—in the league, and in the new party also, if necessary.

But it goes without saying that our position in this regard has nothing in common with the position of those who seek to solve the problem of isolation by desertion of the revolutionary banner and entry into the Socialist Party. Gitlow and Zam, by this shameful performance, only complete the evolution which began with their crusade against "Trotskyism" in the CP. They were among the originators, or at least the earliest practitioners, of the art of misusing the Leninist weapon of denunciation, hurling the epithet "renegade" at honest revolutionists until the word lost all meaning. How hollow that all sounds now.

They even console themselves with the thought that the horrible misuse of epithets by the Stalinists has engendered such a cynicism on the subject of renegacy, that their own return to the "party of revolutionary unity" without a program, without a banner, without—as they announce—the slightest intention to even form a faction in this "united" party, will escape the indignant denunciation of the revolutionary workers. Never mind. The sword of Lenin has been blunted, but it will be sharpened again.

A really serious analysis of the situation, the trade unions, and the currents in the workers' political movement in the United States does not lead to the conclusion that the Socialist Party is or will be the revolutionary party of the future, or that it is the best field for the activities of the revolutionists today. Of all the groups in the SP there is not one that is revolutionary, that is, Bolshevik. There is not one leader that deserves the name of revolutionist. As for revolutionists entering the SP from the outside, they cannot do it, as the case of Gitlow and Zam proved, unless they give up their program and their banner. When revolutionists do that they cease to be revolutionists. The leaders of the Militants who, it must not be forgotten, are the leaders of the party nationally, exacted from Gitlow and Zam a public declaration that they have no intention of forming a communist faction, or any other kind of a faction, in the party. Then, to avoid a conflict with the Old Guard over their admittance, they chivied the ex-communists over to New Jersey—to join the SP, so to speak, as second-grade members.

Some people attempt to find an analogy between the contemptible course of Gitlow and Zam and the section of the French Bolshevik-Leninists in entering the French Socialist Party (SFIO) as a group. But in reality there is no similarity at all. Shaken to its foundations by the crisis of the democratic state, the French Socialist Party reacts with the broadest possible democracy in its own ranks; the leadership is not in a position to place limitations upon it. The Bolshevik-Leninists are able to enter the party without any conditions; they openly retained their whole program, their name, their banner, their press. They work within the Socialist Party for the same ideas that governed their activity as an outside group, and they do it openly. What does this course have in common with the skulking, shamefaced conduct of Gitlow?

We have supported the action of our French comrades. Under the exceptional circumstances prevailing in the French labor movement, we think it was the correct tactical step. But it is obvious that the situation in this country is entirely different. Here the road is open for the creation of an independent party. It is a hard road, let us not deceive ourselves about that, but there is no other for those who have serious revolutionary aims and do not shrink from the implications of a struggle for them. It will be a hard, uphill fight. Those who have no stomach for it can be expected to stand aside on one pretext or another.

How else is one to explain the action of Albert Goldman in jumping over the fence into the SP at the moment our plans for fusion with the AWP and the formal proclamation of the new party were nearing completion? What is that but the act of a strikebreaker? Goldman, like Gitlow, forswearing any intention to form a faction in the SP, still less to proclaim the need of a split with the Black Hundred gang of the Old Guard, imagines that he has discovered a new political recipe. He is going to work wonders in the Socialist Party all by himself by means of personal diplomacy, back-slapping the centrist leaders, and the devil knows what other clever tricks.

It has been said that he even expects to remain a "friend" of the league and the new party. We have no need of such friends. The new party needs revolutionary militants who are firm in their convictions and loyal to their own organization. We have had a good chance in recent years to find out who they are. There are enough to make a start. Others will follow, and we will train them in the same spirit.

Our road is the road to the new revolutionary party. And, by that, not to conciliation with the parties of reformism and centrism but to irreconcilable struggle against them. If we are equal to our tasks we have the opportunity to succeed. The perspective of a rising labor movement is all in our favor; a genuinely Marxist party cannot fail to thrive in the period of labor revival and mass activity. Our rivals—the CP and the SP—are irremediably bankrupt, as the experience of the two big strike waves demonstrated once again. Our forces are not too numerous, but they are of better quality. They are firm in principle and, taking them all together, they embody a rich experience in trade union and mass activity. The task is a colossal one. But we can accomplish it if we have nerve to begin it and the will to carry it through.

We need a declaration of principles that speaks out clearly on every important question. The first draft, taken as a basis, is naturally to be edited, revised, and clarified on every point. The bulk of this work of improving and clarifying the program has already been accomplished by the joint committee. The second draft, embodying important amendments and reformulations, will go to the convention delegates of each organization and then to the joint convention for final revision.

The work in the joint program committee has demonstrated beyond any doubt that we have a common standpoint on all the fundamental questions of principles and tactics. What remains now is primarily a literary task of formulating each and every point with such precision that it cannot have two meanings to anybody. In the program declaration of the new party there should be no trace of ambiguity. We are confident that the final draft which passes the convention will meet this Marxian test and become the charter and guide of all the revolutionary militants in the country.

If, as all signs indicate, the sixth anniversary of our struggle is to culminate in the conclusion of our existence as a separate group and the beginning of a new period of joint struggle with the members of the AWP in a single party, it can only mean that we carry with us that system of ideas and methods which, thanks to our international collaboration, and above all to the aid of our great teacher, we have so firmly acquired.

Our conviction is unshakable. We "Trotskyites" are convinced to the marrow of our bones that our fight was justified and necessary. We renounce nothing and repent nothing. Revolutionary internationalism remains as before our central, unifying idea. The great task now, as we understand it, is to carry this idea into the realm of organization and action. That means concretely: united forces to build the new party of the Fourth International. We hope to contribute our full share to the accomplishment of this great historic task.

Record of the CLA leadership

November 30, 1934

The following was a resolution signed by Cannon, Swabeck, and Shachtman on the organizational report of the National Committee given at the CLA's national convention.[140]

The outgoing National Committee has been in office for three years since the Second National Convention of the league and is virtually identical with the committee that has led the organization during the entire six years of its existence. As such, it must be judged from the standpoint of its achievements as well as of its shortcomings.

1. On the positive side, the Third National Convention records the following facts of outstanding importance:

a. The National Committee led the organization throughout the whole period of its existence, maintained a continuity of leadership, avoided the organizational splits which have disrupted and disorganized so many of the other national sections, conducted a firm political struggle against disintegrating elements (Weisbord, Field, etc.), succeeded in isolating them by political methods and eliminating them from our ranks without serious convulsions such as similar elements introduced into various European sections.

b. The National Committee directed the work of the organization in such a manner as made possible the increase of the league membership from a scattered handful at its inception, to its present strength, and finally established it as a national organization, together with a national youth organization.

c. It maintained a firm line of principle and led the work of consolidating a strong cadre of Bolshevik-Leninists well-equipped with our basic ideas and principles for the task facing them in the new party.

d. It enormously aided the development of these cadres and a broad group of sympathizers around our organization by the systematic publication of the fundamental documents and works of Comrade Trotsky.

e. In the face of the greatest difficulties and sacrifices it continued uninterrupted the publication of the *Militant* as our weekly organ, an achievement which proved to be beyond the power of any other independent political grouping.

f. It firmly supported the progressive revolutionary current in our international organization and gave timely assistance in the solution of the internal crises in other sections on the Bolshevik-Leninist basis.

g. It led the organization unitedly and without internal difficulties in the turn from the position of a faction of the CI to the road of an independent organization working for the creation of new revolutionary parties and a Fourth International.

h. It overcame, at the same time, with the aid of our international organization, the deep internal crisis and factional fight which threatened the existence of the league, succeeded in liquidating the old factions as the resolution of the International Secretariat demanded, and in effecting a working political and organizational collaboration of the most responsible and influential comrades from all the former factions (Cannon, Shachtman, Carter groups)—an accomplishment which alone made possible the fruitful progress of the past year and without which the league would have fallen victim to disintegration and splits and a complete impotence for the great tasks facing it. Without the liquidation of the old faction fight and the loyal collaboration of the leading members of the National Committee from both sides on a political basis, such as has been effected during the past year, our three main accomplishments—the Minneapolis strike, the launching of our theoretical organ, the work for fusion into a new party—would have been impossible.

Above all, the convention establishes the fact that the policy and leadership of the National Committee has brought our organization today to the point of fusion with the American Workers Party on a satisfactory principled basis for the launching of the first party of the Fourth International—an event of the greatest international historical significance.

2. On the negative side, the national convention is obliged to register a series of defects and shortcomings on the part of the National Committee which require the criticism of the membership of the league.

a. The committee failed to attain a good and necessary collective work which would have made it possible for it and for the organization to react more promptly and effectively to situations and problems confronting it, tolerated individualistic methods, gave way to internal dissension which at one time endangered the unity of the league and adversely affected its striking power.

b. Throughout the six years of our existence, the leading committee carried on the administrative work of the organization poorly and inefficiently, failed to give the branches the necessary organizational and informational guidance, or else failed to give it in time.

c. Adequate contact was not maintained between the National Committee and the membership, to the detriment of the work of both, so that the National Committee was not sufficiently sensitive to the feelings and requirements of the membership and the latter was left without the necessary political aid in the solution of their problem and the organizational direction of their work.

d. The committee was especially lax in its international duties, failing to give the international organization sufficient information about the development and problems of the league, failing even to supply the International Secretariat with a minimum of material aid so imperative for its functioning.

e. The National Committee was slow in reacting to events and issues, often giving its position after the event, and in many cases failing to take a position at all. This sluggishness communicated itself to the membership and contributed to the development of tendencies toward passivity and routine in the organization. In addition, the NC gave inadequate attention and aid to our youth movement, which was thus compelled to develop its activity largely by itself.

f. In general the National Committee throughout the six years of the existence of our organization did not function as a rounded and well-organized collective leadership, which would have served enormously to consolidate the league and to enhance the prestige of the NC itself. The national convention, therefore, demands of its leading body, individually and collectively, that it make a radical correction and improvement in its habits and methods of work, and above all, that systematic collaboration, politically and organizationally, be established in the new party.

3. The foregoing criticism is directed at the National Committee as a whole, not merely at its functioning members in the national office. Comrades Swabeck, Shachtman, and Cannon, who carried the main political responsibility since the Second National Convention and led the struggle for the political line of the league, and who, together with Comrade Oehler, carried the entire burden of the administrative responsibility for the National Committee, are herein specifically criticized for grave faults of commission and omission in the conduct of their work.

But the other members of the National Committee—Abern, Spector, and Glotzer, Edwards (alternate), Morgenstern (alternate), Dunne, Skoglund, and Coover (alternate)—each and every one of them must also be taken to account by the organization at this convention.

As for Comrades Dunne, Skoglund, and Coover—the convention declares that these comrades have conducted systematic and unremitting activity in the trade union movement, have thereby brought credit and glory to our organization, not only on a national but on an international scale. At the same time, although far removed from the center and unable to function in it directly, they have at all times carried out their responsibilities as nonresident members and have given the center loyal support in its work. If they have not functioned directly in the center, it has not been because of a refusal on their part, but because they were not called upon to do so.

As for Comrade Oehler, the convention records that he carried out functions assigned to him by the NC, quitting private employment on two occasions for this purpose and in collaboration with other functioning members of the NC. Even during the heated struggle between him and the majority of the NC over important and clearly defined political questions, a measure of responsible collaboration with him was possible. Against Comrade Oehler the convention records the fact that he formed a faction in the league despite the fact that normal democratic processes were never denied to him.

As for Comrade Morgenstern, who was elected at the last convention to the responsible position as an alternate to the National Committee, the Third Convention records the fact that his personal conduct was not in keeping with such a responsibility and called forth the severe censure of the National Committee and his simultaneous resignation from it. Following that, his conduct in the Philadelphia organization and his entirely inadequate personal activity deprived that organization of the political and organizational contribution which he owed to it and contributed heavily to impeding its growth.

As for Comrades Abern, Glotzer, Spector, and Edwards (alternate)—these comrades were guilty of greater derelictions than any other members of the committee. Comrade Abern failed to collaborate with the other members of the National Committee in a comradely manner, although no political differences among them were discerned which would in any way justify the sharp and even poisonous antagonism which he continually engendered, even after the unanimous adoption of the resolution of the International Secretariat calling for a cessation of the old factional fight. He refused to take any kind of responsibility, either political or organizational, assigned to him by the National Committee. Even his present post was assumed by him only after the most vigorous intervention of other committee members who for months encountered his stubborn refusal. He stirred up antagonism against the National Committee without any established political foundation. He absented himself regularly from general membership meetings at which the most serious problems of the league [were dealt with], with or without excuse, and repeatedly and persistently refused to speak for the league at public meetings, although constantly requested to do so by the New York organization. He gathered around himself a clique of discontented comrades without visible political grounds. His whole destructive, negative, and spiteful position is epitomized in his attitude toward the present convention, the final gathering of the organization at which a six-year balance sheet is being drawn.

Comrade Glotzer, who has been one of the most insistent critics of the most obvious shortcomings of the National Committee, failed to preserve his position as a responsible functionary, together with others, at the center, to which he had at first been summoned for the purpose of strengthening the weight, the collectivity, the functioning, and the efficiency of the resident committee. As a member of the National Committee, having no serious differences with its political line and presenting none contrary to it, he nevertheless failed to maintain his solidarity with the committee which, from a Bolshevik standpoint, would logically follow from such a relationship. Devoting himself mainly to criticism, in itself largely justified, he directed his attacks exclusively at those comrades who carried responsibilities and tried to function, even if poorly, while completely ignoring or shielding from all criticism the scandalous conduct of Abern with whom, indeed, he associated himself. At this convention, he even went so far as to associate himself with Abern, who has no right to speak at all on this matter, in a condemnation of the functioning committee members. He appeared at the convention not as a member of the National Committee with which he is presumably in political solidarity, but as a leading spokesman for a clique which includes Abern and which has no political platform of its own.

Comrade Edwards, whose political knowledge and experience in the revolutionary and labor movements entitled us to expect the political attitude of a leader, completely failed the National Committee in this respect, concerned himself with minor grievances, refuses to give the resident committee the solidarity and support which ought to follow from his membership on the National Committee and his agreement with its main line, and instead associates himself with the conduct of Comrade Glotzer and through him of Comrade Abern. In addition, he was far from measuring up to the activity on a local scale which the Chicago organization was entitled to receive from an alternate to the National Committee who has the political qualifications of Comrade Edwards.

Comrade Spector, even if excused from direct participation in the work of the resident committee, by virtue of his leadership and work in the Canadian section, nevertheless owed the resident committee the obligation of political solidarity and the influence of his prestige and personal relationships with other individual members to facilitate that loyal and comradely collaboration without which all talk of a collective leadership is a mockery. The convention regretfully establishes the fact that Comrade Spector appears to have exerted his influence in a contrary direction, devoting himself to attacks on the resident committee, shielding Abern from criticism, and identifying himself with a clique against the National Committee which has no political platform or basis.

4. The convention condemns clique tendencies, personal combinations, the shielding of individuals from just

criticism, and the one-sided criticism of others out of personal considerations and outworn factional reminiscences. The convention categorically demands the dissolution of any clique or factional grouping and the consolidation of the entire league and of the entire leadership on the basis of the political decisions of this convention.

The 'New Militant'

Published December 15, 1934

The following editorial was published in the first issue of the *New Militant*.

The *New Militant* makes its appearance as the official weekly organ of the Workers Party.[141] As such, it will not be independent or neutral but will strive in all respects to represent the aims and ideals of the party as laid down in the Declaration of Principles and to reflect its revolutionary spirit.

The vanguard political party is the highest expression of working-class organization and a party organ, consequently, is the highest type of paper. Our aim, however, is not to publish a "house organ" for restricted party circles, but a political organ for the masses. We hope to popularize the *New Militant* without diluting its political and party character. Such a combination is what is needed to serve the aims we have in mind. If we succeed in this endeavor the *New Militant* will soon make a place all its own in the field of labor journalism.

The main line of the *New Militant* will be the attack against capitalism, the exposure of its frauds and infamies, and the advocacy of the socialist order of society. As we see the situation, the chief recruiting grounds of the new party, even in the early stages of its struggle, is among the politically unorganized but grievously oppressed and bitterly discontented masses of American workers. The main appeal of the *New Militant* will be directed to them.

They are the forces for the new party. They are the troops of the American revolution. They have long remained indifferent to working-class politics of any kind. The political labor movement, reformist as well as revolutionary, has been a comparatively small and isolated circle. But the conditions have matured for a great and rapid transformation. The two gigantic strike waves we have seen were heralds of a mass participation in the political movement as well.

The American workers are moving now in true American style—rapidly and with militant disregard for any kind of obstructions. The *New Militant* will march with them in their struggle. To awaken the discontented workers to class consciousness and draw them toward the party in the course of their experiences in the class struggle—this will be the chief endeavor of the *New Militant*.

The road to the masses is through the vanguard. Our paper can become a power among the masses only if it organizes and educates the advanced workers as it goes along. The fundamental nucleus of revolutionary militants which has been assembled at the foundation of the Workers Party is only a beginning. Thousands of others, scattered and disorganized by the long period of disintegration in the movement belong with the party right now. The *New Militant* will help them to find their place in the party ranks.

In this field quality is what counts. Every class-conscious worker is important. Every honest rebel against capitalism is dear to us and we hope to make our paper their paper. To that end the *New Militant* will provide them with accurate information about all phases of the movement, about the activities of other labor organizations at home and abroad, and strive to illuminate all the important questions of the day with the light of Marxist principle.

We must make our revolution in America, not in some other country and not on the moon. That means, if we are to go at our work seriously, that our paper must concern itself primarily with the actualities of American life and talk to the workers in their own language. It is necessary to show that we understand them in order to make them understand us.

The American people have not inherited conservatism nor the tendency to balk at revolutionary solutions. They overthrew the rule of a king and broke the institutions of chattel slavery by means that were far from polite. The history of the labor movement of the country, on the whole, is a magnificent history of militant struggle. Our paper can and should appeal to these traditions in its agitation among the masses. It can and should be distinctively American in its methods of approach and its realistic concentration on the concrete tasks at hand.

But the world we live in is a unit, and the liberating workers' revolution, as our Declaration of Principles truly says, is by its very nature international in character. One cannot even begin to think straight about a national revolution unless he proceeds from this point of view. We don't believe in the dogma of "socialism in one country," for the United States or for Russia. We see our American revolution as one link in the chain of revolutions which will emancipate the world from capitalism and establish world socialism. This conception stands in the center of the system of ideas which binds us together and animates all our work on national grounds. The *New Militant*, in all its departments, will reflect this revolutionary internationalist point of view.

Non-Partisan Defense

Published December 15, 1934

The following editorial was published in the *New Militant*.

The Workers Party founding convention went on record for the idea of a militant defense organization embracing workers and sympathetic elements of diverse political views, for a united class fight for mutual defense interests. Earlier, the AWP and the CLA had vigorously supported this idea when it was broached by the Provisional Committee for Non-Partisan Labor Defense.

The NPLD, while limited in forces, has won a good name in struggle. When the ILD refused to raise a finger for four young German workers deported from Holland to fascist Germany, the NPLD organized the protest movement in this country. The NPLD played an important part in the fight against New York police brutality which led to the resignation of Commissioner O'Ryan. It was to the fore in local protest movements against government strikebreaking moves on the Gulf Coast, in Toledo,

Minneapolis, and San Francisco.

Last week the NPLD was able to announce that it had saved Antonio Bellussi, militant antifascist, from danger of deportation to fascist Italy. Now comes news that a committee set up on the initiative of and led by members of the NPLD, has won a signal victory in obtaining the release from Sing-Sing of Harold Robins and Andres Gras, strikers framed on a charge of beating scabs in the New York hotel strike. The two workers may have to undergo a new trial, but in any case their first conviction is reversed through the legal fight of the NPLD. The superior court admitted that Robins and Gras were convicted due to the prejudiced conduct of the notorious antilabor trial judge, Corrigan.

Revolutionary workers now in the WP played an important part in the united front for Robins and Gras. The NPLD was also able to draw into active work the Socialist Lawyers Association, one of whose members was Robins's counsel in the appeal.

The WP is ready to go further in support of NPLD's plans. Ever since June, when the NEC of the SP gave favorable, though formal, recognition to the idea, we have urged conclusive action. Almost three months ago a draft plan was approved by representatives of the CLA, the AWP, and the SP. Since then the SP representatives have taken no action. That some elements in the SP are opposed in principle to collaboration with revolutionaries even against the worst reactionaries, everybody knows. What rank-and-file Socialists should ask, however, is why the Militants, who claim to have a majority in the NEC, constantly avoid a final decision on the pressing question of setting up a broad, militant defense organization.

The history of the ILD in the Dutch case; in the Bellussi case, where it sabotaged the defense because the defendant was suspected of "Trotskyism"; in the Robins-Gras case, where it refused all collaboration and constantly maneuvered to sabotage the united front committee; in Scottsboro, where its policies have jeopardized the whole cause and where it is now begging the reactionary Samuel S. Leibowitz for a united front—all these facts and many more make clear that the ILD is not to be thought of as a defense instrument of the workers.

A militant, nonpartisan defense organization is a crying class need today. The Workers Party has put the building of such an organization on its program. It is ready and willing to cooperate with other organizations to build it. The Socialist Party ought to give some definite answer to the NPLD, or to make clear that it is unable or unwilling to carry out in action its verbal commitment of last June. The NPLD, far from having confirmed the diagnosis made last April by the ILD—that it "died aborning"—has grown constantly stronger. Its further work should not be jeopardized by anybody's passivity. The WP calls for action on this matter.

The real issues in the Soviet Union

Published December 29, 1934

The following editorial was published in the *New Militant*.

These are times which impose upon all revolutionary workers an attitude of the greatest responsibility and the most sober judgment in regard to the Soviet Union. Those who have seen the Russian revolution, and its product the Soviet state, as the star of hope and inspiration of the international working class must in no case allow their vision to be obscured by the happenings of the recent days.[142] It is necessary now to hold fast to fundamental conceptions, and to view all the happenings in their light.

The greatest danger of all is that the sympathetic and partly sympathetic masses will be alienated from the Soviet Union itself by the things taking place now. It is the duty of the conscientious revolutionists to counteract this trend. The indignant protest against the Stalinist frame-up of Trotsky, Zinoviev, and other working-class critics—which is voiced instinctively by every honest revolutionist—has to be combined at all times with the defense of the Soviet state against its class enemies and an unqualified condemnation of all terrorist acts and tendencies which can only facilitate the eventual downfall of the Soviet state.

The idea that the Soviet state is immune from this danger is a profound illusion. As long as the Soviet Union is surrounded by a capitalist world it is never free from the danger of a counterrevolutionary overthrow. Lenin and all the Bolsheviks who made the revolution always said this, and that is why they looked for the final solution of the difficulties and contradictions of the Soviet Union in the arena of the international revolution. The theory and practice of "socialism in the Soviet Union alone" could work only to isolate the Soviet Union from its chief and, in the final analysis, its only real source of reinforcement, the international working-class movement. The Opposition, treacherously described as counterrevolutionary and now even branded as terrorist, was animated from the first by this internationalist and fundamentally revolutionary conception. The purpose was to save the Soviet Union by spreading the revolution to other countries.

The accusation that the oppositionist political groups which originated in the Communist Party are responsible for the assassination of Kirov, or any other acts of terrorism, is a monstrous and fantastic slander. Such accusations hurled at the Marxist opponents of Stalin are not believed anywhere, least of all in the circles of the advanced and class-conscious workers. The uncompromising hostility of the Marxists to the methods of terrorism is too well known. The chief result of this infamous attempt to foist the assassination of Kirov onto the oppositionists is to sow confusion and demoralization in the ranks of the working-class supporters of the Soviet state and thereby to weaken its position internally and externally.

By resorting to such methods the Stalin bureaucracy testifies to the weakness of its position and the fear of proletarian criticism. The suspicion inevitably grows that further steps to the right in the field of foreign policy are contemplated, and that the aim is to silence criticism and smash proletarian opposition in advance. The bureaucracy can derive political and factional profit from the use of such methods only at the expense of the Soviet Union itself. Therein lies their condemnation.

We know nothing of the details surrounding the latest incidents—and neither does anybody else except the official circle which keeps it secret. We do not know what the political position of Zinoviev, for example, is at the present time, and consequently cannot take any responsibility for it. But we do know that the attempt to "connect" Trotsky and his adherents with White Guards and with the assassination of Kirov is a transparent frame-up. We know that secrecy serves such ends, not the exposure and defeat of class enemies. For these reasons we demand open trials and full information. Opposition to this demand in the present circumstances is a confession of guilt. The working class of the world must be armed with the truth for the effective defense of the workers' state.

Appendix: Four letters by Trotsky on CLA crisis

The following four letters are reprinted from *Writings of Leon Trotsky (1932–33)* and *Writings of Leon Trotsky Supplement (1929–33)*, © 1972 and 1979 by Pathfinder Press and reprinted by permission.

1. THE SITUATION IN THE AMERICAN LEAGUE
MARCH 7, 1933

To the International Secretariat

Dear Comrades:

The situation in the American League demands, as you have already indicated, a prompt and decisive intervention on the part of our organization. To the extent that I have been able to judge from the minutes of the Secretariat and the correspondence, we haven't any differences with your evaluation of the situation in the American League.

Nevertheless I consider it my duty to explain to you as clearly as possible how I, after very detailed conversations with Comrade Swabeck and a study of the documents, regard the situation in the League and what measures appear to me to be necessary from our side.

1. For several years the action of the League bore mainly a literary propagandist character. The number of members hovered around the same figures, varying according to the improvement or worsening of the work at the center. The lack of progress in the movement which has been the case aroused all sorts of personal antagonisms, group antagonisms, or local antagonisms. The same lack of progress in the movement does not permit these antagonisms to take on a political character. This has given and still gives the struggle an exceedingly poisoned character in the absence of a principled content clear to everybody. Members of the organization do not learn anything from such a struggle. They are forced to group themselves according to personal attachments, sympathies and antipathies. The struggle of the groups becomes in its turn an obstacle to the further progress of the movement.

2. It is quite possible that in this struggle there are contained valid principled differences in embryonic form. Nevertheless it is unfortunate that the two groups anticipate too much and sharpen the organizational struggle between the groups and the members altogether out of proportion with the development of political work and of the questions raised by the latter. In the impatient organizational maneuvers which in a disruptive fashion are agitating the entire League by bringing prejudices to bear upon each group separately, it is impossible not to see the harmful influence of the methods and the procedure of the epigone Comintern, which has accustomed an entire generation to seek a way out of all sorts of difficulties

through apparatus combinations at the expense of the whole organization. Therein lies one of the worst traits of bureaucratism!

3. A genuine solution to the internal difficulties can only be found along the path of expanding mass work. The League has taken that path. It is developing magnificent energy in this work in three directions: (a) campaign on the subject of the victory of fascism in Germany and the capitulation of the Communist International; (b) participation in the unemployed movement; (c) participation in the independent miners union (Illinois). In all these fields, the League has already achieved moral successes. But—and that is the most important feature of the present situation—these first successes are accompanied not by a lessening but by an aggravation of the internal struggle. What does this signify?

4. Of course it is theoretically possible that with the transition to broader work, the potential differences can assume an open and active political character. But up to now this has not at all been expressed in anything. More or less fully developed, serious, and firm differences have not been revealed in any of the three fields of work mentioned above. There remains another explanation: the aggravation of the crisis has been called forth by the very mechanics of the transition from one stage of work to another. This does not exclude the birth of serious differences in the future, but those do not necessarily have to correspond with the lineup of the present groupings.

5. A solution is impossible except by broadening and deepening the mass work, by drawing to the League fresh proletarian elements, by drawing all the centers of the League into the mass organizations. The beginnings have been made for this work. But the struggle of the groupings has taken on such sharpness that *a split is being put*

on the order of the day automatically. A split under these conditions would have a purely a priori character, a preventive one, so to speak, one that is incomprehensible to all except those who initiate the split. If it is difficult for us, the leading members of the International Left Opposition, to grasp the motives of the ferocious struggle, the American workers, including the members of the League itself, would be all the less capable of understanding the causes of a split. This kind of split at the top would infinitely shatter the authority of both groups and compromise the cause of the Left Opposition in America for a long time. It would suffice today for the Stalinist bureaucracy to publish the numerous declarations of the two groups fighting each other in order to poison all sources of sympathy for the Left Opposition. In case of split, the situation would become a hundred times worse.

The two groups should fully understand that in case of a split neither of them could nor would be recognized as a section of the International Left Opposition. The two halves, condemned to impotence for a long time, would find themselves in a situation similar to that of the present groups in Czechoslovakia, who are not now members with full rights in the international organization but only sympathizing groups.

6. The preparation for the national conference of the League is taking place under the sign of the struggle between the two groups. At present one can already to a certain degree picture the perspectives of the conference: more or less unanimous acceptance of the principled political resolutions side by side with a poisoned struggle on the questions of approving the mandates and the composition of the future central committee. If we assume that the two groups are more or less the same size, the changes at the conference would be reduced to the group possessing 49 percent obtaining 51 percent and vice versa, with the further application

of the same methods that would mean a split.

7. The task of our international organization is, it seems to me, quite evident: not to permit a split in any case at present, on the threshold of the transition of the League to mass work; to explain to all the members of the League that the leaders of the two groups are sharpening the struggle by means of impermissible organizational methods and by poisoned polemics; to condemn these methods resolutely; and to call upon the members of the League for the defense of its unity.

8. Independently of the possible opinions of any one of us separately on which of the two groups in the League will acquire a serious and genuine preponderance in mass work, we must as an organization leave the solution of this question to the future (it is quite possible that the leadership, after some regroupments, will be constituted from elements of both the present groups). But the *next* conference cannot in any case assure the domination of one group, due to the absence of political ground in preparation for this as well as of objective criteria. *The task of the next conference should consist of saving the League from a preventive split imposed from the top and of preserving the authority of the League and its combativity for the near future.* It is necessary to pose this task in quite an imperative form before all the local groups involved in the struggle of the central committee.

9. To the extent that it is possible to judge from correspondence, a considerable number of the members of the League, perhaps a majority, do not belong to either of the two groups and speak with indignation of the danger of a split. Given the absence or at least the nonobviousness of the principled basis of the struggle between the groups, *conciliationism is quite justified and progressive in the League's internal life.* It is necessary *now, at the present stage,* to support this tendency with all the authority of the international organization.

10. The preparation of the conference should, it seems to me, be conducted in the spirit of the considerations made above. That means:

a. All the local organizations should demand of the leaders of the two groups that they reduce their clashes within such limits that their speeches, declarations, etc., on both sides, cannot become a weapon in the hands of the enemy.

b. All the theses, countertheses, and amendments should be sent out in time, not only to all the members of the League but also to the International Secretariat so that a discussion of all the phases can take place before the eyes of all the sections and under the control of the latter.

c. The final time of the conference should be designated in agreement with the IS so that the latter will have the opportunity, in case of need, to delegate its representative to it.

d. Up to the time of the conference the present central committee, which of course remains in office, should enjoy the entire support of all the members of the organization. On its part, the central committee will abstain from artificial organizational manipulations within the committee which bear a factional character.

e. The local organizations should be guided in the election of delegates by consideration of sufficient firmness and independence in their representatives on the question of safeguarding the unity of the League; the instructions to the delegates should be voted upon in the same sense.

f. The forthcoming central committee should of course include leaders of both groups now engaged in the struggle; but along with them should be placed some *solid comrades, possessing authority, not having engaged in the struggle of the two groups, and capable of bringing about a healthier atmosphere inside the central committee.* To this end the size of the committee should be considerably enlarged.

g. In case of need, the Secretariat should call a special

plenum devoted to American problems with the participation of representatives of both groups.

Historical developments place exceptional tasks before the American League. Tremendous possibilities are opening for it. Our American friends must be aware that we are following their work with the greatest attention, that we are ready to bring them our support with all the forces at our command and with all our means, and that we firmly hope that they will put an end to the internal malady and that they will issue forth upon a broader path.

G. Gourov [L. Trotsky]

2. LETTER TO SWABECK
MARCH 7, 1933

Dear Comrade Swabeck:

After having a series of discussions with you and becoming acquainted with the documents, I think—entirely apart from any assessment of the minority's attitude—that in the organizational policy of the majority of the central committee there are elements of formal intransigence which may appear as bureaucratism and which in any case will injure rather than enhance the authority of the central committee and its influence.

1. After the June plenum, where all the decisions were approved unanimously, your group attempted to have recourse to cooptation in order to guarantee a majority for itself in the central committee, although nobody could understand in what respects the majority is different from the minority.

2. The proposal of the central committee to the New York branch concerning proletarianization was a mistake not in its general tendency but in its mechanical approach

to the issue and the manifestly practical hopelessness of the proposal under the given conditions.

3. In consideration of the fact that the two groups have approximately the same weight it would be, it seems to me, reasonable for the majority to make a concession to the minority and the designation of Comrade Cannon as assistant secretary.

4. It appears to me absolutely impermissible to deprive Comrade Abern of his vote on the occasion of the departure of Comrade Swabeck.

5. The elaboration, behind the backs of the minority, of a draft thesis on the prospects of American imperialism represents an obviously factional step, all the less justified as on this question no differences have appeared up until now. The situation became that much worse as the document was destined for discussion with foreign comrades who in that way learned about the draft thesis before the minority members of the central committee of the American League.

6. The proposal to immediately transfer the headquarters to Chicago is practically equivalent to a split.

7. Not convincing, it seems to me, is the allegation that in spite of the hopes of any "optimists" the situation became even more acute after the League began to pass from the propaganda to the agitation stage. It is by passing from one stage into another that the malady usually comes to the surface. But serious successes in the field of mass work will inevitably produce a favorable influence upon internal relations and in every case provoke a radical regroupment by gradual isolation of demoralized elements.

A split now would have an a priori character, understandable to nobody but its initiators, and would destroy the authority of the Left Opposition in America for a long time to come. In the meantime it is particularly clear from the letters of Comrade Cannon that great perspectives are opening up for the American League.

I permit myself to establish the following axiom: The Opposition minority has a certain right to manifest impatience but the majority leadership has no such right.

Fraternally,

3. LETTER TO SHACHTMAN
MARCH 8, 1933

Dear Comrade Shachtman:

I have not written to you for a long time. A collection of many causes has made my response to your latest letters difficult. Even now I write you quite briefly. The situation in the League now constitutes our greatest worry. You are heading toward a split, and that will mean catastrophe for the League. It is actually a matter of complete indifference which side in the fight is more wrong, for neither side will be in a position to explain to the workers what caused the split. And that will completely compromise both groups. In one of your letters you gave expression to the hope that the next conference will settle the disputes. That is not my opinion at all. If your group gets 51 percent that would not change anything at all. The determined intervention of the International Secretariat is necessary. I am in correspondence with the Secretariat on the matter, and I hope that you will get word on this in the next period.

I would like to touch fleetingly on just one question. It seems to me that you were mistaken in undertaking the big protest campaign against delegating Comrade Swabeck. Had he come to Copenhagen at that time, it would have been most opportune. We badly needed a Danish-speaking comrade, and with his help we could certainly have built a good section. His participation in the Copenhagen consultations would have been of the greatest significance. Perhaps under this condition the internal struggles in the American League in the course of the last months would not have taken on the current unprecedentedly sharp character. The preconference took on a much greater significance than it seemed to have, on the evening before, to many of us, including me. Comrade Swabeck's participation was very useful. And his stay here is for me and the other members of our local group, of great value. I also hope that Comrade Swabeck will not regret his stay here. Without contact with him the intervention of the International Secretariat would not come off so effectively.

I would really like to implore you, as well as your friends, not to be so nervous, so impatient, to adopt a longer-range perspective and not for a moment to forget that we have an international organization that is not at all inclined to adopt a one-sided view and in whose eyes the "aggressor," the instigator, has much more to lose than to win.

This is it for now. Thanks for sending the fishing line, which I received in good time.

With best greetings,

Yours,

L. *Trotsky*

4. MORE ON THE AMERICAN DISPUTE
APRIL 17, 1933

To the International Secretariat
(Copy to the Central Committee of the American League)

Dear Comrades:
It has appeared to you that my letter could be interpreted

as being more favorable to the minority than to the majority of the central committee of our American section. If this is your impression, that shows that I have expressed myself badly. In intervening in this question, I strove to discount completely our experiences on an international scale (case of Comrade Shachtman) and to follow step by step, without the least interference on our part one way or the other, the development of the internal conflicts and differences in the American section.

It seemed to me—and it still seems to me—that the minority is exaggerating enormously the importance of the national conference; not as a regular political meeting of a revolutionary organization, but as the means of solving the internal struggle by organizational means, that is to say, by an eventual small majority of several votes. For me, the whole of political wisdom is that, at the present stage, there is no organizational means of bringing about a decision favorable for the development of the organization itself. Quite the contrary, it is necessary to advance policies by guarding sharply against rushing things too much.

It also seemed to me that the majority, as the leading faction in the central committee, showed a certain impatience and applied or attempted to apply organizational measures which, without giving permanent results, could not help but sharpen the conflict.

I notice with satisfaction that the majority has withdrawn on its own initiative one of the measures which consisted in depriving Comrade Abern of a deciding vote in the committee in the absence of Comrade Swabeck. And if I understand the sense of the latest minutes the reaction of the minority seems to me quite disquieting.

There is the matter of our possibilities in the miners federation in Illinois. Cannon is well known down there; he enjoys a certain authority there based especially on his past trade union activity. Everything appeared to indicate that it was he who should have gone there again with a situation that is promising enough. The continuity of the work already begun also demands it. But the minority opposed it with the candidacy of Comrade Shachtman and it is to be feared that the central committee will remain undecided.

Such a measure on the part of the minority cannot be justified except by deep differences about our work among the miners. I do not get the impression that the minority is correct in its criticisms. Far from it. Comrade Allard is reproached for not sufficiently emphasizing the point of view of the Left Opposition in the trade union paper of which he is the editor. Comrade Cannon is reproached for having presented himself as a representative of progressive workers and not as a representative of the League. I cannot see any good grounds for the first reproach; I have only read two issues of the paper in question. In one of them, the editors played up the speech of Comrade Cannon quite big, which is of course of great importance for us. It is quite possible that Comrade Allard does not utilize all the possibilities; but he was quite alone—or at least he was up to very recently. And then, it is a question of trade union paper, the editing of which requires a great deal of prudence. The reproach against Comrade Cannon appears to me to be dictated by purely formalistic intransigence. I do not think that it was the task of Comrade Cannon to present himself as a delegate of the League, the latter being a political organization. Not much is accomplished with political demonstrations inside of the trade unions; it is important to get into them, to gain authority within them, to work inside, to create a fraction there, which in its turn must not abuse the name of the League on every occasion, especially not as long as it remains a tiny minority. The mass union is not a meeting called by some political organization. Naturally, for such things there are no cut-and-dried rules; it is a matter of concrete circumstances. But it appears to me—I can very well be mistaken from afar—that there is in the objections of the minority a certain spirit of sectarian formalism. In any case, these objections do not at all appear to me to be sufficient to prevent Comrade Cannon from fulfilling so important a task as that among the miners.

Since I have decided to follow the development of the internal struggle from step to step, I beg you not to consider this letter as "final." Its purpose is to supplement the preceding letter in the light of new experience.

L. Trotsky

Glossary

Abern, Martin (1898–1949) – Joined Socialist movement in 1912; jailed for refusing to register for draft in World War I; founding member of CP; Central Executive Committee member from 1920; first national secretary of CP youth, 1923; Chicago district organizer, 1924–26; International Labor Defense staff, 1926–28; member of CLA NC 1929–34; split from SWP in 1940 with Shachtman to form Workers Party.

Allard, Gerry (b. 1908) – Western UMW miner expelled from CP for protesting expulsion of Left Opposition, 1928; readmitted to CP in 1929; but rejoined CLA in 1931; leader of Progressive Miners of America in Illinois; left CLA in 1933 to join CPLA; after merger of CLA with Musteites in 1934 participated in entry into SP and stayed there after expulsion of Trotskyist faction.

Allen, Devere (1891–1955) – Member of Socialist Party and long-time activist in pacifist organizations.

American Federation of Labor (AFL) – Craft union federation formed in 1880s to protect jurisdictional boundaries, encourage favorable labor legislation, and assist in organizing skilled workers; split in 1936–37 when industrial-type unions formed CIO; merged with CIO in 1955.

American Workers Party (AWP) – Founded December 1933 as successor to Conference for Progressive Labor Action led by A.J. Muste; led Toledo Auto-Lite strike in 1934; fused with CLA to form Workers Party of the U.S., December 1934.

Amter, Israel (1881–1954) – Journalist and musician; joined CP in early 1920s; representative to Comintern, 1923–24; CP leader in New York; arrested in 1951 after first convictions of CP members under Smith Act.

Angelo, Joseph – Left-wing miners' leader in Illinois; founding member of National Miners Union and Progressive Miners of America; expelled from CP and joined CLA in 1929.

Anglo-Russian Trade Union Unity Committee – Founded in May 1925 by British and Soviet trade union leaders to promote peace and progress; British members used this alliance to ward off criticism of their betrayal of 1926 general strike; they walked out of Anglo-Russian Committee in September 1927.

Anti-Socialist Law – German law adopted in 1878 on initiative of Chancellor Otto von Bismarck; banned all Social Democratic organizations and publications, allowing only parliamentary activity; in midst of repression Social Democrats carried out vigorous underground activity; repealed in 1890.

Baldwin, Roger (1884–1981) – Founder of American Civil Liberties Union and its executive director until 1950; collaborated with Cannon on civil liberties work in 1920s when Cannon headed ILD.

Basky, Louis (1882–1938) – Former member of Socialist Labor Party; leader of CP Hungarian section in 1920s; joined CLA in 1929; supporter of Cannon in 1932–33 faction fight; coopted to NC in 1932 but action was rescinded by membership referendum; elected to Workers Party of U.S. NC, 1934; left 1935 with Oehlerites.

Bauer, Eugene (1906–1988) – Leader of German section of Left Opposition; member of IS, 1932–33; broke with Trotskyist movement in 1934 over "French turn" and joined centrist SAP.

Bauer, Otto (1881–1938) – Central leader and theoretician of Austrian Social Democrats after World War I.

Belor, John – Unemployed Minneapolis worker and supporter of Teamster strikes; killed in 1934 in police massacre.

Bernstein, Eduard (1850–1932) – Early German Social Democrat and Engels's literary executor; in 1890s proposed theory of gradual transformation of capitalism, which became known as revisionism.

Billings, Warren (1894–1972) – Class-war prisoner; framed up with Tom Mooney in 1916 for supposed bombing plot in 1916; released in 1939.

Bleeker, Sylvia (1901–1988) – Russian immigrant; participant in Russian revolution; left-wing leader in garment industry; CP candidate for Congress in 1930 when she was expelled for supporting Left Opposition; member of *Unser Kamf* editorial board.

Blum, Leon (1872–1950) – leader of French SP (SFIO); premier in popular front government, 1936–37.

Bordiga, Amadeo (1889–1970) – founding leader of Italian CP; expelled from Comintern in 1930 and adhered to Left Opposition; left ILO in 1932 because of ultraleft sectarian views.

Brandler, Heinrich (1881–1967) – German CP leader in 1920s; expelled 1929 for sympathy with Right Opposition in Soviet CP; continued an independent group until World War II.

Browder, Earl (1891–1973) – SP left-winger; imprisoned two years for draft law violation in World War I; founding member of CP; elected to CEC in 1921; Foster's assistant in trade union work; general secretary of CP 1930–34; head of Communist Political Association, 1944–45; made scapegoat for continuing CP wartime policy as U.S. stepped up pressure on USSR following World War II; expelled in 1946.

Brown, Bill (1897–1938) – President of Minneapolis Teamster Local 574 1921–38; collaborated closely with CLA members in leadership of 1934 strikes.

Bukharin, Nikolai (1886–1938) – Joined Bolsheviks in 1906; editor of *Pravda*, 1918–29; head of Comintern, 1926–29; formed Right Opposition in 1928; removed by Stalin, 1929; tried and executed for "treason" in Moscow purge trials.

Caldis, Aristodimos (1899–1979) – CLA member active in New York hotel workers' strike; expelled February 1934 together with B.J. Field for indiscipline; later left politics.

Carlson, Oliver – CP youth leader in 1920s; elected alternate member of CLA NC in 1929; suspended for indiscipline in Minnesota clothing workers' strike in September 1929.

Carmody, Jack (1905–1950) – Captain in Irish Republican Army; escaped to U.S. in 1922; early recruit to CLA and longtime member of Trotskyist movement.

Carter, Joseph (1910–1970) – Joined Young People's Socialist League, 1924; suspended for left-wing views and joined CP youth, 1928; expelled from YWL and a founding member of CLA; led anti-Cannon clique in New York branch; elected as NC alternate of Workers Party, 1934; left SWP with Shachtman in 1940.

Clarke, George (1913–1964) – Founding member of CLA; elected to Workers Party NC in 1934; left SWP in 1953 split.

Class Struggle – organ of Weisbord's Communist League of Struggle, 1931–37.

Communist International (Comintern) – Founded in March 1919 on initiative of Russian Communist Party as revolutionary leadership of world working class; after 1923 began to degenerate under the influence of degeneration of Soviet CP.

Communist Party (CP) – U.S. section of Comintern; 13,000 members at beginning of 1932, 24,000 in early 1934; published *Daily Worker* and numerous other foreign-language newspapers.

Communist Party (Majority Group) – Organization founded by Jay Lovestone following expulsion from CP in 1929; supported Right Opposition in Soviet CP and Comintern; later became Independent Labor League; dissolved in 1940.

Conference for Progressive Labor Action (CPLA) – Formed in 1929 by Muste and others wanting to rally labor elements who accepted neither AFL nor CP leadership; became American Workers Party in December 1933.

Coover, Oscar (1887–1950) – Minneapolis railroad worker and union organizer; joined CP in 1920 and became a district leader; expelled in 1928 and was founding member of CLA; alternate member of CLA NC, 1931–34; leader of SWP until his death.

Coughlin, Charles (1891–1979) – Detroit-based Catholic priest who organized fascist movement in 1930s.

Cowl, Carl – Expelled from Minneapolis CP youth, 1928; secretary of Minneapolis CLA branch in early 1930s; later became member of Oehler group.

Daily Worker – Founded 1924 as organ of CP.

Darrow, Clarence (1857–1938) – noted civil liberties attorney who defended a number of class-war prisoners.

Dunne, Vincent R. (1890–1970) – Joined Western Federation of Miners in 1905; founding member of IWW; active in free speech and labor battles; joined CP in early 1920s; red-baited out of union posts; a leader of CP Minnesota district; expelled November 1928 and became founding member of CLA; alternate member of CLA NC, 1929–31; regular member of NC, 1931–34; a central leader of 1934 Teamsters strikes; imprisoned under Smith Act in World War II.

Dunne, William F. (1887–1953) – Older brother of Vincent; founding member of CP and close collaborator of Cannon until 1928; co-editor of *Daily Worker,* 1924–27, then assistant editor; expelled from CP in 1946 for "left deviationism."

Edwards, John – CP youth leader in 1920s; delegate to Fourth Congress of Comintern; founding member of CLA in Chicago; supported Shachtman in 1932–33 faction fight; NC alternate, 1931–34.

Engels, Frederick (1820–1895) – Collaborator with Marx in codifying the foundation principles of scientific socialism; outstanding leader of revolutionary workers' movement until his death.

Everest, Wesley – IWW member and World War I veteran castrated and lynched by right-wing mob November 1919 in Centralia, Washington.

Farrington, Frank (1873–1939) – President of UMW District 12 in Illinois; led opposition to Lewis, 1921–26; suspended from post 1926; delegate to 1930 Reorganized UMW convention in Springfield.

Felix (Michiel Mayliak) (1900–1943) – A leader of Jewish group in French Communist League until resignation in 1932.

Field, B.J. (1900–1977) – Joined CLA in August 1931; expelled for indiscipline in 1932; readmitted March 1933 but expelled again in February 1934 for indiscipline in New York hotel workers' strike while he was secretary of hotel workers' union; formed League for a Revolutionary Workers Party, which survived into war years.

Forward – Yiddish-language daily newspaper published by SP members.

Foster, William Z. (1881–1961) – Joined SP in 1901, IWW in 1910; became syndicalist; AFL official, 1915 to early 1920s; led 1919 steel strike; founded Trade Union Educational League, 1920; joined CP, 1921 and led its trade union work; allied with Cannon against Lovestone and Pepper, 1923–25, 1927–28; headed CP, 1945–57.

Frank, Pierre (1905–1984) – Expelled from French CP, 1929; leader of French Communist League; secretary to Trotsky, 1932–33; leading member of Fourth International for over three decades.

Freiheit – Yiddish-language daily newspaper of Communist Party.

Gitlow, Benjamin (1891–1965) – Joined SP in 1907; imprisoned three years under criminal syndicalist law, 1919–22;

CP vice-presidential candidate, 1928; one of three CP national secretaries, 1929; expelled with Lovestoneites in 1929; led 1933 split that formed Workers Communist League; joined SP, 1934; later became right-wing anticommunist author.

Glotzer, Albert (1908–1999) – Joined CP youth, 1923; leader of Chicago CP district; elected to CP youth National Executive Committee, 1927; expelled November 1928; a founder of CLA and member of NC, 1929–34; leading member of Shachtman faction, 1932–33; left SWP in 1940 with Shachtman and became leader of Workers Party; later became right-wing Social Democrat.

Goldman, Albert (1897–1960) – Lawyer and CP leader in Chicago in late 1920s and early 1930s; joined CLA in 1933 but expelled in 1934 for decision to join SP; rejoined Trotskyists in 1936 inside SP; left SWP in 1946 to join Shachtmanites.

Gomez, Manuel (Charles Philips) – Journalist won to Communism after Russian revolution; worked with M.N. Roy in founding Communist Party of Mexico and attended Second Comintern congress in 1920; later participated in Latin American CPs; after returning to U.S., became secretary of All-American Anti-Imperialist League and was supporter of Cannon faction within CP; elected to Comintern Executive Committee, 1928; expelled from CP in 1929 although not a supporter of Left Opposition.

Gompers, Samuel (1850–1924) – President of AFL, 1886–1924; outspoken class collaborationist and supporter of U.S. imperialism.

Goodman, Leon – Expelled from CP youth and founding member of CLA; served ninety-day prison term with Bernard Morgenstern under Pennsylvania antisedition law, 1931–32; left SWP in early 1950s.

Gordon, Sam (1910–1982) – Joined CLA in 1930; supporter of Cannon faction, 1932–33; coopted onto NC in 1932, later rescinded following membership referendum; long-time leader of SWP; active as Fourth Internationalist in Britain following exclusion from U.S. by immigration authorities in 1950s; retired from active involvement in Fourth International in 1960s.

Gorkin, Julian (1902–1987) – Leader of Spanish Left Opposition who split in early 1930s; later became a leader of Workers Party of Marxist Unification (POUM).

Gorman, Daniel (b. 1870) – Became director of United Hatters of North America in 1922.

Graham, James D. (b. 1879) – President of Montana Federation of Labor and a leading member of Socialist Party.

Green, William (1873–1952) – AFL president, 1924–52; conservative craft unionist.

Groves, Reg (1908–1988) – Expelled from British CP in 1932 and became a leader of Left Opposition; opposed entry into ILP and split from ILO, although joined ILP in 1935 as a centrist.

Hathaway, Clarence (1892–1963) – Joined CP in early 1920s; IAM official, 1920–24; attended Lenin school in Moscow on Cannon's recommendation, 1926–28; editor of *Daily Worker* in 1930s; expelled for drunkenness in 1940.

Hays, Arthur Garfield (1881–1954) – Prominent civil liberties attorney.

Hillquit, Morris (1869–1933) – A founder of SP in 1901; its central leader at time of his death.

Hoan, Daniel (1881–1961) – SP member and mayor of Milwaukee; allied with Militant caucus at 1934 SP convention.

Hoover, Herbert (1874–1964) – Republican president of U.S., 1929–33.

Horner, Henry (1879–1940) – Democratic governor of Illinois, 1933–40.

Howat, Alexander (1876–1945) – President of UMW District 14 in early 1920s; led militant Kansas strikes; expelled by Lewis; readmitted 1927; president of "reorganized" UMW in 1930.

Independent Labour Party (ILP) – British centrist party; disaffiliated from Labour Party in 1932, but rejoined in 1939; adhered to London Bureau, 1932–39; 12,000 members in August 1932.

Industrial Workers of the World (IWW) – Founded 1905 as revolutionary industrial union movement; developed syndicalist views opposing political action; suffered severe government repression during and after World War I; sharply declined during 1920s into small sect.

International Labor Defense (ILD) – United front defense organization initiated by CP in 1925 with Cannon as secretary; following Cannon's expulsion in 1928, became a factional tool of CP in labor movement; prominent in Scottsboro case in 1930s; merged into Civil Rights Congress in 1946.

International Ladies' Garment Workers' Union (ILGWU) – Founded 1900; suffered split in mid-1920s following expulsion of CP-led left wing; affiliated to CIO in 1937 but rejoined AFL in 1940.

International Left Opposition (ILO) – Forerunner of Fourth International founded in 1930; formed International Secretariat as coordinating body; changed name to International Communist League in 1933.

Johnson, Hugh S. (1882–1942) – Brigadier general who served as administrator for National Recovery Act, 1933–34.

Kaplan, David – Class-war prisoner framed up in 1910 together with McNamara brothers and Schmidt on a bombing charge and sentenced to ten years' imprisonment.

Karsner, Rose (1889–1968) – Came to U.S. from Romania; joined SP in 1908; founding member of CP; companion and collaborator of Cannon from 1924; assistant secretary of ILD; founding member of CLA; manager of Pioneer Publishers and *Militant* business manager during 1930s.

Kautsky, Karl (1854–1938) – Regarded as outstanding Marxist theoretician within Second International until 1914, when he abandoned internationalism; bitter opponent of October revolution and Soviet Union.

Kellogg Pact – 1928 agreement of fifteen countries renouncing war as instrument of national policy; eventually ratified by sixty-three countries, including USSR; engineered by U.S. Secretary of State Frank B. Kellogg.

Keracher, John – Leader of Michigan SP, which briefly affiliated to CP in 1919; later founded Proletarian Party and was national secretary for many years; became head of Charles H. Kerr Publishing Co. in 1920s.

Kerensky, Alexander (1881–1970) – Prime minister of Russian Provisional Government, 1917; overthrown by October revolution.

Kilbom, Karl (1885–1961) – Swedish CP leader who split in 1929 over Comintern ultraleft turn; led centrist group affiliated to London Bureau; later rejoined Social Democracy.

Kirov, Sergei (1886–1934) – Member of Soviet CP Political Bureau and secretary of Leningrad party organization; repression following his assassination heralded beginning of Moscow trials.

Kling, Lazar – Journalist; met Trotsky in New York in 1917; lived in Moscow during 1920s and became supporter of Bolshevik-Leninists; member of CLA during early 1930s; on editorial board of *Unser Kamf*.

Krzycki, Leo (1881–1966) – Vice-president of Amalgamated Clothing Workers; chairman of SP until 1936 when resigned from party to support Roosevelt.

Labor Age – Monthly edited by Louis F. Budenz; unofficial organ of CPLA.

Lafargue, Paul (1842–1911) – An organizer of early Marxist movement in France; son-in-law of Karl Marx.

Landau, Kurt (1903–1937) – Leader of German Left Opposition, 1930–31; split from ILO in 1931; later went to Spain during civil war and was kidnapped and murdered by

Stalin's secret police.

Lassalle, Ferdinand (1825–1864) – Founder of General Association of German Workers in 1863, which later fused with Marxists to form Social Democratic Party.

Lenin, V.I. (1870–1924) – Founder and central leader of Bolshevik Party from 1903; chairman of Soviet Council of People's Commissars, 1917–24; outstanding leader of Comintern.

Lewis, John L. (1880–1969) – President of United Mine Workers, 1920–60; principal leader of CIO, 1935–40.

Lewit, Morris (1903–1998) – Joined CLA in 1930; editor of *Unser Kamf;* supporter of Shachtman in 1932–33 faction fight; elected member of Workers Party NC, 1934; long-time leader of SWP under name of Morris Stein.

Lhuillier, Rene (1909–1968) – Leader of small group in French Communist League opposed to entry in SP; eventually entered SP but remained there after Bolshevik-Leninists were expelled.

Liebknecht, Karl (1871–1919) – German Spartacist; symbol of revolutionary internationalism during World War I; arrested January 1919 on orders of Social Democratic government and assassinated.

Liebowitz, Samuel S. – Prominent civil liberties attorney; one of ILD lawyers for Scottsboro defendants.

Little, Frank (1880–1917) – IWW organizer lynched by company thugs in Montana during copper miners' strike.

London-Amsterdam Bureau – Loose federation of centrist parties during 1930s opposed to Second and Third Internationals, but opposed to founding of Fourth International.

Lore, Ludwig (1875–1942) – Immigrated from Germany in 1903; active in IWW and SP left wing; edited German-language CP paper from 1919; supported Russian Bolshevik-Leninists in 1924 and expelled from CP; member of AWP who participated in fusion with

CLA; expelled from Workers Party in 1935; later became pro-war journalist.

Lovestone, Jay (1898–1990) – Founding member of CP; became general secretary in 1927; expelled in 1929 and founded Communist Party (Majority Group); later became rabidly anticommunist chief adviser on foreign policy to top AFL-CIO officialdom.

Luxemburg, Rosa (1871–1919) – Leader of Polish and German Social Democratic parties before World War I; leader of revolutionary left within German party and founding leader of Spartacists; arrested on orders of Social Democratic government in January 1919 and murdered.

McLevy, Jasper (1888–1962) – Right-wing Socialist; mayor of Bridgeport, Conn., 1933–57, 1959–60; left SP in 1950.

McMahon, Thomas F. (1870–1944) – President of United Textile Workers, 1921–36.

McNamara, James B. (1881–1941) – Class-war prisoner framed up for 1910 bombing together with Kaplan, Schmidt, and brother John J.; sentenced to life imprisonment.

McNamara, John J. (d. 1941) – Secretary of AFL Bridge and Structural Workers framed up for 1910 bombing; sentenced to fifteen years' imprisonment.

Malkin, Maurice L. – CP member imprisoned for activity in furriers' strike; expelled November 1928 but made statement repudiating Left Opposition in October 1929 when ILD threatened to withdraw from his defense and stop aiding his aged parents; retracted statement in September 1930; expelled from CLA in May 1931 for making deal with bureaucrats to get back into furriers' union.

Marx, Karl (1818–1883) – Collaborated with Engels in codifying foundations of scientific socialism; leader of First International.

Matthews, J.B. (1894–1966) – Member of Socialist Party in New York and a leader of Revolutionary Policy Committee; later became key aide to Sen. Joseph McCarthy and chief investigator of witch-hunting Dies Committee.

Militants – Centrist tendency within Socialist Party led by Norman Thomas that won majority at 1934 SP convention.

Mill, M. (1905–1937) – Member of Jewish Group of French Communist League; became a Stalinist agent.

Minor, Robert (1884–1952) – Radical cartoonist; became anarchist in 1912; joined CP in 1920; editor of *Daily Worker* from 1927; was a chief lieutenant of Lovestone and then of Browder, remaining in CP after each was expelled.

Molinier, Raymond (1904–1994) – A founder and leader of French section of Left Opposition until 1935 when expelled for indiscipline; a supporter of Fourth International in later years.

Mooney, Thomas J. (1882–1942) – Leader of left bloc in California AFL; framed with Warren Billings and three others for bombing at 1916 "Preparedness" parade in San Francisco; sentenced to death but execution stayed in 1918 due to international defense campaign; pardoned in 1939.

Morgenstern, Bernard (1907–1981) – CP youth leader in Philadelphia; founding member of CLA; elected alternate member of NC at 1931 national conference; supporter of Cannon faction in 1932–33 fight; left SWP for personal reasons within subsequent decade.

Muste, A.J. (1885–1967) – Born in Netherlands; trained as preacher; a leader of Lawrence and Paterson textile strikes in 1919; head of Brookwood Labor College; founding leader of CPLA and AWP; became national secretary of Workers Party of the U.S. in 1934 fusion with CLA; returned to church in 1936; established American Forum for Socialist Education in late 1950s and was a leader of antiwar movement in 1960s.

National Miners Union (NMU) – CP-led coal miners' union founded September 1928; dissolved in 1934.

National Recovery Administration (NRA) – New Deal agency set up in 1933 to prepare and enforce codes of business practices; while establishing minimum wage and maximum hours and recognizing right of workers to join unions, primarily designed to help capitalists who needed price floors and other measures as a way out of depression; ruled unconstitutional by Supreme Court in 1935.

National Textile Workers Union (NTWU) – CP-led union founded in September 1928; dissolved in 1934.

Naville, Pierre (1904–1993) – A founder and leader of French Communist League; opposed entry into SP in 1934 and split; later joined SP and reunited with Bolshevik-Leninists; broke with Fourth International at beginning of World War II.

Needle Trades Workers Industrial Union – CP-led union formed January 1, 1929; dissolved when fur workers section merged with AFL union and dress workers joined ILGWU individually around 1935.

Neue Zeit – Theoretical journal of German Social Democrats; founded in 1883 and edited by Kautsky until 1917.

New Masses – Monthly U.S. literary journal under CP control.

Non-Partisan Labor Defense (NPLD) – United front working-class defense organization formed in 1934 as result of collaboration between CLA and AWP.

Oehler, Hugo (1903–1983) – CP unionist in 1920s; district organizer in Kansas City; protested expulsion of Left Opposition but stayed in CP; a leader of National Textile Workers Union organizing drive in North Carolina in 1929; declared for Left Opposition in June 1930; elected to CLA National Committee in 1931; key supporter of Cannon in 1932–33 CLA faction fight; formed sectarian opposition faction in late 1934 and was expelled from Workers Party in 1935 for indiscipline; formed Revolutionary Workers League, which survived into 1950s.

O'Flaherty, Thomas J. (1889–1936) – Former activist in Irish freedom struggle; moved to U.S. in 1912 and joined SP; founding member of CP and member of Central Executive Committee; expelled November 1928 for supporting Left Opposition; co-editor of *Producers News* in Plentywood, Montana; called for farmer-labor party and publishing a common paper with Lovestoneites; dropped from CLA membership in 1931; reapplied in 1932; returned to Ireland in 1934.

Old Guard – Right-wing leadership of SP, which became minority in 1934; split from SP and formed Social Democratic Federation in 1936.

Olgin, Moissaye J. (1874–1939) – Immigrated from Russia in 1915; a leader of Workers' Council group that joined CP in 1921; editor of *Freiheit*; author of anti-Trotsky slander booklet.

Olson, Floyd (1891–1936) – Farmer-Labor Party governor of Minnesota, 1931–36.

Panken, Jacob (1879–1968) – Member of SP elected New York municipal judge in 1917; supporter of Old Guard.

Paz, Maurice (1896–1985) – Early leader of Left Opposition in France; broke with Trotsky in 1929 and joined SP.

Pepper, John (1886–1938) – Hungarian Social Democrat who joined Comintern after defeat of Hungarian revolution; came to U.S. in 1922 and became central leader of CP until 1925; supervised expulsion of Left Opposition as a leader of Lovestone faction; ordered back to USSR in 1929 and expelled; disappeared during Moscow trials.

Progressive Miners of America (PMA) – Independent union formed 1932 in Illinois; affiliated to AFL in 1938 after expulsion of UMW from federation; unsuccessfully attempted to challenge UMW outside Illinois.

Proletarian Party – Originally Michigan SP; expelled for left-wing views in 1919; led by Dennis E. Batt and John Keracher; briefly adhered to CP but split in 1920; a small propaganda sect that abstained from practical action;

suffered several splits in early 1930s that took majority of members; dissolved in late 1930s; some members became officials in United Auto Workers.

Rakovsky, Christian (1873–1941) – Leader of Balkan Social Democratic movement from before World War I; president of Ukrainian Soviet, 1919–23; leading member of Bolshevik-Leninists; expelled from party and exiled to Siberia in 1927; recanted in 1934; framed up and jailed in 1938 Moscow trial.

Ray, George – CLA youth leader; member of editorial board of *Young Spartacus*.

Revolutionary Age – Organ of Lovestoneites; became *Workers Age* in 1932.

Riazanov, David B. (1870–1938) – Russian Marxist scholar and director of the Marx and Engels Institute in Moscow during 1920s; arrested during Moscow trials and died in Siberian exile.

Robins, Harold (1908–1987) – Joined CLA, 1928; imprisoned nine months for participation in 1934 New York hotel workers' strike; left SWP in 1960.

Rolph, James (1869–1934) – Governor of California, 1931–34.

Roosevelt, Franklin D. (1882–1945) – Democratic president of U.S., 1933–45.

Rosmer, Alfred (1877–1964) – Leading French syndicalist during World War I; joined CP in 1920 and was editor of *L'Humanité;* leading member of Red International of Labor Unions; expelled from CP in 1924 as supporter of Bolshevik-Leninists; leader of French Communist League until resigning in 1930; renewed political collaboration with Trotsky and Fourth Internationalists after 1936.

Ruthenberg, Charles (1882–1927) – Leader of SP left wing until 1919; a founder of CP; general secretary at time of death.

Sacco, Nicola (1891–1927) – Italian immigrant, anarchist, and shoe-factory worker framed up on murder charges together with Bartolomeo Vanzetti, 1920; executed after long appeals and mass defense campaign.

SAP (Socialist Workers Party) – German centrist party formed in 1931 as split from Social Democratic Party; in 1932, fused with split-off from Brandlerite Right Opposition; signed Declaration of Four in August 1933 calling for formation of Fourth International, but soon retreated and became opponent of new International.

Schlesinger, Benjamin (1876–1932) – President of ILGWU, 1914–23, 1928–32; manager of Chicago *Jewish Daily Forward* from 1923.

Schmidt, Matthew – Class-war prisoner, framed up in 1910 on bombing charges together with McNamara brothers and Kaplan; received sentence of life imprisonment.

SFIO (French Section of the Workers' International) – Initials used to designate French Socialist Party, affiliated to Second International; central leader during 1930s was Léon Blum.

Shachtman, Max (1903–1972) – Emigrated from Poland in 1904; came to CP through Workers' Council group in 1921; a leader of CP youth, 1923–27; editor of *Labor Defender,* 1926–28; founding leader of CLA and its first international representative; led opposition to Cannon, 1929–33; collaborated closely with Cannon from 1934; led 1940 split of petty-bourgeois opposition to form Workers Party; this became Independent Socialist League, which dissolved into right wing of SP in 1958.

Sharts, Joseph W. (b. 1875) – Novelist and National Executive Committee member of Socialist Party; supporter of extreme right wing within SP.

Sifakis, James – Early member of CP and supporter of Foster group; dropped out in 1928; joined CLA, 1929.

Sigman, Morris (1880–1931) – President of the ILGWU, 1923–28.

Skoglund, Carl (1884–1960) – Swedish Socialist, came to U.S. in 1911; a leader of SP Scandinavian Federation and a founder of the CP; expelled in 1928 and a founder of CLA; member of CLA NC, 1929–34; a central leader of 1934 Minneapolis Teamster strikes; president of Teamsters Local 544, 1938–40; elected member of International Executive Committee of Fourth International, 1938; imprisoned during World War II under Smith Act; faced government deportation threats during 1950s.

Socialist Labor Party (SLP) – Formed in 1877; came under leadership of Daniel De Leon in 1890; degenerated into a sect after founding of Socialist Party in 1901, combining sectarian opposition to fight for immediate demands with electoralist view of fight for socialism; 2,500 members in 1932.

Socialist Party of America (SP) – Founded in 1901; left-wing majority split in 1919 to form Communist movement; regained some influence in late 1920s and early 1930s; 10,000 members in 1931; 24,000 in 1934; right-wing leadership displaced in 1934 by centrist Militant group and split in 1936 to form Social Democratic Federation; two groups reunited in 1957; split in 1972 into Social Democrats USA, a group that became Democratic Socialists of America, and a small group that retains the name Socialist Party.

Soderberg, John G. – Secretary-treasurer of boatman's union; framed up on charges of conspiracy to dynamite barges; CLA played leading role in defense activities; convicted and sentenced to 25 years' imprisonment.

Spector, Maurice (1898–1968) – A founder of Canadian CP and its national chairman, 1924–28; expelled in 1928 for supporting Bolshevik-Leninists; elected to CLA NC in 1929 and a central leader of Canadian Trotskyism; resigned from movement in 1939.

Stachel, Jack (1900–1964) – Left SP to join CP, 1924; CP national organizational secretary, 1927; prominent Lovestoneite; broke with Lovestone in 1929; headed Trade Union Unity League, 1932–35; leading CP member until his death.

Stalin, Joseph (1879–1953) – Joined Bolshevik Party in 1904; became CP general secretary in early 1920s; leader of anti-Leninist wing in Soviet CP from 1923; over time eliminated all opponents and became dictator of CP and Soviet government.

Swabeck, Arne (1890–1986) – Originally from Denmark; joined German Social Democratic Party before World War I; immigrated to U.S. in 1916 and joined SP; member of IWW 1918–20; editor of SP Scandinavian weekly before 1919 split; member of CP's Central Executive Committee; Chicago district organizer; leader of left wing in Chicago Federation of Labor and director of CP's miners' campaign; expelled November 1928; CLA national secretary in early 1930s, and a key leader of Cannon group in 1932–33 faction fight; long-time leader of SWP; later became Maoist; expelled from SWP for disloyalty in 1967.

"Third Period" – Period of final collapse of capitalism and triumph of socialist revolution according to Comintern theory elaborated in 1929; it followed period of revolutionary upheavals (1917–23) and period of capitalist stabilization, ending in 1928; term was dropped after Hitler's rise to power and shift to "popular front" line.

Thomas, Norman (1884–1968) – Six-time SP presidential candidate, 1928–48; led centrist Militant tendency in 1934.

Trachtenberg, Alexander (1885–1966) – Joined SP in 1906; joined communist movement in 1921; founder and head of International Publishers.

Trade Union Unity League (TUUL) – CP-led trade union front formed in 1929 at fourth convention of Trade Union Educational League with William Z. Foster as general secretary; aimed to organize unorganized into industrial unions; failed due to ultraleft sectarian "red union" policy and dissolved in 1935.

Tresso, Pietro (1893–1944) – Joined Italian Bolshevik-Leninists in 1930; leader of ILO and Fourth International; killed after escaping French prison, probably by Stalinists.

Trotsky, Leon (1879–1940) – Joined Bolsheviks in August 1917 and became a central leader of party, Soviet state, and Comintern; organized Red Army during civil war; after 1923 led opposition in Soviet CP and Comintern to preserve Leninist program and strategy; expelled from party and exiled to Siberia, 1927; deported from USSR, 1929; central leader of ILO and Fourth Internationalist movement; assassinated by Stalinist agent.

2½ International (International Association of Socialist Parties) – Formed in 1921 by centrist groups that had left Second International; reunited with it in 1923.

United Textile Workers (UTW) – AFL textile union.

United Workers Party – Formed 1932 from split in Proletarian Party; leadership of Paul Mattick viewed USSR as state capitalist, thought trade unions reactionary, and held antiparliamentarism as a principle; some other leaders briefly moved toward Marxism; led unemployed organization called Workers Leagues.

Unser Kamf – Yiddish-language newspaper published by CLA.

Unser Wort – Newspaper of German section of ILO; later published in U.S. by emigres.

Urbahns, Hugo (1890–1947) – German CP member expelled in 1926, holding ultraleft positions; helped form Leninbund in 1928; expelled Bolshevik-Leninists in 1930; authored "state capitalist" theory of class nature of USSR.

Van Overstraaten, Edouard (1891–1981) – Leader of Belgian CP until 1929; leader of Belgian Left Opposition until breaking with it in December 1930.

Vanzetti, Bartolomeo (1888–1927) – Italian immigrant worker and anarchist; framed on charges of murder in 1920 together with Nicola Sacco; executed in 1927 after long appeals and mass defense campaign.

Vladeck, B. Charney (1886–1938) – Leading SP member; manager of *Jewish Daily Forward*, 1921–38; supporter of SP Old Guard.

Waldman, Louis (1892–1982) – Right-wing leader of SP Old Guard; a founder of Social Democratic Federation.

Walker, John H. (1872–1955) – President of Illinois Federation of Labor; signed call for dissident UMW convention in Springfield in 1930.

Weber, Jack (b. 1896) – Joined CLA in 1930; elected member of Workers Party NC, 1934; leader of Abern group until 1936; left SWP in 1944.

Weisbord, Albert (1900–1977) – SP youth leader, 1921–24; joined CP in 1924; leader of Passaic textile strike, 1926; expelled for "Lovestoneism" in 1929; headed Communist League of Struggle, 1931–37; became AFL organizer but was fired during World War II despite support for war.

Well, Roman (1901–1962) – Stalinist agent inside German Left Opposition until 1932, when he led split toward CP.

Wicks, Harry M. (1889–1956) – CP leader; Comintern emissary in Australia and Far East; expelled from CP in 1937 on charges of having been anticommunist for eighteen years.

Winter, Carl (b. 1906) – CP member; secretary, Unemployed Councils of Greater New York, 1932–33; long-time editor of *Daily Worker*.

Wolfe, Bertram D. (1896–1981) – Leading supporter of Stalin within U.S. CP during 1920s; expelled in 1929 as leader of Lovestone group; apologist for Moscow trials until 1937; later became anticommunist author.

Workers Communist League – Formed 1933 by Gitlow; united with Field group in 1934 to form Organizing Committee for a Revolutionary Socialist Party.

Workers Leagues – Unemployed organizations led by members of United Workers Party; centered in Chicago.

Workmen's Circles – Fraternal organization led by SP; CP-led left wing split in 1930.

Wortis, Rose (1894–1958) – CP leader in needle trades.

Young Spartacus – Monthly publication published by CLA youth from December 1931 until December 1935; organ of Spartacus Youth Clubs, which became Spartacus Youth League.

Zam, Herbert – Founding member of CP; national secretary of Young Workers League, 1925; expelled with Lovestone in 1929; left Lovestoneites in 1934 and joined SP, where he became a leading centrist.

Zimmerman, Charles S. (1897–1983) – Leading trade unionist in CP and then Lovestoneites; business manager of ILGWU Local 22 in New York; vice-president of ILGWU, 1934–72; later chairman of AFL-CIO Civil Rights Committee.

Zinoviev, Gregory Y. (1883–1936) – Close collaborator with Lenin before 1917; head of Comintern, 1919–26; allied with Stalin against Trotsky, 1923–25; allied with Trotsky in United Opposition, 1926–27; capitulated at end of 1927; framed up and executed during Moscow trials.

Notes

1. The CLA had begun publishing a Greek-language paper *(Communistes)* in December 1931 and was preparing to launch a Yiddish-language paper to be called *Unser Kamf.*
2. Cannon is referring to the Lovestone group, which had been expelled from the CP in 1929 and called itself the Communist Party (Majority Group).
3. The Proletarian Party (see Glossary) was undergoing a split, with half of its 400 members being expelled or resigning because of differences with the party leadership. Cannon believed that throughout its existence the Proletarian Party had been characterized by "sectarian passivity, garnished with high-sounding, pseudo-Marxist talk" (*Militant,* January 11, 1932), and saw the rebellion against the leadership as an opportunity to influence these militants in the CLA's direction. However, few of the former Proletarian Party members were won to the CLA; in Cleveland and New York, many joined the CP. Out of the split the United Workers Party was founded; the Proletarian Party itself maintained a sectarian existence until its decline in the late 1930s. Some of its members later became officials in the United Auto Workers.
4. The Scottsboro case was one of the major civil rights battles of the 1930s. In 1931, nine Black youths were indicted in Scottsboro, Alabama, on charges of having raped two white women. In a series of trials they were convicted and sentenced to death or to long prison terms. The struggle to free the defendants was led by the CP through the International Labor Defense. In 1937, after one of the alleged victims recanted her testimony, five defendants were freed. Three were paroled in the 1940s, and the last escaped to Michigan in 1948.
5. In late 1930, Albert Weisbord had formed the Communist

League of Struggle, which, while criticizing the CLA for a lack of orientation to the "mass movement," oriented virtually all its activity to influencing the CLA. Cannon describes the politics of this group more fully in *The Left Opposition in the U.S. 1928–31* (New York: Pathfinder Press, 1981).

6. The review of the book *Lassalle* by Arno Shirokauer was written by Max Geltman, who later used the pen name Martin Glee. The sharpness of Cannon's criticism of the review reflected his opposition to the nonproletarian elements in the New York branch who he felt tended to denigrate the movement's revolutionary traditions in a light-minded way. These forces were the base of an opposition faction then taking shape in the CLA.

The Marxist appreciation of Lassalle's role was summarized in an 1868 letter by Karl Marx. Lasalle's "immortal service," Marx wrote, was that he "re-awakened the workers' movement in Germany after its fifteen years of slumber. But," he added, "he committed great mistakes. He allowed himself to be governed too much by the immediate circumstances of the time. . . . Thus he was driven into making concessions to the Prussian monarchy, the Prussian reaction (feudal party) and even the clericals. . . . Moreover, like everyone who maintains that he has a panacea for the sufferings of the masses in his pocket, he gave his agitation from the outset a religious and sectarian character." In an 1891 letter Engels wrote that "However highly one may estimate Lassalle's services to the movement, his historical role in it remains an equivocal one. Lassalle the socialist is accompanied step by step by Lassalle the demagogue. . . . the same cynicism in choice of methods, the same preference for surrounding himself with rowdy and corrupt people who can be used as mere tools and discarded."

7. The International Left Opposition (ILO) had been formed in April 1930 with an administrative center (International Secretariat) in Paris and later Berlin. Almost from its inception the IS was weak, isolated, and torn by internal crises. At the center of these fights was the struggle to develop a

strong leading cadre and to free the ILO from the influence of elements who resisted the organizational norms of a proletarian party, many of whom played a leading role in most of the European sections. Numerous splits and defections in these groups, especially France and Germany, greatly weakened the influence of the IS. This situation led Trotsky to propose its reorganization. Plans had been made to hold an authoritative international conference in 1931 or 1932, but disagreement on perspectives and representation prevented its occurrence until February 1933.

The CLA had been a part of the ILO from its founding, but because of poverty and distance had played little direct role in its affairs. Shachtman had represented the CLA at the ILO founding in 1930, and basically functioned as the league's international secretary through 1931. However, his handling of this responsibility came under the criticism of Cannon and other CLA leaders who felt he handled the assignment in an overly individualistic way, and took positions on disputed international questions without adequate consultation with the CLA leadership. At the CLA's September 1931 national conference, this friction came out in the open. Shachtman subsequently refused to serve as editor of the *Militant* and took a personal trip to Europe. While there, he tended to associate with opposition currents in the ILO who were disrupting the movement's progress. This led Trotsky to send a letter to the CLA on December 25, 1931, inquiring whether Shachtman's actions also represented the position of the CLA National Committee. That letter can be found in *Writings of Leon Trotsky (1930–31)* (New York: Pathfinder Press, 1973).

As a result, the NC in early 1932 prepared a resolution expressing its position on the internal disputes within the ILO. In February it was decided to combine an original draft by Albert Glotzer with notes prepared by Cannon. Disliking the combined draft written by Cannon, however, Glotzer refused to vote for it when it was submitted by Cannon and Arne Swabeck to the resident National Committee, where it received only their two votes. Glotzer resubmitted his original draft, Abern put forth his own motions, and Shachtman abstained on all the resolutions. Only after the nonresident NC members submitted written votes was Cannon's resolution officially adopted. This dispute became the opening round in the 1932–33 faction struggle that was to bring the CLA to the verge of a split.

While originating as a minority document of Cannon and Swabeck within the NC, this statement was adopted unanimously two months later.

8. "A Letter to National Sections," reprinted in *Writings of Leon Trotsky (1930–31)*. This circular dealt with problems of the German, French, Spanish, and U.S. sections and the need to reorganize the IS. In particular, Trotsky singled out for criticism the group of Kurt Landau which had split from the German section in May 1931; and the groups in France led by Pierre Naville and Alfred Rosmer and by the Jewish group of the French section, all of whom were leading a faction struggle against the section's leadership.

9. This resolution, adopted at the 1931 CLA national conference, was published in the September 19, 1931, *Militant*.

10. On March 7, 1932, police fired on a peaceful march organized by the Detroit Unemployed Council at the Ford Motor plant in Dearborn, Michigan, killing four. On March 12, Chicago police fired on a march of several thousand at the Japanese consulate protesting Japan's war against China and the Dearborn massacre. One worker was critically wounded and many were arrested. These events were followed by a red-baiting campaign in the media, aimed at placing the blame for these incidents on members of the Communist Party.

11. Following a bitter miners' strike in Harlan County, Kentucky, a number of miners' leaders were framed up and convicted for the murder of several deputies in May 1931. Several of the miners received life sentences. Some were pardoned in 1935, and the rest were eventually freed in 1941.

12. An anticommunist witch-hunt began in 1919. During the notorious Palmer raids of January 1920, some 5,000 foreign-born radicals were rounded up and deported. As a result

of this and other repressive actions, the recently formed Communist movement made the decision to go underground following a debate on open versus underground functioning. The CP decided in 1921 to launch a public organization, the Workers Party; Cannon was elected its first national chairman. In 1923 the CP itself resumed open political work and dissolved the underground organization into the Workers Party. From 1925 to 1929, the party was known as the Workers (Communist) Party.

13. In September 1931, Japanese imperialism invaded and occupied the province of Manchuria as a step in its drive to take control of all of China. Demonstrations in solidarity with China were held throughout the world. While the other imperialist powers condemned the Japanese action, they did nothing to interfere with it.

14. In the January 1932 issue of *Young Spartacus,* CLA youth leader Joseph Carter had written an article "Honor Bolshevik Leaders," where he stated that "the tactics advocated by Marx and Engels in the *Communist Manifesto* in 1847–48 [were] later proclaimed by Engels as outlived." Carter referred to Engels's 1895 introduction to Marx's *The Class Struggles in France, 1848–50.* (This can be found in Marx and Engels, *Selected Works,* vol. 1 [Moscow: Progress Publishers, 1969].) Swabeck wrote a reply to Carter's article in the March 5, 1932, *Militant* entitled "Uphold Our Revolutionary Classics." Shachtman wrote a reply to Swabeck ("Statement by Shachtman on the Article 'Uphold Our Revolutionary Classics' in *The Militant* of March 5, 1932"), which was printed in the Internal Bulletin, along with Cannon and Swabeck's answer to it reprinted here. Shachtman's reply to Swabeck's *Militant* article stated, "The procedure [of Swabeck] is unprecedented and unwarranted, the tone of the article is disgraceful, rude, and uncomradely, the contents of the article are ridiculous both from the historical and theoretical points of view." Shachtman then went on to launch an attack against Cannon for allegedly waging a factional campaign to discredit Shachtman. This exchange marked the start of the open polemics that led

to the formation of rival factions.

15. Trotsky had written, "The crisis in America creates premises for revolutionary work on a broad scale for the first time. It is to be hoped that, thanks to the preceding systematic education of cadres, the American League will enter the new period well enough prepared, although it should not be concealed that the real test for the cadre is still ahead." *(Writings of Leon Trotsky [1930–31]).*

16. For Cannon's account of the Joseph Fox case, see p. 117. Malkin had been expelled when it was discovered that, behind the back of the CLA, he collaborated with the right-wing union officialdom to get back into the fur workers' union.

17. Shachtman had fought to put Morris Lewit on the NC.

18. Cannon's insert read: "The Opposition, whose strength lies in its ideas and which constitutes a faction, has especially rigid requirements and cannot have any hesitation in enforcing them. For that reason, the American section of the Left Opposition also endorses the struggle conducted by our French section against the right-wing group of Gourget and against the ambiguous attitude of other members of the Ligue, such as Naville, who did not join in rejecting categorically the ideas and conduct of this group, and whose attitude, instead, comforted it, just as it comforted the Landau group in its destructive work in the ranks of the German opposition."

19. In an attempt to justify its electoralist perspective, the SLP had published the Engels introduction in 1924 under the title *The Revolutionary Act.* (New York: New York Labor News, 1924). Following Riazanov's uncovering of Engels's unexpurgated original manuscript, the SLP issued a pamphlet denying the authenticity of the new version entitled *Who Are the Falsifiers? Documentary Evidence Proving Correctness and Authenticity of the S.L.P. Translation of Frederick Engels' Introduction to "Class Struggles in France" by Karl Marx and—An Exposure of the "Communist" or Burlesque Bolshevik Falsification and Garbling of that Same Introduction* (New York: New York Labor News, 1926).

20. The full text of Luxemburg's speech at the founding congress of the German Communist Party can be found in *Rosa Luxemburg Speaks* (New York: Pathfinder Press, 1970).
21. Translated from Riazanov's "Engels's Introduction to Marx's *Class Struggles in France 1848–50*" in *Unter dem Banner des Marxismus,* no. 1.
22. The full quotation, in a different translation, can be found in the chapter "Summing Up" in Trotsky's *1905* (New York: Random House, 1972).
23. Trotsky's 1928 criticism of the Stalin-Bukharin draft program of the Comintern is included in *The Third International After Lenin* (New York: Pathfinder Press, 1970).
24. Carter and George Ray had brought the NC meeting a protest of the National Youth Committee, condemning Swabeck's tone and procedure.
25. This refers to "Left Wing Needle Trades Crisis" in the May 24, 1930, issue of the *Militant.*
26. For Cannon's account of this discussion and Trotsky's role in it, see *The First Ten Years of American Communism* (New York: Pathfinder Press, 1973), pp. 83–87 [2010 printing]. This book also contains Cannon's accounts of other chapters in early CP history that are traced in this article.
27. Foster, who was an AFL official during World War I, had supported the U.S. war effort and had sold war bonds.
28. Trotsky's letter of March 7, 1932, is included in *The Spanish Revolution (1930–39)* (New York: Pathfinder Press, 1973).
29. Glotzer went on national tour to report on a trip to Europe and had submitted a report on this tour to the NC on April 11. About his three-day trip to Minneapolis he reported: "It appears that for some time prior to my arrival in Minneapolis, the older comrades had not been playing the role that falls upon their shoulder. . . . Both Comrades Dunne and Skoglund are working at present on a job that allows for little time for activity. In addition neither of the two comrades are well physically. There are circumstances that must be taken into account. But in spite of that better efforts could have been made by them to help in the

direction of the work." Glotzer went on to criticize the work Dunne and Skoglund were doing—organizing coal drivers—saying that they should be organizing helpers instead, and that they were guilty of "fraternization with the bosses" for organizing a fund-raising social that bosses were allowed to attend.

30. In his letter of April 18, Dunne wrote: "We have formed certain opinions about Abern, Shachtman, and Glotzer; we have not forgotten the spectacle these comrades presented in the meetings of the [National] Committee when we first came to the center, the poverty of their argument and discussion, the total lack of political groundwork for the assault upon you. And what has followed since then has not changed our views."

31. The elections in Cloakmakers Local 9 were shady because the right-wing leadership threw its support to the left candidates to block the election of representatives of the strongest group in the union—a "Progressive Bloc" of anarchists and Lovestoneites. This gave the CP-led left wing five of the seven delegates from that local.

32. In the mid-1920s, the right-wing leadership of the ILGWU under President Schlesinger, desperate as a result of the strength of an organized left wing under Communist Party leadership, expelled a number of opposition locals and leaders. The split left the ILGWU in a greatly weakened state. In 1929 the left wing formed the Needle Trades Workers Industrial Union.

33. For a different translation, see "'Left-Wing' Communism—An Infantile Disorder," in V.I. Lenin, *Collected Works* (Moscow: Progress Publishers, 1966), vol. 31, pp. 42, 49, and 41 respectively. Volapük was a proposed international language based largely upon English, devised in 1879.

34. One letter was from a CP member, the other from a Lovestoneite. The CPer said that the party Central Executive Committee had demanded that Lovestone repudiate Brandler and state that "the party line is right and always has been right." Lovestone offered to submit to discipline after readmission but refused to issue such a statement first.

According to a report by Lovestone, the Lovestoneite said, the negotiations had begun with a meeting with a Comintern representative, who proposed that they return to the party and work everything out gradually. Lovestone had demanded a full discussion and a party convention, to which the Comintern representative replied, "That would mean the end of Stalin."

35. In 1927, while he was CP general secretary, Lovestone had advanced a perspective that came to be known as "American exceptionalism," which saw little prospects for a working-class radicalization in the United States because of U.S. capitalism's apparent strength and stability.

36. Bukharin and the right wing were defeated in April 1929 at the Sixteenth Congress of the CPSU; he lost his post in the Comintern in July and was removed from the CPSU Political Bureau in November, although remaining in the party. The International Left Opposition predicted that a right turn would follow. Only shortly after these events, however, the ultraleft "third period" began, lasting until 1933–34. At that point Stalin did make a sharp right turn.

37. The case of marine workers John Soderberg, Thomas Bunker, and William Trajer is described in *The Left Opposition in the U.S. 1928–31*.

38. Morgenstern and Leon Goodman of Philadelphia were arrested and charged with sedition in February 1931 for handing out a leaflet about unemployment that called for international proletarian revolution. They were released May 17, 1932, after serving ninety days in prison.

39. In March 1920, Friedrich Kapp led an attempted revolt to overthrow the German bourgeois republic and establish a military dictatorship. A massive general strike of the German working class smashed this rightist coup attempt. The British general strike of May 1926, sparked by a coal miners' strike, lasted nine days before being called off by the union officialdom at the peak of its effectiveness, thereby betraying the miners.

40. The reference to Kentucky refers to the bloody Harlan

County battles between state deputies and miners. During 1917–20, Butte, Montana, was the scene of armed vigilante attacks and lynchings, frequent periods of martial law, and the use of agents provocateur, all of which successfully smashed the formerly well-entrenched trade union movement there. Mussolini's fascist movement in Italy had taken power in 1922 and proceeded to dismantle the organized workers' movement.

41. "The Organizational Structure of the Communist Parties, the Methods and Content of Their Work: Theses." A translation of this document is contained in *Theses, Resolutions and Manifestos of the First Four Congresses of the Third International* (London: Ink Links, 1980).

42. Trotsky's article, "What Next—Vital Questions for the German Proletariat" can be found in *The Struggle Against Fascism in Germany* (New York: Pathfinder Press, 1971).

43. In 1931 an internal dispute leading to a split had broken out in the Toronto branch, then functioning as a unit of the CLA. After hearing reports by the leaders of both groups, Maurice Spector and William Krehm, the plenum adopted the following motions:

"1. That we make another effort for comradely collaboration, without recrimination, of the Toronto membership within one branch, including all of those who are now members.

"2. That the National Committee supports fully the political tendency represented by Comrade Spector and considers it as the basis for united collaboration.

"3. The National Committee demands from the Toronto membership that this be adhered to on penalty of measures to be taken against those who fail.

"4. That we accept as a perspective the proposals made by Comrade Spector for an autonomous Canadian section of the Left Opposition in the sense that the first practical steps in that direction, such as the launching of a paper, establishment of an editorial board, etc., to be taken as soon as the branch has reached a sufficient degree of collaboration and stability."

A reunification was eventually achieved, but the Krehm group split shortly thereafter, forming the League for a Revolutionary Workers Party, which collaborated with a group of the same name in the U.S., led by B.J. Field. The Canadian branches of the CLA formed the Workers Party of Canada in 1934.

44. This document was entitled "The Situation in the American Opposition: Prospect and Retrospect." It attempted to trace the origins of the dispute, pinning the blame on Cannon's attitude and conduct going back to early 1930. The document's theme was Cannon's alleged "conservatism," lack of administrative ability, and opposition to the younger leaders. Differences on international questions were minimized, and Cannon's emphasis on them was alleged to be a factional ploy.

45. The June 29 document signed by Abern, Glotzer, and Shachtman was entitled "The Results of the Plenum of the National Committee."

46. The NC majority's point-by-point reply to this document was entitled "Reply of the N.C. to the Minority Statement" and was signed by Cannon and Swabeck.

47. Bulletin no. 3 contained Shachtman's statement on the Swabeck article, as well as the March 22 answer to it by Cannon and Swabeck, "Internal Problems of the Communist League of America (Opposition)," printed earlier in this volume.

48. At an NC meeting on July 14, 1932, Shachtman insisted that "The Situation in the American Opposition: Prospect and Retrospect" be published in the Internal Bulletin. Cannon made a motion that this be done "only after adequate reply has been made by the NC." The minutes do not show that a formal assignment was made to prepare the reply, but this is apparently a draft of it. Neither Cannon's draft reply nor the Shachtman-Glotzer-Abern document was ever printed in the bulletin.

49. No such appendix was found in the Cannon archives.

50. Shachtman's letter of December 1, 1931, expressed a

favorable opinion of the Spanish section leadership (which Trotsky said was committing "all imaginable mistakes") and attacked Molinier for "antagonizing" them. Shachtman called for liquidating the International Secretariat because he thought it lacked political authority and was dependent on Molinier for material support. He also proposed a series of changes in the leadership of the French section.

51. The Bordigists, led by Amadeo Bordiga, were the first Italian group to adhere to the International Left Opposition, before splitting from it in late 1932. Their ultraleft politics included opposition in principle to the united front tactic.

52. Cannon's introduction, published in the February 15, 1931, *Militant,* is reprinted in *The Left Opposition in the U.S. 1928–31.*

53. Shachtman's statement at the plenum condemned the activities of Landau, Naville, Mill-Felix, and other groupings within the ILO. Regarding his association with the attacks against the Molinier leadership of the French section, he stated, "I repudiate of course any association of my name with such a campaign." He further stated, "The proposal made by me in my Paris letter to Comrade Trotsky looking towards a solution of the sharp situation in the [French] Ligue, were not based on fundamental considerations. I regard them as a casual episodic opinion, which I now view as incorrect and superseded by what is said in the present statement."

54. A draft on the situation in the New York branch was found with this document in the Cannon archives; it was later incorporated into Cannon's report on the results of the membership referendum, published December 29, 1932, in the Internal Bulletin and reprinted in this volume.

55. This committee was the U.S. affiliate of the World Congress Against War, led by Henri Barbusse, Romain Rolland, H.G. Wells, Albert Einstein, Theodore Dreiser, Maxim Gorky, and others. The August 8 New York conference was attended by 200 people, mostly CP members. The CLA was represented by Cannon, Oehler, and Shachtman. At the height of its "third period" politics, the CP had called

Baldwin a "social fascist."

56. The CLA resolution, published in the same issue of the *Militant* as this open letter, gave a class analysis of imperialist war and exposed the hypocrisy of capitalist peace conferences and disarmament plans. It went on to state that "The imperialists have a permanent hatred for the Soviet Union not only because of the economic advances it has made, but primarily because it is the fatherland of the workers everywhere, the beacon light which inspires the proletariat through the world to intensify its fight for emancipation from capitalism. . . . War against Russia is a military continuation and prolongation of the attack upon the proletariat in every country."

    In opposing pacifist and liberal leadership of the antiwar movement, it stated, "The struggle against war, therefore, is primarily the struggle against one's own ruling class and does not begin only when war has broken out. It must be carried out in the same class spirit: before, during and after the outbreak of war." Concretely, it urged a united front in Germany to defeat fascism and called for an international congress of the Second International, Third International, and all workers' organizations to organize a united front against the imperialist war danger and the threat of fascism in Germany.

57. Baldwin answered Cannon's letter on August 12. He wrote that he had been assured by the organizers of the conference that all opponents of war would be admitted. He also said that he had been informed that all delegates who had arrived before the police shut the doors had been seated, and that Shachtman had given a long presentation on the CLA resolution. Actually Shachtman had only been able to read the resolution.

58. Clarke and Jack Carmody had run out of money in their field organizing, and Clarke went to Chicago to try to raise some more. After a speech to the Chicago branch, he collected $40; this windfall put them back on the road.

59. The Illinois miners' strike began on April 1 over a wage cut to below $6.10 a day. After the official UMW leadership

signed a contract for $5 a day, miners protested with demonstrations and continued the strike. In the midst of this battle an independent union, the Progressive Miners of America, was formed in Gillespie, Illinois, on September 1. It represented 35,000 miners. Carmody had written a *Militant* article on the strike maintaining that it was revolutionary and that the miners showed revolutionary consciousness because of their willingness to use arms. He thought it was a harbinger that the rest of the proletariat was "passing over from the defensive to the offensive." Clarke thought Carmody's article should be changed to say that this was only true of the vanguard. The new union leaders themselves eventually accepted the pay cut in exchange for union recognition.

60. B.J. Field, a member of the New York branch, was expelled for violating discipline in 1932. Shortly thereafter, he made a personal trip to Turkey where he visited Trotsky and offered his collaboration on several projects. The publication on Trotsky's recommendation of some of Field's articles on economic matters in the European Opposition press touched off an angry response by Cannon and other CLA leaders; they saw it as a disregard for the decisions of the American league.

The CLA leadership was especially sensitive because it followed on the heels of an experience involving Albert Weisbord that seemed in their eyes to indicate a pattern of conduct by Trotsky. Weisbord had also made a trip to Turkey and held discussions with Trotsky. Trotsky later urged the CLA to open a bridge to Weisbord and explore the possibility for fusion, a proposal the CLA leadership was skeptical about. The *Militant* subsequently published several of Weisbord's documents as part of a public discussion. But instead of pursuing common work and discussions on a leadership level, Weisbord called public meetings where the CLA branches and members were invited to discuss unity. The CLA NC answered Weisbord politically in a statement in the *Militant* and broke off unity discussions in late October 1932.

61. An international conference of the Left Opposition was held in February 1933. Documents from that meeting are contained in *Documents of the Fourth International: The Formative Years (1933–40)* (New York: Pathfinder Press, 1973).
62. In Des Moines, three CLA sympathizers had been expelled from the CP, and ten other members walked out in protest. In Davenport, three CP members had called for studying the program of the Left Opposition, and they subsequently formed a CLA branch. In Pittsburgh, the CP rank and file had rebelled against the bureaucratic practices of the party's district organizer and had succeeded in getting him replaced; Gordon had reported an openness to the CLA's ideas on the part of some CP members there.
63. The Shachtman faction was on a campaign against sending Swabeck to Europe to represent the CLA in discussions with Trotsky and with other sections of the International Left Opposition.
64. F. Petras, a Greek CLA member from New York, had written a letter to Pete Vomvas, a Greek sympathizer in Pittsburgh, commenting on the internal debate in the CLA. The NC meeting of January 5, 1933, discussed the matter and voted to demand an explanation from Petras of this violation of discipline.
65. In a letter dated October 20, 1932, Trotsky wrote, "The fact that the article of Comrade Field appeared in the Opposition press without a previous agreement with you is really not correct. For this I will assume the major responsibility and I am ready, if you consider it useful, to submit a corresponding apology to all of the sections." *(Writings of Leon Trotsky [1932])* But Trotsky advised the CLA to find some way to neutralize the effects of Field's organizational conduct while continuing to collaborate with him in work on questions related to economics. Soon after this the league resumed collaboration with Field. He was readmitted to membership in March 1933, only to be expelled again in February 1934 for indisciplined conduct in a strike of hotel workers in New York. This incident is covered later in this volume.

66. Trotsky was able to get a visa to visit Denmark in November 1932 when a Social Democratic student group invited him to give a lecture on the Russian revolution. While there, he held a number of discussions with members of various European sections of the Left Opposition to help prepare the upcoming international conference. Although these were informal discussions, the Soviet government charged that Trotsky was using his visit in Copenhagen to hold a political conference. Under this pressure, the Danish government withdrew his visa.

67. In addition to the demagogic factional use of this issue by Shachtman's supporters, Cannon also feared that this issue could be picked up by the CP, which was then calling for a "militant workers' antireligious movement."

68. This is a reference to the CP's "mass trial" of one of its members—Finnish immigrant August Yokinen—on March 1, 1931, on charges of racist treatment of Blacks at a CP Finnish dance in Harlem. A trial was held before 1,500 people where Yokinen was condemned by a "workers' jury." As a result of the publicity, Yokinen was arrested and deported to Finland. Cannon's comments on this affair are contained in *The Left Opposition in the U.S. 1928–31*.

69. In his letter of December 26, Dunne wrote, "The Minneapolis motion on the international delegate does not have any of the significance that you apparently attribute to it; we were not satisfied with the formulation, neither was Cowl: it came at the end of an almost unlimited debate on the whole question of our attitude toward international questions, during which the factional attitude of Cowl and his friends was brought out in the open for the enlightenment of the comrades; it was an unusually small meeting and in the small hours of the morning, due principally to sheer exhaustion—we let it slide."

70. In their statement to the January 10 NC meeting, Swabeck and Oehler said: "The proposal of Comrades Abern and Shachtman to restrict the functioning of Comrade Cannon to the service he can render in [his] spare time while working for a living elsewhere . . . can only tend to

narrow down the scope of our activities, to render the financial crisis chronic and to consecrate the league to stagnation as a literary circle. The difference reflected in the contrasting proposals are not mere disagreements over a 'practical' matter. They go to the heart of the conflict concerning the *kind* of organization that is to be built, its opportunities, perspectives, and tasks—a conflict which is going deeper and taking on a fundamental character. To dispense with professional functionaries; or to restrict their selection to those having private means of support; or to propose an editor as the sole full-time functionary of the league—this corresponds in no way with the true conception of the present tasks of the league. . . . The course now must be to tighten the organization internally, to strengthen its political-organizing staff, to establish communist discipline and responsibility, to cleanse the league of triflers, windbags, and bohemians, to insist on activities and sacrifices from every member. The Bolshevik struggle for these aims is inextricably bound up with any serious orientation toward increased and more effective participation in the class struggle and in the party movement. Talk of the latter without supporting the former is only phrase-mongering."

71. On January 11, 1933, the *Daily Worker* printed a call for a conference of New York State Trade Union Committee for Unemployment Insurance, on January 22, inviting representatives from other workers' organizations to attend. This partial turn toward united–front-type activity marked the beginning of a radical shift away from the CP's "third period" policy.

72. The Amsterdam congress was held August 27–29, 1932. After having put forward an ultraleft stance for several years in which they referred to their opponents as "social fascists," this conference signaled a turn by the Stalinists toward collaboration with bourgeois liberal forces on a pacifist basis.

73. This was the first time that the CLA was officially recognized by a Stalinist-organized conference. In addition to

its own delegate, the league had delegates from five trade unions, the Spartacus Youth Club, the Greek Workers Club, and the *Unser Kamf* Jewish Workers Club.

74. On December 28–29, 1932, a student antiwar conference of 500–600 was held in Chicago sponsored by the National Students League as an offshoot of the international congress held in Amsterdam in August. The CLA's Spartacus Youth Clubs issued a statement to the conference signed by its twenty delegates (printed in the January 7, 1933, *Militant*), calling for united actions led by working-class youth, denouncing the League of Nations, and calling for defense of the Soviet Union. However, the SYC delegates voted in favor of the main resolution at the conference, which had a pacifist character, and one member—Manny Geltman—was elected to the permanent committee that was established.

    At the CLA NC meeting of January 9 Cannon criticized the affirmative vote and the *Militant* coverage, and moved that Geltman be instructed to resign from the permanent committee. At the NC meeting of January 23, Shachtman and Abern defended the actions of the youth delegates. They called for Geltman not to resign, but rather to propose that the antiwar organization established by the conference be converted into a predominantly working-class united front. On a number of motions related to the conference, the NC was divided two against two. The dispute was finally resolved, and the February 20 *Militant* printed Geltman's statement of resignation from the permanent committee.

75. Trotsky's October 1932 letter, "Mill as a Stalinist Agent," (signed "Gourov") is reprinted in *Writings of Leon Trotsky (1932)*.

76. Frank Farrington and Alexander Howat were "progressive" miners' officials who broke with the Lewis leadership of the UMW and formed a "Reorganized United Mine Workers of America" in March 1930. Under their leadership, which was supported by Muste and the CPLA, the new movement was unable to stand up to the Lewis forces,

which had the backing of the government and employers. Following a March 1931 court decision backing the legality of the Lewis union, the Howat leadership brought the movement back into the official UMW. This collapse had a disorienting effect on militant forces among the miners.

77. On January 30, 1933, German President Hindenburg appointed Adolf Hitler as chancellor and head of a coalition cabinet of the Nazis, Nationalists, and other ultraright forces. Hitler began using the power of his office to destroy his political opponents and crush the German workers' movement. The Social Democrats and Stalinists failed to put up any serious resistance. The International Left Opposition launched a campaign to get out the truth about the German situation through mass meetings and stepped-up sales of its press. The CLA organized big meetings throughout New York City, sent Hugo Oehler on a speaking tour, and put out the *Militant* three times a week for a month.

78. In the course of his speeches on the German crisis, Cannon had raised the need for the Soviet Union to be prepared to use the Red Army to come to the defense of the German workers against Hitler should the need or the opportunity arise—especially given the danger that a fascist victory posed for the Soviet Union. The CP accused Cannon of a "provocation" to precipitate an imperialist war against the Soviet Union. In reply to these slanders Cannon submitted an article for the *Militant* entitled "The Red Army and the German Revolution." In that article he denied he had called for a Soviet "march on Germany," and wrote, "The Stalinist demagogy around this question is in essence a capitulation before bourgeois public opinion. . . . It is not the danger of provoking a war on the Soviet Union that might be avoided. It is the danger that the Soviet Union and the world working class will be taken unawares and fail of the necessary preparation in a war that is inevitable if fascism triumphs in Germany."

However, when Cannon submitted the article to the NC for discussion, Shachtman prepared a counterstatement. Cannon felt that Shachtman's statement, while containing generalities about having no objection in principle to using the Red Army, tended to give credence to the Stalinist arguments. Cannon subsequently introduced the resolution printed here, as well as a reply to Shachtman's statement. These and other documents of the controversy were printed in Internal Bulletin no. 10. In his "Note on Shachtman's Statement on Germany and the Red Army," printed in that bulletin, Cannon added the following postscript:

"The recent alarming information from Comrade Trotsky about the internal condition of the Red Army, which directly affects its *capacity* to fulfill its proper role in the present circumstances, places an extraordinary restriction on public utterances on the question. That alone compels me to refrain from publishing my article on the Red Army in the *Militant.* But the fundamental question of the international tasks of the Red Army remains unaffected. From the standpoint of an internationalist the new information about the internal *weakness* of the Red Army—a weakness resulting from the accumulated effects of Stalinist policy—is not a reason to make concessions to the Stalinist conception of its nationally limited *role*. On the contrary it is a reason to oppose it all the more firmly."

79. In March 1920 the bourgeois government of Poland invaded the Ukraine. The Red Army counteroffensive successfully pushed the invaders out, and began a drive into Poland that reached the outskirts of Warsaw. However, the Red Army was then driven back and the USSR was forced to accept peace terms that ceded to Poland territory in the Ukraine and Byelorussia.

80. August 4, 1914, was the date that the German Social Democratic Party voted war credits in the Reichstag, thereby indicating its support to German imperialism in World War I. Other major Social Democratic parties followed suit, and that date is therefore generally synonymous with the collapse of the entire Second International.

81. This article can be found in *The Struggle Against Fascism in Germany* (New York: Pathfinder Press, 1971).

82. The article referred to is "I See War with Germany," which

can be found in *Writings of Leon Trotsky (1932)*.

83. Shachtman's motion had a sectarian slant; it criticized the CLA fraction in the PMA, especially Gerry Allard, for not counterposing the CLA's politics to those of the "progressives." It amalgamated with this an attack on Cannon for speaking at the Gillespie conference as a representative of "left-wing workers in New York" rather than as a delegate of the CLA. After further discussion in the NC and a letter from Trotsky that supported Cannon's tactical approach in this situation, Cannon and Shachtman reached agreement on tactics in the Progressive Miners union.

84. This CP-organized conference for unemployment insurance and relief was held March 5–7. As with the New York City conference held in January, CLA members were again able to be officially recognized as delegates and to address the conference.

85. The conference organizers had proposed the meeting adopt the call for a general strike.

86. Dewitt C. Webb was a World War I veteran active in the 1932 march on Washington of 20,000 demanding immediate payment of the bonus that had been promised veterans. Webb was an honorary member of the PMA and a CLA sympathizer. He and John Wang were framed on weapons charges during a picket at the Peabody Coal Company. The PMA "progressives" had decided not to appeal their sentence, and Angelo wanted advice on how to continue the defense effort.

87. Twenty-two miners had been put on trial in Taylorville, Illinois, on charges of murdering a Peabody mine boss in Kincaid in 1931. Rather than organizing a militant class-struggle defense, the PMA leadership, on the advice of its lawyers, had adopted a stance that stressed reliance on the courts.

88. This Open Letter was published together with a "Manifesto of the Left Opposition" that was addressed "to the members of the C.P.U.S.A. and to all Communist Workers."

89. Trotsky's criticisms were outlined in a letter to Arne Swabeck

on March 7, 1933, which is reprinted as an appendix to this volume.

90. The NC minutes include the following statement preceding this final motion: "On the point to follow, we send you two motions, one by Cannon, and one by Shachtman, which, as is to be seen, represent different shadings and emphasis. Since a matter of tactics alone is involved, we have decided to leave the execution to the steering committee of Allard, Angelo, Glotzer, and Oehler."

    Shachtman's countermotion stated: "In the Executive Committee of the conference our comrades shall propose to invite fraternal delegates from labor political organizations to greet the conference, pointing out that they are much closer to the heart and nature of the conference than the 'farmers' organizations' that were invited. Should this be turned down by the EC, our steering committee should bring in the proposal as a minority report, without allowing themselves to be maneuvered into a position where this becomes the central issue of dispute at the conference. Should it be adopted, Comrade Oehler should submit a credential from the CLA(O) and greet the conference in its name, pointing out our position as outlined in the motions adopted by the NC and giving a lead for the crystallization of the left-wing and progressive elements away from the right-wing and job-selling elements."

91. Oehler had proposed that the conference should set up a national left-wing trade union center similar in program to the old Trade Union Educational League.

92. Cannon's motions of April 5, 1933, included the following: "(1) All decisions in regard to the national conference of the league, arrangements, representation, and other organizational questions, shall be subject to ratification by the International Secretariat in case of disagreement in the National Committee. (2) The functioning NC is to consist of all members resident in New York. Disputed questions may be appealed by referendum to the full committee. (3) As previously decided, Comrade Cannon shall arrange a speaking tour to the West, timing his schedule so as to be

in Chicago as a delegate of the league to the Mooney congress on April 30. Thereafter he is to go into the Illinois field for a period of work among the miners in cooperation with Comrade Oehler, who is also to remain in the field. (4) During the absence of Comrade Cannon, Comrade Abern shall conduct the work of the national office as acting secretary. . . ." At the next meeting Shachtman made countermotions that would have put off Cannon's trip; since Cannon and Shachtman were the only PC members in New York to vote on the motions, there was a deadlock.

93. Unity discussions with Weisbord were resumed in March 1933; in April a joint statement was published and some joint public meetings were planned. This process was broken off in November after Weisbord made public attacks on the league and it became clear that the politics of the two groups were diverging.

94. The ILO held a plenum in May attended by both Swabeck and Shachtman, where the CLA faction fight was discussed. In a letter written to Cannon on May 15, Swabeck wrote the following: "At the plenum we have arrived at an agreement for the discontinuation and final liquidation of the factional struggle in the league. Comrade Shachtman and myself are in accord and have undertaken to carry the agreement out." This agreement was codified in a resolution adopted by the plenum, which was printed in CLA Internal Bulletin no. 14. The eleven points of this resolution were based on the general propositions of Trotsky's proposals.

In a letter written on June 9 to his supporters, following a discussion with Trotsky, Shachtman made a criticism of his faction's conduct: "Take our opposition to Swabeck's leaving for Europe: it was neither well-formulated nor well-founded, and it is necessary to acknowledge that frankly. . . . It is true that I feel now more confirmed than ever in the opposition we manifested to all the bureaucratic actions and conduct of the majority in the past period. But even here, where I still feel we were so thoroughly correct, our position, and the position of the league, would have been strengthened immeasurably if we had tried ten times harder to see to it that we, at least, did nothing, by word or deed, that would contribute to the tension in the league."

While remnants of the factional situation flared up occasionally in the next few months, this agreement was generally upheld and marked the end of the Cannon-Shachtman faction fight.

95. The Rank and File movement in Illinois was an insurgent miners' movement formed in April 1931 led by Ray Edmondson that opposed the Howat-Farrington capitulation to the Lewis-led UMW. It itself eventually was forced back into the UMW.

96. At the Gillespie conference, right-wing Socialists had presented a motion to endorse and send delegates to a "Continental Congress of Workers and Farmers for Economic Reconstruction" in Washington, from which Communists and left-wing forces were to be excluded. Oehler, Glotzer, and other left-wing delegates opposed this motion, and proposed instead that an inquiry be sent to the Washington congress organizers as to whether all working-class organizations would be invited; if not, then the PMA would refuse to send delegates. Allard and the CP delegates voted for the original motion.

97. Following the red-baiting attacks launched against Allard and the PMA, Allard published a statement in the April 14 *Progressive Miner*, limiting himself to denying membership in the Communist Party.

98. The CLA leadership was able to reach an agreement with Allard, at least temporarily (in late 1933 he left the CLA and joined the CPLA); shortly afterward, he was removed from his position as editor of the *Progressive Miner* as part of the rightward shift of the PMA leadership.

99. On January 21, 1933, Tom Mooney, the country's most famous class-war prisoner, issued a call for a national congress in Chicago April 30–May 2, under the auspices of the Tom Mooney Molders' Defense Committee. Declaring that "The time has come when all organizations fighting for my freedom must be welded into the widest possible

united front," Mooney addressed his appeal "to every AFL union and all working-class organizations." Mooney's authority forced the CP, which had dominated his defense activities, to go along with what turned out to be a broad united front gathering, despite attempts to sabotage it by the leaderships of the AFL and SP.

The conference was attended by 1,048 delegates, including 39 from the Left Opposition. Cannon addressed the congress on the first day and presented the CLA's proposals. These were submitted to the Resolutions Committee, of which Cannon was a member. The committee subsequently issued a majority report by CP leader Clarence Hathaway. On behalf of the Resolutions Committee minority, Cannon told the congress that all the main points of the Left Opposition resolution had been incorporated, and he proposed an amendment to Hathaway's resolution reading: "Each organization entering the united front obligates itself to discipline in action but retains its full independence and its right to criticism." When put to the vote, the Left Opposition resolution received 63 votes. Cannon was subsequently elected to the National Mooney Council of Action on behalf of the CLA. Almost immediately after the congress, the CP again began to undercut the movement in sectarian fashion.

100. The CLA was in the midst of a fund-raising campaign to aid the German Left Opposition, a drive coordinated by Martin Abern. In a letter to Cannon who was on a trip to Minneapolis, Rose Karsner had written that Abern was in favor of sending money to Germany even if it meant skipping an issue of the *Militant*. Karsner had raised with Abern that the CLA should also be raising money to enable Swabeck to return to the United States. This suggestion was evidently the source of the "agitation" within the New York branch being waged by Abern's factional supporters. While Swabeck was stuck in Europe for lack of money, Shachtman had received $200 to attend the May ILO plenum (where the agreement to end the faction fight was reached), when only $150 had been allocated.

101. The Gourov "letters" were actually three documents: a letter dated July 15, 1933, signed by G. Gourov (Trotsky); a discussion article written in the form of a conversation, dated July 20, 1933; and the minutes of a discussion of July 27, 1933. The letter is reprinted in *Writings of Leon Trotsky (1932–33)*; the other two documents are in *Writings of Leon Trotsky (1933–34)*.

102. The program of action included twelve points: (1) issuing a public manifesto on the new course, following the completion of the branch discussions; (2) moving the national office to Chicago; (3) transforming the *Militant* into a popular agitational paper at a cheaper price; (4) establishing a theoretical magazine; (5) accepting members on a broader basis; (6) establishing united front relations and joint activities with other working-class organizations, especially left-wing groups inside reformist or centrist groups; (7) forming nuclei within reformist and centrist organizations; (8) forming peripheral organizations on a broad basis; (9) getting members into mass organizations, especially trade unions; (10) strengthening the central apparatus, including putting on at least one field organizer; (11) organizing tours by NC members; and (12) raising a special fund for this.

    The move to Chicago was later postponed, and eventually the idea was abandoned.

103. The Conference of Left Socialist and Communist Organizations held in Paris, August 27–28, 1933, was attended by fourteen predominantly centrist organizations, as well as by the ILO. The ILO issued a declaration (manifesto) written by Trotsky calling for the creation of the Fourth International and outlining its principles, a document reprinted in *Writings of Leon Trotsky (1933–34)*. At the conference, the ILO was able to form a Bloc of Four with three other organizations, which issued a common declaration in favor of a Fourth International that can be found in *Documents of the Fourth International: The Formative Years (1933–40)*.

104. A series of strikes was occurring at the time. Most prominent was a strike by 60,000 silk workers, centered in Paterson,

New Jersey, that began in August. Also on strike were 35,000 miners in Pennsylvania, 60,000 dressmakers in New York, and numerous other workers in New York's garment industry.

105. In August 1933 a general strike forced the ouster of Cuban dictator Gerardo Machado. Out of the continuing revolutionary upsurge emerged a nationalist government, which was eventually ousted by Fulgencio Batista, who then became Cuba's strongman.

106. A subsequent article by Trotsky dated October 1, 1933, "The Class Nature of the Soviet State," (contained in *Writings of Leon Trotsky [1933–34]*) was designed to answer the questions that were being raised as to whether the break with the Comintern signified a change in the class character of the Soviet state. After reaffirming defense of the October revolution and the Soviet Union, Trotsky wrote: "How [can we] approach the reorganization of the Soviet state? And, is it possible to solve this task with peaceful methods?

"We must set down, first of all, as an immutable axiom that this task can be solved only by a revolutionary *party*. The fundamental historical task is to create the revolutionary party in the USSR from among the healthy elements of the old party and from among the youth. . . . After the experiences of the last few years, it would be childish to suppose that the Stalinist bureaucracy can be removed by means of a party or soviet congress. . . . No normal 'constitutional' ways remain to remove the ruling clique. The bureaucracy can be compelled to yield power into the hands of the proletariat vanguard only by *force*.

"The question of seizing power will arise as a practical question for the new party only when it will have consolidated around itself the majority of the working class. In the course of such a radical change in the relation of forces, the bureaucracy would become more and more isolated, more and more split. As we know, the social roots of the bureaucracy lie in the proletariat, if not in its active support, then, at any rate, in its 'toleration.' When the proletariat springs into action, the Stalinist apparatus will remain suspended in midair. Should it still attempt to resist, it will then be necessary to apply against it not the measures of civil war but rather the measures of a police character. In any case, what will be involved is not an armed insurrection against the dictatorship but the removal of a malignant growth upon it.

"A real civil war could develop not between the Stalinist bureaucracy and the resurgent proletariat but between the proletariat and the active forces of the counterrevolution. In the event of an open clash between the two mass camps, there cannot even be talk of the bureaucracy playing an independent role. Its polar flanks would be flung to the different sides of the barricade. The fate of the subsequent development would be determined, of course, by the outcome of the struggle. . . .

"Which is closer: the danger of the collapse of the Soviet power that has been sapped by bureaucratism or the hour of the consolidation of the proletariat around a new party that is capable of saving the October heritage? There is no a priori answer to such a question; the struggle will decide. A major historical test—which may be a war—will determine the relation of forces. It is clear, in any case, that, with the further decline of the world proletarian movement and the further extension of the fascist domination, it is not possible to maintain the Soviet power for any length of time by means of the internal forces alone. The fundamental condition for the only rock-bottom reform of the Soviet state is the victorious spread of the *world revolution.*"

In line with this perspective, Trotsky called for the formation of a new party of the Fourth International in the Soviet Union.

107. In 1932, on Trotsky's initiative, the CLA had changed its previous position advocating the formation of an independent labor party in the United States. This new position was held by the CLA and its successors until 1938 when, again on Trotsky's initiative, the Socialist Workers Party adopted the position of advocating the formation of a labor party based on the unions. Trotsky's 1932 article, "The Labor Party Question in the United States," is printed

in *Writings of Leon Trotsky (1932)*. His position in 1938 is outlined in *The Transitional Program for Socialist Revolution*, (New York: Pathfinder Press, 1977). A review of the SWP's thinking on this question during the 1930s can be found in Farrell Dobbs's *Teamster Power* (Pathfinder Press, 1973, 2008).

108. Trotsky's letter, contained in *Writings of Leon Trotsky (1933–34)*, suggested to the tiny British section that it consider entering the left-centrist Independent Labour Party.

109. At Trotsky's suggestion, Cannon had written Groves on September 19 offering to send the British section a free weekly bundle of 100 *Militants* and an assortment of literature for its work in the ILP.

110. These eleven points, contained in "The International Left Opposition, Its Tasks and Methods," read as follows:

"In accordance with the spirit and the sense of the decisions of the first four world congresses [of the Comintern], and in continuation of these decisions, the Left Opposition establishes the following principles, develops them theoretically, and carries them through practically:

"1. *The independence of the proletarian party*, always and under all conditions; condemnation of the policy toward the Kuomintang in 1924–28; condemnation of the policy of the Anglo-Russian Committee; condemnation of the Stalinist theory of two-class (worker-and-peasant) parties and of the whole practice based on this theory; condemnation of the policy of the Amsterdam Congress, and by which the Communist Party was dissolved in the pacifist swamp.

"2. Recognition of the international and thereby of the *permanent character of the proletarian revolution;* rejection of the theory of socialism in one country and of the policy of national Bolshevism in Germany which complements it (the platform of 'national liberation').

"3. Recognition of the *Soviet state as a workers' state* in spite of the growing degeneration of the bureaucratic regime; the unconditional obligation of every worker to defend the Soviet state against imperialism as well as against internal counterrevolution.

"4. Condemnation of the economic policy of the Stalinist faction both in its stage of *economic opportunism* in 1923 to 1928 (struggle against 'superindustrialization,' staking all on the kulaks) as well as in its stage of *economic adventurism* in 1928 to 1932 (overaccelerated tempo of industrialization, 100 percent collectivization, administrative liquidation of the kulaks as a class); condemnation of the criminal bureaucratic legend that 'the Soviet state has already entered into socialism'; recognition of the necessity of a return to the realistic economic policies of Leninism.

"5. Recognition of the necessity of systematic Communist work in the proletarian mass organizations, particularly in the reformist trade unions; condemnation of the theory and practice of the Red trade union organization in Germany [RGO] and similar formations in other countries.

"6. Rejection of the formula of the *'democratic dictatorship of the proletariat and the peasantry'* as a separate regime distinguished from the *dictatorship of the proletariat*, which wins the support of the peasant and the oppressed masses in general; rejection of the anti-Marxist theory of the peaceful 'growing-over' of the democratic dictatorship into the socialist one.

"7. Recognition of the necessity to mobilize the masses under *transitional slogans* corresponding to the concrete situation in each country, and particularly under *democratic slogans* insofar as it is a question of struggle against feudal relations, national oppression, or different varieties of openly imperialistic dictatorship (fascism, Bonapartism, etc.).

"8. Recognition of the necessity of a developed *united-front policy* with respect to the mass organizations of the working class, both of trade union and political character, including the Social Democracy as a party; condemnation of the ultimatistic slogan 'only from below,' which in practice means a rejection of the united front and, consequently, a refusal to create soviets; condemnation of the opportunistic application of the united-front policy as in the Anglo-Russian Committee (a bloc with the leaders without the masses and against the masses); double condemnation of the policy of the present German Central Committee, which combines the ultimatistic slogan 'only from below' with the opportunistic practice of parliamentary pacts with the leaders of the Social Democracy.

"9. Rejection of the theory of *social fascism* and of the entire practice bound up with it as serving fascism on the one hand and the Social Democracy on the other.

"10. Differentiation of *three groupings* within the camp of communism: the Marxist, the centrist, and the right; recognition of the impermissibility of a political alliance with the right against centrism; support of centrism against the class enemy; irreconcilable and systematic struggle against centrism and its zigzag policies.

"11. Recognition of *party democracy* not only in words but also in fact; ruthless condemnation of the Stalinist plebiscitary regime (the rule of usurpers, gagging the thought and the will of the party, deliberate suppression of information from the party, etc.).

"The fundamental principles enumerated above, which are of basic importance for the strategy of the proletariat in the present period, place the Left Opposition in irreconcilable hostility to the Stalinist faction which currently dominates the USSR and the Communist International. Recognition of these principles, on the basis of the decisions of the first four congresses of the Comintern, is an indispensable condition for the acceptance of single organizations, groups, and persons into the International Left Opposition."

The entire resolution can be found in *Documents of the Fourth International: The Formative Years (1933–40).*

111. At the joint committee meeting the CLA and Gitlow's Workers Communist League had each proposed their own draft statements. Agreement was not reached, however, largely because of the Gitlowites' rejection of the Declaration of Four.

112. The Fifty-third AFL annual convention began October 10 in Washington, D.C., attended by some 600 delegates.

113. The United Workers Party, formed as a result of the 1931–32

split in the Proletarian Party, was composed of two main tendencies: an ultraleft, anarcho-syndicalist wing led by Paul Mattick; and a tendency led by Tom Dixon, Oscar Peterson, and Sinclair, which was moving in a Marxist direction. The CLA's negotiations with the UWP were designed to win over the latter grouping. The UWP's primary area of activity was the unemployed movement, where it had formed an organization, the Workers Leagues, which were located in Chicago and several other places, with a membership of over 1,000.

114. The Cook County Federation of the Workers League was under the control of the CP. It was preparing a conference in several weeks, and a discussion was under way among the UWP and CLA forces on how to combat its plans to link the Cook County Federation to the CP's national unemployed councils.

115. The Friends of the *Militant* Club in Chicago had been founded in October 1932 by sympathizers of the CLA to give financial support, help circulate the *Militant,* and hold public meetings; it began with about 25 members. In a letter to Cannon of November 24, 1933, Glotzer had written of the frictions that had arisen between the club and the CLA.

"The leaders of the club," Glotzer wrote, "have embarked on a course of open sabotage of the league's activities. If this is what that organization desires nothing can stop them—but they cannot do it under the label of an auxiliary of the Left Opposition. The branch here wasted—I say this advisedly—more time with this group of self-glorifying petty bourgeois, than was worth. . . . We are dealing here with a couple of dilettantes, who ran the club with such an iron hand that they succeeded in narrowing it down to about as narrow as it could be. They desired to be the unofficial kingpins of the Chicago Opposition. They wanted to know everything and still retain their exalted position of sympathizers. Their dissatisfaction springs from this desire to be taken in confidence, which never could take place. We tried to treat them as sympathizers and they won't accept this role. . . . We will take up the question openly and frankly with the club and tell the members, those who are left in the club, just what the situation is and try to bring about a solution in this manner. If this is impossible then we shall propose that their relation to us as an auxiliary be liquidated."

116. A Conference of Revolutionary Socialist Youth Organizations was actually held in late February, at first in Holland and then moved to Belgium. It set up an International Bureau of Revolutionary Youth Organizations. Glotzer was one of several Fourth Internationalist delegates who attended.

117. In San Jose, California, on November 27, a mob lynched two men who were being held for kidnapping and murder. The following day, California Gov. James Rolph stated, "This is the best lesson which California has ever given the country." On October 19 in Princess Anne, Maryland, a young Black man who was being held in jail on suspicion of attacking a white woman, was lynched by 1,000 whites. On November 28, a young Black man being held on the same charge was lynched by 9,000 whites in St. Joseph, Missouri.

118. A general strike of New York hotels began on January 24, 1934, called by the Amalgamated Hotel and Restaurant Workers Union (referred to by Cannon as the Amalgamated Food Workers), an independent union whose secretary was CLA member B.J. Field. Workers at over fifty hotels and restaurants went out on strike, and mass picket lines were set up, including one of over 3,000 at the Waldorf Hotel. On January 30, a rally of 10,000 was held at Madison Square Garden where Cannon was one of the main speakers. The CLA threw all its energies into the strike, assigning a number of leading members to assist, and putting the *Militant* out three times a week.

119. The hotel strike quickly ran up against attempts by the Federal Labor Board to mediate the conflict. Field increasingly began to bend to the pressure of the board and to the labor officialdom; at the same time he disregarded the collaboration of the CLA fraction and national leadership.

In his *History of American Trotskyism, 1928–38* (New York: Pathfinder Press, 1944, 1972, 1995, 2002), Cannon described what happened:

"[Field] had suddenly gone through a certain transformation; from nothing he had suddenly become everything. His picture was in all the New York papers. He was the leader of a great mass movement. . . . He began to carry out his negotiations with these people, and to conduct himself generally, like a Napoleon. . . . He disregarded the fraction of his own party in the union. . . .

"We wanted to help him because we were bound up in the situation as much as he was. All over town, and all over the country in fact, everybody was talking about the Trotskyist strike. Our movement was on trial before the labor movement of the country. All our enemies were hoping for disaster; nobody wanted to help us. . . . No matter how far Field might depart from party policy, it would not be Field who would be remembered and blamed for the failure, but the Trotskyist movement.

"Eventually the hotel strike bogged down for lack of militant policy because of a crawling reliance on the Labor Board which was aiming to scuttle the strike. Days were wasted in futile negotiations with Mayor LaGuardia, while the strike was dying on its feet for proper leadership. . . . We were in danger of having our movement compromised. If we should condone what was being done by Field and his group we could only spread demoralization in our own ranks."

Consequently, in the midst of the strike, the CLA put Field and Aristodimos Caldis on trial for violating party discipline. They were expelled on February 18. The hotel strike was finally called off in early March having failed to achieve its major objectives. Several weeks later, because of the strike's outcome, the CP was able to take over the union leadership and remove Field from his position as secretary; in response, Field led a split from the union.

120. The Conference for Progressive Labor Action had renamed itself the American Workers Party at a convention held in Pittsburgh, December 2–3, 1933. On January 27, 1934, the

Militant printed an open letter from the CLA to the AWP proposing a discussion with the aim of agreeing on a program as the basis for a new, united party. Preliminary discussions began shortly thereafter, and the CLA NC took up this question at its February 26 meeting.

Cannon's motion printed here was opposed by one presented by Hugo Oehler. Oehler stressed that, "The LO will not compromise on principle to form a new party. We will not enter a party that has a non-Marxian program through omissions. Compromise on other questions only on the basis of a fight for these points first." Oehler's position on this question, which had a sectarian bent, was to foreshadow a growing divergence with the CLA's course on this and other questions that eventually led him to form an opposition faction later during the year.

At the March 8 meeting of the National Committee, Cannon reported on the progress of the negotiations with the AWP, outlining an agreement reached for organized collaboration in three areas: trade union work, where the two parties would work together in common unions and industries; unemployed work, where the CLA agreed to support and build the AWP's Unemployed Leagues; and work in a new labor defense organization that would include other working-class forces as well—this became the Non-Partisan Labor Defense.

121. The March 17 *Militant* contained a letter on the situation of the fur workers, most of whom belonged to the CP-led Needle Trades Workers Industrial Union. The letter described how the fur workers had no confidence in the AFL's International Fur Workers' Union, and supported the CP-led union, but that the weakness of this union made it unable to stand up to the united opposition of the ILGWU and the employers. It further stated that the lack of democracy within the CP-led union played into the hands of the ILGWU officialdom.

122. In mid-April, Trotsky's residence at Barbizon, France, was publicized by the local police, and he became the target of a furious witch-hunt campaign in the press, with both the

fascists and the Stalinists demanding his deportation. The government complied and issued a deportation decree, but the expulsion could not be carried out because no other country would accept Trotsky. He remained in France until June 1935, when he was able to move to Norway.

123. During the days of February 11–16, 1934, the Austrian government of Englebert Dollfuss capped a year of repression by shutting down the Social Democratic press. A general strike was called. Armed resistance by Social Democratic workers broke out, which was crushed by the government. Hundreds were killed and thousands imprisoned. That same week, a coup attempt by French fascist and royalist forces, and the subsequent imposition of a right-wing government, led to a one-day general strike and protest demonstrations throughout France.

124. This is apparently a reference to the declaration written by Trotsky entitled "France Is Now the Key to the Situation," in *Writings of Leon Trotsky (1933–34)*.

125. On February 16, 1934, the SP and various New York trade unions had called a rally at Madison Square Garden in solidarity with the Austrian workers' uprising. That meeting, which drew 22,000, was disrupted and physically broken up by an organized group of CP members.

126. According to a report in the *Militant,* the two May Day marches drew a total of 150,000 between them. *Workers Age,* the newspaper of the Lovestoneites (who also supported the SP-led united front rally), reported that 25,000 participated in the CP-sponsored Union Square march, and that 35,000 had marched in the Madison Square event, including a contingent of 15,000 from the ILGWU. Cannon and Manny Garret spoke at the rally following the Madison Square march on behalf of the CLA.

127. Antonio Bellussi was an Italian refugee being threatened with deportation, who was receiving no assistance from the CP's International Labor Defense; as a result of the NPLD's defense campaign, the deportation was prevented and Bellussi found refuge in South America. The four German Communists included one Trotskyist and three members

of the centrist SAP who had been arrested by Dutch police and handed over to the Nazis during the February 1934 international youth congress held in Holland. Harold Robins and Andres Gras were members of the New York hotel workers' union who had been framed up and sentenced to prison terms on assault charges for their participation in the hotel strike.

128. The Minneapolis strikes of Teamsters General Drivers Local 574 began in February 1934 with a strike by coal-yard drivers that helped put the union in a position to organize other sections of the trucking industry. A key role in this and subsequent strikes was played by CLA leaders V.R. Dunne, Carl Skoglund, and others. On May 16, Local 574 launched a strike of 5,000 workers aimed at winning union recognition. The ten-day strike was marked by mass picketing and flying picket squads that effectively shut down the trucking industry. In addition, it saw several massive battles at the city market of organized strikers against police and special deputies, where the repressive forces were driven off the streets. A Women's Auxiliary was also created. The strike was concluded by a victorious settlement that gave the workers union recognition. A third strike took place in July–August, culminating in the complete victory of Local 574. A full account of these strikes is contained in Farrell Dobbs's *Teamster Rebellion,* (New York: Pathfinder Press, 1972, 2004).

129. Under the impact of the rising labor upsurge, auto workers had begun forming a union in 1933, the Mechanics Educational Society. Due to its success in recruiting workers, the AFL reluctantly began to give its support to the drive. A strike date was set for March 20, 1934. As the strike loomed, the federal government intervened to prevent the workers from going out, and got a postponement from the AFL leaders, after which President Roosevelt personally held negotiations with AFL President William Green. On March 25, the AFL accepted a settlement whereby a three-person board would be set up composed of representatives from the employers and the union, and an "impartial" professor.

This "impartial" board reached an agreement that maintained the open shop and gave the company union a firm base.

130. The Toledo Auto-Lite strike, led by members of the American Workers Party, did win union recognition when the bosses signed a six-month contract on June 4 recognizing the union and granting a 5 percent wage increase.

131. The convention of the Socialist Party, held July 1–4, 1934, was the scene of a sharp struggle for control of the party between the right wing (the "Old Guard"), which had previously controlled the party, and a centrist grouping (the "Militants") led by Norman Thomas, the party's most prominent spokesperson. By a substantial majority, the convention adopted the resolutions of the Militants, which was to set the stage for a split by the Old Guard in early 1936. A third current emerged on the eve of the 1934 convention, the Revolutionary Policy Committee, which had issued a programmatic statement signed by 47 members. In an article in the May 5, 1934, *Militant,* Cannon wrote that "for the first time since 1921, a group of more or less influential party members takes issue with the reformist position on fundamental principle questions and approaches the standpoint of revolutionary Marxism, that is, of communism." The CLA sought out the leaders of this current for discussion, with the aim of winning over a number of them. Cannon was sent to Detroit to observe the convention, as well as to hold discussions with RPC members and evaluate the political prospects for further collaboration.

132. A conference of the Second International had been held in Paris, August 21–25, 1933, under the impact of the fascist victory in Germany. Three currents emerged at the conference: a right wing led by the German, British, and Scandinavian parties; a center led by the Austrian party; and a small left wing led by the Polish Bund. Although still within the framework of centrism, the Bund's resolution condemned many aspects of Social Democratic policy and called for the destruction of the capitalist state and establishment of the dictatorship of the proletariat. Four

of the six delegates from the American SP supported this resolution.

133. Waldman had been a central defender of the Old Guard position at the convention. On the first day of the gathering, he created a scandal by refusing to rise for the singing of the *Internationale*. Sharts caused a stir during the debate on the Declaration of Principles when he declared that "I, as an American, loving America above all nations on the earth, hereby register my declaration that I will stand by America when I see fit, and I will not yield to those red internationalists who have written into this platform the right to say that I must attack my country under all circumstances that they select."

134. Following protracted negotiations and discussions and the publication of a draft program, the CLA addressed a letter to the AWP on September 7 urging the two organizations to take further steps forward in discussing some of the concrete organizational and political questions involved in achieving unification. At the AWP's Active Workers Conference, held September 8–9 outside of Pittsburgh, Muste reported on the progress in the negotiations. The organization gave its approval to continuing the progress toward unification. Subsequently the CLA's New York branches held a membership meeting where the NC's course was unanimously approved.

135. Roosevelt had appointed a three-person board headed by former New Hampshire Gov. John Winant to mediate the strike. The board's proposal was to call for the strikers to return to work, after which the workers' grievances would be investigated.

136. Cannon attended the October 1934 enlarged plenum of the International Communist League (formerly the International Left Opposition) in Paris. While there, he was assigned the task of conducting discussions with leaders of a sizable minority in the French section who were opposed to Trotsky's proposal to enter the French Socialist Party (SFIO), (which became known as the "French turn"), a proposal approved by the ICL plenum. The goal of these

discussions was to maximize the unity of the French section and to reduce the impact of any splits that could not be healed immediately. This letter was Cannon's report to the ICL leadership on the results of his discussions. Upon returning to the U.S., Cannon found the CLA itself was confronted with an organized faction opposed to the "French turn," led by Hugo Oehler.

137. Following continuing negotiations between the CLA and AWP, a preliminary declaration had been drafted by Muste and Shachtman in October as the basis for the united party. At the CLA NC meeting of October 22, where this document was adopted, Oehler attacked it as "entirely inadequate." Shortly thereafter, a series of organizational agreements were arrived at, calling for parity on all leading bodies, and plans were worked out for a unity convention following separate conventions of each party at the end of November. When Cannon returned from France, he took over Shachtman's role in the negotiations with Muste over the programmatic declaration, and a second draft was approved by the CLA NC on November 19, with Oehler voting in favor, despite what he viewed as "serious shortcomings." This draft was to be submitted to conventions of both organizations at the end of November prior to a joint convention of the fused organization.

138. The Gitlow and Field groups had formed an Organizing Committee for a Revolutionary Workers Party in May 1934, although there was no agreement between the two groups on major programmatic questions.

139. Gitlow and Zam both joined the SP, having both recently split from the Lovestoneites. Goldman was expelled from the CLA by the National Committee on October 29, 1934, for his decision to join the SP regardless of the CLA's decisions, and for holding discussions about his views on this with Gitlow, Zam, and others in violation of CLA discipline. Goldman stated that he was in full agreement with the league on all questions except entry into the SP. Relations with Goldman were reestablished in 1936 following the entry of the Trotskyist movement into the SP.

140. The CLA held its third and final convention November 28–30, 1934, in New York, at the same time that the AWP was holding its convention. The CLA gathering was the scene of a bitter factional struggle, with Hugo Oehler and Tom Stamm leading a sizable faction opposed to the "French turn." They also criticized the upcoming fusion with the AWP as being on an inadequate programmatic basis, although they joined in the unanimous vote that approved it. Also vocal at the convention was an antileadership grouping led by Martin Abern and Jack Weber that Cannon characterized as an unprincipled clique. This convention revealed the new alignments that had taken shape in the CLA since the liquidation of the old faction fight. Cannon, Shachtman, and Swabeck teamed up to defend the positions of the NC majority; while Oehler and Stamm (former supporters of Cannon-Swabeck) and Weber and Abern (former supporters of Shachtman) made common cause against the leadership. The organizational report to the convention, upon which this resolution was based, was delivered by Swabeck.

141. The fusion convention of the CLA and the AWP was held November 30–December 2. It adopted the name Workers Party of the United States. AWP leaders had originally proposed that the fused organization should continue to use the name American Workers Party. However, as Muste pointed out in a confidential memorandum to the AWP leadership, dated October 10, 1934, the CLA leaders "raised that both Canadians and Latin Americans strongly object to monopoly of term American by USA and feeling in these countries that this is an unconscious reflection of U.S. imperialism." It was therefore agreed to call the new organization Workers Party *of the U.S.* As part of the unity agreement, the new party organ was named *New Militant,* with Cannon designated as editor. Muste was elected national secretary of the new party.

142. On December 1, 1934, Sergei Kirov, Communist Party secretary in Leningrad, was assassinated by an obscure Soviet employee. The Soviet press claimed the assassination was

the work of a "Zinovievite-Trotskyite conspiracy," and used this slander to whip up a campaign against all potential political opponents. A series of secret trials and executions were quickly held. This marked the beginning of Stalin's purge that eliminated most of the surviving cadres of the Bolshevik Party leadership team assembled by Lenin.

Index

Abern, Martin, 26, 169, 606–8, 637g
  and faction fight, 76, 218–20
Albany State Conference for Labor Legislation, 357–59, 361, 365–71
Allard, Gerry, 333, 364, 382, 399, 637g
  attack on, 411–13
  differences with CLA leadership, 399–400, 406–10
Allen, Devere, 551, 555, 637g
Amalgamated Clothing Workers, 16, 35
Amalgamated Food Workers, 481–86
American Committee for the World Congress Against War, 255, 258
American Federation of Labor (AFL), 16–18, 35–36, 532–33
  affiliation to, 501–2, 541
  Fifty-third Annual Convention of, 453–54
  leadership of, 425–26
  and textile strike, 579–82
American Workers Party (AWP), 36, 39, 637g
  fusion with, 489–92, 573, 576–77
  and internationalism, 492–95
Amsterdam Congress Against War, 312
Amter, Israel, 123–26, 637g

Anarchism, 208–9
Angelo, Joseph, 363, 638g
Anti-Cannon agitation, 145–46
Anti-Cannon group, 226, 228–29
Anti-Semitism, 470
Anti-Socialist Law, 96, 104, 638g
Antiwar movement, 257–58
Antiwar slogans, 69–71
Appeals, 266–67
Argentina, 461
Aristocracy of labor, 163
Armed insurrection, 90, 94–95, 106, 204
Attacks on strikes, 63
Austria, 506–7, 575

Baldwin, Roger, 54, 255–58, 638g
Basky, Louis, 220, 638g
Bauer, Eugene, 586, 638g
Belgium, 461
Bernstein, Eduard, 92, 638–39g
Billings, Warren, 417, 639g
Blacks, 18, 34
  and lynchings, 469
  and Scottsboro case, 127–30
Bleeker, Sylvia, 341–42, 639g
Bolshevik method, 232
Bolshevik-Leninists, 14–15, 198, 374
Bolshevism, 509–10
Bordigists, 242–43, 298, 670n
Bourgeoisie, 343
Brandlerites, 434–35
Brazil, 462

Bridges, Harry, 36
British section, 437–39
Brooklyn transit workers strike, 124
Brown, Bill, 439–40, 536, 639g
Bukharin, Nikolai, 15, 19, 180, 639–40g, 667n
Bulgaria, 200
Bureaucratism, 15, 500, 625
  and CLA, 114–16, 226, 340–41, 629

Cadre building, 148
Cannon group, 25–27, 144
Carmody, Jack, 259–62, 284, 640g
Carter group, 169, 218–19, 290–91
Carter, Joseph, 85–86, 110–11, 563, 640g
  and *The Class Struggles in France*, 89–93, 95–96
Centrism, 548
Chiang Kai-shek, 15
Chicago branch, 166–67
China, 200, 240–41
Clarke, George, 259, 284, 640g
Class Struggle, 182, 640g
Class society, 473
Classes, origin of, 202
Cliques, 165, 285, 607–9
Coal operators, 411–13
Communism, 459
Communism and Syndicalism (Trotsky), 244
Communist International, 14, 195, 443–44, 492, 640g
  break with, 442, 475
  and Germany, 32–33, 373–74
  on leadership, 212
Communist International (*continued*)
  and "third period," 19–20
Communist Manifesto, 492
Communist Party, 19–21, 160–61, 177–78, 208–9, 277, 310–12, 462, 474, 548, 640g
  attacks on Cannon by, 341
  and defense work, 526–27
  and farmers, 20
  and German events, 373
  and Japanese militarism, 69–70
  and May Day, 514–19
  and miners, 324, 329–31
  and Minneapolis strike, 544–45
  proposals from CLA to, 197, 373–75
  and Red Army, 345–46
  and unemployed movement, 309, 311–12, 365–68, 476
  and unions, 152–55, 426, 428–29, 500, 571–72
Communist Party (Germany), 31–33, 373, 445
Communist, 433
Communists, 66–67, 162, 208–9, 414–15
Company unionism, 211
Composition of CLA, 24–25, 279
Concessions to minority, 282–83, 395–96
Conference for Progressive Labor Action (CPLA), 18, 39, 389, 438, 489–90, 641g
  and Gillespie conference, 327–29
Conference of the Left Socialists and Independent Communist Parties, 424

Contract demands, 334–35, 381–82
Cooptations to National Committee, 220, 269–70, 290, 629
Coover, Oscar, 605, 641g
Correspondence, 80–81
Coughlin, Father Charles, 470, 641g
Cowl, Carl, 283, 641g
Craft unionism, 17–18, 483
"Criticism of the Draft Program" (Trotsky), 105
Cuba, 433

Darrow, Clarence, 51–52, 641g
Declaration of Principles (SP), 554–55, 558, 563
Declaration of Principles (WPUS), 611
"Declaration of the Four," 435, 449
Defense strategy, 51–52, 128–30, 417–18
Defense work, 417–18, 525–28, 615–17
Democratic centralism, 15, 209, 213, 447
Democratization of unions, 210–11
Dialectics, 103
Dictatorship of the proletariat, 203, 205
Disputes with branches, 116
See also Specific branches
Dobbs, Farrell, 36
Dual unionism, 20, 429
Dunne, Vincent R., 25–26, 269, 605, 641g
and Minneapolis strikes, 36, 536

Dunne, William F., 240–41, 544–45, 641g

Economic crisis, 260
Economic hardships, 137
Education, 273, 291–92
Edwards, John, 606, 608, 641g
Ellis, Clifford B., 199
Engels, Frederick, 89–99, 105–7, 492, 642g
European sections of ILO, 186–89
See also Specific countries
Everest, Wesley, 472, 642g
Expulsions, 119, 265

Faction fight, 25–27, 76–103, 221–24, 269–72, 395–96
causes of, 186–87, 190
deepening of, 340–41
end of, 30, 602–3, 681–82n
international questions in, 78–80
and principles, 291
and Shachtman, 167–69
Trotsky on, 623–35
Factionalism, 165–67
Farm Holiday Association, 20
Farmer-Labor Party, 38
Farmer-labor movement, 388
Fascism, 567
in France, 506–7
in Germany, 31–33, 200, 344, 519
in Italy, 200
in U.S., 470–74
Field work, 259–60, 277–79, 281
Field, B.J., 265–68, 273–76, 334, 397–98, 642g
and hotel strike, 487–88

Finances, 133, 259–60, 278, 283–88, 297–99, 339–40, 378, 392, 407, 419
Finland, 343
First National Conference (1929), 76, 116–17
"Ford-Dubner" thesis, 125
Foreign-language-speaking workers, 43–44
Forward, 54, 642g
Foster group, 171–72
Foster, William Z., 172, 642g
and trade unions, 179
Foster-Cannon group, 171
Fourth International, 33, 421, 441–42, 492, 494–96, 506–7, 575–76
norms of, 495–97
Fourth World Congress (Communist International), 246
Fox, Joseph, 117
France, 505–8
See also French Communist League
Frank, Pierre, 583, 642g
Free Tom Mooney Congress (1933), 417–18
Freedom of speech and discussion, 201, 256–57, 447
Freiheit, 462, 642g
French Communist League, 60–61, 82–83, 461, 583–87
French Section of the Workers' International (SFIO), 584–86
Friends of the *Militant* Club, 468
Full-timers, 139, 259–60, 299, 307–8, 320–22
Fur workers, 499–503

Fusion, 39, 489–92, 573–74, 589–91, 603

Geltman, Max, 660n
General Drivers Union No. 574, 35–36, 533–36, 541
General strike, 204, 362, 567–70
German campaign, 338–39
German section of ILO, 83, 166, 187–88, 320–21
Germany, 31–32, 200, 333, 575
crisis in, 343–44, 373–75
Germany—The Key to the International Situation (Trotsky), 347
Gillespie Trades and Labor Council, 323
Gillespie conference, 323–26, 330–31, 338, 379–81, 405–6
and political organizations, 382–83
and trade union federation, 385
Gitlow group, 434–35, 449–50
Gitlow, Benjamin, 398, 434–35, 449, 594, 642–43g
and new International, 495
and Socialist Party, 596–97
Glotzer, Albert, 26, 169, 606–8, 643g
and faction fight, 76, 218–19
and Minneapolis branch, 138
Goldman, Albert, 598, 643g
Gomez, Manuel, 237–38, 240–41, 643g
"Goose caucus," 125–26
Gordon, Sam, 220, 242–43, 277, 281, 643–44g
Gourov. *See* Trotsky, Leon
Gras, Andres, 616–17

Great Depression, 13, 16–17, 34
Greek-language press, 43, 45
Green, William, 455, 457, 568, 579–81, 644g
Groves, Reg, 437, 644g

Hathaway, Clarence, 341, 366–67, 644g
Hays, Arthur Garfield, 51–52, 644g
Hillquit, Morris, 549, 644g
Hitler, Adolf, 31
Homogeneity, 168
Hotel strike, 482–84, 487–88, 540
Howat, Alexander, 403, 414, 644g
Hungary, 200
Hunger, 359

Imperialism, 344–45
Inactivity of leaders, 142
Independent Chicago Teamsters, 387
Independent Labour Party, 437–39, 645g
Independent unions, 387–88, 428–29
Industrial Workers of the World (IWW), 199, 204–6, 244, 548, 645g
  and leadership, 213
  and needle trades, 208
Industrial unionism, 17, 324, 455
Infantile Sickness of "Left" Communism (Lenin), 162
Internal Bulletin no. 6, 320
Internal crisis, 337–38, 341–42, 356, 624–27
  See also Faction fight

International. *See* Fourth International; New International
International delegate, 282, 285, 287–88, 297–98, 302–3
International Fur Workers Union, 499
International Labor Defense, 51–52, 526, 645g, 659n
International Ladies' Garment Workers Union, 35, 501, 645g
  convention of, 151–52, 156, 159
  strikes of, 154
International Left Opposition (ILO), 24–25, 59–61, 645g, 660–62n
  and B.J. Field, 265–68
  and CLA, 266–67, 274–76, 626–27
  and Germany, 32–33, 60
  NC resolution on, 218
  and new International, 33, 441–42
  origins and development of, 187–90
International Preconference of the Left Opposition, 443
International questions, 189–90, 226, 230–31
International Secretariat, 61, 298, 604, 660–61n
International work, 61–62, 78–80
International Youth Conference, 468
Internationalism, 198, 238–39, 444, 575–76, 613–14
  and defense of the USSR, 349–51
  and new party, 492–95, 575–76

"Introduction to *The Class Struggles in France*," 77
Italy, 200

Japan, 69–71
Jewish committee, 461–62
Jewish-language press, 43
Johnson, Hugh S., 454, 457, 645g
Justice, 472–73

Kautsky, Karl, 92–93, 645–46g
Keracher, John, 47–48, 646g
Kerensky, Alexander, 511, 646g
Kirov, Sergei, 620–21, 646g
Kling, Lazar, 463, 646g

Labor Age, 327–28, 646g
Labor bureaucracy, 163, 208–9, 317–18, 458, 566
 and strikes, 579–81
Labor legislation, 324–25, 360, 368–69
Labor party, 38, 434–35
Landau, Kurt, 60, 82–83, 150, 646–47g
Lassalle, Ferdinand, 57–58, 647g, 660n
Leadership, 75, 138–39, 142–43, 276
 formation of, 187–88
 of unions, 159, 207–9, 541–42
Left wing in unions, 152–53, 425–31, 459–60, 545–46, 581
Legality and illegality, 64–65, 90–92, 105, 125
Lenin, V.I., 14, 511, 620, 647g
 and Lassalle, 58
 on leadership, 161–62
 and united front, 315
Lewis, John L., 457–58, 647g

Lewit, Morris, 463, 647g
Lhuillier, Rene, 586–87, 647g
Little, Frank, 472, 647g
London-Amsterdam Bureau, 586, 647g
Longshore strike. *See* San Francisco strike
Lovestone group, 177–80, 434, 562
 and marine workers' trial, 182–83
 and needle-trades unions, 500–501
Lovestone, Jay, 19, 170, 398, 594, 648g
Lovestone-Pepper faction, 140
Luxemburg, Rosa, 90, 92, 98–101, 648g
Lynchings, 469–72

Madison Square demonstration, 515, 517
Majority errors, 377–78
Malkin, Maurice L., 144, 648g
Marine workers' trial, 182
Marx, Karl, 202–3, 492, 648g
 and Lassalle, 660n
Marxism, 65, 195, 199, 201, 493–94
Mass meetings, 338–39
Mass picketing, 571
Masses, illusions of, 427
Materialist conception of history, 202
Matthews, J.B., 557, 561, 648–49g
Mattick group, 465
May Day, 513–19
May Day Labor Conference, 514–15, 518–22
Membership, 624

Militant group, 179, 550, 553–54, 561–62, 590, 597, 649g
Militant, the, 38, 220, 299, 439, 466, 563, 602
  and factionalism, 133
  and National Committee, 111–13
  sixth anniversary of, 589
Mill, M., 61, 280, 649g
Miners, 262, 333–34
  See also Progressive Miners of America
Minneapolis branch, 276, 282–83
  and unemployed movement, 476–78
Minneapolis strikes, 35–37, 529–38
  organization of, 541–43
  results of, 540–41, 570, 576
Mob violence, 470–73
Molinier, Raymond, 252–53, 583, 649g
Mooney, Thomas J., 417–18, 649g
Morgenstern, Bernard, 185, 299–302, 605–6, 649g
Municipal Socialists, 550
Muste, A.J., 39, 649g

National Committee, 27–28, 87–88, 220–21, 391–92
  balance sheet on, 601–9
  and control of the *Militant,* 111
  disputes in, 131, 139–40, 149–50, 165–66, 235
  June 1932 plenum of, 217–21
  and new International, 423–24, 433–34
"National communism," 14

National conference, 302, 321
National Council of Unemployed, 18
National Industrial Recovery Act, 35
National Miners Union, 329
National Recovery Administration (NRA), 425–27, 454–57, 649–50g
  code of, 481–82
  and strike wave, 537–40, 565–66
National Youth Committee, 109–10
Nationality groups, 60–61
Naujoji Gadyne, 44–45
Naville, Pierre, 61, 82–83, 245, 247, 583–85, 650g
Needle Trades Industrial Union, 499–500
Needle trades, 19, 151–57, 499–503
  influence of syndicalism in, 208
  left wing in, 208–11
New Deal, 34
New International, 563
New International, 423–24, 433–36, 441–42
New Militant, 611–14
New party, 441–43, 447–48, 546, 558–59, 582, 589–92
  and AWP, 489–90, 573
  and Gitlow group, 449–51
  and internationalism, 492–95
New York branch, 225, 270–71, 292–95
  composition of, 23–24, 78, 119–21, 147–48, 169–70
  NC resolution on, 218–19, 289

New York branch (*continued*)
   struggle in, 84–86, 169–70
New York Unemployed Conference, 313–14
Non-Partisan Labor Defense (NPLD), 525, 527, 615–17, 650g

Oehler, Hugo, 26, 144, 319, 382, 409, 605, 650g
   tour of 333, 339
Olgin, Moissaye, 256, 651g
Olson, Floyd, 543–44, 651g
Organizational work, 278–79
Our Revolution, 58

Pacifism and pacifists, 255–56, 258, 555–56
Parliamentarism, 311–12
Party democracy, 196–97, 447
Pepper, John, 171, 651g
Pepper-Lovestone group, 125–26
Poland, 343, 345
Police, 63–64
Political Committee, 28, 319
Preliminary international conference, 298, 320, 356
Primitive communism, 202
Principled differences, 624
Principles of new party, 443
Progressive Bloc, 156
Progressive Miner, 364, 399, 401–2
Progressive Miners of America, 37, 262, 321, 325–27, 338, 387, 400, 411, 414, 651g
   and contract, 334–35, 381–82
   and defense cases, 363–64
   and Gillespie conference, 324–27, 380–82
   leadership of, 401–3

Prohibition, 472
Proletarian Opposition Bulletin, 48–49
Proletarian Party, 47–50, 590–91, 651–52g, 659n
Proletarianization, resolution on, 341, 629
Propaganda work, 73–74, 278
Provisional Committee for Non-Partisan Labor Defense, 525–26

Radicalization, 200–201, 565
Rakovsky, Christian, 374, 652g
Rank and File movement, 403, 682n
Rank and file control, 210, 212–13, 447
"Rank and file leadership," 159–63, 207, 211–13
Recruitment, 74, 397, 612–13
Red Army, 343–47, 349–50
"Red unions," 20, 428–30, 446, 540
Red-baiting, 411–15, 458
Referendum on plenum decisions, 220, 289–90
Reformism and reformists, 90, 312, 361
Regroupment, 591–93
Religion, 300
"Resolution on the Red Army and the German Revolution," 343–53
Revolution, 200–201, 205, 343
Revolutionary Age, 44–45
Revolutionary Policy Committee (RPC), 551, 555, 557–59, 561–63
   work within, 562–63

INDEX / 709

Riazanov, David, 91–94, 97, 652g
Robins, Harold, 526, 616–17, 652g
Rolph, James, 470–72, 652g
Romania, 343
Roosevelt, Franklin D., 34–35, 426–27, 454, 457, 565–66
Rosmer, Alfred, 61, 245–46, 652g
Ruthenberg, Charles, 171, 652g

Sacco-Vanzetti Defense Committee, 52
San Francisco strike, 36–37, 567–68
Scottsboro case, 51–52, 127–30, 659n
Second International, 492, 559
Second National Conference (1931), 75–76, 85–87, 116–17, 185, 601
Shachtman faction, 352–53
Shachtman, Max, 25–26, 76, 319, 605, 653g
  and Carter group, 218–19, 270–72
  and correspondence, 80–82
  and Engels's introduction, 96–97, 102–4
  in Europe, 26, 79–80, 87–88, 252–54
  and faction fight, 76, 84–88, 173, 218–19, 249–50, 351–53
  and international questions, 81–84, 140, 218, 222, 230–33, 242, 247, 249–52
  and New York branch, 84–86
  and Red Army, 346–47
Sharts, Joseph, 564, 653g
"Situation in the American Opposition: Prospect and Retrospect, The," 226
Skoglund, Carl, 25, 319, 605, 653–54g
  and Minneapolis strikes, 36, 536
Slander, 227–28, 236–38
Social Democratic Party (Germany), 31–32
Social Democracy, 492, 547–48
"Social fascism," 445
Socialism, 203
"Socialism in one country," 104–5, 178, 444–45, 492
Socialist Labor Party, 90–91
Socialist Lawyers Association, 616
Socialist Party, 18, 314–16, 327, 517–18, 548–49, 553, 596, 654g
  convention of, 547–57
  and international question, 551–52, 563–64
  and Jewish workers, 462
  and May Day, 515–16
  and NPLD, 616–17
  Old Guard in, 19, 549–52, 558
  and Soviet Union, 556
  and unions, 552–54
  work within, 562–64, 596–98
Socialist Workers Party (SAP) (Germany), 586, 653g
Soderberg, John G., 182, 654g
South Africa, 461
Soviet Union, 343–46
  defense of, 343–47, 349–51, 444–45, 619–20
  trade with, 360
  and Trotsky, 509–11

Spanish section, 251–53
Spector, Maurice, 26, 118, 606, 608, 654g
Speedup, 426
Splits, 29–31, 135, 148–50, 590–92, 625–27, 630
  actions against, 395
Split with Foster, 171–72, 191, 270
Staff, 133, 259, 283–84, 321–22
  See also Full-timers
Stalin, Joseph, 14–15, 178, 508, 655g
Stalinism and Stalinists, 50, 159, 179–80, 310–12, 443–47, 474, 492, 510–11, 516–18
  and fight against war, 256
  struggle against, 195, 478
  and Trotsky, 506, 509–10
  See also Communist Party
State power, 202–3
"Statement on the Motion for a Plenum" (Shachtman), 148–49
Steelworkers, 540
Strike wave, 34–35, 426–27, 430–31, 453–54, 456, 537–40, 565–66
Strikes, 64, 154, 209–10, 472, 530–31, 566–67
Suppression of party, 65
Swabeck, Arne, 26, 138–39, 303–4, 337, 377–78, 605, 655g
  answer to Carter by, 77, 89
  attacks on, 226
  as international delegate, 297, 631–32
  national tour of, 260
Sympathy strikes, 532, 567
Syndicalism and syndicalists, 161–62, 205, 208

Taylorville Defense Committee, 364, 382
Teamsters union, 533–34
  See also General Drivers Union No. 574
Textile workers, 566, 569–70, 579–82
Theoretical magazine, 133
Third Conference of the Needle Trades Left Wing (1925), 210–11
Third World Congress (Communist International), 212
"Third period," 19–20, 32
Thomas, Norman, 549–51, 555, 655g
Toledo strike, 36, 540, 567, 571–72
Toronto branch, 118, 174–75, 668–69n
  NC resolution on, 289
Trade union bureaucracy. *See* Labor bureaucracy
Trade union democracy, 207, 324
Trade union federation, 323, 327–28, 379–80
  and Gillespie conference, 385–87
Trade union fetishism, 428–29, 501
Trade Union Unity League (TUUL), 328, 389, 540, 655g
Trade union work, 37, 321–22, 338
Tresso, Pietro, 584, 655–56g
Trotsky, Leon, 14–16, 58, 87–88, 101–2, 656g
  attacks on, 505–12, 619
  and B.J. Field, 267, 274–75

Trotsky, Leon (*continued*)
  and CLA, 27–30, 80–83, 140, 273–74, 288, 377–78, 395–97
  and ILO, 59–62, 166, 437
  and Lenin, 249
  and new International, 421, 423
  and rank and file control, 214
  on the trade unions, 244–45
Turn to mass work, 37, 337–38, 397, 592–94, 625, 627
Two-and-a-half International, 496

Unemployed Councils, 476–77
Unemployed movement, 18, 309–10, 320, 338, 466–67, 476–78
Unemployed workers and strikes, 571
Unemployment, 66, 200, 314–15, 358–60, 365, 426, 476–77
Unemployment insurance, 324, 360, 368
Union affiliation, 499–503, 540–41
Union recognition, 535–36, 539–41, 543–44
Unions, 35, 204, 454–56, 542–43
  See also Specific unions
United Auto Workers, 659n
United front, 20, 314–15, 360–61, 445, 515–16, 519, 522, 525–26
  in France, 506–7
  in Germany, 31–32, 374
  and May Day, 513–19
"United front from below," 20, 155, 445, 516
United Front Conference Against the Sedition Law, 118

United Mine Workers (UMWA), 16, 35, 329
United Textile Workers Union (UTW), 579–80
United Workers Party, 465, 467, 656n
Unity, slogan of, 151, 154–57, 314–15
  and revolutionary vanguard, 193–97
Unity of CLA, 121, 132, 219
Unity of right wing and centrists, 177–78
Unser Kamf, 461–62, 656g
Uruguay, 461

Vanguard, role of, 612
Voice of Labor, 449

Wages, 66, 426
Waldman, Louis, 564, 657g
War, fight against, 255
Weisbord, Albert, 53–55, 84–85, 117–18, 144–46, 397–98, 657g, 659–60n
  and marine workers' trial, 181–83
Well, Roman, 320, 657g
What Is to Be Done? (Lenin), 58
White Guards, 506, 510
Who Are the Falsifiers?, 93, 97–98
Winter, Carl, 366, 657g
Women, 531–32
Work day, 324, 360
Workers, 33–34, 65–67, 359–62, 425–26
  respect for organizations by, 316–17
  and Roosevelt administration, 538–39

Workers League, 465–67
Workers Party of the U.S., 14, 39, 611
  and defense work, 615–17
Workers' Council group, 590
Workers' militia, 512
Workers' school (Chicago), 467–68
Workers' state, 444
Wortis, Rose, 212–13, 658g

Young People's Socialist League (YPSL), 563
Young Spartacus, 563, 658g
Youngstown branch, 282
Youth, development of leadership among, 144
Youth clubs, 169

Zam, Herbert, 594, 596–97, 658g
Zinoviev, Gregory, 619, 621, 658g

ALSO BY JAMES P. CANNON

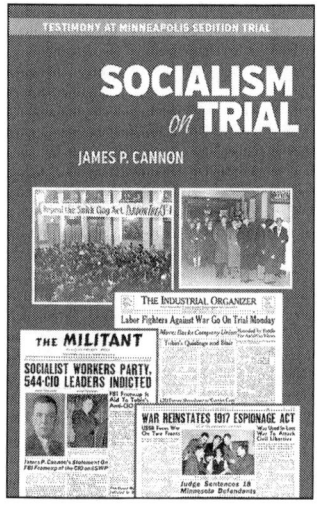

Socialism on Trial
Testimony at Minneapolis Sedition Trial

The revolutionary program of the working class, presented in response to frame-up charges of "seditious conspiracy" in 1941, on the eve of US entry into World War II. The defendants were leaders of the Minneapolis labor movement and the Socialist Workers Party. $15. Also in Spanish, French, and Farsi.

The History of American Trotskyism, 1928–38
Report of a Participant

"Trotskyism is not a new movement, a new doctrine," Cannon says, "but the restoration, the revival of genuine Marxism as it was expounded and practiced in the Russian Revolution and in the early days of the Communist International." Talks by a founding leader of American communism on building a proletarian party in the United States. $17. Also in Spanish and French.

Notebook of an Agitator
From the Wobblies to the Fight against the Korean War and McCarthyism

Spans four decades of working-class battles—defending IWW frame-up victims and Sacco and Vanzetti; battles on the San Francisco waterfront; labor's fight against the McCarthyite witch-hunt. Includes the 1934 strike call and seven articles from *The Organizer*, daily bulletin of the Minneapolis Teamster strike. $20

WWW.PATHFINDERPRESS.COM

'THE HISTORY OF EXISTING SOCIETY IS THE HISTORY OF CLASS STRUGGLES'

Labor, Nature, and the Evolution of Humanity
The Long View of History

FREDERICK ENGELS, KARL MARX, GEORGE NOVACK, MARY-ALICE WATERS

Why is it important to know that social labor, transforming nature, has been the motor force of humanity's evolution for millions of years? Because without that knowledge, working people are unable to see beyond the capitalist epoch, beyond the class exploitation that warps all human relations, ideas, and values. The dictatorship of capital had a beginning ... and it will have an end. But only the revolutionary conquest of state power by the working class can open the door to a world free of capitalism's dog-eat-dog social reality. A world built on human solidarity. A socialist world. $12. Also in Spanish and French.

The Communist Manifesto
KARL MARX AND FREDERICK ENGELS

Communism, say the founding leaders of the revolutionary workers movement, is not a set of ideas or preconceived "principles" but workers' line of march to power, springing from a "movement going on under our very eyes." $5. Also in Spanish, French, Farsi, and Arabic.

Understanding History
Marxist Essays

GEORGE NOVACK

How did capitalism arise? Why and when did this exploitative system exhaust its once revolutionary role? Why is revolutionary change fundamental to human progress? $15

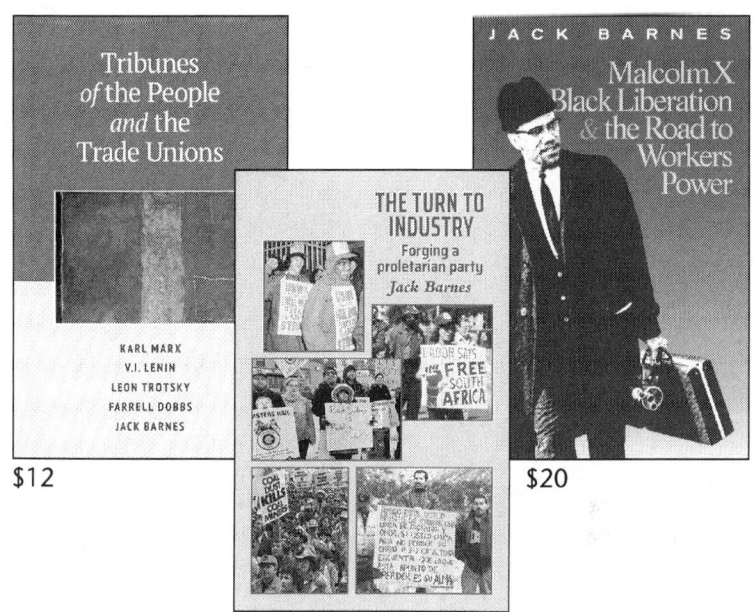

$12 $20

$15

Three books to be read as one . . .

about building a party that's working class in program, composition, and action. One that recognizes, in word and deed, the most revolutionary fact of our time . . .

. . . that working people have the power to create a different world as we act together to defend our own class interests—not those of the privileged classes who exploit our labor, not of those who fear us as "deplorables," or just plain "trash."

As we advance along a revolutionary course toward workers power, we will transform ourselves and awaken to our own worth. Also in Spanish and French.

Special Offer!
All three $30

The Turn to Industry and *Tribunes of the People and the Trade Unions* $20

Either book plus *Malcolm X, Black Liberation, and the Road to Workers Power* $25

WWW.PATHFINDERPRESS.COM

CAPITALIST CRISIS AND THE FIGHT FOR WORKERS POWER

Are They Rich Because They're Smart?
Class, Privilege, and Learning under Capitalism
JACK BARNES

Exposes growing class inequalities in the US and the self-serving rationalizations of well-paid professionals who think their "brilliance" equips them to "regulate" working people, who don't know what's in our own best interest. $10. Also in Spanish, French, Farsi, and Arabic.

The Clintons' Anti-Working-Class Record
Why Washington Fears Working People
JACK BARNES

What working people need to know about the profit-driven course of Democrats and Republicans alike over the last three decades. And the political awakening of workers seeking to understand and resist the capitalist rulers' assaults. $10. Also in Spanish, French, Farsi, and Greek.

The Transitional Program for Socialist Revolution
LEON TROTSKY

The Socialist Workers Party program, drafted by Trotsky in 1938, still guides the SWP and communists the world over. The party "uncompromisingly gives battle to all political groupings tied to the apron strings of the bourgeoisie. Its task—the abolition of capitalism's domination. Its aim—socialism. Its method—the proletarian revolution." $17. Also in Farsi.

In Defense of the US Working Class
MARY-ALICE WATERS

Drawing on the fighting traditions of the oppressed and exploited of all colors and national origins, in 2018 tens of thousands of teachers and other working people in West Virginia, Oklahoma, and other states waged victorious strikes. They fought for dignity and respect for themselves, their families, and for all working people. $7. Also in Spanish, French, Farsi, and Greek.

Is Socialist Revolution in the US Possible?
A Necessary Debate among Working People
MARY-ALICE WATERS

Fighting for a society only working people can create, it is our own capacities we will discover. And along that course we will answer the question posed here with a resounding "Yes." Possible but not inevitable. That depends on us. $7. Also in Spanish, French, and Farsi.

Malcolm X Talks to Young People

"The young generation of whites, Blacks, browns, whatever else—you're living at a time of revolution," said Malcolm in 1964. "And I for one will join with anyone, I don't care what color you are, as long as you want to change this miserable condition that exists on this earth." Four talks and an interview in the last months of Malcolm's life. $12. Also in Spanish, French, Farsi, and Greek.

WWW.PATHFINDERPRESS.COM

New International
A MAGAZINE OF MARXIST POLITICS AND THEORY

Capitalism's Long Hot Winter Has Begun
JACK BARNES

Today's global capitalist crisis is but the opening stage of decades of economic, financial, and social convulsions and class battles. Class-conscious workers confront this historic turning point for imperialism with confidence, Jack Barnes writes, drawing satisfaction from being "in their face" as we chart a revolutionary course to take power. In *New International* no. 12. $14. Also in Spanish, French, Farsi, Arabic, and Greek.

Imperialism's March toward Fascism and War
JACK BARNES

"There will be new Hitlers, new Mussolinis. That is inevitable. What is not inevitable is that they will triumph. The working-class vanguard will organize our class to fight back against the devastating toll we are made to pay for the capitalist crisis. The future of humanity will be decided in the contest between these contending class forces." In *New International* no. 10. $14. Also in Spanish, French, Farsi, and Greek.

U.S. Imperialism Has Lost the Cold War
JACK BARNES

The collapse of regimes across Eastern Europe and the USSR claiming to be communist did not mean workers and farmers there had been crushed. In today's sharpening capitalist conflicts and wars, these toilers are joining working people the world over in the class struggle against exploitation. In *New International* no. 11. $14. Also in Spanish, French, Farsi, and Greek.

BUILDING A PROLETARIAN PARTY

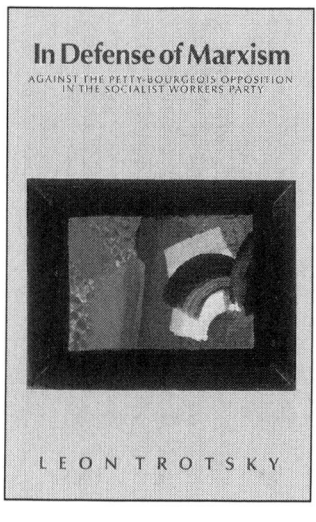

In Defense of Marxism
Against the Petty-Bourgeois Opposition in the Socialist Workers Party
LEON TROTSKY

A reply to those in the revolutionary workers movement in the late 1930s bending to bourgeois patriotism during Washington's buildup to enter World War II. Trotsky explains why only a party fighting to bring workers into its ranks and leadership can steer a communist course. In the process, he defends the materialist and dialectical foundations of Marxism. $17. Also in Spanish.

The Struggle for a Proletarian Party
JAMES P. CANNON

"The workers of America have power enough to topple the structure of capitalism at home and to lift the whole world with them when they rise," Cannon asserts. On the eve of World War II, a founder of the communist movement in the US and leader of the Communist International in Lenin's time defends the program and party-building norms of Bolshevism. $20. Also in Spanish and Farsi.

Their Trotsky and Ours
JACK BARNES

To lead the working class in a successful revolution, a mass proletarian party is needed whose cadres, well beforehand, have absorbed a world communist program, are proletarian in life and work, derive deep satisfaction from doing politics, and have forged a leadership with an acute sense of what to do next. This book is about building such a party. $12. Also in Spanish, French, and Farsi.

WWW.PATHFINDERPRESS.COM

THE CUBAN REVOLUTION AND ITS IMPACT FROM AFRICA TO THE US

October 1962
The 'Missile' Crisis as Seen from Cuba
TOMÁS DIEZ ACOSTA

In October 1962 Washington pushed the world to the edge of nuclear war. Here the full story of that historic moment is told from the perspective of the Cuban people, whose determination to defend their sovereignty and their socialist revolution blocked US plans for a devastating military assault. $17

From the Escambray to the Congo
In the Whirlwind of the Cuban Revolution
VÍCTOR DREKE

Dreke was second in command of the internationalist column in the Congo led in 1965 by Che Guevara. He recounts the creative joy with which working people have defended their revolutionary course—from Cuba's Escambray mountains to Africa and beyond. $15. Also in Spanish.

Socialism and Man in Cuba
ERNESTO CHE GUEVARA, FIDEL CASTRO

"Man truly reaches his full human condition when he produces without being compelled by physical necessity to sell himself as a commodity," wrote Guevara in 1965. $5. Also in Spanish, French, Farsi, and Greek.

Cuba and the Coming American Revolution
JACK BARNES

This is a book about the struggles of working people in the imperialist heartland, the youth attracted to them, and the example set by the Cuban people that revolution is not only necessary—it can be made. It is about the class struggle in the US, where the revolutionary capacities of workers and farmers are today as utterly discounted by the ruling powers as were those of the Cuban toilers. And just as wrongly. $10. Also in Spanish, French, and Farsi.

Cuba and Angola: The War for Freedom
HARRY VILLEGAS ("POMBO")

Cuba and Angola
Fighting for Africa's Freedom and Our Own
FIDEL CASTRO, RAÚL CASTRO, NELSON MANDELA

Two books that tell the story of Cuba's unparalleled contribution to the fight to free Africa from the scourge of apartheid. And how, in the doing, Cuba's socialist revolution was also strengthened. $10 and $12. Also in Spanish. *Cuba and Angola: The War for Freedom* is also available in Farsi and Greek.

How Far We Slaves Have Come!
South Africa and Cuba in Today's World
NELSON MANDELA, FIDEL CASTRO

Speaking together in Cuba in 1991, Mandela and Castro discuss the role of Cuba in the history of Africa and Angola's victory over the invading US-backed South African army. That victory accelerated the fight to bring down the racist apartheid system. $7. Also in Spanish and Farsi.

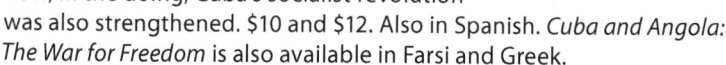

WWW.PATHFINDERPRESS.COM

THE RUSSIAN REVOLUTION'S WORLD EXAMPLE

Lenin's Final Fight
Speeches and Writings, 1922–23
V.I. LENIN

In 1922 and 1923, V.I. Lenin, central leader of the world's first socialist revolution, waged what was to be his last political battle—one that was lost following his death. At stake was whether that revolution, and the international communist movement it led, would remain on the revolutionary proletarian course that brought workers and peasants to power in October 1917. $17. Also in Spanish, Farsi, and Greek.

The History of the Russian Revolution
LEON TROTSKY

How, under Lenin's leadership, the Bolshevik Party led millions of workers and farmers to overthrow the state power of the landlords and capitalists in 1917 and bring to power a government that advanced their class interests at home and worldwide. Unabridged, 3 vols. in one. Written by one of the central leaders of that socialist revolution. $30. Also in French and Russian.

The Revolution Betrayed
What Is the Soviet Union and Where Is It Going?
LEON TROTSKY

In 1917 workers and peasants of Russia were the motor force for one of the deepest revolutions in history. Yet within ten years a political counterrevolution by a privileged social layer, whose chief spokesperson was Joseph Stalin, was being consolidated. The classic study of the Soviet workers state and its degeneration. $17. Also in Spanish, Farsi, and Greek.

WOMEN'S LIBERATION AND SOCIALISM

Cosmetics, Fashions, and the Exploitation of Women

Joseph Hansen, Evelyn Reed, Mary-Alice Waters

How big business reinforces women's second-class status and uses it to rake in profits. Where does women's oppression come from? How has the entry of millions of women into the workforce strengthened the battle for emancipation, still to be won? $12. Also in Spanish, Farsi, and Greek.

Women in Cuba: The Making of a Revolution Within the Revolution

From Santiago de Cuba and the Rebel Army, to the Birth of the Federation of Cuban Women

Vilma Espín, Asela de los Santos, Yolanda Ferrer

The integration of women in the ranks and leadership of the Cuban Revolution was intertwined with the proletarian course of the leadership of the revolution from the start. This is the story of that revolution and how it transformed the women and men who made it. $17. Also in Spanish, Farsi, and Greek.

WWW.PATHFINDERPRESS.COM

EXPAND YOUR REVOLUTIONARY LIBRARY

The Jewish Question
A Marxist Interpretation
ABRAM LEON

Why is Jew-hatred still raising its ugly head? What are its class roots—from antiquity through feudalism, to capitalism's rise and current crises? Why is there no solution under capitalism? The author, Abram Leon, was killed in the Nazi gas chambers. Revised translation, new introduction, and 40 pages of illustrations and maps. $17. Also in Spanish and French.

The Struggle against Fascism in Germany
LEON TROTSKY

Writing in the heat of struggle against the rising Nazi movement, a central leader of the Bolshevik Revolution in Russia draws lessons from that first victorious proletarian revolution, examines the petty bourgeois class roots of fascism, and presents a revolutionary political course to defeat it. $25

The Left Opposition in the U.S.
Writings and Speeches, 1928–31
JAMES P. CANNON

How veteran leaders of the American communist movement, expelled in 1928 by a growing Stalinist faction, joined with Bolshevik leader Leon Trotsky to continue building a party to carry out the program for world revolution developed by the Communist International under Lenin's guidance. $23

Puerto Rico: Independence Is a Necessity
RAFAEL CANCEL MIRANDA

One of the five Puerto Rican Nationalists imprisoned by Washington for more than 25 years and released in 1979 speaks out on the brutal reality of US colonial domination, the example of Cuba's socialist revolution, and the ongoing struggle for independence. $5. Also in Spanish and Farsi.

Thomas Sankara Speaks
The Burkina Faso Revolution, 1983–87

Under Sankara's guidance, Burkina Faso's revolutionary government led peasants, workers, women, and youth to expand literacy; to sink wells, plant trees, erect housing; to combat women's oppression; to carry out land reform; to join others worldwide to free themselves from the imperialist yoke. $20. Also in French.

Maurice Bishop Speaks
The Grenada Revolution and Its Overthrow, 1979–83

The triumph of the 1979 revolution in the Caribbean island of Grenada under the leadership of Maurice Bishop gave hope to millions throughout the Americas. Invaluable lessons from the workers and farmers government destroyed by a Stalinist-led counterrevolution in 1983. $20

WWW.PATHFINDERPRESS.COM

Teamster Rebellion
FARRELL DOBBS

The 1934 strikes that won union recognition for truckers and warehouse workers in Minneapolis and helped pave the way for the working-class social movement that built the industrial unions. The first of four volumes by a central leader of these battles. $16. Also in Spanish, French, Farsi, and Greek.

Labor's Giant Step
The First Twenty Years of the CIO: 1936–55
ART PREIS

The story of the explosive labor struggles and political battles in the 1930s that built the industrial unions. And how those unions became the vanguard of a mass social movement that began transforming US society. $27

Revolutionary Continuity
Marxist Leadership in the United States

The Early Years, 1848–1917
Birth of the Communist Movement, 1918–1922

FARRELL DOBBS

"Successive generations of proletarian revolutionists have participated in the movements of the working class and its allies. ... Marxists today owe them not only homage for their deeds. We also have a duty to learn what they did wrong as well as right so their errors are not repeated." —Farrell Dobbs. Two volumes, $17 each.

Capitalism's World Disorder
Working-Class Politics at the Millennium
JACK BARNES

The social devastation and financial crises, the coarsening of politics, the cop brutality and acts of imperialist aggression accelerating around us—all are products not of something gone wrong with capitalism but of its lawful workings. Yet the future can be changed by the united struggle and selfless action of working people conscious of their power to transform the world. $20. Also in Spanish and French.

Cointelpro
The FBI's Secret War on Political Freedom
NELSON BLACKSTOCK

An in-depth look at the 1960s and '70s covert FBI disruption and counterintelligence program—code-named COINTELPRO. Contains reproductions of FBI documents released through the Socialist Workers Party suit against government spying. $15

The Founding of the Socialist Workers Party
Minutes and Resolutions, 1938–39
JAMES P. CANNON

At founding gatherings of the Socialist Workers Party in 1938–39, revolutionists in the US codified two decades of experience in building a communist party. They charted a working-class course in resisting the coming imperialist war, fighting fascism and Jew-hatred, the struggle for Black rights, forging an alliance with exploited farmers, and the battle to transform the unions into revolutionary instruments of struggle by working people. $23

WWW.PATHFINDERPRESS.COM

PATHFINDER AROUND THE WORLD

UNITED STATES
(and Caribbean, Latin America, and East Asia)
  Pathfinder Books, 306 W. 37th St., 13th Floor
  New York, NY 10018

CANADA
  Pathfinder Books, 7107 St. Denis, Suite 204
  Montreal, QC H2S 2S5

UNITED KINGDOM
(and Europe, Africa, Middle East, and South Asia)
  Pathfinder Books, 5 Norman Rd.
  Seven Sisters, London N15 4ND

AUSTRALIA
(and Southeast Asia and the Pacific)
  Pathfinder Books, Suite 2, First floor, 275 George St.
  Liverpool, Sydney, NSW 2170
  Postal address: P.O. Box 73, Campsie, NSW 2194

NEW ZEALAND
  Pathfinder Books, 188a Onehunga Mall Rd.
  Onehunga, Auckland 1061
  Postal address: P.O. Box 13857, Auckland 1643

JOIN THE PATHFINDER READERS CLUB
BUILD YOUR LIBRARY!

$10 / YEAR
25% DISCOUNT ON ALL PATHFINDER TITLES
30% OFF BOOKS OF THE MONTH

Valid at pathfinderpress.com and local Pathfinder book centers

Go to: www.pathfinderpress.com/products/pathfinder-readers-club